The Cambridge Companion to Twentieth-Century Irish Drama

The essays in this collection cover the whole range of Irish drama from the late nineteenth-century melodramas which anticipated the rise of the Abbey Theatre to the contemporary Dublin of theatre festivals. A team of international experts from Ireland, the UK, the USA and Europe provide individual studies of internationally known playwrights of the period of the Literary Revival – Yeats, Synge, Lady Gregory, Shaw, Wilde, O'Casey – contemporary playwrights Brian Friel, Tom Murphy, Frank McGuinness and Sebastian Barry, and emerging playwrights such as Martin McDonagh and Marina Carr. In addition to studies of individual playwrights the collection includes examination of the relationship between the theatre and its political context as this is inflected through its ideology, staging and programming. With a full chronology and bibliography, this collection is an indispensable introduction to one of the world's most vibrant theatre cultures.

THE CAMBRIDGE COMPANION TO
TWENTIETH-CENTURY IRISH DRAMA

EDITED BY
SHAUN RICHARDS

CAMBRIDGE
UNIVERSITY PRESS

PUBLISHED BY THE PRESS SYNDICATE OF THE UNIVERSITY OF CAMBRIDGE
The Pitt Building, Trumpington Street, Cambridge, United Kingdom

CAMBRIDGE UNIVERSITY PRESS
The Edinburgh Building, Cambridge, CB2 2RU, UK
40 West 20th Street, New York, NY 10011–4211, USA
477 Williamstown Road, Port Melbourne, VIC 3207, Australia
Ruiz de Alarcón 13, 28014 Madrid, Spain
Dock House, The Waterfront, Cape Town 8001, South Africa

http://www.cambridge.org

First published 2004

Printed in the United Kingdom at the University Press, Cambridge

Typeface Sabon 10/13 pt.   *System* LATEX 2$_\varepsilon$ [TB]

A catalogue record for this book is available from the British Library

ISBN 0 521 80400 0 hardback
ISBN 0 521 00873 5 paperback

CONTENTS

Contents

CONTRIBUTORS

Richard Allen Cave is Professor of Drama and Theatre Arts at Royal Holloway College, University of London. He is the editor of the Chadwyck-Healey *Theatre in Focus* series, his contributions to which include *The Gate Theatre Dublin: 1928–1978*. Recent publications are Penguin editions of *W. B. Yeats: Selected Plays* (1997) and *Oscar Wilde: Selected Plays* (2000).

Adrian Frazier is Director of the MA in Drama and Theatre Studies at NUI, Galway. He is the author of *Behind the Scenes: Yeats, Horniman, and the Struggle for the Abbey Theatre* (1990) and *George Moore 1852–1933* (2000).

Claire Gleitman is an Associate Professor of Dramatic Literature and chair of the English Department at Ithaca College, NY. She has published numerous articles on contemporary Irish drama, and other subjects, in such journals as *Comparative Drama*, *Eire/Ireland*, the *Canadian Journal of Irish Studies* and *Modern Drama*. She is currently co-editing an anthology of dramatic literature.

Nicholas Grene is Professor of English at Trinity College, Dublin and Director of the Synge International Summer School. He has published widely on Irish theatre, most recently *The Politics of Irish drama: Plays in context from Boucicault to Friel* (1999) and the edited collections *Interpreting Synge: Essays from the Synge Summer School, 1991–2000* (2000) and *Talking About Tom Murphy* (2002).

John P. Harrington is Dean of Humanities and Social Sciences at Rensselaer Polytechnic Institute, New York. His books on Irish literature include *The Irish Beckett* (1991) and *The Irish Play on the New York Stage* (1997). He is editor of Norton's anthology *Modern Irish Drama* (1991) and, with Elizabeth J. Mitchell, the collection of essays *Politics and Performance in Contemporary Northern Ireland* (1999).

Mary C. King is Visiting Professor in Irish Studies at Goldsmiths College, London. She has written, lectured and broadcast widely on Irish literature and theatre, recently contributing articles on Wilde, Joyce and Synge to journals in Britain, Ireland and the USA. Her book *The Drama of J. M. Synge* was published jointly in 1985 by Fourth Estate in the UK and by Syracuse University Press in the USA.

Cathy Leeney is a Lecturer at the Drama Studies Centre, University College, Dublin and co-founder and director of Carysfort Press. She is the editor of *Seen and Heard: Six New Plays by Irish Women* (2001) and, with Anna McMullan, of *The Theatre of Marina Carr: Before Rules was Made* (2002).

Joep Leerssen is Professor of Modern European Literature at the University of Amsterdam, specializing in the literary dimension of European national thought and in the formation of national stereotypes and national identities. Among his publications on Irish literature and culture are *Mere Irish and Fíor-Ghael* (1986; rpt. 1996) and *Remembrance and Imagination: Patterns in the Historical and Literary Representations of Ireland in the Nineteenth Century* (1996).

Helen Lojek is Professor of English at Boise State University, Idaho, where she teaches American literature and contemporary English language drama. Articles on Brian Friel, Frank McGuinness, Anne Devlin and the Charabanc Theatre Company have appeared in such journals as *Contemporary Literature*, *Modern Drama* and *Irish University Review*. Her study of Frank McGuinness is forthcoming from the Catholic University Press.

Ronan McDonald teaches at the School of English and American Literature, University of Reading. He was co-editor of *Bullán: An Irish Studies Journal* and has research interests in modern Irish and British literature and drama, literary theory and film studies. His book *Tragedy and Irish Writing: Synge, O'Casey, Beckett* was published in 2002.

Vic Merriman is Lecturer in Contemporary Irish Theatre and Drama at Dundalk Institute of Technology. He is currently completing a PhD at Staffordshire University on 'Postcolonial desires and representations of subjectivities in contemporary Irish theatre'. He publishes regularly on contemporary Irish theatre, arts policy and drama pedagogy.

Gearóid O'Flaherty is a Lecturer with OSCAIL, the National Distance Education Centre at Dublin City University. His research interests include Anglo-Irish literature and drama, Gothic literature and the literature of the *fin de siècle*.

Contributors

James Pethica teaches Irish and modern British literature at Williams College in Massachussetts. He is currently working on the authorized biography of Lady Gregory, and a critical book on her creative partnership with Yeats. His publications include *Lady Gregory's Diaries, 1892–1902* (1996), an edition of the drafts of *Yeats's Last Poems* (1997) and *Yeats's Poetry, Drama and Prose: A Norton Critical Edition* (2000).

Lionel Pilkington is a Lecturer in English at NUI, Galway and author of *Theatre and the State in 20th Century Ireland: Cultivating the People* (2001), as well as numerous articles on Irish theatre and cultural politics.

Shaun Richards is Professor of Irish Studies at Staffordshire University. He has published widely on Irish drama and cultural politics and is the co-author of *Writing Ireland: Colonialism, Nationalism and Culture* (1988).

Marilynn Richtarik is an Associate Professor of English at Georgia State University in Atlanta. She is the author of *Acting Between the Lines: The Field Day Theatre Company and Irish Cultural Politics 1980–1984* (Oxford University Press, 1995; Catholic University of America Press, 2001). She is currently working on a critical biography of Belfast playwright Stewart Parker.

Neil Sammells is Dean of Academic Development at Bath Spa University College, co-editor of *Irish Studies Review* and author of *Wilde Style: the Plays and Prose of Oscar Wilde* (2000). He is currently editing a special issue of *Gothic Studies* devoted to Wilde, and preparing a study of Anglo-American dandyism.

Brian Singleton is Senior Lecturer at the School of Drama, Trinity College, Dublin. He is the editor of *Theatre Research International*, and a member of the Executive Committees of the International Federation for Theatre Research and the American Society for Theatre Research. He has published books on Antonin Artaud and articles on twentieth- century Irish theatre in numerous journals including *Modern Drama* and *European Review*.

Stephen Watt is Professor of English and Cultural Studies at Indiana University-Bloomington. His most recent books include *Postmodern/Drama: Reading the Contemporary Stage* (1998), *Keywords: A Devil's Dictionary for Higher Education* (1999), co-authored with Cary Nelson, and *A Century of Irish Drama: Widening the Stage* (2000), edited with Eileen Morgan and Shakir Mustafa.

1892: National Literary Society founded.

1899: First productions of Irish Literary Theatre: W. B. Yeats's *The Countess Cathleen* and Edward Martyn's *The Heather Field*.

1900: Founding of Inghinidhe na hÉireann (Daughters of Ireland).

1901: Douglas Hyde's *Casadh an tSúgáin* (*The Twisting of the Rope*) premiered by the Irish Literary Theatre.

1902: W. B. Yeats's and Lady Augusta Gregory's *Cathleen ni Houlihan* premiered by the Irish National Dramatic Company.

1903: National Theatre Society tours to London.

1904: Abbey Theatre opens with W. B. Yeats's *On Baile's Strand*, Lady Gregory's *Spreading the News* and their joint-authored *Cathleen ni Houlihan*.

1905: Founding of Sinn Féin.

1906: National Theatre Society Limited registers as a company.

1907: Premiere of J. M. Synge's *The Playboy of the Western World* (greeted by riots at Abbey Theatre).

1908: Founding of Cork Dramatic Society.

1909: Abbey stages G. B. Shaw's *The Shewing-up of Blanco Posnet* in protest over censorship. Death of J. M. Synge.

1913: Defeat of Home Rule Bill. Formation of Ulster Volunteer Force (January) followed by that of Irish Citizen Army and Irish Volunteers (November). Irish Transport and General Workers' Union calls strike in Dublin, which escalates into general lock-out.

1914: Outbreak of World War One.

1916: Easter Rising led by Irish Volunteers and Irish Citizen Army. The Rising (24–9 April) is followed by the execution of sixteen of its leaders.

1917: Sinn Féin wins four by-elections.

1918: End of World War One. Sinn Féin wins seventy-three seats (and becomes largest party) in general election.

1919: War of Independence (Anglo-Irish War, 1919–21). First meeting of Dáil Éireann; Eamon de Valera elected President. Dublin Drama League Founded.

1920: Black and Tans recruited. Six-county parliament and administration established in North.

1921: Truce between British Army and IRA. Anglo-Irish Treaty signed establishing Irish Free State (with six northern counties remaining part of United Kingdom).

1922: Anglo-Irish Treaty approved by Dáil Éireann. Anti-Treaty forces occupy Four Courts, Dublin, which is then attacked by Provisional government troops. Outbreak of Civil War (1922–3).

1923: W. B. Yeats awarded Nobel Prize for Literature. Film censorship law passed. Irish Free State joins League of Nations.

1925: Irish Free State begins subsidizing of Abbey Theatre. G. B. Shaw awarded Nobel Prize for Literature. Legislation prohibiting divorce in Free State passed.

1926: Eamon de Valera founds Fianna Fáil.

1928: Gate Theatre founded by Hilton Edwards and Micheal MacLiammoir; first production is Ibsen's *Peer Gynt*. Sean O'Casey's *The Silver Tassie* rejected by Abbey Theatre.

1929: Censorship of Publications Act passed.

1932: Fianna Fáil under Eamon de Valera wins general election (it remains in power until 1948). Amateur Dramatic Association founded. Death of Lady Augusta Gregory.

1933: Fine Gail formed.

1935: Sale and importation of contraceptives made illegal in Free State. Public Dance Halls Act passed.

1936: IRA declared illegal.

1937: New Irish Constitution. Ulster Group Theatre founded.

1939: Outbreak of World War Two. Éire states intention of remaining neutral. Death of W. B. Yeats.

1941: Ernest Blythe becomes Managing Director of Abbey; he remains in post until 1967.

1943: Eamon de Valera's St Patrick's Day radio broadcast evokes an idealized Ireland of 'frugal comfort'.

1945: End of World War Two. Eamon de Valera sends condolences to German embassy on death of Hitler.

1948: Ireland declared a Republic.

1949: Ireland leaves (British) Commonwealth.

1950: Death of G. B. Shaw.

1951: Abbey Theatre building destroyed by fire. Belfast's Lyric Theatre founded. Republic of Ireland Arts Council established.

1953: Pike Theatre founded.

1954: Death of Sean O'Casey.

1955: Ireland joins United Nations.

1957: Dublin Theatre Festival established. Tennessee Williams's *The Rose Tattoo* closed under censorship law and director imprisoned.

1958: T. K. Whitaker's Report on Economic Development encourages economic modernization. Episcopal opposition forces cancellation of Dublin Theatre Festival.

1959: Eamon de Valera elected President (until 1973). Sean Lemass becomes Taoiseach.

1960: Radio Telefís Éireann (RTE) founded. Yeats International Summer School established.

1963: American President J. F. Kennedy visits Ireland.

1966: Opening of new Abbey Theatre.

1969: Samuel Beckett awarded Nobel Prize for Literature. People's Democracy March from Belfast to Derry attacked by Protestants at Burntollet Bridge. British troops sent into Northern Ireland.

1970: IRA splits into Officials and Provisionals.

1972: 'Bloody Sunday' in Derry when British paratroopers kill fourteen people. Brian Friel's *Freedom of the City* (1973) clearly echoes this event.

1973: Ireland joins European Economic Community.

1974: Strike called by Ulster Workers' Council brings Northern Ireland to a halt (subject of Stewart Parker's 1987 play, *Pentecost*).

1975: Druid Theatre Company founded in Galway.

1977: *Crane Bag* journal founded.

1980: Field Day Theatre Company founded in Derry. Start of first hunger strike by Republican prisoners in Long Kesh/Maze Prison.

1981: Deaths of ten hunger strikers in Long Kesh/Maze Prison.

1983: Charabanc Theatre Company founded.

1984: Trinity College, Dublin establishes School of Drama and Theatre Studies.

1985: Anglo-Irish (Hillsborough) Agreement.

1990: Mary Robinson elected President.

1994: IRA ceasefire followed by that of Loyalist paramilitaries.

1995: Seamus Heaney awarded Nobel Prize for Literature. Divorce legalized in Republic after referendum.

1997: Mary McAleese elected President.

1998: Good Friday Agreement. David Trimble and John Hume share Nobel Peace Prize. Arts Council budget for theatre in the Republic reaches £8 million.

2000: New building for Abbey Theatre projected with budget of £50 million.

I

SHAUN RICHARDS

Plays of (ever) changing Ireland

The idea of 'nation', as both theme and setting, has haunted the development of Irish theatre. From the originary Irish National Theatre Society to the present National Theatre Society Limited, Irish theatre is marked by the 'national' appellation and all its implications. Whether the specific 'national' theatre is that of Britain, the United States, France or Ireland, the assumption is that its role is to stage the pressing concerns, or historical foundations, of the nation and, as in the case of the origins of the national theatre of Ireland, define the characteristics according to which the aspirant nation could be identified and distinguished. As observed by Lauren Kruger, the impulse to '*theatrical nationhood* manifests itself fully only in the course of the nineteenth century'[1] and particularly as 'representations of the ruling bloc confront the (counter) hegemonic claims of emergent groups' (*The National Stage*, 6). Ireland shares the nineteenth-century onset of this phenomenon, and while the Irish case differs somewhat from that of Europe and the United States in that the confrontation is of national rather than specifically class factions, it parallels their use of the stage in the contest for economic and political power. While Ireland had already enjoyed theatre as an art form and entertainment for several centuries, drama in its late nineteenth- and early twentieth-century manifestation sought to define and determine the basis of Irish claims for political independence from Britain. What this involved was a complex series of definitions and exclusions which resonate across the practice and criticism of Irish theatre. Any study of this terrain is necessarily engaged in a consideration of the basis for the original definitions and their implications for the theatre – and state – which subsequently evolved up to, and into, the contemporary moment.

The relationship between England and Ireland was for centuries one of ruler and ruled which, despite the advances made across the nineteenth century with regard to ameliorating its most negative aspects, continued up to the establishment of the Free State in 1922 and, from a republican/nationalist perspective, continues in Northern Ireland to the present day. At the heart of this relationship were images circulated through 'histories', travel writings, 'scientific' studies of race, cartoons, and plays which suggested the inferiority of the Irish at worst, their infantile dependency at best. The late eighteenth-century image of Ireland portrayed in David Hume's *History of England* captures the brutal end of this spectrum: 'The Irish from the beginning of time had been buried in the most profound barbarism and ignorance . . . distinguished by those vices alone to which human nature, not tamed by education or restrained by laws, is for ever subject.'[2] In the same period an apparently less offensive portrayal is that of Sir Lucius O'Trigger in Sheridan's *The Rivals* (1775), but it is one whose comic illogicality makes it only a less condemnatory complement to Hume's derogatory judgement.

Late nineteenth- and early twentieth-century Irish nationalist intellectuals were alert to the implications of such negative representations for any attempts to mobilize the population to assert its independence. In an explicit acknowledgement of the political dimension of theatre, the nationalist polemicist D. P. Moran asserted, 'The English mind has had for many years a mighty weapon in the stage for one of its great enterprises – the conquest of the Irish mind.'[3] The fact that Irish audiences willingly attended the performances of plays which were exhibitions of 'vulgar, pointless, uninteresting drivel'[4] only increased the demands for, and expectations of, a truly Irish national theatre. As declared by the founder of Sinn Féin, Arthur Griffith, in 1902, 'We look to the Irish National Theatre primarily as a means of regenerating the country. The Theatre is a powerful agent in the building up of a nation. When it is in foreign and hostile hands, it is a deadly danger to the country. When it is controlled by native and friendly hands it is a bulwark and a protection.'[5] What was then required was a substitute for a theatre which was perceived as antinational and the institution of a stage which would cultivate 'Art as the handmaid of Irish nationalism.'[6]

It was against this backdrop of cultural-political expectations and the perceived inability of the contemporary stage to achieve their realization that Lady Augusta Gregory, Edward Martyn and W. B. Yeats met in 1897, when their 'talk turned on plays'.[7] The result of this discussion was a letter composed by Lady Gregory and Yeats which sought funding for a theatrical venture whose stress is explicitly on the issue of representation: 'We will show that Ireland is not the home of buffoonery and of easy sentiment, as it has been represented, but the home of an ancient idealism' (*Our Irish Theatre*, 20). While the impetus behind the venture was perhaps more concerned with the perceived artistic inadequacies of a commercially driven mainstream theatrical world than it was with any overt political agenda, the political context of a frustrated demand for Irish Home Rule, coupled with the nationalist perception that theatre was a prime mover in the subjugation of any separatist impulses, meant that whatever the intention, the initiative which was to culminate in 1904 with the establishment of the Abbey Theatre, Dublin, could not be immune to the complex political realities of the moment.

These were what D. P. Moran described as 'The Battle of Two Civilizations' in which the members of the Anglo-Irish Ascendancy, who enjoyed economic and political power as a result of their physical, property-based, representation of British interests in Ireland, would necessarily be removed. The full implications of this for theatrical representations of Ireland are revealed in the response to Yeats's *The Countess Cathleen* (originally *The Countess Kathleen*, 1892) which was to share the bill in Dublin on 8 May 1899 with Martyn's *The Heather Field* in the first performances to be realised after their initial 1897 discussions.

The play is set in a famine-struck Ireland of the sixteenth century which, although historically distant, is given a more contemporary charge by its evocation of the Potato Famine of the 1840s through images of people with mouths 'green from eating dock and nettles'.[8] That the Famine was popularly believed to have been caused by British malevolence made it a highly emotive subject. In this politically charged context Yeats's drama concerned the attempts of two merchants who take advantage of the desperation of the starving peasants by offering them money to purchase food if they will only commit their immortal souls to their master, the Devil. Here, Yeats's play carried an allusion to the practice of 'Souperism' by which starving Catholics were offered sustenance at the price of converting to Protestantism. And as a final blunder into the sensibilities of a Catholic/nationalist audience Yeats had the Countess Cathleen offer her soul in place of those of her peasant tenants, who acknowledge the significance of this gesture of munificence because their souls 'are not dear to God as your soul is' (*Variorum Plays*, 146). Given that the landowners of Ireland were predominantly Anglo-Irish and Protestant, Yeats was exacerbating nationalist sensibilities by suggesting that the social hierarchies on earth were given divine confirmation in heaven. The response to the published version of play expressed in the pamphlet 'Souls for Gold' is a useful insight into the complexities of dramatic representation at the foundational moment of an Irish national theatre.

As summarized by the pamphlet's author, F. Hugh O'Donnell, 'Out of all the mass of our national traditions it is precisely the baseness which is utterly alien to all our national traditions, the barter of Faith for Gold, which Mr. W. B. Yeats selects as the fundamental idea of his Celtic Drama!' (*Our Irish Theatre*, 261). And following on from a scathing condemnation of Yeats's ignorance of Irish actuality, the extent to which O'Donnell's anger was derived from what has been termed 'colonial discourse' became clear:

'Mr. W. B. Yeats seems to see nothing in the Ireland of the old days but an unmanly, an impious and renegade people, crouched in degraded awe before demons, and goblins, and sprites, and sowths and thivishes, – just like a sordid tribe of black devil-worshippers and fetish-worshippers on the Congo or the Niger' (264).[9] While Yeats and Lady Gregory were 'confident of the support of all Irish people, who are weary of misrepresentation' (20), O'Donnell's pamphlet reveals the problematic nature of such claims.

Irish theatre, in Christopher Murray's phrase, may be 'a mirror up to nation', but 'the mirror does not give back the real; it gives back images of a perceived reality.'[10] This is strikingly demonstrated in the scene in J. M. Synge's *Playboy of the Western World* (1907) when Christy Mahon gazes into a mirror. Encouraged by the idolization (and idealization) he receives from the villagers as a result of supposedly killing his father, Christie rejects the mirror he had used at home as 'the divil's own mirror . . . would twist a squint across an angel's brow'. Now he sees the 'truth': 'Didn't I know rightly I was handsome.'[11] However, the play's comic celebration of savagery constituted the most fundamental challenge to what nationalist audiences deemed an acceptable representation of Ireland. Typical of the many letters of protest received by the Dublin press is that from 'A Western Girl' who claims that being as she was 'well acquainted with the conditions of life in the West' she could authoritatively assert that 'this play does not truly represent these conditions'. Her rhetorical question, 'Could any Irish person accept this as a true picture of Irish life?'[12] implied that to do so was to exclude oneself from all claims to being Irish. While riots greeted the inadequacy of representation in *Playboy*, Synge had first-hand experience of a performance which audiences did accept as an adequate representation of their reality: Douglas Hyde's Irish-language play *Casadh an tSúgáin* (*The Twisting of the Rope*) (1901), in which it is the peasant community, rather than the savage outsider, whose success is celebrated. In his review of the evening for *L'Européen*, Synge noted that, during an interval, the enthusiastic nationalist audience reacted with emotional tears to the singing of old Irish songs, and he felt as if 'the soul of a people' had entered the theatre.

Here, theatre creates a self-enforcing loop in which image accords with audience desire for self-representation in which only validated images are deemed to be 'in the true'. As defined by Marco De Marinis, these are 'closed performances' which 'anticipate a very precise receiver and demand well-defined types of "competence" . . . for their "correct" reception.'[13] The danger here is the potential for cultural and dramatic stasis in which the audience-stage loop permits no alternative images to those approved, and prescribed. Dipesh Chakrabarty poses the question which pertains to all decolonizing contexts: 'How could one reconcile the need for these two different and contradictory ways of seeing the nation: the critical eye that sought out the defects in the nation for the purpose of reform and improvement, and the adoring eye that saw the nation as already beautiful or sublime?'[14] This tension was to run throughout the early years of the Irish national theatre, in which only 'the adoring eye' was admitted and only one scene was acceptable.

The dominant play style at the Abbey Theatre was 'the peasant play'. However, although the sets were accurate with regard to physical dimensions, and often stocked with genuine artefacts, this was far from gritty realism. Rather it was an idealised representation of the life felt to be expressive of the very core of the nation; a connection between the present and a precolonial authenticity which could not be severed (or mocked) without, by implication, polluting the fountain source of the nation itself. As Brenna Katz Clark observes, 'Many of the audiences, only a generation removed from the land, looked to the Irish peasant as a symbol of their lost identity . . . A national theatre must be popular, and the peasant play met the requirements of that demand.'[15] For '[w]hat is given in the theatrical space is never an image of the world, but the image of an image. What is "imitated" isn't the world, but the world recast according to the fiction and in the frame of a culture and a code' (my translation).[16] This 'code' expressed the state which was to develop after 1922, and the plays which it deemed adequate representations of its self-image. In Terence Brown's account the Irish Free State was deeply informed by the often inhibiting values expressed through the peasant play in which individual desire was subordinate to communal dictates. What emerged was an 'attitude of xenophobic suspicion' of all manifestations of modernisation and a 'deep reverence for the Irish past'.[17] This was a petit-bourgeois state culture informed by 'the prudent and inhibiting values of farm and shop' (136).

As a result there was an effective consensus as to what should be represented, and Sean O'Casey's *The Plough and the Stars* (1926), which critiqued the Easter Rising through a savage inversion of the call for self-sacrifice in Yeats's and Lady Gregory's *Cathleen ni Houlihan* (1902), was condemned as bitterly as *Playboy* had been two decades earlier; and in almost identical terms. It was not, Hannah Sheehy-Skeffington argued, an adequate representation of 1916. Above all she objected to the fact that it was 'a supposedly national theatre, which held up to derision and obloquy the men and women of Easter week'.[18] However, O'Casey's critical realism was more an echo of an earlier, failed, phase of a theatre based on the 'critical eye' than a prelude to a new phase of national self-analysis. Theatre progressively came tacitly to support the new state where oppositional forces had hardened into a mirror-image of the colonial structures they had so recently displaced, even outdoing them in censoriousness and repression as a rigorous conservatism held sway over all debate.

Indeed, in Lennox Robinson's *Drama at Inish* (1933), theatre's socially transformative power becomes the source of comedy rather than the dynamic of a national liberation. While the manager of the small repertory company sees Irish theatre as the inheritor of the socially conscious dramas of Ibsen, Strindberg and Tolstoy, the result of these productions is to induce a destructive bout of self-condemnation in their audiences. The point is serious, but the conclusion is comic, as the owner of the town theatre decides that gritty naturalism will be replaced by a circus. The play ends as the music of the circus band coincides with the outbreak of sunshine to dispel the rain which has accompanied the theatre of social engagement. Theatre's representation of society, Robinson is satirically observing, is required to fall far short of any socially corrective accuracy.

The implication of this freeze-framing of the stage representations of Irish society is that it could not accommodate aspects of a modernity which was inimical to the self-image of the state. The issue had already been debated in the pages of Dublin's *Daily Express* in 1899 when Yeats overruled John Eglinton's declaration in 'What Should be the subjects of a National Drama?' that Ireland's theatre should 'exchange the patriotism which looks back for the patriotism which looks forward'.[19] While Eglinton rejected 'the forms and images in which old conceptions have been embodied – old faiths, myths, dreams' (*Literary Ideals* 26), Yeats stressed that the arts should be liberated from 'their age', and be more concerned with the revelation of 'a hidden life' (36). Yeats's repeated conception of this life differed significantly from that envisaged by the architects of the new Irish state, but it united with them in excluding the supposedly anti-Irish qualities of modernization.

The classic expression of this is the 1943 St Patrick's Day radio broadcast of the Taisoeach (Prime Minister), Eamon de Valera, which evoked an Ireland embodying the qualities that the Abbey Theatre introduced into the discourse of the nation through its plays and stage sets. It was an essentialist vision of both the nation and the social, political and economic structures that sustained that dearly achieved authenticity, with 'frugal comfort' enjoyed around the 'firesides' of 'cosy homesteads' set in 'fields and villages'; an Ireland which would be 'the home of a people living the life that God desires that man should live'.[20] By the end of the next decade it was glaringly obvious that this dream was not to be realised: 'De Valera's "dream" Ireland had never existed.'[21]

De Valera's broadcast was made in the 1940s, but the economic tensions within the state, and their effect on the drama, had already been signalled in the 1930s as economic problems forced the nominally self-sufficient Irish state into what many regarded as a Faustian pact with the all-consuming capacity of an increasingly Anglo-American global economy. However, from the American perspective of Curtis Canfield the theatrical consequences of social change were to be celebrated for forcing the theatre away from 'the picturesque naiveté which was so much a part of Irish plays twenty years ago'.[22] What was changing Ireland, he argued, was the importation of mass communication and entertainment systems which smoothed away the differences between Dublin, London and New York; and the most significant indicator of these changes was the hydro-electrification of the River Shannon. The emblematic significance of this event, which had been planned from the earliest years of the Free State, cannot be overestimated, for while the new state had taken the lifestyle and economy of the west as expressive of its authentic reality, the hydro-electrification scheme was opposed by the embodiments of that authenticity, the salmon fisherman of the Shannon who resisted this enforced erosion of their long-established lifestyle. According to Canfield, 1930s Ireland was becoming modern in its economy and experimental in its drama, but, as demonstrated in Denis Johnston's Shavian *The Moon in the Yellow River* (1931), the tension between economic, as opposed to cultural, necessity was a vital aspect of a debate which was to run into the 1960s – and beyond.

While the play is set in 1927, with a plot driven by the armed resistance of 'die-hards' to the establishment of a partitioned Ireland, the thematic drive is more directly concerned with the extent to which the economy of the country expresses its innate cultural values. 'We are engaged in *Kulturkampf*',[23] as the German engineer in charge of the electric power station declares to his opponent intent on its destruction. And this cultural struggle is explicitly related to 'The Battle of Two Civilizations' essayed by D. P. Moran, the conflict being between the engineer's intention of transforming the country 'from the sordid trivialities of peasant life to something newer and better' (*Selected Plays*, 121) and the Irish idealist's determination to 'keep one small corner of the globe for the unfortunate human race' (139). While opposition to 'some place-hunting industrialist with a small technical education and with neither culture nor religion to guide them' (147) is out of line with Canfield's sense that '[i]n the midst of this stirring of new forces another Ireland is merging, one which, if early symptoms are correct, is more than content to allow its romantic predecessor in the grave' (*Changing Ireland*, xi–xii) it is far more indicative of the indigenous cultural resistance to change which informed the period.

But it was a conservatism whose results fell short of the ecologically and politically 'green' agenda of Johnston's finally defeated idealist. According to J. J. Lee, even in the nominal heyday of independent Ireland it 'continued to be characterized by a high incidence of mental disease, by hideous family living conditions in its urban slums, and by a demoralized casual working class, urban as well as rural' (*Ireland 1912–1985*, 159). And far from heralding an embrace of European theatrical experimentation commensurate with the nominal social modernization, the drama of the 1930s can be seen as initiating 'a long period of decline and decadence'.[24]

Chris Morash's survey of theatre criticism of the 1940s indicates that conservatism continued to dominate, as a 'sense of belatedness – of living in a time after all the great dreams have been dreamed – runs through all cultural criticism of the period'.[25] What was now in evidence was 'an aesthetic of strategic boredom' (79). But as it became increasingly obvious that Ireland had not engaged in a form of modernization which could sustain a viable independent state, economic conservatism came under increasing pressure, resulting in the 1958 Report on Economic Development and its wholehearted commitment to modernization and foreign investment. While the theatrical aesthetic which had informed the development of Irish theatre across the first half of the twentieth century had been based on an 'ancient idealism' and its expression in the peasant play, the new style was informed by the economic directive that '[i]t would be well to shut the door on the past and to move forward.'[26] Four years earlier Brendan Behan's *The Quare Fellow* (1954) contained the observation that 'the Free State didn't change anything more than the badges on the warders' caps'.[27]

All this was to change radically, for the Report marked a watershed in cultural as well as economic terms: 'New class forces, new divisions of urban and rural, new consumer choices were making themselves in Ireland, so that "Ireland" itself, as a fixed and coherent notion, ceased to exist, either in social life or in literature.'[28] What sort of 'Ireland' was to be represented on stage was now a matter of fierce and continuing debate. And if the economic impulse was directed towards modernization, the stage image of the society, which for so long had suggested the essential continuity of tradition and unity of culture, had also to be contested.

While the plays of Brian Friel and Tom Murphy frequently demonstrate a sophisticated appreciation that the past has to be accommodated rather than simply rejected, they are equally alert to the necessity of reclaiming the stage for representations of the emerging Ireland. And this necessitated deconstructing an image whose power echoed through from its appearance in Yeats's and Lady Gregory's *Cathleen ni Houlihan*; namely Ireland as the old woman who, if redeemed by sacrifice, would become a young girl with the walk of a queen. In Friel's *The Loves of Cass Maguire* (1966) the invalid Cass is described as one who, if she were able to move, 'would have the authority and self-possession of a queen'[29] but whose present immobility removes all positive resonances. Similarly, Murphy's *Bailegangaire* focuses on the bedridden and senile old woman, Mommo, who is restored to sanity by engaging with the inadequacies, rather than the glories, of the de Valerean past.

Above all, both playwrights expose the redundancy of an Ireland evoked through the perpetuation of the stage set of the peasant cottage. Recollecting the genesis of his first play, *On the Outside* (1959), written with his friend Noel O'Donoghue, Murphy recalled O'Donoghue's assertion that 'one thing is fucking sure, it's not going to be set in a kitchen'. Which, commented Murphy, was 'the most progressive thing anybody had ever said to me.'[30] Friel's *The Communication Cord* (1982) goes even further in destroying the kitchen set and all its connotations. The set, that of a converted byre which still contains the posts and chains used for tethering cows during milking, is 'too "authentic" . . . an artefact of today making an obeisance to a home of yesterday'[31] which ensures that it is read as an image in the 'critical eye'. The limiting and frequently hypocritical aspects of such a homage to the past are captured in Senator Donovan's accidental imprisonment in the milking chains which changes his idealization of the cottage as 'the absolute verity' into its rejection as 'that shit' (*The Communication Cord*, 75). All 'obeisance' before this cultural icon ends with the cottage's collapse into 'Total Darkness' (93) and the implication that the world which this set once suggested needs to be radically reappraised if theatre is to do anything more than parade shadows of the past before the audience's eyes.

Marina Carr and Martin McDonagh are instructive in this context as, for their critics, their dramatizations of rural Ireland too often topple over into representations which recycle rather than critique disabling images. McDonagh in particular exemplifies the extent to which a nominal liberation effects another incarceration when, in *The Cripple of Inishmaan* (1997), the islanders watch a preview of Robert Flaherty's 1935 film *Man of Aran* which has just been shot on a neighbouring island. Filmed with financial support from de Valera's government, the film was a paean to the life of the Aran islanders as expressive of an authentic Ireland. As McDonagh's islanders sit through the lengthy shark-fishing sequence, the precocious Slippy Helen starts to complain, and she greets the end of the film with the declaration, 'Oh thank Christ the fecker's over. A pile of feckin shite.'[32]

While the iconoclastic urge is evident, the extent to which it was a still critical necessity in the Ireland of the 1990s is open to question, as even iconoclasm can serve to reinforce the centrality of the images it seeks to displace. Whether such impulses are overt, as in McDonagh's head-on engagement with plays of the west, or, as in work such as Enda

Walshe's *Disco Pigs* (1996) and Mark O'Rowe's *Howie the Rookie* (1999), a rejection of the rural in favour of a complete emersion in the lifestyle and argot of street-level Ireland, there is the danger that one aesthetic is replaced by another which is no more accurate in its representations for being couched in the contemporary vernacular of urban rather than de Valerean Ireland.

Nicholas Grene has coined the term 'black pastoral' to describe plays which self-consciously invert the earlier idealizations of life in the west of Ireland by presenting it as brutal and unidyllic. The urban equivalent to this impulse emerged under the title of 'North Side Realism' after the works' location among the high-rise estates of Dublin's economically depressed North Side. De Valera's image of the cosy homestead set in fields and villages has mutated into the Dublin evoked in Dermot Bolger's *The Lament for Arthur Cleary* (1989): 'Everywhere closed except the burger huts, all the buses gone, everyone milling around drunk, taking to the glittering lights like aborigines to whiskey.'[33] And to confirm the completeness of this revolution in representation, Fintan O'Toole asserted that now it is Bolger who best captures the state of a nation for whom '[s]ex and drugs and rock 'n' roll are more important . . . than the old Irish totems of Land, Nationality and Catholicism'.[34]

A century on from the founding of the Irish national theatre, the original model of a national theatre intent on 'articulating a unified national image and unified cultural traditions' has become socially obsolescent.[35] But despite this perception '[t]he bulk of theatre work being presented in Ireland continues . . . to preoccupy itself with issues of history and national identity'.[36] The most powerful articulation of the consequent crisis of representation affecting contemporary Irish theatre is Declan Hughes's essay 'Who the Hell Do We Think We Still Are?', which asserts that the rural image no longer resonates culturally, and that even in plays intent on iconoclasm, 'the iconography remains powerfully the same: half door, pint bottle, sacred heart'.[37] The point is that much of the new drama is concerned with the demolition of images which are known through repetition rather than felt through lived experience, and a consideration of Hughes's own work reveals that more is required than a simple substitution of city for country in terms of set and theme. His drive is away from plays which recycle essentialism in either celebratory or cynical mode and into an embrace of the postmodern collapse of identity: 'It's the condition. Simple as that. Not only but also. The future not the past. Bring it all on' (*Theatre Stuff*, 14). Accordingly, the Dublin of *Digging for Fire* (1991) is not that of the drugged streets but that of the diaspora, for whom '*there* [New York] is as much *here* as *here* is . . . and I don't believe the *here* you're describing [village Ireland] exists here. To me, *here* is more like . . . *there*.'[38]

While this sense of plural identity is a liberating world away from the frequently reductive essentialism which marked the period of the Literary Revival a century before, it is no less problematic in terms of the theatre(s) through which it is staged and confirmed. If representations of Ireland are now recognized as multiple, refracted across the globe as much as across the island then, argues O'Toole, '[b]ecause we no longer have one shared place, one Ireland, we can no longer have a naturalistic theatre of recognition in which a world is signalled to us through objects and we tacitly agree to recognize it as our own' ('Irish Theatre', 174). To adapt a statement by Seamus Deane, what is now required is a drama 'unblemished by Irishness, but securely Irish'[39] as Irish audiences of the twenty-first century may, once again, be 'weary of misrepresentation'.

* * * * *

The chapters which follow trace out the major contours of the complex century-long development which constituted an Irish 'national' theatre, largely, though not exclusively, through the playwrights and productions of the Abbey Theatre but also, as the dynamism of that venture infused cultural life as a whole, the developments of, and reactions to, that original impulse to take control of 'representation'. The first essay, by Stephen Watt, necessarily focuses attention on Irish theatre before the Abbey, particularly the productions of the playwrights of the popular theatres of Dublin, a theatrical world whose productions were deemed by Hugh Hunt, former Director of Plays at the Abbey Theatre, to be 'best forgotten'. It is this assertion which Watt critiques, acknowledging that while this popular form of theatre was that disparaged by Yeats and Lady Gregory in the 1890s as the home of 'buffoonery', it was in reality far from the realm of 'casual comedy' to which Yeats relegated it in his poem 'Easter 1916'. Irish melodrama, as Watt reads it, staged as strong a 'nationalist' message as that nominally advanced by the Abbey. Indeed, in its intentionally accessible and popular form it spoke to – and for – an audience whose interests and appetites frequently fell far short of the more elitist and intellectual art to which the Abbey was dedicated.

It is precisely the implications – and origins – of the Abbey's artistic policy which are variously interrogated by the essays from Adrian Frazier, Joep Leerssen, James Pethica, Mary King and Richard Allen Cave. All the contributions work in the context established by Frazier's study of the 'ideology' of the Abbey; namely the political world – and preferences – from which the Abbey directorate (and major playwrights) were drawn. This was the world of Ascendancy Ireland, the politically and economically dominant 'class' in Ireland whose Protestantism declared its origins in England as much as it separated it from the rising power of an Irish, Catholic, middle class. Frazier defines the founders of the Abbey as 'class renegades' in their engagement with Irish nationalism but is alert to the extent that these sympathies were tempered (and sometimes compromised) by strong elements of self- and class interest.

Joep Leerssen's chapter on Yeats develops this analysis but within a European framework where Yeats is seen alongside conservative figures such as T. S. Eliot and Ezra Pound. Leerssen, moreover, reads Yeats as looking towards the practices of the European avant-garde; this was part of his general hostility to the rising power of middle classes but also the cause of a profound disillusion captured in his 1919 letter to Lady Gregory, 'A People's Theatre', where he acknowledged that the 'art theatre' of which he had dreamed had been defeated by the popularity of plays whose orientation was material rather than metaphysical. While Lady Gregory was for long read as a marginal figure whose role in the composition of *Cathleen ni Houlihan* was ignored in favour of Yeats, James Pethica's detailed account of her career makes the case for her serious consideration, not least as the 'charwoman of the Abbey' whose practical skills maintained the theatre through times of discord. Moreover, as his reading of *The Rising of the Moon* (1903) suggests, she, as much as any of the Abbey figures, was marked by the tension between her allegiance to her Ascendancy origins and her emotional ties to Irish nationalism.

Similar tensions have been found by various critics in the work of J. M. Synge but Mary King's analysis extends beyond this established position, reading Synge's 'post-Protestant' imagination as one which saw the limitations of the emerging Irish nationalism and, equally, stands as a prescient critique of contemporary Ireland. King's concept of Synge's dramatic style as one of 'transfigured realism' whose 'monochrome' quality masks the subtle depths of meaning orchestrated within his stage world is complemented by Richard Allen Cave's detailed analysis of the 'ideological' dimension of Abbey stage sets. This chapter echoes many of the concerns of those which precede it, here grounded in the specifics of theatre where the 'poor' stage sets of the Abbey are read as a deliberate refutation of the excesses of England made manifest in its dense and cluttered stages, and where the Abbey stage's evocation of a world beyond 'the door' was intended to suggest a superior, Irish, dimension of being.

It is this concept of an essential Irish nature which is the concern of the chapters on Oscar Wilde and George Bernard Shaw by Neil Sammells and Gearóid O'Flaherty respectively. Wilde's Irishness has been 'rediscovered' by critics such as Declan Kiberd and Terry Eagleton[40] but Sammells extends their theses through close reading of the major plays, which suggest that, for Wilde, both 'Irishness' and 'Englishness' were surface styles beneath which there was no such thing as an innate national essence. O'Flaherty's detailed account of Shaw's engagement with concepts of national identity through, particularly, *John Bull's Other Island* (1904), builds on this interrogation of national essences, concluding that while sympathetic to aspects of the nationalist endeavour, it was marked, for Shaw, by its limitations. Indeed, argues O'Flaherty, Shaw saw nationalism, in all its manifestations, as an obstruction to the progress of his real conviction – international socialism.

It was international socialism which informed the work of Sean O'Casey from the Dublin Trilogy through to his late plays such as *The Start Turns Red* (1940). Yet, as Ronan McDonald argues, the position of the Trilogy is far from the simple humanist interpretation of socialism suggested by David Krause in *Sean O' Casey: The Man and his Work*. Reading the Trilogy – and O'Casey – as symptomatic of postindependence Ireland, McDonald suggests that these are complex works riven by O'Casey's confusion over the principles to which he was committed and their deliverability in the new state from which they were so evidently absent.

O'Casey's 'confusion' is of the 1920s in the immediate aftermath of Irish independence when the possibility of socialism was at least a recent memory. However, by the 1930s the innate conservatism within Irish nationalism was manifest in the state whose constitution of 1937 circumscribed the position of women to hearth and home, with the resultant alienation and 'exile' of women playwrights which is analysed by Cathy Leeney. In telling readings of the 1930s work of Teresa Deevy and the contemporary plays of Marina Carr, Leeney argues that what differentiates the work of the two playwrights, and sheds light on their respective societies, is the extent to which the female protagonists are, in Deevy, oppressed by systems of control from which fantasy is the only release, while, in Carr, equally frustrated protagonists rage violently against their continuing repression.

It is precisely the presence of other, exiled voices which is addressed by John P. Harrington's study of the countertradition in Irish theatre exemplified by Samuel Beckett. Indeed, as Harrington reads Beckett, there was a rigorous exclusion of the specifics of locality from his work which implicitly refuted the obsession with 'Irishness' which marked the Abbey under the management of Ernest Blythe from 1941 to 1967. Above all, suggests Harrington, Beckett's work reconnected Irish theatre with the work of the European avant-garde (a realization, in part, of Yeats's aspirations) and provided a liberating model for those contemporary playwrights whose forms and themes looked to set the Irish experience within a consciously international context.

On one level Brian Friel's drama could be seen as perpetuating those concerns with the local which were stripped out by Beckett, and the commitment to national essence deconstructed by Wilde. But as Helen Lojek argues, Friel is above all 'testing' what once were certainties to establish their contemporary relevance. Indeed, it is this highly conscious interrogation of established parameters of national narrative and identity which characterizes the works discussed by Lojek, Marilynn Richtarik, Nicholas Grene and Claire Gleitman. The idea of 'testing' which Lojek identifies in Friel was the stated intention of the Field Day Theatre Company (of which Friel was a director) whose brief, productive history is discussed by Richtarik. Central to the company's purpose, argues Richtarik, was to present alternative visions of the past and present and, particularly, to enable audiences to engage with enabling, rather than restrictive, narratives of history. A concern with history in its broadest sense, in fact, is paramount in the work of the contemporary playwrights discussed in these chapters. As Grene maintains, Tom Murphy's *Famine* (1968) powerfully locates the origins of 'famine' – emotional, cultural and political as much as physical – in the trauma of the potato famine of the 1840s which continues to mark contemporary society and which his drama is dedicated to dramatizing – if not exorcizing. It is this engagement with history in all its multiplicity of narratives which is addressed by Claire Gleitman through her analysis of Sebastian Barry and Frank McGuinness. Following on from the earlier chapters – including those on Wilde and Shaw – which have addressed their subjects' impulse to fracture the monolithic and exclusive identity of 'Irishness', Gleitman sees McGuinness's *Observe the Sons of Ulster Marching Towards the Somme* (1985) and Barry's *The Steward of Christendom* (1995) as opening up what we term 'history' into a more fluid range of stories which can accommodate, rather than exclude, those who do not fit neatly into prescribed national categories.

The concluding chapters by Lionel Pilkington, Vic Merriman and Brian Singleton readdress many of the impulses and debates which characterized the founding decades of the Irish national theatre in the early years of the twentieth century. The provocative thrust of these chapters is established by Pilkington's study of the relationship between the Abbey and the Irish state which extends the Adrian Frazier's analysis of the ideology of the early Abbey into the contemporary moment. Above all, argues Pilkington, the theatre was regarded as a key element in establishing and maintaining the stability of the state. Accordingly, he suggests, the values of 'traditional' nationalism – which could be seen as threatening that state stability in its demands for an all-Ireland political entity – were not staged unless the subject was treated satirically or, as in Friel and Murphy, as a crisis which was more existential than political.

The paradox of a theatre whose origins were in the first blaze of nationalism having its ability still to engage with the provocative and contemporary tempered by the pragmatic demands of a modern, wealthy European state runs through the chapters by Merriman and Singleton. In an echo of Leeney's discussion of the 'exiled' state of Irish women playwrights, Merriman addresses the socially marginalized and theatrically muted presence of the rural and urban proletariat who have not benefited from Ireland's current economic success. In particular he reads the commercial and critical success of Martin McDonagh and Marina Carr as demonstrating an abandonment of the revolutionary impulse of Synge in favour of a crowd-pleasing mockery of those whose social and economic circumstances have not improved markedly from the time of the founding of the Abbey. Singleton, too, refocuses attention on the productions of the early Abbey – and its heirs – within a contemporary context in which productions of Yeats can be sponsored by Coca-Cola. As once-radical plays become commodified and commercialized though income-generating 'festivals', Singleton questions the extent to which they have a genuinely contemporary relevance unless those productions are radically reconceived in terms of pressing social concerns. Here, the issue of 'misrepresentation' which provided the dynamic of the Abbey Theatre in 1904 effects a century-long cycle as, once again, the question is as to the adequacy of the theatrical images of the society whose truths – and needs – they purport to stage. It is to this historically informed interrogation of a society and its theatre that this *Companion* is dedicated.

NOTES

1. Lauren Kruger, *The National Stage: Theatre and Cultural Legitimation in England, France and America* (Chicago: University of Chicago Press, 1992), 3.
2. Quoted in Liz Curtis, *Nothing But the Same Old Story* (London: Information on Ireland, 1984), 36.
3. 'The English Mind in Ireland – The Drama', in *The Leader*, 8 September 1900, 22.
4. 'The English Mind in Ireland – Drivel at the Gaiety', in *The Leader*, 22 September 1900, 56.
5. Editorial, *The United Irishman*, in 8 November 1902, 1.
6. 'Cugan', 'The Play's The Thing', *The United Irishman*, in 14 November 1903, 3.
7. Lady Augusta Gregory, *Our Irish Theatre* (Gerrards Cross: Colin Smythe, 1972), 19.
8. *The Variorum Edition of the Plays of W. B. Yeats*, ed. Russell K. Alspach (London: Macmillan, 1966), 16.
9. According to Homi Bhabha, 'colonial discourse' is an 'apparatus of power' whose objective 'is to construe the colonized as a population of degenerate types on the basis of racial origin, in order to justify conquest and to establish systems of administration and instruction'. See Homi Bhabha, 'The Other Question: Stereotype, discrimination and the discourse of colonialism', *The Location of Culture* (London: Routledge, 1994), 70.

10. Christopher Murray, *Twentieth-Century Irish Drama: Mirror Up to Nation* (Manchester: Manchester University Press, 1997), 9.
11. J. M. Synge, *The Playboy of the Western World*, in Anne Saddlemyer (ed.), *J. M. Synge, Collected Works, Volume IV, Plays* (London: Oxford University Press, 1968), 95.
12. Quoted in James Kilroy (ed.), *The 'Playboy' Riots* (Dublin: Dolmen Press, 1971), 9–10.
13. Marco De Marinis, 'Dramaturgy of the Spectator', in *The Drama Review*, 31:2 (1987), 103.
14. Dipesh Chakrabarty, *Provincializing Europe: Postcolonial Thought and Historical Difference* (Princeton: Princeton University Press, 2000), 151.
15. Brenna Katz Clark, *The Emergence of the Irish Peasant Play at the Abbey Theatre* (Ann Arbor: UMI Research Press, 1982), 94.
16. Anne Ubersfeld, *L'Ecole du Spectateur* (Paris: Editions Sociales, 1981), 6.
17. Terence Brown, *Ireland: A Social and Cultural History 1922–1985* (London: Fontana, 1985), 147.
18. Quoted in Robert G. Lowery, (ed.), *A Whirlwind in Dublin* (Westport, CT: Greenwood Press, 1984), 58.
19. John Eglinton, W. B. Yeats, A. E., and W. Larminie, *Literary Ideals in Ireland* (Dublin: T. Fisher Unwin, 1899; rept. New York: Lemma Publishing Corporation, 1973), 12.
20. Eamon de Valera, 'The Deserted Village Ireland', in Seamus Deane (ed.), *The Field Day Anthology of Irish Writing, Volume III* (Derry: Field Day, 1991), 748.
21. J. J. Lee, *Ireland 1912–1985 Politics and Society* (Cambridge: Cambridge University Press, 1989), 334–5.
22. Curtis Canfield (ed.), *Plays of Changing Ireland* (New York: Macmillan, 1936), xiii.
23. Denis Johnston, *The Moon in the Yellow River*, in *Selected Plays of Denis Johnston* (Gerrards Cross: Colin Smythe, 1983), 139.
24. Fintan O'Toole, 'Irish Theatre: The State of the Art', in Karl-Heinz Westarp and Michael Boss (eds.), *Ireland: Towards New Identities?* (Aarhus: Aarhus University Press, 1998), 166.
25. Chris Morash, '"Something's Missing": Theatre and the Republic of Ireland Act', in Ray Ryan (ed.), *Writing in the Irish Republic, Literature, Culture, Politics 1949–1999* (London: Macmillan, 2000), 66.
26. See *Economic Development*, Pr. 4808, 1958, 9.
27. Brendan Behan, *The Quare Fellow*, in *Brendan Behan, The Complete Plays* (London: Methuen, 1978), 59.
28. Fintan O'Toole, 'Islands of Saints and Silicon: Literature and Social Change in Contemporary Ireland', in Michael Kenneally (ed.), *Cultural Contexts and Literary Idioms in Contemporary Irish Literature* (Gerrards Cross: Colin Smythe, 1988), 22.
29. Brian Friel, *The Loves of Cass Maguire* (Oldcastle: Gallery Press, 1984), 11.
30. Quoted in Thomas Kilroy, 'A Generation of Playwrights', *Irish University Review*, 22:1, (1992), 139.
31. Brian Friel, *The Communication Cord* (Oldcastle: Gallery Press, 1989), 11.
32. Martin McDonagh, *The Cripple of Inishmaan* (London: Methuen, 1997), 61.

33. Dermot Bolger, *The Lament for Arthur Cleary*, in *A Dublin Quartet* (Harmondsworth: Penguin, 1992), 26.

34. Fintan O'Toole, 'Introduction', *A Dublin Quartet*, 1.

35. Eileen Morgan, 'Introduction: Re-Thinking the Abbey and the Concept of a National Theatre', in Stephen Watt, Eileen Morgan and Shakir Mustapha (eds.), *A Century of Irish Drama, Widening the Stage* (Bloomington: Indiana University Press, 2000), xxv.

36. Karen Fricker, 'Travelling Without Moving: *True Lines* and Contemporary Irish Theatre Practice', in Dermot Bolger (ed.), *Druids, Dudes and Beauty Queens: The Changing Face of Irish Theatre* (Dublin: New Island, 2001), 118.

37. Declan Hughes, 'Who the Hell Do We Think We Still Are? Reflections On Irish Theatre and Identity', in Eamonn Jordan (ed.), *Theatre Stuff: Essays on Contemporary Irish Theatre* (Dublin: Carysfort Press, 2000), 12.

38. Declan Hughes, *Digging for Fire*, in *Declan Hughes, Plays: I* (London: Methuen, 1998), 38.

39. Seamus Deane, 'Heroic Styles: The Tradition of an Idea', in *Ireland's Field Day* (London: Hutchinson, 1985), 58.

40. Declan Kiberd, *Inventing Ireland: The Literature of the Modern Nation* (London: Jonathan Cape, 1965), 33–50; Terry Eagleton, 'Foreword', *Saint Oscar* (Derry: Field Day, 1989), vii–xii.

2

STEPHEN WATT

Late nineteenth-century Irish theatre: before the Abbey – and beyond

[A] thing that endures – that is the sole redress we have, against history and all its crimes.

(Stewart Parker, *Heavenly Bodies*)

The longstanding notion that Irish melodrama before the founding of the Irish Literary Theatre is scarcely worthy of our attention is a well-worn myth. Like many clichés, this one about popular drama is minimally informed by fact, for there were no Shakespeares or Molières plying their crafts for popular audiences during the last half of the nineteenth century. In the past two decades or so, however, popular genres like Irish melodrama once dismissed as ephemeral or culturally negligible have been reclaimed. Equally important, as these once-neglected texts expand our purchase on turn-of-the-century Irish culture, they also enhance our understanding of greater, more canonical plays and playwrights. This essay, then, although focused on nineteenth-century melodrama, necessarily concerns both the popular and the more 'literary'.

Until recently, melodrama was regarded as too insignificant to inform serious discussion of modern Irish drama. Hugh Hunt, former Director of Plays at the Abbey Theatre, writes in the 'Prologue' to his 1979 history of the theatre that popular playwrights of the nineteenth century represented Ireland as largely 'a mythical land of blarney and blather'; hence their names – he mentions J. W. Whitbread, John Baldwin Buckstone and Fred Cooke specifically – and the plays they wrote are 'best forgotten'.[1] Recalling the Dublin theatre of his youth, Bernard Shaw in a 1946 essay exceeded even Hunt's condemnation. His reminiscence begins generously enough with the 'nobly spacious, lofty, beautifully proportioned' Theatre Royal in Hawkins Street and the Gaiety Theatre founded in 1871, which, though a mere 'bandbox' compared to the Theatre Royal, afforded Shaw his first taste of Gilbert and Sullivan as well as a salutary dose of the comedian Edward Royce, whom Shaw hailed as 'the only perfect harlequin I have ever seen'.[2] In fact, both theatres during the 1890s, the decade in which the Irish Literary Theatre was founded, scheduled similar calendars of attractions: five to seven weeks of German opera at the Gaiety versus Italian opera at the Royal; rival pantomimes after Christmas that often ran into mid-February; touring London stars in revivals of Shakespeare, Goldsmith and Sheridan interspersed with the contemporary social drama of Arthur Wing Pinero, Henry Arthur Jones and others; and varieties of melodrama, on occasion Irish melodrama.

To enjoy Irish melodrama more consistently by the now largely forgotten playwrights that Hunt disparages, and revivals of such better-known plays as Dion Boucicault's *The Colleen Bawn* (1860), *Arrah-na-Pogue* (1864) and *The Shaughraun* (1874), most Dublin playgoers at the turn of the century and later visited the Queen's Royal Theatre. And it is the Queen's, as it was commonly abbreviated, for which Shaw reserves his most acid prose: 'There was one other theatre, the Queen's in Brunswick street . . . but respectable people did not then frequent it, as it served not only as a theatre for crude melodrama but as a market for ladies who lived by selling themselves' ('Preface', 13).

Not surprisingly, then, when Peter Kavanagh observed in *The Irish Theatre* (1946) that it might prove 'interesting to remember' a play such as Hubert O'Grady's *The Famine* (1886), staged in theatres across Ireland for move than two decades, few scholars heeded his recommendation.[3] It is not hard to understand why. Until the 1980s and 1990s, save in the case of Boucicault's dramas, it was difficult even to locate copies of O'Grady's and J. W. Whitbread's plays, let alone critical analyses of them, outside of the Manuscript Division of the British Library or other special collections.[4] Moreover, when such preeminent figures as W. B. Yeats and Lady Augusta Gregory adverted to native melodrama, they did so to help define precisely what sorts of works the Irish Literary Theatre would *not* produce. Announcing the Theatre's second season in the *Irish Literary Society Gazette* (January, 1900), Yeats promised plays that 'expound Irish characters and ideas', plays composed as 'one writes literature, and not as one writes for the Theatre of Commerce'.[5] Yeats and Lady Gregory proffered a more direct criticism of the 'theatre of commerce' in 1897 while outlining their ambition to nurture a 'literary' Irish drama that might rival the best work from ancient Greece or contemporary Scandinavia:

> We will show that Ireland is not the home of buffoonery and of easy sentiment, *as it has been represented* [my italics], but the home of an ancient idealism. We are confident of the support of all Irish people, who are weary of misrepresentation, in carrying out a work that is outside all the political questions that divide us.[6]

For Yeats and Gregory, if most drama had *mis*represented Ireland and her people, none did so more egregiously than melodrama. Yet, as Nicholas Grene has concluded, given the widespread success of Boucicault's and similar plays with middle- and working-class audiences in Dublin, London and America, this misrepresentation must have been more various – or at least been received differently by various audiences – than any blanket indictment of the genre would suggest.[7] One typical charge, as replicated in the manifesto of the Irish Literary Theatre, is that popular drama advanced a stereotype of Irish men and women as low-comic figures – 'buffoons' better known as 'Stage Irishmen' – a hypothesis troubled by much of what follows. Moreover, as Grene asks, what more realistic depiction of Irish people, or of Irishness, obtains in plays produced by the Irish Literary Theatre, later the Abbey Theatre, and what enabled playwrights to create such authenticity?

Through all of this, to return to my epigraph from Stewart Parker's *Heavenly Bodies* (1986), Irish melodrama has 'endured'. Indeed, as *Heavenly Bodies* is based on Dion Boucicault's career, one might argue that melodrama survived the entire twentieth century, thus affecting its 'sole redress' against 'history'.[8] It remained an attraction at the Queen's for decades, well past the years of World War One. Boucicault and his wife made their Dublin debuts at the Theatre Royal in 1861 in *The Colleen Bawn* and appeared again in 1864 in *Arrah-na-Pogue*; thirty years later, throughout the 1890s, both plays and *The Shaughraun* were revived *every* year in Dublin. In 1899, the year of the Irish Literary Theatre's inaugural productions, all three were staged in July: *The Shaughraun* at the Queen's, the other two at the Theatre Royal. In mid-December they were revived again for a two-week run at the Theatre Royal, with *Arrah-na-Pogue* reprised for the last week of the year at the Queen's. Much the same pattern was repeated in December 1904, when the Abbey Theatre opened its doors on the 27th with Yeats's *On Baile's Strand*, Gregory's farce *Spreading the News* and a revival of *Cathleen ni Houlihan*. In the week before, the Queen's mounted *The Shaughraun* and *The Colleen Bawn*, and the Yeats-Gregory evening at the Abbey was rivalled by a pantomime at the Gaiety, opera at the Theatre Royal and Whitbread's patriotic melodrama *Sarsfield* at the Queen's.[9] In his history of the Queen's – one of several studies of the Dublin popular theatre published in the 1980s and 1990s[10] – Séamus de Búrca includes a playbill for a 1928 revival of *Arrah-na-Pogue*, and in his diaries of playgoing Joseph Holloway recalls seeing *The Shaughraun* in the spring of 1935.[11] More recently, in 1988 Britain's National Theatre staged *The Shaughraun* in London starring Stephen Rea, and the Abbey produced *The Colleen Bawn* in 1998.

This brief on behalf of Irish melodrama is intended neither to deify the popular theatre, nor to deny the preeminence of low-comic Irishmen (and women) in the most long-lived – and long-loved – examples of the genre. Rather it is to advance two quite different claims: first, that in entertaining audiences of several classes in different venues such comic characters accomplished a more complex cultural work than many commentators have recognised; and second, that peasant drama at the Abbey – and, as my title is intended to imply, Irish drama 'beyond' the Abbey – is better understood in a context in which popular drama is included. To take up the former point, in his poem 'Easter 1916' Yeats ponders the 'terrible beauty' of Irish nationalism. In the poem's first two stanzas, nationalist green replaces the multicoloured 'motley' of jesters and of many Stage Irishmen on the London stage. The events of Easter 1916, we are told, have persuaded Irishmen of all classes and occupations to resign their parts in the 'casual comedy' of daily life, assuming more significant roles in emulation of the heroes who died for Ireland's freedom.

On the popular stage, however, no such opposition existed: there, such eloquent historical figures as Wolfe Tone, Robert Emmet and Edward Fitzgerald happily coexisted with their peasant countrymen and women – and the 'blarney and blather' Hunt excoriates. Sophisticated aristocrats and vivacious peasants, priests and Fenians, even the 'King's English' and English as they 'spake' it in Ireland – all of these potential oppositions met in nineteenth-century melodrama. And, whether the action of melodramas moved towards comic or tragic denouements, they often communicated to legions of admirers as strong a nationalist message as any play in the Abbey's repertory. A century ago, J. M. Synge and the young Sean O'Casey could be counted among these legions, as, more recently, was the late Stewart Parker. More important, the conventions of Irish melodrama have influenced the development of modern Irish drama in discernible ways, a point to which I shall return after sketching the most prominent features of the era's most enduring plays.

Amid the playwrights whose works consistently drew enthusiastic audiences in Dublin during the later nineteenth century, three names stand out: Dion Boucicault (1820–90), a Dublin-born actor-writer who, at age twenty-one, wrote a successful comedy of manners for one of London's most celebrated actor-managers and whose plays were staged in the United States, England and Ireland; James W. Whitbread (1848–1916), an Englishman who managed the Queen's Theatre from the early 1880s until 1907 and authored numerous patriotic melodramas based loosely on Irish history, particularly the 'rising' of 1798; and Hubert O'Grady (1841–99), a native of Limerick, manager of a touring company and actor whose appearance during the 1876–7 season in *The Shaughraun* first brought him to the attention of Dublin playgoers. In addition, dozens of other melodramatists turned to

Irish topics, many in imitation of Boucicault, and several rose to prominence not only in Ireland, but in England and the United States as well. Edmund Falconer, for example, seized upon the success of Boucicault's *The Colleen Bawn* in London, and wrote dramas such as *Peep o' Day* (1861), *Killarney* (1862) and *Eileen Oge; or, Dark's the Hour before the Dawn* (1871) for West End audiences. C. H. Hazlewood followed suit with *Poul a Dhoil; or, The Fairy Man* (1865), *The Ballanasloe Boy* (1867) and *For Honour's Sake* (1873) for the working-class, largely immigrant audiences that frequented such East End theatres as the Britannia and Shoreditch.[12] In sum, the most accomplished of Irish dramas, like Boucicault's, appealed to a wide range of theatregoers: from the fashionable patrons of Wallack's Theatre in New York, where *The Shaughraun* premiered, to West End and working-class audiences alike in London; from playgoers who enjoyed Shakespeare and Sheridan at Dublin's Theatre Royal, to a popular audience that supported 'crude melodrama' at the Queen's.

While Boucicault is the acknowledged master of the genre, he was hardly the first to exploit its conventions to achieve broader cultural work. For while he was basking in critical accolades after the 1841 production of his comedy *London Assurance*, Irish plays were drawing audiences in London, New York, Boston and Philadelphia. Given the influx of Irish immigrants to both England and the United States in the 1840s and 1850s, many attempting to escape the ravages of the Great Famine, this success is hardly surprising. In the decade of the 1830s plays based on popular Irish novels by Samuel Lover and Charles Lever, the most famous of them starring the celebrated star-actor Tyrone Power (1795–1841), were produced at London's Adelphi and Haymarket theatres. During the next two decades J. H. Amherst's *Ireland As It Is* (1848) and several plays by James Pilgrim – *The Limerick Boy; or Paddy's Mischief* (1850), *Shandy Maguire; or, The Bould Boy of the Mountain* (1851), *Ireland and America; or, Scenes in Both* (1851) and *Irish Assurance and Yankee Modesty* (1854) – consistently garnered audiences in New York, Philadelphia and Boston. Boucicault's greater Irish plays soon followed, as did his antebellum drama *The Octoroon; or, Life in Louisiana* (1859). But, apart from entertaining audiences, how did such plays represent the Irish and how did these representations, however stereotypical and low-comic, facilitate their assimilation into a society not always eager to embrace them?

All of Pilgrim's plays featured comic Stage Irishmen like Paddy Miles the title character of *The Limerick Boy*, Shandy Maguire, and Jimmy Finnegan in *Ireland and America*. Bearing a distinct family resemblance to their counterparts in Boucicault, O'Grady and Whitbread, Jimmy is a 'rolicking blade' whose unrequited love for his female counterpart Peggy has 'made him ten times worse'; and, replicating the stereotype Yeats and Lady Gregory despised, Paddy enters *The Limerick Boy* exhibiting strong proclivities for 'eating, drinking, loving, and fighting'.[13] A quarter of a century later in *The Gommock* (1876), O'Grady describes Larry as a 'quare boy, fond of fairies, fortune-telling, fighting and fun'.[14] Even the greatest of these characters, Conn in Boucicault's *The Shaughraun*, resembles these comic Irishmen. Waiting for Conn early in the play, Mrs O'Kelly, his loving mother, laments to Moya, his peasant girlfriend, that the 'shebeen' has been his home when 'he's not in gaol', and offers what might qualify as one of the most negative descriptions, however unintended, ever uttered about the comic Irishman. Yet her characterisation is immediately parried by Moya's keen social insight, clarifying one of several ways in which class is invoked in Irish melodrama:

> *Mrs O'Kelly.* Conn nivir did an honest day's work in his life – but dhrinkin', an fishin', an' shootin', an' sportin', and love-makin'.
> *Moya.* Sure, that's how the quality pass their lives.
> *Mrs O'Kelly.* That's it. A poor man that spoorts the sowl of a gentleman is called a blackguard.[15]

Herein lies one paradoxical quality of the later Stage Irishman: while he may be a peasant inclined to drink too much and work too little, he possesses the 'sowl of a gentleman'. Inside Conn's soul and Sean the Post's in *Arrah-na-Pogue* exist other qualities as well, such as loyalty and bravery. More important, in *The Shaughraun*, Boucicault's later *Robert Emmet* (1884) and a host of Whitbread's historical melodramas – *Lord Edward or '98* (1894), *Wolfe Tone* (1898), *The Ulster Hero* (1903) and *Sarsfield* – another attribute resides there as well: patriotism.

The Stage Irishman, in other words, however entertaining or fond of liquor, was often much more than a 'buffoon'. On American stages at mid-century Pilgrim's transplanted peasants demonstrated a self-reliance and industry that confirmed their ability to thrive in the emerging industrial economy of their new home. In *Ireland and America* Jimmy Finnegan not only wins the love of Peggy Anderson, but also becomes a prosperous businessman; in *Irish Assurance and Yankee Modesty* the comic Irishman Pat also secures the affection of his female counterpart while moving his Brahmin employer to concede that he is a 'd–d clever fellow' who 'plays his cards well'. Comic Irishmen on the late Victorian London stage were often damned clever as well, especially in matters pertaining to business. That is to say, far from replicating the stereotypes of an indolent Irish deployed in anti-Irish accounts of the Famine to paper over British complicity in the disaster, or of the pugnacious, simianized Irish portrayed in British responses to Fenian aggression – both of which helped rationalize England's continued hegemony over its colonial possession – the comic Irishman in Hazlewood's East End plays is often as industrious as he is amusing. Crotty in *For Honour's Sake* (1873) is one such character, as he explains in the exposition of Act 1 when recounting his economic rise in the world:

> It's industry that's the fine thing . . . It's the poor boy I was at first . . . I was the prudent boy, and wid the first money I scraped together I bought a donkey, then a pony, and then a horse with a car. And the beast and myself are now Crotty and Co., carriers in general.[16]

Such business acumen results from the comic Irishman's frequently displayed ingenuity, a characteristic manifested in several ways.

In most Irish melodrama save for the most reverent of Whitbread's historical plays and Boucicault's *Robert Emmet*, one of the comic Irishman's most vigorous displays of ingenuity – and manliness as well – emerged in his comic trouncing of the villain. In Pilgrim's *Irish Assurance and Yankee Modesty* Pat unsettles the nefarious schemes of a prissy Englishman, Clifford, who rues the day he ever came to the United States. Even more typical is Shandy Maguire, wrongly imprisoned on the trumped-up charges of his English rival for the hand of Mary Connor; his omnipresent shillelagh may suggest an unfortunate stereotype but his courage nonetheless cannot be matched by his adversary. But when it comes to creating such characters, few playwrights can match O'Grady, Whitbread and Boucicault (who believed he had transformed the 'buffoon' whom Lady Gregory and Yeats despised into a far more admirable character).[17] In the majority of examples, in fact, the comic Irishman's uncanny ability to detect plots against his aristocratic master or friend – and then effect a daring rescue or escape – drives the action of the play.

The Stage Irishman's wit in O'Grady's and Whitbread's plays accentuates his physical gifts and vivacity. In O'Grady's *The Gommock*, for example, Larry warns the villainous Hickey, 'I'll put my fist through you and shake hands with the wall' (13); and in Whitbread's 1891 play *The Nationalist* Denny O'Hea pledges to tutor Paddy Flynn, a lecherous attorney, in 'the science ov boxology' by giving him a sound thrashing.[18] Even when cast in historical moments such as the Williamite invasion of the 1690s depicted in Whitbread's *Sarsfield*, a comic knockabout like Gallopin' Terry Hogan seems always poised to defeat his opponent, in this case Hans Oosterdam, servant to the lascivious Duke of Wurtemberg. Hans, following his master's lead, has become smitten with an Irishwoman (another convention in such plays), in this instance the lovely Eilly Blake, Terry's romantic interest. As a consequence Hogan is required to perform two roles: to protect Eilly from Hans's rapacity *and* save the historical hero from capture by the enemy, always a suspenseful possibility. The dramatic action of *Sarsfield*, then, alternates between intrigue and rescue, romance and military manoeuvring, with Gallopin' Terry finding abundant opportunities to flex both his muscle and his wit. Rescuing Eilly from Hans's clutches in Act 3, he informs his nemesis that if he catches him 'attemptin' to annoy this gisha' wid any of [his] dirthy, greasy, Dutch cheese attentions . . . I'll blow ye into the bog ov Allen' (70). Later, moments before the final curtain when Sarsfield is forced to surrender and leave for France, Terry foils Hans's plans to marry Eilly – who was never interested in the Dutchman in the first place – and in the closing scene he and Sarsfield profess their love both for Ireland and for freedom.

It is conventional in Irish melodrama that villains like Hans and Wurtemberg share perhaps as many stereotypical attributes as the so-called Stage Irishman exhibits. For example, even when they are not merely avaricious or cowardly, such figures are often lustful and unprincipled in their pursuit of Irish women. If they are foreign – British, or Williamite Dutch as in the case of *Sarsfield* – they tend to see Irish women as an irresistible 'spitfire' they must possess (Wurtemberg) or as a figure of natural beauty they are driven to admire (the sympathetic Captain Molineux in *The Shaughraun*). If they are Irish, like Corrigan in *The Colleen Bawn*, they tend to view women as property and a woman's body as a synecdochal figure for land or an estate. 'I'll take a lien for life on *you*, instead of the mortgage' (*Selected Plays*, 197), Corrigan threatens Mrs Cregan.

The worst of the Irish villains pervert both the law and their positions as lawyers or land agents to further their own ends; and, in the case of historical melodramas, they manipulate their friendships with nationalists only to betray them. Emulating Judas, in other words, such characters as Francis Magan and Francis Higgins in Whitbread's *Lord Edward, or '98*, Joey Rafferty in *Wolfe Tone* and the infamous Harvey Duff in *The Shaughraun* betray their Christ-like friends by becoming informers. Most often their plans are foiled by the comic Irishman, who recognises their potential for treachery long before the gentlemen-patriots do. Thus in *The Shaughraun*, after saving the young Fenian Robert Ffolliott in a series of sensational escapes and rescues – so-called 'sensation scenes' exploited in posters at the time in the way that film 'trailers' feature explosions and car chases today – Conn confronts Harvey Duff near the end of the play. On a precipice high above a rocky shoreline Conn batters Duff with the names of all the people he has destroyed. Pleading for mercy, Duff is then surrounded by the community he has terrorized and leaps over the side. In the rare instances in this genre of such malevolent characters actually succeeding, as is the case with Higgins (aka "The Shamado") in *Lord Edward*, they are reminded that their victory will be short lived: he will inevitably become an 'object of hatred and contempt for every passerby to cast a stone at' (*For the Land They Loved*, 169). At the same time the patriot whose life he has sacrificed, Edward Fitzgerald, will be revered wherever green is worn.

In addition to abusing their power as attorneys, informers in historical melodrama are often confederates of reprehensible British officers, raising the question of how such characters played to American and especially British audiences. The most infamous of these is Major Henry Charles Sirr, who appears in both Whitbread's *Lord Edward* and Boucicault's *Robert Emmet*, which premiered in Chicago. In the latter play Sirr's sadistic attempts to coerce information from Ann Devlin, another historical figure, rival the most ruthless of actions on the melodramatic stage. Early in the play he vows to get Ann ('my beauty') in his 'clutches' and make things 'hot' for her (*Selected Plays*, 337); and by Act 3 he gets the opportunity to do so by preparing to repeat the atrocity performed by his historical predecessor: hanging her until she talks. Although the undaunted Ann is spared this torture, Sirr finally achieves at least one part of his ongoing project: Emmet's capture and sensationally staged execution. So how could audiences in Britain countenance such brutality, even taking into account the numerous rationalizations for colonialism that existed at the time?

At least three possible answers exist. First, as in all these melodramas, greedy Irish informants enable Sirr's villainy. By comparison, the British officer appears at least partially motivated by an admirable nationalism, not personal enrichment, the sole concern of Emmet's former friends Michael Quigley and Patrick Finerty in *Robert Emmet*. Second, Sirr's perversity is counterbalanced by the nobility of another British officer, young Captain Norman Claverhouse. Much like Captain Molineux in *The Shaughraun*, Lieutenant Frank Tracy in O'Grady's *The Fenian* (1888) and – to take up an example from the contemporary stage – Yolland in Brian Friel's *Translations* (1980), Claverhouse loves an Irishwoman with a selflessness usually found in heroic drama. In fact, he had one day hoped to marry Sarah Curran and had been encouraged by her father to pursue her. But Sarah loves Emmet unreservedly. Whereas villains pay little regard to such niceties in forcing themselves upon the objects of their lust, Claverhouse's love for Sarah is such that he resolves never 'to quit' her side until she becomes Emmet's wife (*Selected Plays*, 339). Third, and most important, the contrast provided by British officers like Sirr and Claverhouse allowed audiences to 'read' perversity as originating in the excesses of a single character, not in the brutalities of a system of colonial domination. Purnima Bose traces the origins of such a reading in British accounts of colonialist atrocities in both India and

Ireland, and their representation of a 'rogue colonialism'.[19] That is to say, violent British reprisals against natives in both countries – 'Bloody Sunday' at Croke Park in 1920, for instance – are attributed to – in a more psychoanalytic register one might say projected upon – a single officer who tragically exceeds his authority.[20] In this way, while one audience might 'read' the display of physical forces as inherent to a colonialist regime, another might locate its provenance in the pathology of an individual whose excesses in no way implicate the larger imperial project.

In many of these more overtly political melodramas women's roles also evolved, modifying earlier formulae which relegated women to parts either as heroines in peril or as their loyal friends, servants or mothers. Such characters still appeared, of course, but the range of roles expanded to include more independent women like Ann Devlin in Boucicault's play and Honour O'Neill in C. H. Hazlewood's *For Honour's Sake* (1873), who does something earlier heroines simply dare not contemplate: she kills a pursuer who 'wouldn't take no for an answer' in order to save her brother, who had come to her aid and was being overpowered by her assailant.[21] The most effective plays of Hubert O'Grady, for example, known for his creation of both comic Irishmen and villains like Sadler in *The Famine*, offered such a range of parts. Female characters in *The Famine* resemble those of Boucicault's *The Colleen Bawn*: the wronged peasant girl Nelly O'Connor and the aristocratic Lady Alice Raymond who befriends her. Like Boucicault's's Eily O'Connor, Nelly has proved an attractive inconvenience to a marriage that will financially benefit a former lover; like Anne Chute, Lady Alice provides a kind of moral centre expansive enough to include unfortunate women like Nelly. In such plays class antagonism is toppled by a larger sense of moral propriety and human sympathy.

In *The Fenian* such roles expand to include not only peasant beauties and Anglo-Irish gentlewomen but also another favourite character on the popular stage: the older peasant woman of ingenuity and patriotic fervour. In *The Fenian* this is 'Old Nancy' who frequently foils the machinations of the villainous Maxwell and offers at times a metacommentary on the action. Her most memorable speech, in many ways a prescient one, concerns her love for Ireland and her willingness to fight for her freedom. After following the romantic lead, Colonel Frank Tracy, who is in love with the peasant girl Ellen Lynch, to a Fenian meeting place, Nancy expresses her desire to join in the struggle:

> Begorra, maybe the Lieutenant is a fenian, and more power to him if he is. I wonder do they take females in the society, for although I'm a female myself, I [am] as good a man as any of them.[22]

As, indeed, she proves to be. Like the Stage Irishman, she is fond of drink and her speech is replete with 'begorras' and 'mushas', but, also like her male counterparts, she is loyal, intrepid and – at base – a nationalist.

At working-class theatres in Dublin, Liverpool, the East End of London and elsewhere, O'Grady's plays provided audiences with excitement, humour and a not insignificant element of Irish nationalism. For O'Grady's obituary in December 1899 *The Irish Playgoer* recalled the recent success of an October revival of *The Famine* and hailed O'Grady as the 'best of all the latter-day Irish comedians'.[23] Perhaps he was. More important for the purposes of this essay, as another eulogist phrased it, *The Famine* and *Eviction* (1879), performed frequently in England, amounted to sermons 'preached from behind the footlights' about conditions in Ireland and appealed to 'popular feeling in a curiously successful fashion'.[24] So did Boucicault's and Whitbread's plays, which grew in nationalist sentiment as the nineteenth century came to a close. Whitbread's plays based on the 1798 rising, for instance, and Boucicault's *Robert Emmet* 'preached' an even more relevant message as far as the plays of the emergent Irish Literary Theatre are concerned. Finally, in many of Whitbread's plays in particular, the comic Irishman (and occasionally Irishwoman) not only shared the stage with aristocratic United Irishmen like Wolfe Tone and Henry Joy McCracken, they also matched these heroes' nationalistic fervour. In this way, melodrama depicted the nationalist project as one that united social classes, one that in fact required the cooperation of brave peasants and Anglo-Irish gentry alike. The peasant, therefore, as he (*and* she) was in the early years of the Abbey Theatre, played a key role on the melodramatic stage, as did representations of a rural Ireland that in some ways anticipated the greater work of the Abbey Theatre.

In the 1890s many Irish actors and writers, however much they shared Yeats's and Lady Gregory's disdain for the 'theatre of commerce', knew about it, worked in it, and in many cases enjoyed it. Willie (W. G.) and Frank Fay, often credited with transforming a 'predominantly literary movement into a living theatrical entity with its distinct national flavour and form' (*The Abbey*, 32), played a crucial role in the Irish National Theatre Society founded in 1903. Willie Fay had acted in several of Whitbread's plays in the early 1890s, and later in the decade his brother Frank's theatre reviews for the *United Irishman* criticized Queen's Theatre productions of Whitbread's patriotic melodramas. What was needed, Fay inveighed repeatedly in his writing, were literary dramas and Irish acting that transcended the stock gestures of the conventional characters discussed above. The Fay brothers, along with such actors as Maud Gonne, Dudley Digges and Maire T. Quinn, aided enormously in this latter enterprise.[25]

The young Sean O'Casey and J. M. Synge were also quite familiar with Irish melodrama and admired its energy and verve. In his autobiography O'Casey remembers the painful days after the riot in the Abbey in 1926 sparked by *The Plough and the Stars* and his subsequent exodus from the theatre. His amazement and indignation trigger memories of *The Shaughraun*, *The Colleen Bawn* and other melodramas which, as a 'kidger', he had seen or read, "ere ever the Abbey Theatre had entered its beginning'.[26] Albeit in revised and more complex ways, the Stage Irishman emerges clearly in O'Casey's plays, particularly in his 'Dublin Trilogy': *The Shadow of a Gunman* (1923), *Juno and the Paycock* (1924) and *The Plough and the Stars* (1926). A number of O'Casey's recent detractors see a direct correlation between the Stage Irishman and O'Casey's depiction of 'inner city Dubliners as jabbering leprechauns', a representation that in Declan Kiberd's view appealed to the 'new middle-class elites which dominated the Free State' by casting the proletarian in roles once reserved for 'the stage-Irish peasant'.[27] Perhaps. Like his low-comic predecessors, Fluther Good, one such Irishman in the *Plough*, promises his adversaries a trouncing they will not soon forget in terms just as animated as any nineteenth-century peasant ever pronounced. Yet, like his predecessors, Fluther also exhibits considerable bravery when searching for a distraught Nora Clitheroe in the midst of the Easter Rising and bringing her safely home. And, near the end of the play, he challenges two British soldiers to put down their guns and fight fair; then he would 'beat th' two o' yous without sweatin'!'. In short, as was often the case on the late nineteenth-century stage O'Casey so much enjoyed, a Stage Irishman like Fluther may not always be reducible to a buffoon or denigrating stereotype.

Like O'Casey, J. M. Synge enjoyed melodrama and, however transformed by his ethnographic knowledge of peasant Ireland, his formal study of French literature and his sadly short-lived genius, it endures in the texts of his plays. Maurice Bourgeois refers to Synge's 'fond study of melodrama' and his contemplation of the 'Irish National Theatre's relation to the "Stage Irishman" school', a 'study' comprised both of his criticism of the 'absurdity' of Boucicault's plots and of his praise of the 'acting parts' of plays like *The Shaughraun*.[28] Writing about a 1904 Queen's Theatre revival, Synge admired Conn, Mrs Kelly and Moya's 'naive humour', a kind of characterization 'now rare on any stage' and 'useless to expect from the less guttural vocal capacity of French or English comedians' (*The Queen's Royal*, 12). So, while Christopher Fitz-simon, among others, brilliantly foregrounds the Rabelaisian spirit of *The Tinker's Wedding*, its 'robust humour' might also be regarded as containing echoes of earlier melodrama.[29] Juxtapose, for example, Michael Byrne's taking off his coat in pique and advising the priest who threatens to expose to the authorities his sundry crimes, 'Go up to your own shanty, or

I'll beat you with an ass's reins till the world would hear you roaring,' with the similar threats of the comic Irishmen when confronting informants. Or compare, as Christopher Morash has recently done, the riots in the Abbey Theatre over its production of *The Playboy of the Western World* with a popular audience's animated response to the opening scene of Whitbread's *Wolfe Tone* in which the comic Irishman (and college porter) is abused by a group of students. Here, as Morash argues, issues both of social class and the construction of audience arise; when confronted with the events of *Playboy*, therefore, an audience accustomed to reacting vigorously to melodrama simply could not manifest the passivity the Abbey attempted to cultivate.[30] It reacted, in short, as a popular audience might.

Traces of popular *fin-de-siècle* melodrama might be recognized in contemporary drama as well. And not necessarily only in such overt instances as Stewart Parker's *Heavenly Bodies*, in which an elderly Boucicault is the protagonist. When Jack McNeilis tells a friend in Brian Friel's *The Communication Cord* (1982) that the peasant cottage 'shaped our souls' and 'determined our first pieties', to what extent is this a reference to a literal edifice or an allusion to the representations of Irish peasantry that have endured at least since Boucicault's time? More obviously, when Major Lancey near the end of Friel's *Translations* threatens to level Ballybeg and slaughter the village's livestock unless the missing Lieutenant Yolland is found, in what ways does this excess resemble that of sadistic 'rogue officers' like Major Sirr? How do Hugh and Jimmy Jack in the same play both reproduce and transform their comic antecedents on the popular nineteenth-century stage? However one chooses to answer such questions, the mere possibility of their formulation confirms that Irish melodrama, whatever its limitations, has indeed endured into our new millennium. In this way, as Parker's fictive Dion Boucicault insists, it has redressed a picture distorted by both its detractors and a theatre history at times hesitant to accord it any significant place in the story of modern Irish drama.

NOTES

1. Hugh Hunt, *The Abbey: Ireland's National Theatre 1904–1979* (Dublin: Gill and Macmillan, 1979), 5.
2. See Shaw's 'Preface: Fragments of an Autobiography', in David H. Grene and Dan H. Laurence (eds.), *The Matter with Ireland* (London: Rupert Hart-Davis, 1962), 11–14.
3. Peter Kavanagh, *The Irish Theatre* (Tralee: Kerryman Limited, 1946), 401.
4. Manuscript copies of popular Irish plays can be found in the Lord Chamberlain's Collection, Manuscript Division, British Library, London. The Raymond Mander-Joe Mitchenson Theatre Collection in Kent contains several printed, not published,

copies of J. W. Whitbread's plays; and the Dion Boucicault Collection is located at the University of South Florida Library.

5. John P. Frayne and Colton Johnson (eds.) *Uncollected Prose by W. B. Yeats, Volume II* (New York: Columbia University Press, 1976), 197.

6. Lady Gregory, *Our Irish Theatre* (Gerrards Cross: Colin Smythe, 1972), 20. Lady Gregory refers to Ibsen several times in *Our Irish Theatre*, and in his essay 'The Literary Movement in Ireland' (1899) Yeats compares the intellectual movement in Ireland to the 'awakening' of consciousness in ancient Greece, Elizabethan England and contemporary Scandinavia.

7. Nicholas Grene, *The Politics of Irish Drama: Plays in context from Boucicault to Friel* (Cambridge: Cambridge University Press, 1999), 6.

8. Stewart Parker, *Plays: II* (London: Methuen, 2000), 116.

9. For a calendar of theatrical attractions in Dublin 1898–1904, see the Appendix to my *Joyce, O'Casey, and the Irish Popular Theater* (Syracuse: Syracuse University Press, 1991), 199–239.

10. See also Cheryl Herr (ed.), *For the Land They Loved: Irish Political Melodramas, 1890–1925* (Syracuse: Syracuse University Press, 1991), from which all the quotations from J. W. Whitbread's *Lord Edward, or '98* (1894) and *Wolfe Tone* (1898) come; and a special issue of *The Journal of Irish Literature* 14 (1985); 3–49, which contains two plays of Hubert O'Grady discussed here: the short *Emigration* (1880) and *The Famine* (1886). Quotations from these two plays refer to this issue, while those from O'Grady's *The Fenian* (1888) come from the manuscript copy of the play in the British Museum's Lord Chamberlain's Collection.

11. See the playbill section of Séamus de Búrca's *The Queen's Royal Theatre Dublin, 1829–1969* (Dublin: Séamus de Búrca, 1983); and Robert Hogan and Michael J. O'Neill (eds.), *Joseph Holloway's Irish Theatre, Volume II 1932–1937* (Dixon, CA: Proscenium Press, 1969), 43.

12. For a discussion of Irish melodrama in working-class London at the end of the nineteenth century, see Julia Williams and Stephen Watt, 'Representing a "Great Distress": Melodrama, Gender, and the Irish Famine,' in Michael Hays and Anastasia Nicolopoulou (eds.), *Melodrama: The Cultural Emergence of a Genre* (New York: St Martin's Press, 1996), 245–65.

13. James Pilgrim, *Ireland and America; or, Scenes in Both* (New York: Samuel French, 1856), 19; and *The Limerick Boy; or, Paddy's Mischief* (Boston: William V. Spencer, 1855), 8. These acting copies were published a few years after the initial productions of the plays.

14. Hubert O'Grady, *The Gommock*, Lord Chamberlain's Collection, British Library Manuscript Division, BL Add MS 53185H.

15. Dion Boucicault, *The Shaughraun*, in *Selected Plays: Dion Boucicault* (Gerrards Cross: Colin Smythe, 1987), 271.

16. C. H. Hazlewood, *For Honour's Sake: An Original Romantic Irish Drama in Three Acts* (London: Samuel French, n.d.), 18.

17. In his polemical *A Fireside Story of Ireland* (London: Bradbury, Agnew, and Company, 1881), Boucicault announces his 'vocation' to 'abolish' the Stage Irishman and all his 'ridiculous capers' from the stage.

18. J. W. Whitbread, *The Nationalist* (Dublin: W. J. Alley and Company, 1892), 5. Alley printed several scripts for Whitbread authorised 'For Private Use Only'.

19. See Purnima Bose, *Organizing Empire: Individualism, Collective Agency, and India* (Durham: Duke University Press, 2003).

20. After the IRA's assassination of eleven British officers on 21 November 1920, the Black and Tans (British auxiliary troops) fired into a football crowd at Croke Park, which resulted in twelve deaths.

21. C. H. Hazlewood, *For Honour's Sake: An Original Romantic Irish Drama in Three Acts* (London: Samuel French, n.d.), 7.

22. Hubert O'Grady, *The Fenian*. British Library Manuscript Division, Lord Chamberlain's Collection, Add. MS 53416G.

23. Hokey-Pokey, 'Hubert O'Grady's Death,' *The Irish Playgoer*, 28 December 1899, 4.

24. 'Hubert O'Grady's Death,' *The Evening Herald*, 22 December 1899, 4, col. 7.

25. For a discussion of the cultivation of a distinctly Irish acting style in the early years of the Abbey Theatre, see Nelson O. Ritschel's dissertation, '"Rouse This Sleeping Land": The Aesthetics of the Irish Theatre Movement, 1899–1916', Brown University, 1997.

26. Sean O'Casey, *Inishfallen, Fare Thee Well*. 1949. In *Autobiographies II* (London: Pan Books, 1980), 157.

27. Declan Kiberd, 'The Elephant of Revolutionary Forgetfulness', in Maírín Ni Dhonnchadha and Theo Dorgan (eds.), *Revising the Rising* (Derry: Field Day, 1991), 18.

28. Maurice Bourgeois, *John Millington Synge and the Irish Theatre*, 1913. (New York: Benjamin Blom, 1965), 262.

29. Christopher Fitz-simon, *The Irish Theatre* (London: Thames and Hudson, 1983), 154.

30. Christopher Morash, 'All Playboys Now: The Audience and the Riot', in Nicholas Grene (ed.), *Interpreting Synge: Essays from the Synge Summer School, 1991–2000* (Dublin: Lilliput Press, 2000), 137–8.

3

ADRIAN FRAZIER

The ideology of the Abbey Theatre

I

'Ideology' is not simply, though a thesaurus equates them, 'thought'; it can also refer to unconscious assumptions that place a boundary beyond which thought cannot go. The most influential definitions of the concept are those of Karl Marx: 'The nature of individuals thus depends on the material conditions determining their production,' and, more particularly, 'The ideas of the ruling class are in every epoch the ruling ideas.'[1] Such ideas 'rule' because it is only through them that a person can imagine a relationship to 'transpersonal realities such as the social structure or the collective logic of History'.[2] Both the dominant and subordinate classes live within a historical thought-world, which holds all the thought the masters have and all the mastered get. 'False consciousness' is thus unconscious of all that is false in its picture of the world. The landlord class cannot see the tenant truly and the tenants can't either; similarly for workers and employers and all other echoes of the master/slave relationship. Ideology is given glamour by the best minds that schools can educate, publishers can publish or money can buy. Seeking instruction or entertainment, people become willing partners in their own subjection. It is a sorry state of affairs as Marx describes it, this prison-house of ideology.

The problems with this formulation of the concept of ideology are obvious. How does any person, someone like Marx for instance, ever debug his or her mental system and think independently? How does social change come about, much less revolution? How is one to speak of the traditional outlooks of ordinary people, the ones not picked up in the market of representations? For instance, it was not from the ruling class that the peasants came by the belief that the land by right should belong to the peasant, the workers that labour deserves an honest wage, or the colonized that the colony was once a happy nation with its own 'natural' customs.[3] Marx was aware of these problems, and in *Theses on Feuerbach* he argued that 'the doctrine that men are the product of circumstances and upbringing forgets that circumstances are changed by men and that it is essential to educate the educator'(*Karl Marx*, 156). His own political programme depends on a 'vanguard' breaking away from the elite and identifying with the working class, which it penetrates with its theoretical unmasking of ideology and organizes by means of manifestos for change.

More generally Marx spoke of types of societies succeeding one another as generations do, each sowing the seeds of its own supplanting. In this sense not just the 'vanguard', but the bourgeoisie as a whole, 'historically has played a most revolutionary part' and will continue to do so, the *Communist Manifesto* warns, by digging its own grave (223). While each hegemony aims to maintain its dominion for the years to come, the ideas of the ruling class teach others to rule as well. Early modern rhetoric about liberty (originally referring to privileges of the few), and the creed that as individuals the masters are second to none, becomes universalized in the modern period among the many: freedom and equality become the Rights of Man, then of women, and finally of all races and groups. The prison-house of ideology thus does night-duty as the incubator of historical change.

II

The unconscious and class-related aspects of ideology can be seen in a little conversation W. B. Yeats had in February 1898 with Augusta, Lady Gregory, in her London apartment at Queen Anne's Mansions. Yeats had been working with his beloved Maud Gonne in organizing a commemoration of the Rebellion of 1798, more Gonne's sort of thing than his own; he was 'terribly cut up' by the squabbles among the nationalist and republican groups. Worse yet, he told Lady Gregory, Gonne had a new plan to go to distressed areas in the west of Ireland. With the Irish Marxist James Connolly she had already written a leaflet for distribution that said Church doctrine held that 'no human law can stand between starving people and their RIGHT TO FOOD'.[4] To crowds of hungry tenants she aimed to give speeches telling them to kill the landlords' cattle for food (a rather startling attempt by a vanguard to penetrate the masses with 'theory'). Should the government then shoot the thieves, Maud Gonne foresaw the bloodshed as excellent publicity for the overall cause. Yeats had advised her that this incendiary strategy was a mistake, but still offered to come along on her tour, fearing harm might otherwise come to her.

Hearing this tale, Lady Gregory was 'aghast'. She told Yeats she doubted there was any famine, but if there were:

we who are above the people in means and education, ought . . . to be ready to share all we have with them, but that even supposing starvation was before them it wd be for us to teach them to die with courage [rather] than to live by robbery . . . In all the crimes that have been condoned in Ireland, sheep-stealing has always been held in horror by the people, & it wd be a terrible responsibility to blunt their moral sensitiveness by leading them to it.

Yeats was thunderstruck; suddenly he saw 'how wrong such a line would be' and promised to throw his efforts against the rabble-rousing plan. The rapidity with which Yeats is reeled in by the incendiarism of Gonne, and then reeled back the other way by the patrician morality and containment strategies of Gregory is fascinating: not just two women, but fundamental ideologies are in a fight for life.

There are at least three ideological elements in Augusta Gregory's outburst. One is that of hierarchy, entailing upon the few responsibilities to the many. The ruling ideas ought, of course, to be the ideas of the ruling class, those 'who are above the people in means and education'. Lady Gregory shows her excellent tact by pleasantly including within the 'we who are above' her guest, although Yeats at the time had little means and no property. He was not a member of the Ascendancy – largely the estate-owning, Anglo-Irish, Church of Ireland Protestants in Ireland, people like the Persses of Roxborough (Gregory's family) and the Gregorys of Coole (her husband's family). It is possible that Yeats was dizzily aware for a moment how far he had fallen out of the ways of thinking of the Anglo-Irish, and was relieved to be able to take his bearings from Lady Gregory.

A second ideological element in Gregory's remonstrance is the belief that robbery is the crime of all crimes, a belief she attributes to the peasants themselves. Yet in doing so she changes the crime from cattle-killing to sheep-stealing. It is generally landlords who own cattle, and clear peasants from their holdings in order to graze them. Tenants own sheep, and put them out to pasture on the commons. Stealing sheep could get the robber killed, judicially or otherwise. Fear of such punishment may have had as much to do with prevention of this crime, when it was prevented, as a belief in the rights of property. The sacralization of property by Lady Gregory is ideological.

A third ideological element suggests that it is the duty of the Anglo-Irish, once they have done all they can to relieve distress, to teach the starving tenant to die with honour rather than to rob. Obviously, in this scenario the owners have not shared *all* their possessions with the poor, or there would be nothing to steal, but putting this technical contradiction aside, notice that a story is hinted at like those found in popular seafaring tales. A captain in the British navy teaches the common sailor to give up his life fighting for the ship. It would be unholy to mutiny, run up the white flag or hide below decks; you should give your life to protect the cargo, other people's goods. The heroicization of the starving peasant, like that of the martyred sailor, is ideological. The core of all three elements is a golden rule: *don't touch our property!*

III

The ideas of Maud Gonne and the rebels of 1798 are equally open to scrutiny. The bloody-minded personal aggrandizement in Gonne's scheme is spotted straightaway by Lady Gregory, if belatedly by Yeats. Maud Gonne was a woman in love not with a poet but with the standing ovation and long columns on the front page. Her celebrity had its roots in ideological elements of the revolutionary era that have their own radioactive influence on Irish history, with a half-life measured in centuries.

In July 2000 the owner of an old guesthouse beside the bridge in Castlecomer, Co. Kilkenny remarked bitterly to a visitor that when the town was burnt in 1798 by rebels up from Wexford his house was one of the few to survive. It is appropriate to take a little time over those events in Castlecomer because the ideologies that brought about the Rebellion, and the ideologies that grew up in its aftermath, haunted the interval between 1898 and 1916, during which the Irish dramatic revival occurred.

The assault on Castlecomer occurred on a Sunday, 24 June 1798. On the night before, the United Irishmen rebels had killed seven of their prisoners, all Protestant Orangemen. Under the leadership of Father John Murphy, the army of 5,000 set off in early morning for Castlecomer, where 300 militia led by James Butler guarded Lady Ormond's castellated mansion. Butler wept when he could not rouse his troops to leave the castle and oppose the rebels, just then pouring into the town from two directions. The rebel commander wished to deliver an order of surrender to the garrisoned militia, and for that dangerous job he selected an African, the only one among the 5,000.[5] In the course of the day Father Murphy's rebels fired the town and castle, drank up the contents of the Castlecomer wine cellar, and then fled when they heard that General Asgill's troops were on the horizon, riding to relieve the town. Asgill halted short of Castlecomer, set up his cannon, and shelled the burnt and empty town.

From Castlecomer to Vinegar Hill things grew worse and worse for the rebels, especially after the surrender of Father Murphy, and the glorious standards of the United Irishmen – Equality of Man, Universal Reason, Democracy and Freedom of Religion – were dragged in the dirt. Irishmen were anything but United. The victors celebrated the defence of tradition and property by the pitch-capping of captives and the military slaughter of pike-bearing troops of farmers. The myth of croppies' graves opening to release new rebels continues into the present, inspiring hope in one place, fear and anger in another.[6]

Days like that Sunday in Castlecomer write their own stories into people's memories, shreds of narrative that structure responses to the present. They can emerge in the 1880s as a story that priests are behind the Land League, or a contrary story that Rome failed and will always fail Ireland; or in the 1890s as a story that nonsectarian republicanism is either beautiful or horrible. In the run-up to 1916 the Rebellion of '98 could generate narratives showing on one hand that justice is not justice but conquest, and on the other that rebellion is just robbery and murder. One rising was being hatched from the memory of the other. Similarly the burnings of Catholic homes in Belfast in July and August of 2000 by Loyalist paramilitaries is hardly news so much as history murderously ritualised, a reenactment glorified by the ruling ideas of one group. Ideology structures history as commemorative cycle: 1898 is 1798, 1688 is every July Twelfth, and the 1845 Famine is any season of poverty and hunger. Had Maud Gonne ever succeeded in stirring up a wildcat outrage on property in the Erris peninsula of Co. Mayo (where in fact in 1898 there was distress but no 'famine'), it, too, would have left its radioactive trace, energizing and poisoning the area for years to come, making the actual geography into symbolic space, the theatre of ideologies in which all play roles.

IV

In 1898 Lady Gregory was not just steering Yeats away from Maud Gonne and into the company of reform-minded unionist landlords like Sir Horace Plunkett (a system of cooperative creameries was his long-term solution to distress in the west); she was also giving her friend the benefit of her advice, energy and social connections in the formation of the Irish Literary Theatre. George Moore and Edward Martyn, landlords like Gregory, were on board for the new venture, which aimed to 'show that Ireland is not the home of buffoonery and of easy sentiment, as it has been represented, but the home of an ancient idealism'.[7] This manifesto sounds very much like an anti-ideological intervention of 'theory'. It promises to replace representations with realities. That those writing the plays and bringing the productions to Dublin were themselves members of the Ascendancy does not necessarily imply that they defended it.

In fact, Gregory, Yeats, Martyn and Moore resemble the class renegades who make up the 'vanguard' in the thinking of Marx. Gregory had a soft spot for the rebel ballads which she sang as a child. Yeats, after bitter boyhood experiences in English schools, was capable of hating 'England' though he lived happily in London; in the company of Gonne he had made common cause with militant republicans. Martyn's strict Catholicism put him at odds with Protestant England, and Moore, the son of an Irish patriot member of Parliament, was ready to turn his back on an England that did not properly appreciate his novels and even condescended to him on account of his Irish background. They would all have voted for Home Rule; however, they would also have thought it right that they should continue to rule at home after that distant day arrived. In short, they could play a revolutionary role vis-à-vis the Union, and a counter-revolutionary one vis-à-vis a domestic democracy.

Yeats's contribution to the first season of the Irish Literary Theatre, the *Countess Cathleen*, performed 8 May 1899 in Dublin, is a spectacular example of colliding ideologies. Although first written in the early 1890s, the play dramatizes the very issue that arose in his aforementioned conversation with Lady Gregory about Maud Gonne's plan to save the peasants from famine in 1898. The play stages the story of a time of famine in which devils went about Ireland buying souls for gold. While the peasants are ready to trade, and get prices according to their relative sinfulness, the great landlord Countess Cathleen is horrified by the eternal loss of so many helpless souls. She gives away her money, permits the tenants to take her property, and finally sells her own soul (worth a great deal more than anyone else's), to buy back those of her tenants. In the denouement angels rescue the countess because God, we are told, judges the intention rather than the deed.

Apart from paying a fantastic compliment on behalf of God to Maud Gonne, the play has a number of progressive and patriotic aims. It shows how to turn an Irish folktale into a verse-play, how landlords should care for their tenants, how all Irish people should care more for their souls than their bellies, and how the English are devils who buy and sell. Somewhat to Yeats's surprise, many Irish people protested against the performance, and it was not all because an old Parnellite enemy of Yeats, F. Hugh O'Donnell, published a pamphlet against the play, and Cardinal Logue on this basis condemned it. Some in the audience (for example, university classmates of James Joyce but not Joyce himself) thought Yeats displayed offensive ignorance of both the history of his own country and the theology of its majority religion, Roman Catholicism. There had been a great famine in Ireland in 1845 and following years, and a stock conception essential to the whole ideology of the Land War in the 1880s was that the landlords did not save their misguided and hungry tenants, even if some tried to do so (notably, George Moore's father in Co. Mayo), but had offered them soup on condition they convert to Protestantism, which most refused to do. The cottiers had been well taught by their priests 'to die with courage [rather] than to live' by loss of their soul, to quote once again Lady Gregory's advice to Yeats on the hungry tenants of Erris.

The vast reallocation of land in Ireland from landlords to tenants, underway from the late 1880s to 1910, was based on an emerging nationalist consensus that landlords were bankrupt stewards of the country, and Irish feudalism was an unworkable anachronism. Yeats's play was an ideological counterfiction flattering to patriotic members of the ruling class by means of its depiction of the value of the chivalric tradition, noble manners and a feudal way of life. Significantly, it was more successfully staged as tableaux by titled ladies at the Lodge in Phoenix Park for the pleasure of Arthur Balfour, the Chief Secretary.[8] 'The only worthwhile revolutions for Yeats,' John Kelly remarks, 'are counter-revolutions.'[9] He wanted to achieve unity of culture in Ireland, the many under the leadership of the few, consolidated by opposition to England and public amnesia about past internal conflicts ('Race and Class', 139). However, in this revolutionary period a single hegemonic ideology does not dominate in Ireland; ideologies multiply, advance and retreat, change their content but not their form, or retain their significance in spite of a shift in style. The ideology of *The Countess Cathleen* did not remain unconscious, and so did not successfully 'rule'. Instead it brought about a proliferation of ideological interventions.

V

The ideology which motivates a work may be quite different from that work's consequences. Some play-lovers and amateur actors who attended the performance of *The Countess Cathleen* took fire from it – notably Frank and W. G. Fay, James Cousins and Seamus O'Sullivan. By October 1901 the Fays had trained the Irish-speaking cast of Douglas Hyde's *Casadh an tSúgáin* (*The Twisting of the Rope*). This brief curtain-raiser upstaged the big mythological drama by Yeats and Moore, *Diarmuid and Grania*, during the third and final season of the Irish Literary Theatre, held at Dublin's Gaiety Theatre. A few months later the Fay brothers persuaded George Russell (A. E.) to write a play for them, *Deirdre*. It was rehearsed in the Coffee Palace over the winter, and performed in April 1902 along with a one-act play about 1798 mostly written by Lady Gregory yet conceived and signed by Yeats, *Cathleen ni Houlihan*.[10] The production was organized by Inghinidhe na hÉireann (the Daughters of Ireland), Maud Gonne's feminist-nationalist organization, and staged in a Carmelite hall near the Roman Catholic church on Clarendon Street in Dublin. At the curtain 'A Nation Once Again' was sung by the audience.[11] That summer members of 'W. G. Fay's National Dramatic Company' put their savings together and rented a shabby hall in Camden Street to carry on their movement, one that was nearly as political as it was theatrical. They set up a board of officers for their organization, renamed it 'The Irish National Theatre Society', and offered its presidency to George Russell. He declined, but on 9 August 1902 Yeats, next in line, took it up and quickly made the most of its executive potential, though he subsequently struggled with fellow board members Arthur Griffith (editor of *The United Irishman*) and Maud Gonne.

Within these facts are indications of the ideology of the original Irish National Theatre Society. George Russell was a hero of this group, partly on account of his practical kindliness and impractical, fanciful theosophy, partly because of his work with Sir Horace Plunkett's Irish cooperative movement. This sought to relieve rural distress and dependence on England by means of well-organized self-reliance, and self-reliance was crucial to the new theatre group's self-conception. Its members especially hated Dublin's dependence on touring English shows, 'regular night-school[s] of Anglicization'.[12] The new Irish National Theatre Society (INTS) promised to replace these with true Irish manners enacted by Irish citizens. Douglas Hyde, also one of their heroes, was the leader of another great nongovernmental organization, the Gaelic League. It, too, had an ethic of self-help as a means to recovery of both the original language of Ireland and its pride. The Coffee Palace rehearsals link the company with the Total Abstinence League of the Sacred Heart. At the Coffee Palace working men, it was hoped, could be drawn away from pints of Guinness to cups of coffee, improving lectures and inoffensive plays (Padraic Colum and the Fay brothers were habitués).[13] That the plays were staged at a Carmelite temperance hall indicates how comfortable these players were in a Catholic setting (*Abbey Theatre: Interviews and Recollections*, 33). The facts that they billed themselves as 'Irish National' players, and pooled their own money, are marks of their commitment to communalism, national independence, and democratic practices. That they asked not just Yeats, but also Griffith and Gonne to be on their executive board affiliates them with nationalist groups and newspapers that existed to propagandize for Irish independence; most believed they constituted such a group themselves. The members of the INTS meant to bring about their own decolonization, beginning immediately – a core idea of Sinn Féin at its inception in 1905.

The inaugural plays they asked Russell and Yeats to write for them also reveal the ideology of the early INTS. The Fays noticed the first act of *Deirdre* in a journal and prodded Russell to finish it, even giving him an outline for the last act.[14] The play was acted behind a gauze curtain, and the language is equally gauzy. It is a soft-core, soft-focus tableau of Ireland in the mythological ages, a kind of pornography of nationalist self-love, and very popular with the Daughters of Ireland.

The second play performed by the society was also written after a specific request by the ensemble (the authors of the Irish Literary Theatre had written their plays, then hired English actors to stage them). On 4 May 1901 Frank Fay had written in *The United Irishman*: 'Let Mr Yeats give us a play in verse or prose that will rouse this sleeping land. There is a herd of Saxon and other swine fattening on us. They must be swept into the sea along with the pestilent crowd of West-Britons . . . This land is ours, but we have ceased to realize the fact. We want a drama that will make us realise it.'[15] At Coole in the summer of 1901 Yeats went straight to work, or Lady Gregory did. Her *Cathleen ni Houlihan* is a wholly republican play, set in Killala, Co. Mayo in 1798, just before the landing of the French. It depicts a much more romantic and heroic reality than do historical accounts of events on the other side of the country in Castlecomer. A young man is preparing to be married when an old-woman-who-is-Ireland appears and calls him away to her service; he must sacrifice everything (most pointedly, his life) to get back her four green fields, stolen by a stranger. Leaving parents and farm, bride and dowry, he follows after her as in a dream. At the play's end a boy coming into the house says there was no old woman on the road, but he saw 'a young girl, and she had the walk of a queen'.[16] Such simple, romantic, unmistakably incendiary drama is one of the things W. G. Fay's national players most wanted to stage. *Cathleen ni Houlihan* became a foundational myth of grass roots Irish republicanism: its enactments took on the character of a rite of blood sacrifice.

No doubt the INTS expected that its new President would write more *Cathleen ni Houlihan*s, but he could not do twice what he had never done once. Lady Gregory was the author who soon emerged publicly as the supplier of such works, though none quite as hair-raising as her first. The force of later 'rebel plays' such as *Twenty Five* (1903) and *The Rising of the Moon* (1907) is softened by populist comedy and the condescendingly quaint 'Kiltartan dialect' she invented, a stage-poetry quite different from Synge's alarming arias developed out of dialect and translations of Gaelic speech forms. She tended to see country people as winningly childlike and pure at heart; he imagined them as splendidly pagan with a strange kinship with the dark.

A collision between the ideologies of the authors and the players was on course from the start: one group was hierarchical, the other democratic; one was all for keeping the many dependent on the few, the other was wedded to a new ideology of self-reliance; one was rooted in an aristocracy of land, the other in democratic labour; one was for parliamentary Home Rule, the other was sympathetic to Sinn Féin; one was horrified by Jacobin socialism, the other was excited by it. One 'Cathleen' weighed against the other: the fear of those whose families had the most to lose in 1798 was opposed by the long anger of those whose ancestors suffered most in the 1845 Famine.

VI

One of the first points of conflict between the President and the company was in the selection of plays. Part of the constitution of the new INTS laid down that plays proposed for production should be read to the members and voted on, and that no plays should be produced that were offensive to national ideals. One of the actors, T. G. Keller, recalls gathering in Camden Street to vote down a play by Yeats and vote in one by Synge unanimously; if so, it must have been *Riders to the Sea* (1904), for Synge's *In the Shadow of the Glen* (1903) was protested against by Gonne and Hyde as being offensive to national ideals. Were there in fact, as in the play, Irish wives who whistled for a philandering young fellow down the hill, and who left an ageing husband to run off with a tramp? If so, it was not normally so, Griffith argued in print.[17] Along with two actors from the original company, Gonne resigned when outvoted (*Abbey Theatre: Interviews and Recollections*, 25). In another crisis some in the company and many outside it wanted to stage Padraic Colum's *The Saxon Shillin'* (1903), an antirecruiting and antilandlord play, but Yeats and the Fays diplomatically rejected it on aesthetic grounds. Those grounds, more and more, were to be the only ones publicly acceptable to Yeats, and to make sure he got his way he overruled the democratic reading committee then revised its rules so that he could better control it (February 1903), and finally abolished it (September 1905). After a lengthy, complex and politically brilliant campaign by Yeats, democracy and propaganda were rooted out by the executive; the authority of authors (not control by players, audience or purse) and art for art's sake were honoured in their stead.

By the time this victory was complete most of the original members of the Fays' company had resigned in bitterness, and others would follow. It became a public relations problem that those who were driven out tended to be Catholics, and those who remained or were brought on board were not. Among the authors, for instance, George Moore and Edward Martyn – both from Catholic families – were left behind when the Irish Literary Theatre gave way to the Irish National Theatre Society in 1902. The official explanation was that they did not like amateur folk drama or verse plays (which was true), but the sectarian coincidence came to seem ominous. Next came Padraic Colum, a significant talent, who resigned over the extirpation of democracy in the theatre in 1905. All this occurred in a climate where, in the words of Lionel Pilkington, 'constructive unionist cooperation with constitutional nationalism [was collapsing] in a welter of sectarian recrimination'.[18] William Boyle, a writer of popular comedies, quit in 1907 after concluding from a dinner party with theatre-owner Annie Horniman that *The Playboy of the Western World* was part of an 'anti-Irish' drive in the executive (*Behind the Scenes*, 218). The day would come in 1908 when the Fays as well would be shown the door. The caretaker of the Abbey Theatre said to W. G. Fay as he left, 'You'll be the owner of this theatre yet' (*The Abbey Theatre*, 47) – not to be, but a sage assessment of the significance of property to control of the Abbey Theatre.

As Catholic writers and actors were sacrificed, all sacrifices were made for Synge, whose plays caused controversy and did not sell tickets or win friends. From the first he was welcomed by Lady Gregory and Yeats, whether on holidays at Coole or in London at Gregory's apartment where he gave first readings of his plays; in 1905 he officially joined the executive. A comfortable coincidence of fundamental ideologies united the directors and set them apart from the actors. Of course, Synge was not simply a gentleman; he was the one dramatic genius of the early movement. Remarks like that of Yeats that his own 'mission in Ireland [was] to serve taste rather than any definite propaganda' are in keeping with the feeling of all true writers that a message cannot be the highest aim of art; nonetheless, Yeats's conception of taste may originate in class feeling ('Race and Class', 144). Style, he came to think, was 'but high breeding in words and argument'.[19] The Abbey executive believed it had a mission to educate both the actors and the audience, to raise them – whether they liked it or not – to an appreciation of what those who were above them in means and education judged to be finest. Abbey Theatre ticket prices and house customs, for instance, differed from those of popular theatres: late entry was forbidden; the house was darkened during performance; absolute silence was required until the curtain gave the cue for applause, a kind of passive gentility unknown to many Dublin theatregoers.[20] Even Yeats's particular taste for tragedy on stage may in some part have ideological roots: it is for the few to teach the many how to die with dignity. Of course, things can backfire, and an audience might learn instead how to die with dignity in 1916 in a post office, where Patrick Pearse shaped his valour on the model of Cuchulain's last stand.

The ideological work of the repertoire of the NTS often works through one theatrical trope: the stranger in the country kitchen, the importance of which is developed in Nicholas Grene's *The Politics of Irish Drama*. It forms the heart of the Irish play's 'intertextual line of descent'. W. B. Yeats's *The Land of Heart's Desire*, Douglas Hyde's *The Twisting of the Rope*, Yeats's and

Lady Gregory's *Cathleen ni Houlihan*, Synge's *In the Shadow of the Glen* and *The Playboy of the Western World* all develop this situation within the first decade or so of modern Irish drama. That cottage on stage represents the temple of Irish domesticity, the sacred origin, the mystery of mysteries – within it the Irish are themselves. Let us draw the curtain; now listen to the amazingly unique talk of true Irish cottiers, and watch them fight and court in their own way. That voyeuristic revelation of primacy is what the Irish play offers to Londoners, New Yorkers and Dubliners, too, many of whom were themselves a generation or more away from being tillers of the fields.

Equally dangerously, the trope aims to explain the colony to the imperial centre, interpreting Irish domesticity truly, i.e., *not* as 'the home of buffoonery and of easy sentiment'. The ongoing possibilities for violation of privacies or totemic desecrations are endless and inviting, especially to 'strangers' with the affectionate menace of a Synge. Given the incomplete struggle for national independence, echoed by the conflicts within the INTS itself, every performance was played out on a battlefield of ideologies, not in a prisonhouse of false consciousness. On the Abbey stage the progressive potential of plays by authors from a dominant class gave form to the appetite of the audience for historical change, and the repressive potential of the plays was itself a provocation to the public demand for expression of national independence and self-respect. The plays bottle the political energies of the moment of their emergence, and they can still freshly decant them, so that, for instance, *The Playboy of the Western World* has been read by W. J. McCormack as a revenant drama in which the spirit of Parnell is again glorified then once again mocked by an unworthy people, and by Declan Kiberd as a programme for Frantz Fanon-style decolonization.[21]

VII

One key figure remains unaddressed: the owner of the Abbey Theatre, Annie Horniman. This prickly English woman was brought into the Irish theatre movement by Yeats on account of her readiness to spend her wealth on a joint project with her fellow mystic from the Order of the Golden Dawn. She came from the Quaker family that founded Horniman Tea, the first company to put tea in bags for retail sale, and was thus caught up in the practices and beliefs of British capitalism and imperial trade with India. Horniman was a rebel in the family in her mysticism, feminism and passion for theatre; she was a chip off the old block in her dislike of inefficiency, menials who behaved like equals and upstart colonials. In particular she hated Irish people (*Behind the Scenes*, 179–86).

Still, drawn on by her affection for Yeats and the hope of an important role for herself in a new theatrical sensation, Horniman bought the old Mechanics' Institute on Abbey Street. Before the December 1904 opening she had it refitted along the latest bourgeois Celtic lines with stained-glass windows, portraits of authors and, leading ladies and gentlemen, deep carpets, etc. Most significantly, in 1905 she put up a subsidy so that the actors could be paid. Her ideology and her wealth were both important in turning the NTS into a commercial repertory theatre, with frequent tours outside Ireland.

Yet from the start she demanded that the theatre operate according to the 'Samhain principles' published by Yeats with her original offer of the Abbey to the INTS. The first principle required that authors take precedence over actors, the second that actors take precedence over spectacular scenery, and third, most importantly, was a principle interpreted by Horniman so as to prohibit the performance of any 'political' play – i.e., one that was either anti-English or pro-Irish independence. She was determined that no money of hers would be spent advocating 1798-style rebellion or even Home Rule on the Abbey stage.

Of course, Annie Horniman could not entirely stamp out the Irishness of the Irish National Theatre Society, but she strengthened the hand of the one director she liked and even sometimes trusted, W. B. Yeats. In fact, she strengthened it so much that Yeats was able to buy the Abbey for a fraction of its cost from a disenchanted Horniman in 1910. In 1925 when the Irish Free State began subsidizing the Abbey, Yeats preserved the National Theatre Society charter so important to him and to Horniman, a charter that occasionally stiffened the resolve of later artistic directors of the Abbey. The National Theatre Society was intended to remain independent of government control in spite of dependence on government money, friendly to authors and emerging talent, known for script-driven and actor-centred dramas of high talk rather than ensemble pieces or stage-spectacles, with a strong repertory of Irish plays and international masterpieces. The aspiration was still to replace false or dated representations of Ireland with true ones. The prison-house and birthplace of ideologies, the Abbey Theatre remains open to the entrance of the stranger, talking the talk of love, or bearing tales of famine, crime or revolution.

NOTES

1. David McLellan (ed), *Karl Marx: Selected Writings* (Oxford: Oxford University Press, 1977), 161, 176.
2. Fredric Jameson, *The Political Unconscious* (Ithaca: Cornell University Press, 1981), 30.

3. In a supplement to Marx, George Rudé develops the concept of 'popular ideology' in *Ideology and Popular Protest* (Chapel Hill: University of North Carolina Press, 1980).

4. James Pethica (ed.), *Lady Gregory's Diaries 1892–1902* (Gerrards Cross: Colin Smythe, 1996), 166–7 and notes.

5. Art Kavanagh, *Ireland 1798: The Battles* (Bunclody, Wexford: Irish Family Names, 1998), 223. See also Tom Lyng, *Castlecomer Connections* (Castlecomer History Society, 1984).

6. See Seamus Heaney's poem for the 50th anniversary of the 1916 Easter Rising, 'Requiem for the Croppies,' *Opened Ground* (London: Faber and Faber, 1998), 22.

7. Lady Gregory, *Our Irish Theatre* (Gerrards Cross: Colin Smythe, 1972), 20.

8. Roy Foster, *W. B. Yeats: A Life, I: The Apprentice Mage, 1865–1914* (Oxford: Oxford University Press, 1997), 204.

9. John S. Kelly, 'The Fifth Bell: Race and Class in Yeats's Political Thought', in Okifumi Komesu and Masaru Sekine (eds.), *Irish Writers and Politics* (Gerrards Cross: Colin Smythe, 1989), 117.

10. See James Pethica, '"Our Kathleen": Yeats's Collaboration with Lady Gregory in the Writing of *Cathleen ni Houlihan*', in Deirdre Toomey (ed.), *Yeats and Women* (London: Macmillan, 1997), 205–22.

11. Seamas O'Sullivan, 'How Our Theatre Began', in E. H. Mikhail (ed.), *The Abbey Theatre: Interviews and Recollections* (Basingstoke, Macmillan, 1988), 12.

12. D. P. Moran, *The Leader*, 15 September 1900, 40.

13. Padraic Colum, 'Early Days of the Abbey Theatre', *The Abbey Theatre*, 65.

14. See Robert Welch, *The Abbey Theatre 1899–1999: Form and Pressure* (Oxford: Oxford University Press, 1999), 15; and Mikhail, *The Abbey Theatre*, 16.

15. Frank J. Fay, *Towards a National Theatre*, ed. Robert Hogan (Dublin: Dolmen Press, 1970), 53.

16. *The Variorum Edition of The Plays of W. B. Yeats*, ed. Russell K. Alspach (London: Macmillan, 1996), 231.

17. Adrian Frazier, *Behind the Scenes: Yeats, Horniman, and the Struggle for the Abbey Theatre* (Berkeley: University of California Press, 1990), 84–90.

18. Lionel Pilkington, 'The Beginnings of the Irish National Theatre Project', in Eamonn Jordan (ed.), *Theatre Stuff: Critical Essays on Contemporary Irish Theatre* (Dublin: Carysfort Press, 2000), 32. See also Pilkington's *Theatre and the State in Twentieth-Century Ireland: Cultivating the People* (London: Routledge, 2001).

19. W. B. Yeats, 'Poetry and Tradition', *Essays and Introductions* (London: Macmillan, 1961), 253.

20. Christopher Morash, 'All Playboys Now: The Audience and the Riot', in Nicholas Grene (ed.), *Interpreting Synge: Essays from the Synge Summer School, 1991–2000* (Dublin: Lilliput Press, 2000), 138.

21. W. J. McCormack, *Fool of the Family: A Life of J. M. Synge* (London: Weidenfeld & Nicolson, 2000), 312; Declan Kiberd, *Inventing Ireland: The Literature of the Modern Nation* (London: Jonathan Cape, 1995), 183–8.

4

JOEP LEERSSEN

The theatre of William Butler Yeats

I
The European and British background

Nineteenth-century playhouses attracted little original dramatic writing. The emphasis was on dramatizations of novels; on opera, operetta and melodrama; and on the production (often 'theatrical' and 'spectacular' productions, in the more tinselled sense of the words) of established classics. Conversely, romantic and postromantic authors were more inclined to lyric poetry and the novel than to drama – the transition being marked, perhaps, by Goethe's *Faust*, Shelley's *The Cenci* and Hugo's *Hernani*.

A revival of the drama was instigated by Henrik Ibsen. With *A Doll's House* (1879), *Ghosts* (1881), *An Enemy of the People* (1882), *Hedda Gabler* (1890) and *When We Dead Awaken* (1899) he revolutionized and rejuvenated European theatre. While Wagner was taking the large-scale theatrical pomp of dramatic opera to its extreme in Bayreuth, and Labiche was offering ironically comic entertainment in the Boulevard theatres of Paris, Ibsen's drama was spare, verbal rather than spectacular, and offered no amusement or historical-picturesque escapism.

Ibsen's drama gave Europe a signal that the theatre could once again turn from spectacle to dialogue, and his example triggered the rise of the 'literary theatre' or 'art theatre'. His work paved the way for the careers of new playwrights such as Chekhov in Russia, Maeterlinck in Flanders, and Strindberg in Sweden. Some of the new Ibsenites in the European theatre (e.g., Chekhov) emulated his 'problem plays' with their unflinching, analytical realism. Others, like Maeterlinck, adopted his 'literary', textual approach to use the theatre as a medium for lyrical symbolism. All of them took the point that the theatre need not be a large-scale, commercial metropolitan venture, but could be established in out-of-the-way places as a small-scale, innovative and even experimental genre.

Of the three great Irish innovators of English-language theatre (Shaw, Wilde and Yeats), two were Ibsenite, albeit in different ways. Shaw showed Ibsen's influence in his incisive, discursive, analytical realism; Yeats in his symbolist pursuit of a new, small-scale, innovative 'art theatre'.[1]

The dramatic writing of Wilde, Shaw and Yeats originated in an English *fin-de-siècle* atmosphere. The English theatrical scene was already experiencing the influence of the new art theatre, with producers such as J. T. Grein (whose theatrical work was influenced by André Antoine's Parisian *théâtre libre*, and who had begun staging Ibsen in the 1890s), actresses such as Florence Farr and Mrs Patrick Campbell, and financiers of avant-garde symbolist theatre such as Annie Horniman. Many of these figures formed intellectual networks through literary or esoteric coteries, and it was within this environment that Yeats, in the course of the 1890s, developed his theatrical ambitions.

II
Yeats's philosophical, literary and political outlook

In 1890 no one would have guessed that the aspiring poet and artist William Butler Yeats, then in his mid-twenties (he had been born in 1865) was to become Ireland's national *homme de lettres* in later life: a senator in its new parliament, accepting the 1924 Nobel Prize as a representative of that new Free State. Ireland in 1890 was still a recalcitrant province within the United Kingdom, something like Wales aspiring to the status of New Zealand; and young Yeats, though imbued with the familial and regional influences of his family roots in Sligo and Dublin, spent much of his time in the London metropolis and its literary scene.

Yeats's intellectual ambiance in the 1880s was that of the English *fin-de-siècle*.[2] The aestheticism of the Pre-Raphaelites became a negation of that Victorian moralism which had been manifested by Carlyle, Tennyson and Matthew Arnold. The artistic pursuit of beauty was now seen as a radically different thing from the celebration of moral values or virtues like duty, integrity and honesty. Yeats himself saw the pursuit of beauty as an esoteric quest for hidden ideals, as opposed to the pragmatically oriented grain of historical and social circumstances. This poetical and occultist agenda led him to involvement with hermetic societies such as the Order of the Golden Dawn, and a preoccupation with symbols, myths and supernatural beliefs.

Occultism was nothing unusual in these years. Many *fin-de-siècle* artists and poets had links with Freemasonry, Rosicrucianism, Theosophy, or table-rapping séances. A plethora of small but influential societies and individuals mystified the salons of Paris and London with dark hints of unspeakable lore, and with promises to initiate their adepts into the secret knowledge of Tibetan or ancient Egyptian religion. What made Yeats's involvement with occultism (which he never abandoned throughout his life) special was that he linked it not to some vague, exotic orientalism, but rather to his Irish background. To be sure, the Celtic nations of Europe were stereotypically seen as otherworldly, removed from practicality, gifted with second sight and mystically sensitive – but it was Yeats who could take this trite ethnic cliché and use it to develop the outlines of a specifically Irish *fin-de-siècle* literature.

In Yeats's view Ireland was only superficially Christian or modern. Underneath the provincial imperial-British surface he sensed the presence of ancient paganism and the half-remembered myths of Gaelic antiquity. This led him to an interest in folklore and Gaelic legend and myth: he hoped to recuperate a mystical, esoteric closeness to a higher spiritual sphere which had been lost in the drab middle-class suburbs of Britain. Folktale collections like *The Celtic Twilight* (1893; its title gave its name to a whole school of Irish *fin-de-siècle* writing) testify to this attempt to merge three different spheres into a literary programme: a folklore interest in the popular, oral culture of the Irish peasantry; an antiquarian, mythological interest in the ancient legends and epic poems of the Gaels; and an occultist interest in a higher, spiritual enlightenment beyond the realm of positive, practical knowledge. What these three highly disparate interests had in common was in fact a negative quality: all of them were antirealist, antibourgeois, anticonventional. Yeats defined his stance by the rejection of Victorian realism and urban, English, middle-class values. Anything that served to offer alternatives to middle-class Victorianism could be accommodated in his literary and artistic pantheon: Japanese, Byzantine, and Chinese culture all offered inspiration to him in the course of his writing career; and many of his poems and plays feature the conjunction of a beggar and a nobleman, or a fool and a king, who between them share the great value of nonbourgeois existential intensity. Likewise Yeats could see himself alternatively as a bohemian wandering artist or as a latter-day aristocrat, playing both ends of the social spectrum against the middle.

Politically his views led Yeats into political conflicts and perplexities throughout his life; and even after his death the question of Yeats's politics has continued to vex critics. The constant factor in his outlook was an elitist distrust of the middle classes, especially the petty bourgeois lower-middle classes. (Yeats himself was from a mercantile background with some tenuous gentry connections – not-quite-upper-middle class – but he preferred to see himself as the real or metaphorical heir of an aristocratic ancestry.)

As with other elitist modernists of his generation (such as T. S. Eliot or Ezra Pound), his elitism and cultural pessimism could take the form either of aristocratic High Toryism or, especially after World War One, of a certain sympathy with the Fascist creed of collective discipline and a hero-worshipping authoritarianism.

Yet at the same time Yeats was an Irish nationalist. Both contemporaries and later critics (whose postcolonial perspective tends to see separatist nationalism as a subversive, progressive stance) have been bewildered by Yeats's combination of radical national separatism and antidemocratic elitism. Yeats was deeply convinced that Celtic Ireland was congenitally worlds apart from the Victorian empire, that Ireland's subordination within the United Kingdom was unjust, and that a radical divorce between Ireland and Britain was necessary and inevitable. He saw his attempts to create a specifically Irish 'Celtic Twilight' literature as a vindication of Irish national distinctness; his interest in, and admiration for, radical Irish separatists such as O'Donovan Rossa is no less longstanding or intense than his association with occultism. The unlikely crossover between esoteric table-rapping and political activism was also made by the person who probably influenced Yeats most in this regard: Maud Gonne, a radical nationalist with a lifelong interest in the occult, and the great love of Yeats's life. One may even speculate whether Yeats's participation in separatist activities (protests against an Irish visit from Queen Victoria; centenary commemorations of the 1798 Rebellion) should not be seen as largely motivated by his passionate desire for Gonne.

Irish nationalism in the 1890s was by and large a populist movement with its main anchorage in the urban, Catholic petite bourgeoisie. Movements like the Gaelic League, though instigated by men such as Douglas Hyde (from the same Protestant professional classes as Yeats and Gonne), came to be largely controlled by the lower ranks of the Catholic clergy and found their strongest appeal with white-collar workers, clerks and schoolteachers – precisely the class that Yeats despised most.

Accordingly, Yeats's relations with Irish nationalism were uncertain and volatile – both in his public career and within his writings. Sometimes his poetry and drama were almost propagandistically Irish-nationalist, sometimes aloof from contemporary national politics; while in Yeats's theatrical ventures a close association with nationalist forces (in the press and in politics) alternated with serious conflicts. This ambiguity lasted throughout Yeats's active literary life, from around 1890 until his death in 1939. At all times, however, the underlying tension was that between Yeats's mystical-elitist worldview and his sense of responsibility to engage in public affairs.

III
Yeats's theatre: national and literary

Yeats was not only a dramatist and poet, he also organized and led a theatre company and launched an actual theatrical venue, which has become an important focus of worldwide fame: the Abbey Theatre in Dublin.[3] These managerial activities throw light on Yeats's political and literary concerns.

The origins of the Abbey Theatre lie with a literary society founded by Yeats and others in 1892: the National Literary Society. It had branches in Dublin and London, and was flanked by a linguistic counterpart, established in 1893 for the preservation and revival of the Gaelic language, the Gaelic League. The National Literary Society often collaborated with the Gaelic League,[4] drew on an overlapping circle of enthusiasts and occasionally cosponsored initiatives. However, unlike the Gaelic League with its revivalist language concerns, the National Literary Society attracted the more English-language, Anglo-Irish cultural forces.

By 1899 this National Literary Society had spawned a theatrical initiative in the establishment of the Irish Literary Theatre. The main initiators were Yeats, Lady Gregory, Edward Martyn and George Moore, and their venture was to be epoch-making. Its productions included original plays by Yeats and the others, translations from Molière into Hiberno-English dialect, by Lady Gregory, and occasional productions of important non-English plays. Reorganized into the Irish National Theatre Society, it acquired the Abbey Theatre in 1904 (financed by Annie Horniman), forming the focal point of that remarkable episode known as the Irish Literary Revival – the platform for Yeats's plays and drama criticism. It was also the beginning of the entire subsequent tradition of Irish theatre, represented by names such as J. M. Synge, Sean O'Casey, Hugh Leonard and Brian Friel.[5]

Yeats's theatre thus hovered, in its various incarnations, between the appellations 'Literary' and 'National'. It aimed at being 'literary' in the tradition of the new art theatres of the 1890s, with their dreamlike, understated symbolism, their denial of spectacular productions and their preference for small audiences of refined cognoscenti; and it aimed at being 'national' in the sense that it hoped to lift Irish culture out of second-rate drab provincialism and to let Ireland, in terms of theatre and literature at least, take its place among the nations of Europe. Yeats himself wanted to be part of a European avant-garde, and to represent the 'Celtic' contribution to this new symbolist avant-garde, a countermovement against the prevailing realism of the times. He phrased his hopes for a 'Celtic Movement' as follows:

It comes at a time when the imagination of the world is as ready as it was at the coming of the tales of Arthur for a new intoxication. The reaction against the rationalism of the eighteenth century has mingled with a reaction against the materialism of the nineteenth century, and the symbolical movement, which has come to perfection in Germany in Wagner, in England in the Pre-Raphaelites, in France in Villiers de l'Isle-Adam and Mallarmé, and in Belgium in Maeterlinck, and has stirred the imagination of Ibsen and D'Annunzio, is certainly the only movement which is saying new things.[6]

The list of examples is telling. Obviously, for Yeats, a Dublin theatre that could be part of this prestigious Europe-wide avant-garde would by the same token raise the status of Ireland and bolster the cause of Irish nationalism. That is not, however, how Yeats's contemporaries – the Irish nationalists who formed the intended audience for his theatre – saw it . For them nationalism meant anti-British separatism, and conjoint refusal of British values and glorification of Gaelic individuality. Nationalist critics, newspaper editors and audiences were ready to praise the new theatrical initiative as long as it celebrated a pure, unadulterated Gaelic identity – for instance, by setting plays in Ireland's mythical past or among the as yet unanglicized peasantry. Critics and audiences had considerable reservations, however, when Yeats's theatre performed European themes or even plays which they considered 'un-Irish'. While Yeats's definition of national connoted the dignity of being unprovincial, other nationalists used the term in the sense of the purity of being non-British. Even the use of a nationally motivated discourse was at cross-purposes and could generate misunderstandings.[7]

In the early years (1899–1903) the new literary/national theatre did, by and large, cater for the taste and political sensibilities of Irish nationalists. Thus the 'kitchen comedies' by Lady Gregory (set in an idealized rustic Ireland) were greeted with applause, as were the occasional double-bill productions involving actors' groups from the Gaelic League or the nationalist women's association Inghinidhe na hÉireann (Daughters of Ireland). Various plays were written in the national vein by associates of Yeats – notably Edward Martyn's *The Heather Field* (1899) and *Maeve* (1900), Alice Milligan's *The Last Feast of the Fianna* (1900). Yeats himself was quite willing to play to the nationalist gallery. In programme notes, occasional journalism and American lecture tours he proclaimed the importance of national identity and national commitment for the creation of great literature, and the importance of creating great literature for fostering national commitment and national identity. The only point where he allowed himself to depart slightly from the extreme nationalist standpoints of Arthur Griffith, D. P. Moran and the radical separatists was his insistence that the English language was a legitimate vehicle (alongside Gaelic) for pursuing that agenda.[8]

The high point of Yeats's collaboration with separatist nationalism came in 1902. In that year he and Lady Gregory produced *Cathleen ni Houlihan*, which was straightforward nationalist propaganda. It was, significantly, written for Maud Gonne, who played the central, mythical character, and it made use of a theme from traditional anti-English legend and folktale. The figure of Cathleen ni Houlihan is a longstanding poetical figure representing Ireland. Eighteenth- and nineteenth-century poetry and verse can depict her variously as a young woman in distress, importuned and enslaved by wicked men, or else as a divine vision embodying the eternal sovereignty of Ireland and predicting liberation from foreign oppression. Yeats mixes this personage with other themes from legend, folklore and the poetical tradition, to describe how an old crone, bedraggled and down at heel, seeks shelter in a humble peasants' cottage in rural Ireland. The time is that of the Rebellion of 1798; and the woman's words leave the audience in no doubt as to what she represents: Ireland.

> *Bridget.* What was it put you wandering?
> *Old Woman.* Too many strangers in the house.
> *Bridget.* Indeed you look as if you've had you'd share of trouble.
> *Old Woman.* I have had trouble indeed.
> *Bridget.* What was it put the trouble on you?
> *Old Woman.* My land that was taken from me.
> *Peter.* Was it much land they took from you?
> *Old Woman.* My four beautiful green fields.[9]

Towards the end of the short sketch Cathleen ni Houlihan's voice comes to command the allegiance of a young man, Michael, who leaves his fiancée to join the rebel forces. His fighting spirit, his willingness to strike a blow for the nation's sake, have apparently rejuvenated her.

> *Peter.* . . . Did you see an old woman going down the path?
> *Patrick.* I did not, but I saw a young girl, and she had the walk of a queen
> (231).

The symbolism in this play anticipated the discourse and rhetoric of the most radical militant separatists, who, inspired by the 1798 Rebellion and by Gaelic rebel verse, felt that every new generation should be willing to shed its blood for the perennial cause of Ireland's liberty. Notions of blood sacrifice, and a genderized, mythically based relationship between virile prowess and national devotion, would be instrumental in 1916, when a violent insurrection formed the prelude to the Irish War of Independence. Not for nothing did Yeats later muse, in 'The Man and the Echo', 'Did that play of mine send out / Certain men the English shot?'. It certainly helped to fan the fervently nationalistic mood.[10]

But that was in 1902, and the Easter Rising took place in 1916. In the intervening years the relationship between Yeats and the Irish nationalists soured considerably. It should in any case be kept in mind that *Cathleen ni Houlihan*, though one of Yeats's most memorable and notorious plays, is by no means representative of him. It marked the brief, transient phase in his career when he was closest to radical, separatist nationalism, Maud Gonne style. It was not always like that.

Yeats's earlier play *The Countess Cathleen* (1892) had in its 1899 production created some controversy. Catholic circles took exception to the fact that the religious theme of 'indulgence' (acquiring grace to redeem suffering souls in purgatory) was handled by a known Protestant. The play dealt with the paradox of a lady of the manor willing to sell her soul to the devil in order to set free the souls of her peasant tenants – a moral perplexity which Catholics found mishandled from a dogmatic point of view and therefore offensive. Though the episode was soon cleared up, it placed the budding Literary Theatre in a shady position vis-à-vis Catholic, middle-class morality; and in subsequent years the problem was to return with a vengeance.

Two factors contributed to the widening of the rift between Yeats and Catholic nationalism. The first was the fact that in acquiring the Abbey Theatre the Irish National Theatre Society drifted into the ambit of their main financier, Annie Horniman, a wealthy arts patron. She and Yeats knew each other through occultist circles, and Horniman had already helped to finance new aesthetic theatre initiatives in England. Established in the Abbey Theatre building, the venture began to move away from populist propaganda and into more elitist, rarefied and cosmopolitan taste. At Horniman's behest Yeats attempted to go 'upmarket' by suppressing cheap seating in the theatre; and the Irish National Theatre Society was turned from a group of fellow amateurs into a limited liability company, with a board of directors (Yeats, Lady Gregory, Synge) and the actors and producers as employees. All this was anathema to the politically motivated radicals in the company. The flashpoint came with a play by a new talent, J. M. Synge – a discovery and protégé of Yeats – called *In the Shadow of the Glen* (1903). In its bitter and sarcastic view of Irish peasant life the play was closer to Ibsen than to any previous Abbey production; coming in the atmosphere of growing mistrust between Yeats and the populists, it seemed a cynical and supercilious mockery of the rustic genre that had dominated the previous decade. The result was a split in the Society; having lost Martyn in 1902, Yeats now lost his talented and popular producer/directors, the Fay brothers, and some of his most celebrated actors (including Máire Walker) as well as the sympathy of Maud Gonne.

In the years 1905–10 Yeats was left with the Abbey Theatre, the moral backing of Lady Gregory, the financial backing of Annie Horniman (a mixed blessing, since she was a demanding and querulous person) and his own and Synge's talents. But around him there were by now other theatrical splinter groups (Martyn's Players' Club, the Fay brothers' Irish National Dramatic Company, the party-politically based National Players Society and the Walkers' Theatre of Ireland). And he had very little credit with the na-tionalistically minded population.

All this was precipitated into a crisis with Synge's play *The Playboy of the Western World* (1907), which gave rise to one of the most notorious riots in theatrical history. It must be said to Yeats's credit that he never lost faith in the great talent of Synge, and faced the hostile Dublin audiences undaunted, convinced that he took the side of literary innovation against vulgar pettiness and intolerance. He was to do so once more in his career, in 1926, when he once again faced an uproarious audience that loudly voiced its disapproval – this time, of Sean O'Casey's *The Plough and the Stars*.

Thus, from 1905 onwards, Yeats became ever more obviously antina-tionalist. While continuing to believe in a separate cultural identity for his country, he withdrew into a haughty class-bound elitism and made a habit of denouncing the vulgarity of most nationalists. To be sure, the 1916 Rising (undertaken by men whom Yeats had come to despise – one of them, John MacBride, the man who had married his beloved Maud Gonne) forced him to acknowledge that this grand, violent but doomed gesture had restored some tragic dignity to Irish nationalism; but the War of Independence and subse-quent Civil War (1919–23), in which various nationalist factions opposed each other, confirmed him in his mistrust of modern, populist or democratic politics.

In 1919 Yeats wrote an open letter to Lady Gregory, 'A People's Theatre', in which he all but conceded defeat. Even the fact that the Abbey Theatre had become an institution of sorts in Dublin cultural life irked him, and felt like 'a discouragement and a defeat'. He was now convinced, he wrote, 'that the Abbey Theatre can never do all we had hoped. We set out to make a "People's Theatre" and in that we have succeeded. But I did not know until very lately that there are certain things, dear to both our hearts, which no "People's Theatre" can accomplish.'[11]

While his original intention had been to 'bring the old folk-life to Dublin, patriotic feeling to aid us, and with the folk-life all the life of the heart' ('A People's Theatre', 252), the new taste was realistic and cerebral, a 'Theatre of the head' instead of the heart. He denounced a populism which worked 'from sympathy, from observation, never from passion from lonely dreaming'. Instead he yearned for the esoteric, elitist art theatre of the *fin-de-siècle*: 'I want to create for myself an unpopular theatre and an audience like a secret society where admission is by favour and never to many' (254).

Accordingly, Yeats's relations with the new Irish Free State remained ambiguous. He accepted the prestige and trappings of public prominence (becoming a senator, for instance) but was always ready to denounce Ireland's intellectual vulgarity and narrow-mindedness. As a vestigial representative of the country's preindependence elite, he felt himself involved in, but not subordinate to, the Ireland he had helped to create. He spent much time away from Ireland, in London or France. It is typical that the last poems before his death, taking the form of a cultural testament, were addressed to Ireland as from the outside, or even from above; his plays had become less and less 'Irish' in their setting and coloration from the 1910s onwards. Yeats died in France in 1939, when his various misgivings about Ireland, about democracy and about the Western world in general seemed more realistic than they had been at any point before. Only very shortly before his death had he returned, with *The Herne's Egg* (1938) and *The Death of Cuchulain* (1939), to using Gaelic legendary material in his dramatic writing.

IV
Yeats's drama: performance and politics

Yeats was never primarily a playwright; he was, rather, a poet who occasionally wrote drama. He started his writing career when poetry, as a genre, had long been cannibalizing the drama, in the absence of a vigorously functioning theatre. From Shelley's *The Cenci* onwards, dramatic poems, never intended (or at any rate unsuited) for stage production, had flourished, culminating in the dramatic monologues and monodramas of Browning and Tennyson. And the poem that occupied Yeats most deeply throughout the 1890s was a hybrid, *The Shadowy Waters*, which was staged at the Abbey in 1904, and of which he included the 1906 version in his *Collected Poems*, the 1911 version in his *Collected Plays*.

Indeed, in the early years a good deal of effort was put into seeking a fresh demarcation between the genres of poetry and drama. Stage productions in *fin-de-siècle* Dublin were not necessarily dramatic; in some cases the bill included a set of symbolical tableaux vivants, still-life enactments, which were a specialty of the nationalist women's club Inghinidhe na hÉireann under the direction of the Fay brothers. The slow, deliberate delivery of the amateur actors, and their Irish singsong speech, worked in favour of an incantatory rather than realistic production style. Yeats himself explored a 'theatre of stillness', with slow-moving, dreamlike production values and an emphasis on the dialogue rather than on the action and gesticulation. Parisian art theatre *mise-en-scène* was explicitly imitated in Dublin, in the creation of a distant and vague impression by placing the action behind a veil, for example.[12]

Conversely, poetry was always seen as a potential performance. Among the closest artistic collaborators of Yeats in the 1890s was the remarkable post-Pre-Raphaelite actress Florence Farr, who spoke poetry to the accompaniment of a medieval zither, the psaltery. Yeats was as impressed with this performed poetry as he was infatuated − for a while − with Farr. He wrote essays on the topic, and had Farr perform in Dublin; *The Land of Heart's Desire* was dedicated to her and Farr played the leading role in the 1899 production of *The Countess Cathleen*.

If we see Yeats as a poet who also wrote plays, the question becomes what would, from case to case, dictate his choice of genre. One obvious answer is that drama, far more than poetry, is a social form of literary art. It requires the actual congregation of an audience in a theatre, and as such is far more suited to the public and political ambitions of an author than is the printed page − especially if the poetry on that page is meditative, metaphysical and intensely lyrical and personal.

Yeats's *Collected Plays* − the volume which he himself put together and which reflects his own arrangement of his oeuvre as a whole − lists twenty-six plays in not-quite-chronological order.[13] This 'director's cut' does not constitute the *complete* works of Yeats; he revised and reordered his collections throughout his life, and earlier poems (also dramatic ones, like *Mosada*, 1886) are suppressed as a matter of course.

Taken as a whole, Yeats's dramatic output from 1902 runs fairly steady at around one play per year, with productivity troughs in the mid-1910s and mid-1920s, and peaks in the years 1902–04, 1919–22 and 1934–39. These peaks represent three intense periods when Yeats's literary life and his involvement with public life coincided: the beginnings of the Literary Theatre, the deeply troubled period of the War of Independence, and the final 'rush' of his old age. The dramatically less productive period of the 1910s was marked instead by poetry writing, culminating in the collection *The Wild Swans at Coole* (1919), while the mid-1920s led to the collection *The Tower* (1928).

At the same time it would be wrong to see Yeats's life as a conjunctural seesaw between bouts of drama and of poetry. There is a great deal of interpenetration between the two genres. The plays include poems; certain themes and images are taken up in drama and in poetry; many poems are in the mode of dialogue, as are many plays (which are almost barren of action).

Thus Yeats's theatre throughout his life is poetic, much as Shaw's is prosaic. While Shaw uses the dramatic form to pursue dialectical point-counterpoint arguments and confrontations between attitudes and personalities, Yeats uses his actors as a configuration of personae who between them weave a mythical or meditative plotline, each contributing his or her part to a mosaic-form parable. Yeats eschews most of the stock-in-trade of the theatre. There is no use of dramatic themes like mistaken identities or mistaken intentions; there is no use of the *coup de théâtre* (the sudden revelation of background information or unexpected reversal in character quality); the division in acts is like a linear chapter division of the narrative line, rather than a change in action or perspective. Indeed, Yeats's drama is highly undramatic. A story unfolds and winds its course, often in a fatalistic, preordained way; the characters play their parts in a sequence of events which are unsurprising because they are often mythical, inevitable or fatal.

The furthest Yeats goes in the direction of specifically dramatic and theatrical (as opposed to poetic) strategies is in his use of a clown-figure, comparable to Feste in *Twelfth Night* or the gatekeeper in *Macbeth*. These are not intended for comic or farcical relief, but rather as a type of commentative chorus, counterbalancing the lofty, epic-mythical storyline from an extra-social perspective. Thus in *The King's Threshold* the conflict between King and Court-poet is balanced and commented upon by the characters of two cripples; in *On Baile's Strand* the epic story of Cuchulain and Conchobar is taken straight from ancient Gaelic myth, but the figures of a Fool and a Blind Man are added. It bespeaks, once again, the Yeatsian preference for extremes: king and beggar, poet and fool. If there is any sense of dialectics in Yeats's plays, it derives from this dramatic juxtaposition of pauper and nobleman — a juxtaposition which was central to Yeats's moral vision and which he held to be typical of Ireland, of all countries.

In certain plays the personae of beggar, clown and fool can take over the action and become not just ancillary characters but main relayers of the storyline — thus *The Cat and the Moon* has a dramatis personae of a blind beggar, a lame beggar and a musician; *At the Hawk's Well* is carried by three musicians, the Guardian of the Well, an Old Man and a Young Man. Frequently, also, the actors are masked, a gesture that harks back to Greek tragedy but also invokes an idea of impersonality, of a highly unmelodramatic, ritual and even liturgical theatre. Yeats explored the possibilities of such a static and nondramatic theatre further by looking at drama forms outside the modern realistic tradition — a search that started with contemporary, symbolist art theatre in Paris (Maeterlinck, Villiers de l'Isle-Adam) and led to ancient Greek tragedy and to Japanese Noh — theatre forms that involve the ritual, stylized performance of well-known narratives rather than thrills and melodrama.

Yeats was not alone in these experiments towards crosscultural fertilization. One is reminded, for instance, of Puccini's operatic experiments, which used commedia dell'arte in the Chinese theme of *Turandot* (unfinished at his death in 1924) and set grand opera in contemporary Japan or America (*Madama Butterfly*, 1904; *La fanciulla del West*, 1910). But in Yeats's case the attempt to create a literary and national theatre meant that he could set Gaelic or Irish-derived storylines in a setting of cosmopolitan hue. Thus Yeats's national focus does not prevent him from placing Irish material cheek by jowl with different cultural traditions. Although this was anathema to purists at the time, it represents an attempt to emancipate and derusticate Irish culture by way of globalization. This is perhaps Yeats's most original and outstanding contribution to his country's literature, and one in which he was almost a century ahead of his time.

In the wider development of twentieth-century theatre, Yeats's position is less marked. His attempt to create a poetic theatre of stillness and ritual made him an idiosyncratic side-product of Symbolism and the *fin-de-siècle*. Yet, in conclusion, attention should be drawn to two highly remarkable plays which Yeats wrote in the 1930s, and in which he took his drama style to extremes. *Words upon the Window-Pane* (1934) and *Purgatory* (1939) both meditate on a nightmarish vision of history as an uncanny repetition of ancient sins and memories. *Purgatory*, especially, the anguished and hypnotic combination of stillness and repetition anticipates very strongly the later theatre of Samuel Beckett – much as the lame and the blind beggar in *The Cat and the Moon* are not merely symbols for body and soul, but, defamiliarized as they are through the Noh-like setting, become anticipations of *Waiting for Godot*'s Vladimir and Estragon.

NOTES

1. It is perhaps the great originality of Oscar Wilde, the third Irish figure to appear on the theatrical scene, that his drama did not shirk the tradition of middle-brow Labiche-style farces – although this observation applies more to *The Importance of Being Earnest* and *An Ideal Husband* than to the very Aestheticist *Salomé*.
2. Two recent biographies give an excellent contextualization of Yeats in this environment: Terence Brown's *The Life of W. B. Yeats: A Critical Biography* (Oxford: Blackwell, 1999), and, especially, Roy Foster's *W. B. Yeats: A Life, I: The Apprentice Mage, 1865–1914* (Oxford: Oxford University Press, 1997).
3. There are many studies of the Irish Literary Revival, but the most detailed picture emerges from the series *The Modern Irish Drama: A Documentary History*, ed. Robert Hogan and James Kilroy (Dublin: Dolmen Press, 1975 ff.).

4. The moribund Gaelic language was rescued from extinction by the activities of the Gaelic League. Among these was the occasional production of Gaelic-language plays, many of them written by Douglas Hyde and produced with the help of the Literary Society, which form the beginning of modern drama in Irish-Gaelic. On the outlook of the Gaelic League, the best source is Philip O'Leary, *The Prose Literature of the Gaelic Revival, 1881–1921. Ideology and Innovation* (University Park, PA: Pennsylvania State University Press, 1994).

5. This tradition was anything but singular or uniform; it involved a number of schisms, splits, rifts and quarrels. Some of the more nationalistically minded actors were frozen out of the Abbey Theatre between 1902 and 1906; Edward Martyn and George Moore parted ways with Yeats around 1903 by setting up first the Players' Club and then the National Theatre Company. This offshoot started its activities by staging Ibsen's *A Doll's House* in 1903, and after some vicissitudes it established itself in 1929 in the still-active Gate Theatre.

6. W. B. Yeats, 'The Celtic Element in Literature' (1897), in *Essays and Introductions* (Basingstoke: Macmillan, 1961), 187.

7. I have explored this cross-purpose further in my *Remembrance and Imagination: Patterns in the Historical and Literary Representation of Ireland in the Nineteenth Century* (Cork: Cork University Press, 1996), 207–23.

8. The ambivalence of Yeats's stance is illustrated by the two versions we have of an essay entitled 'The Literary Movement in Ireland'. It first appeared in an American review in 1899, then later in 1901 in an essay collection edited by Lady Gregory, *Ideals in Ireland*. In the American 1899 version Yeats was still slightly reticent concerning Gaelic revivalism. Those reservations were dropped in the 1901 version. Both versions are in *Uncollected Prose by W. B. Yeats*, ed. J. P. Frayne and C. Johnston, 2 vols. (Basingstoke: Macmillan, 1970–75), *Volume II*, 87.

9. *The Variorum Edition of The Plays of W. B. Yeats*, ed. Russell K. Alspach (London: Macmillan, 1966), 223. The four fields, traditionally, stand for the four provinces of Ireland; the colour green hammers home the symbolical intent.

10. The most politically influential piece of theatre Yeats wrote was probably *On the King's Threshold* (1904). In this play he drew on the ancient Gaelic theme of 'shaming someone by fasting on his doorstep'. In so doing Yeats brought the archaic and forgotten notion of the hunger strike into renewed currency and extreme fasting has remained an important activist strategy in Ireland ever since.

11. W. B. Yeats, 'A People's Theatre: A Letter to Lady Gregory' (1919), in *Explorations* (London: Macmillan, 1962), 244.

12. The 'veiled' 1902 production of *Deirdre*, by A. E. (George Russell) was based on the production of Maeterlinck's *Pelléas et Mélisande* in Lugné-Poe's *Théâtre de l'Oeuvre*; cf. Hogan and Kilroy, *The Modern Irish Drama, Volume II*, 41.

13. In chronological order, they are: *The Countess Cathleen* (1892); *The Land of Heart's Desire* (1894); *Cathleen ni Houlihan* (1902); *The Pot of Broth* (1904); *The King's Threshold* (1904); *On Baile's Strand* (1904); *Deirdre* (1907); *The Unicorn from the Stars* (1908); *The Green Helmet* (1910); *The Shadowy Waters* (1911); *The Hour-Glass* (1914); *At the Hawk's Well* (1917); *The Only Jealousy*

of Emer (1919); *The Dreaming of the Bones* (1919); *Calvary* (1920); *The Player Queen* (1922); *The Cat and the Moon* (1926); *Sophocles' King Oedipus* (1928); *The Resurrection* (1931); *Sophocles' Oedipus at Colonus* (1934); *The Words upon the Window-Pane* (1934); *A Full Moon in March* (1935); *The King of the Great Clock Tower* (1935); *The Herne's Egg* (1938); *Purgatory* (1938); *The Death of Cuchulain* (1939).

5

JAMES PETHICA

Lady Gregory's Abbey Theatre drama: Ireland real and ideal

From the outset of her career as a cultural nationalist in the late 1890s, Lady Gregory pursued and encouraged both pragmatic and visionary modes of nation-building. The work of restoring 'dignity' to Ireland required practicality as well as idealism, she argued in early essays, with 'adaptable, sagacious' real-world talents needing to be combined with otherworldly, transformative dreams if the country were to achieve both economic and imaginative self-determination.[1] As a writer, activist and patron she consequently sought a balance between the 'real' and the 'ideal' in Ireland – counterpointing her promotion of Irish folklore and legend, for instance, by campaigning against British overtaxation, and encouraging the cause of agricultural organization amid her first flush of enthusiasm for Yeats's writings (*Diaries*, 147, 135–7). Her involvement in the Irish theatre movement epitomised this distinctive mix of pragmatism and idealism. Both her achievements as a playwright and her decades-long financial and directorial guardianship of the Abbey Theatre would be motivated by her conception of the theatre as a forum in which the practical and the visionary might be combined to effect lasting political, social and imaginative change.

Her participation in the theatre movement began, symptomatically, because of her practical skills. Though she had 'never been at all interested in theatres' before meeting Yeats, and at first collaborated with him only as a folklorist, she was captivated by and eager to help him realize his long-harboured hopes for a poetic and romantic school of drama that might counter the rise of Ibsenite realism and the dominance of 'commercial' considerations in the theatre.[2] During a conversation in summer 1897, when Yeats told her of Edward Martyn's plays being declined by London managers, she responded by saying that 'it was a pity we had no Irish theatre where such plays could be given'. Yeats replied that this 'had always been a dream of his' but he thought it impossible on financial grounds. With Lady Gregory suggesting a guarantee fund, however, 'things seemed to grow possible' (*Our Irish Theatre*, 19). They co-wrote an appeal manifesto, sent this out to likely donors, and soon received enough pledges to support a short first season of productions.[3] The published list of guarantors shows how central Lady Gregory's influence was in this success, for the majority were her friends and connections, with few of them noted for prior literary involvements, and some, as she observed to Yeats, not even having 'a very clear idea what they put their names to – just know it was some fad of mine' (*Collected Letters, II*, 339). When their plan to begin productions in 1898 was disrupted by restrictions on the licensing of Dublin theatres, her practical skills were again crucial. She urged a campaign to repeal the existing laws, and, principally through the intervention of her friend W. H. Lecky, this was achieved within the year (*Our Irish Theatre*, 24).

An administrative role would remain central to Lady Gregory's involvement in the movement over the years: the patent establishing the Abbey in 1904 was granted in her name, thereby assigning principal legal responsibility for its operation to her; she long provided the theatre with funds to supplement the strings-attached patronage of Annie Horniman; with Yeats and Synge she engineered its reconstitution as a limited liability company in 1905, a move which gave them absolute directorial control; and it was repeatedly her fundraising skills which sustained it during various financial crises in its first decades. George Bernard Shaw would in 1910 memorably christen her 'the charwoman of the Abbey' in admiring recognition of the ways in which she so often ignored class position and personal pride when tackling the many and sometimes demeaning practical tasks vital to the theatre's success.[4]

In the first two seasons of the Irish Literary Theatre experiment Lady Gregory was thus largely an organizer and functionary, whom Yeats relied on to 'safe guard the interest of the Theatre' (*Collected Letters, II*, 594). During this period she was self-professedly content, as an 'amiable amateur',[5] to focus on promoting Yeats's success – a motivation which remained crucial to her long after her own emergence as a playwright. 'I will do what Yeats decides,' she declared in 1908: 'I went into this Theatre for his sake and his interests have been first with me all through.'[6] Beginning in summer 1900, however, her involvement in the composition of plays by others gradually intensified, thereby paving the way for her own career as a dramatist. Characteristically, it was again her practical skills which provided the impetus. First came a secretarial role, typing a translation of Douglas Hyde's *Casadh an tSúgáin* (*The Twisting of the Rope*) from his dictation in August 1900. As mediator between Yeats and George Moore during their strained collaboration on *Diarmuid and Grania* in autumn 1900, she was more intimately involved in the creative process, to the point of 'altering Moore's words' (*Diaries*, 281). And finally, in autumn 1901, as the Irish Literary Theatre prepared for its final season, she emerged as a fully-fledged collaborator, co-authoring *Cathleen ni Houlihan* with Yeats, and *An Pósadh* (*The Marriage*) with Hyde.

Her involvement in *The Twisting of the Rope* was a crucial stage in this emergence. Based on a scenario by Yeats, and influenced by her essays on the Connaught poet Anthony Raftery (*c.* 1784–1835), the play offered a radical break from the drawing-room concerns of the commercial theatre, and its peasant realism established conventions which would predominate in the early years of the Abbey. The play turns on how a wandering poet, partly based on Raftery, is treated by a peasant community which acknowledges his genius but also fears the power of his poetic curses and condemns him for his wandering, self-indulgent lifestyle. In exploring the poet's relationship to the community which forms his audience, the play is centrally concerned with the capacity of artists to shape and express cultural realities, and with the process by which they turn the raw material of transient life into something more permanent and imaginatively provocative. Its masterplot thus engaged themes vital to Hyde, Gregory and Yeats – each committed to literature as a means of representing and potentially transforming Ireland.

Cathleen ni Houlihan, written in late 1901, would be the first of several collaborative plays by Yeats and Gregory featuring an artist-disturber as its central character, in which they would revisit and complicate Hyde's simple peasant realism in the light of their own distinctive ideological and personal interests. Initially conceived by Yeats in 'a dream almost as distinct as a vision', the play is set in a cottage where there is 'well-being and firelight and talk of a marriage'.[7] The marriage, between Michael Gillane and the daughter of a prosperous farmer, promises to bring both happiness and material security to a family that has long struggled to raise itself from poverty. Into the Gillane cottage, however, comes an Old Woman, who is gradually revealed to be Cathleen ni Houlihan, the personification of Ireland herself. Though he does not seem conscious of her true identity, or fully aware that her call for help in 'putting the strangers out of my house' is a call to fight the British, Michael is moved to sympathy by her seeming vulnerability. When she proclaims, with rising poetic intensity, that those who die in her cause win the immortality of being remembered by 'the people', he follows her from the cottage, entranced, to face almost certain death. As Yeats observed of this central narrative, 'the bridegroom leaves his bride, and all the hopes come to nothing. It is the perpetual struggle of the cause of Ireland and every other ideal cause against private hopes and dreams, against all that we mean when we say the world' (*Variorum Plays*, 234).

Yeats, who had already begun to realize that he needed help in overcoming his tendency to 'symbolise rather than represent life' in his plays, welcomed

Lady Gregory's help, recognizing that her 'knowledge of the country mind and country speech' from her years of gathering folklore ideally suited her to supply the realism needed to make his vision tangible (*Variorum Plays*, 1295–6). The play's opening action, of which she appears to have been sole author – 'all this mine alone' she noted on the first half of the manuscript draft[8] – skilfully evokes the sociology of the Gillane family, and brings dramatic and human specificity to the situation the Old Woman comes to disturb. Its simple opening exchanges quickly hint at strains between a husband whose narrow material interests have left him imaginatively bankrupt, and a wife who cares more for the emotional wellbeing of her family than for their material status; while numerous small details register Lady Gregory's feeling for the precise material realities of peasant life, and her intense focus on the human preoccupations which Cathleen's call disrupts.

Early audiences generally regarded the play as a clarion call to nationalist action. Its famous final line, which announces Cathleen's offstage transformation from an Old Woman into 'a young girl' with 'the walk of a queen' was seen as symbolically dramatizing the kind of renewal of Ireland that patriotic commitment might yield. Shaw recognized that the play 'might lead a man to do something foolish',[9] and Yeats himself would wonder late in life whether it had played some part in fomenting the 1916 Rising and in the death of '[c]ertain men the English shot'.[10] More recent audiences have viewed Michael's susceptibility to her call less positively, however, as a disturbing loss of agency at best, and at worst as his falling victim to a vampiric shape-shifter who feeds on his blood. Rather than celebrating single-minded patriotism, or validating Michael Gillane as a martyr who earns the status of mythic hero, the play's action has instead come to be seen as embodying a tautly conflicted critique of the attractions and dangers of idealistic nationalism.

The ideological tensions at the heart of the play reflect both Yeats's and Lady Gregory's underlying anxieties over their roles as nationalists. Sharing roots deeply embedded in Protestant Ascendancy culture, they recognized that to succumb to the siren call of Cathleen ni Houlihan would involve a potentially irrevocable rejection of and separation from their privileged heritage. As he acknowledged more frontally in 'Easter 1916', Yeats knew that 'excess of love' for country might lead to a ruinous indifference to ordinary desires, and a potentially inhuman sacrifice of selfhood (*Variorum Poems*, 394). The play's conflicts thus revisit in explicitly political terms his long-established vacillation over whether to stay loyal to a known world that seems imaginatively inadequate or to quest for an ideal world which might turn out to be a destructive fantasy. As trustee of the Coole estate for her son Robert, Lady Gregory was explicitly worried that her increasingly nationalist stance might harm his prospects, and was also anxious not to let politics come between them. In the year before co-writing *Cathleen ni Houlihan* she had come close to breaking with several old friends over the increasingly militant tone of her writings, and this experience had already determined her to 'keep out of politics & work only for literature' (*Diaries*, 265–7).

After 1900 Lady Gregory would repeatedly claim to be merely 'preparing for' rather than 'working for Home Rule' (*Diaries*, 259) but she remained deeply drawn to the idea of political self-sacrifice for the good of others, a motivation that had long been central to her self-conception as a liberal landlord. If the initial vision of Cathleen as an artist-figure, luring Michael Gillane away by the persuasive power of poetry, was Yeats's, the central proposition offered in the lines she sings – that to be 'remembered for ever' by 'the people' is worth the loss of one's life and of ordinary desires – reflects Lady Gregory's distinctive preoccupation with folk-memory and nationalist martyrology. In the two years before co-authoring the play she had assembled a large album of broadsheet ballads, mainly commemorating Irish rebels executed or exiled for acts of resistance to British rule, and had drawn on these to write a series of articles that emphasize how the memory of the rebels still endured in what Raftery had called 'the book of the people' – the collective political, literary and historical memory of the Irish country-people.

Her most emphatic celebration of the 'rebel' ballad heritage, 'The Felons of Our Land', written in 1900 and certainly read by Yeats, draws direct analogies between Christ's self-sacrifice in allowing himself to be led to 'a felon's death' and the ennobling sacrifice of those who had been willing to die for their country; and it repeatedly and approvingly endorses the idea that a place in 'the book of the people' was the highest form of acclaim to be won in Ireland. (In *The Gaol Gate* of 1906, the favourite of her plays, the self-sacrifice of a young man who chooses to be hung rather than inform and be freed provides the dramatic climax, as his mother and widow, in tragic pride, call for his name to be entered in the pantheon of martyrs.) Embodying many of the core ideas explored in *Cathleen ni Houlihan*, 'The Felons of Our Land' proposes that Irish poets should concern themselves not with commemorating victories, but instead should 'tell of the meaning of failure, of the gain that may lie in the wake of a lost battle'. If Irish poets 'possessed the faith that is evidence of things unseen', she charges, they 'would strive to give spiritual vision to trembling and discouraged men'.[11] The essay, which evokes Yeats directly in its closure, effectively challenges him to explore the meaning of patriotism more frontally in his work, and to draw back from visionary abstraction towards a more practically consequential mapping of the relationship between the real and the ideal.

In *Cathleen ni Houlihan* the two writers thus achieved a powerful melding of Lady Gregory's realist, practical interests with Yeats's symbolic preoccupations, as well as an intense and fortuitous confluence of their broader shared ideological concerns. The play also gave Yeats the 'real popular success'[12] Lady Gregory had felt he needed, but this proved unrepeatable in their subsequent collaborations. In *Where There is Nothing*, written hastily in 1902, Yeats again aspired to bring together 'the rough life of the road and the frenzy that poets have found' (*Variorum Plays*, 1296), but here his artist-visionary 'disturber', Paul Ruttledge, and the cast of tinkers he consorts with (who seem largely Lady Gregory's work), collide awkwardly rather than combining to dramatic or philosophical effect; and in the play, as in its later variant, *The Unicorn From the Stars*, the two writers' interests and literary styles remain jarringly unblended.

* * * * *

The successful collaboration on *Cathleen ni Houlihan* soon prompted Lady Gregory to write plays alone. In November 1901 she drafted a scenario for *The Marriage*, and the following summer she completed the short peasant play *A Losing Game*. These first efforts treat themes that would remain central to much of her work, and display many of the essential strengths and limitations of her technique as a dramatist. In *The Marriage* a newly married peasant couple face separation, being too poor to retain their cottage. When a blind man enters they generously give him what little they have saved for their wedding meal. Discovering their poverty the blind man reveals himself to be Raftery, commands the locals to come with wedding gifts, coerces even the local miser to give them money, and thus secures their future. When they turn to thank him, though, he has vanished, and a latecomer to the cottage reveals that Raftery had died three days earlier.

While this plot borrows much from *Cathleen ni Houlihan*, especially in its offstage final transformation, it portrays the artist-disturber as someone who reconciles rather than creates conflict between what Yeats had termed 'ideal' causes and 'private hopes'. Whereas idealism and the materialist concerns of ordinary life are held up as mutually contradictory in *Cathleen ni Houlihan*, in *The Marriage* the poet-visionary inspires a fragmented peasant community to pool its resources, thereby strengthening it both socially and spiritually. Lady Gregory thus represents the artist as a Christ-figure, who rewards the generosity and humanism of the young couple by using his healing powers to bring them both literal and symbolic wealth.

The play's plot makes plain the religious and spiritual imperatives at the heart of much of Lady Gregory's writing. As 'The Felons of Our Land' suggests, she believed that art should ideally lead one from the 'seen' to the 'unseen', thereby giving sustenance to the 'discouraged', and inspiring real practical consequences. In the optimistic closure of *The Marriage*, however, idealistic humanism is allowed to triumph quite unproblematically, without requiring the personal sacrifice and significant human costs registered in *Cathleen ni Houlihan*. Perhaps recognizing that the play savoured of wishful thinking, Lady Gregory revisited its central themes the following year in *A Losing Game*. Here, a peasant couple again face dispossession, but their marriage is an uneasy partnership between a jealous older man and a young woman, Kate, who married for security rather than love when her sweetheart, Christie, failed to return from the United States to marry her. As Kate resigns herself to leaving the cottage, Christie enters unannounced with a fortune saved in the United States. Finding her already married, he deliberately loses the money to her husband in a card game, thereby guaranteeing her security and proving the depth of his love.

Yet if Christie, as his name suggests, is, like Raftery, something of a deus ex machina, arriving in timely fashion to prevent her dispossession, *A Losing Game*, unlike *The Marriage*, is far from rosy-eyed about the real costs of such idealism. His self-sacrifice saves her from poverty, but it does nothing to redeem the sterility of her marriage, and indeed merely leaves her more fully aware of what she has lost. And while Christie portrays his self-sacrifice as a desirable escape from the mediocrity of domesticity, this fails to disguise his lasting despair at losing her. In rejecting ordinary reality he becomes a figure for the artist-dreamer whose imaginative power is fully animated only by a loss he is unable to overcome. With his 'wild' talk and his repeated references to Kate as the 'woman of the house',[13] Christie may have influenced the characterisation of Synge's Tramp in *In the Shadow of the Glen* (as well as Synge's choice of name for the artist-disturber in *The Playboy of the Western World*) but his imaginative vitality, unlike the Tramp's, offers Kate little encouragement or consolation in the face of her unhappy marriage and loss of love.

These two early peasant plays embody conflicts that would remain fundamental to Lady Gregory's work throughout her career as a dramatist. While hopeful Christian humanism constantly animates her writings, underpinning her aspiration that art could lead from the 'seen' to the 'unseen', her plays repeatedly acknowledge how idealist aspirations are undercut or complicated by the real-world conditions they seek to alleviate. *The Travelling Man*, begun in early 1903, is characteristic in featuring an artist-redeemer who grants a vision of paradise to a child, but whose presence also troublingly reminds the child's mother that she herself is no longer able to share that vision. As in *A Losing Game*, the example of a higher idealism offers a provocative inspiration and models a path to the 'unseen', yet leaves its witnesses painfully unresolved, desiring the ideal, yet not convinced that it is possible in ordinary life.

* * * * *

These conflicts, and Lady Gregory's continuing ideological self-debate, powerfully animate *The Rising of the Moon* – probably her finest short play, written in summer 1903 – in which an escaped Fenian prisoner arouses a long-buried sense of patriotism in a police Sergeant, who consequently lets him escape. The play's central action offers an optimistic revision of *Cathleen ni Houlihan*, with the Fenian Ragged Man as a disturber who is able to inspire service in Ireland's cause without demanding blood sacrifice or tragic loss, and without Cathleen's chilling absolute requirement that a patriot must 'give me all'. He evokes connection with the Sergeant, agent of imperial control, by singing ballads which show them to have a shared heritage and by stressing the extent to which it is only chance that has made them opponents. Ideological polarization and violence are thus avoided by their reaching together a collective memory, or shared mythology, which is apparently beyond political ideology or at least negates its dialectic tensions.

Yet if the play, like *The Marriage*, dramatizes a seemingly unlikely triumph of humanism, the Ragged Man is far from being an idealized healer. While his talk and song inspire beneficial human connection, they leave the Sergeant acutely conflicted at the end of the play between the claims of political idealism and the materialist concerns of ordinary life, and far from sure he has done the right thing: left mulling over the reward he has forgone, he wonders, 'Am I as great a fool as I think I am?' (*Collected Plays*, I, 67). Nor is the Ragged Man the unambiguously good, if troubling, Christ-figure of *The Travelling Man*. His stage-Irish charm, and his preference for winning the Sergeant over by guile, initially persuade us that he is merely a sentimentalized representation of Fenianism; but his readiness to shoot the Sergeant if necessary near the end of the play starkly reminds us that his charm is only a tool, and that the potential for real violence lurks uncomfortably close beneath the surface humour of the action.

As political drama the play signals Lady Gregory's uncertainty whether to identify with the Ragged Man, an artist-rebel who is both dangerous and the beguiling agent of peaceful transformation, or with the Sergeant, upholder of and representative of the economic and political status quo for the landlord class. Its use of comedy, however, shows her increasing ability to poke fun at the contradictions of her own position, and her confident first use of humour as a means of disarming an audience. The play offers an essentially carnivalesque treatment of serious political issues, with social and ideological faultlines being exposed, and then defused, by the force of humour. With its skilful use of physical comedy (such as the Ragged Man's repeated attempts to sneak past the Sergeant), its proto-Absurdist movements between serious and comic themes, and most of all its stripped, largely static, central action, in which the Ragged Man and the Sergeant sit symbolically back to back on a large barrel as they talk, the play also marks a massive advance in Lady Gregory's sense of stagecraft and dramatic construction, and her emerging penchant for a minimalist action, in which the focus is principally on language itself. A decade later she would write that she had, 'I think, given up an intention I at one time had of writing a play for a man and a scarecrow only, but one has to go on with experimentation or interest in creation fades' (*Our Irish Theatre*, 57). In *The Rising of the Moon* that experimental instinct resulted in a play which is at times almost Beckettian in its technique, and which reflects an innovative drive in her work that is rarely credited.

* * * * *

The opening of the Abbey Theatre in 1904 intensified the theatre movement's need for a broader repertory, and Lady Gregory responded in characteristically pragmatic fashion, writing some two dozen plays over the next decade, many of which became box-office staples at the new theatre. While contemporary critics frequently accused her of taking advantage of her directorial powers to promote her own work, many of her closest associates saw her instead as compromising her artistry for the theatre's benefit by writing too much, too quickly. Yeats would reflect bitterly in 1909 that she had brought herself 'near to death with overwork' in 'giving us enough plays . . . often working much against the will', while Sean O'Casey, years later, would regret the way her overzealousness as 'charwoman' at the Abbey meant that 'a good deal of what she did shows hurry'.[14] Her drama of this period falls predominantly into three categories – one-act comedies, translations and longer historical/political plays – of which the short comedies are the most famous.

The taut construction, fast pacing and farcical humour of *Spreading the News* (1904), *Hyacinth Halvey* (1906) and *The Workhouse Ward* (1908) have long been admired, keeping these and others of Lady Gregory's short comedies in frequent revival, and much anthologized. Following her own somewhat dismissive description of her comedies as being written primarily to provide relief from the seriousness of Yeats's tragedies and verse-dramas at the Abbey, many critics have treated them lightly, or echoed Yeats's own marginalizing description of them as delightful but sentimental trifles 'where the wickedest people seem but bold children'.[15] The robust farce which predominates in most of these plays, however, masks a subversive political content which quietly parallels the more overt carnivalesque dynamics of *The Rising of the Moon*, and which is long overdue for critical recuperation.

These plays are innovative, too, in their exploration of the social construction of reality, and their investigations of the ways in which both individual lives and social beliefs are shaped and influenced by the power of myth and illusion.

Spreading the News, set in the fictive village of Cloon, is characteristic. Its action spins out a single minor incident into fast-paced, extravagant farce, with an old woman's misunderstandings resulting in one man being arrested for murder and another thinking his wife has run off with a lover. The humour of this narrative only partly disguises the ways in which the play offers a telling critique of the Cloon peasants' preference for extravagant 'talk' over reality or productive action, and, by extension, of their inability to assert themselves politically. Nor does the surface humour fully mask the extent to which dysfunction, potential madness and violence lurk uncomfortably close to the surface in this village community. At the same time, however, the play portrays the Cloon peasants as attractive in their imaginative creativity and disingenuousness, and these qualities, moreover, help them remain inscrutable to colonial outsiders who seek to bring them to order (here represented by a laughably earnest Magistrate, formerly an administrator in the Andaman Islands).

Like many of Lady Gregory's Cloon comedies, the play is thus poised between admiration for the distinctive, vibrant culture of the Irish peasantry, and critical impatience with their shortcomings. (In *The Workhouse Ward*, in which an ageing pauper prefers to stay quarrelling in the poorhouse with his lifelong rival rather than accept the prosperous home a sister offers him, Lady Gregory would observe directly that she viewed the squabbling pair as potential symbols of 'ourselves in Ireland' (*Collected Plays*, I, 260) in their preference for the familiarity of antagonistic co-dependency over productive action, and their privileging of linguistic creativity over material advancement.) *Spreading the News* was probably influenced by Synge's tragi-comic vision of the dysfunctions of Irish peasant life in *In the Shadow of the Glen*, but Lady Gregory's play, featuring a community only too ready to believe, erroneously, that a murder has taken place, and quick to elevate its own imaginative projections to the level of fact, in turn surely influenced Synge's more sustained investigation of the power of collective myth and social illusion in *Playboy*, as did her *Hyacinth Halvey*, with its farcical narrative of a meek, ineffectual man who is raised to heroic stature by a community desperate for someone to lionize.[16]

In *The Full Moon* (1910) Lady Gregory would herself subsequently borrow plot elements from *Playboy* for her further narrative of Halvey's increasingly wild efforts to break free of the myths that constrain him. In all these short comedies subversive political humour abounds, focusing most often on the structures of power within Irish society – revealed in the trans-actions and attitudes of shopkeepers, postal workers, policemen, priests' housekeepers and other such representatives of the social order – but also on the ever-present influence of British colonial rule. *Hyacinth Halvey* is charac-teristically wry, featuring a butcher who sends substandard or rotting meat to England and to soldiers at the local barracks, all the while complaining that England is 'a terrible country with all it consumes' (*Collected Plays, I*, 44).

As Shaw shrewdly observed, Lady Gregory's comedies reflect a talent closely reminiscent of that of Molière.[17] Her translations/adaptations of Molière – *The Doctor in Spite of Himself* (1906), *The Rogueries of Scapin* (1908), *The Miser* (1909) and *The Would-Be Gentleman* (1926) – reflect sophisticated collegial appreciation of the French playwright's gift for pacy dialogue and interest in the farcical exposure of social illusions. Her transla-tions make pronounced use of 'Kiltartan' speech – a heavily idiomatic form of English, drawing on the syntactical constructions and verbal emphases used by Irish speakers – with the aim of adapting them more fully into an Irish context. Most audiences and readers, however, have found the idiom overdone and less effective than its use in Lady Gregory's own plays.

* * * * *

Lady Gregory's impulse to write history plays – much like her work as a folklorist, and her redaction of Irish epics – initially stemmed from her wish to provide and popularize mastermyths that would aid the cause of nation-building. The theatre, she hoped, might offer plays that would leave Irish schoolchildren with 'their imagination stirred about the people who made history'.[18] *Kincora*, her first effort in this vein, and her first three-act play, is unwieldy and dramatically ineffective as initially published (1905), and she acknowledged that keeping its action 'too closely to history' had proved dramatically constraining (*Collected Plays, II*, 286). In a substantially re-vised version (1909), however, Brian Boru and his final battle at Kinkora become of secondary importance to a focus on his former wife, Gormleith, who constantly foments disturbance and seeks excitement, and who betrays Brian once he seems to have lost his passion and fire. With her other long his-torical plays, *Dervorgilla* (1907) and *Grania* (1909), which likewise centre on decisive, headstrong female characters, the revised version reflects Lady Gregory's developing interest in powerful or assertive women who challenge or disrupt male authority and order. This interest seems to have gradually subsumed her initial aim of dramatizing actual historical episodes, and when publishing the works together she termed them 'folk-histories'.

In *Dervorgilla* the title-character's role in precipitating the Norman inva-sion of Ireland remains narratively important, but the primary focus is on her determination and guilt rather than political actualities; while in *Grania* historical events merely provide context for the play's concern with the politics of desire. In this long three-act work, which successfully sustains dramatic tension despite containing only three roles, Grania, who elopes with the young and desirable Diarmuid on the eve of her wedding to the ageing King Finn, comes to realize that male desire for her is at root always fuelled by competition between men, and that the homosocial bonds linking Diarmuid and Finn are ultimately more important to them than she is. At the end of the play, her romantic illusions gone, and Diarmuid murdered, she seizes the crown Finn has long offered her, resolutely asserts her determination to follow her own desires, and powerfully faces down crowds who jeer at her as coldly ambitious. *Grania* remained unproduced during Lady Gregory's lifetime, a telling indication that she regarded its content as potentially too revealing.

In her other 'folk-history' plays Lady Gregory would likewise draw but loosely on historical fact. *The White Cockade* (1905), set in the period between the Battle of the Boyne and the final flight of King James, focuses on the contrasting characters of James and his general, Patrick Sarsfield. Sarsfield is the sole figure to combine integrity and practical force in a cast featuring a narrow-minded materialist who cares nothing for politics, an old woman so set in her loyalty to James that she is blind to realities, a boy who seeks the excitement of battle without understanding its dangers, cynical turncoats, and a king who is a craven coward. With his blend of visionary energy and pragmatic sense, Sarsfield is a figure both for Lady Gregory's ideal of a transformative Irish political leader, and for the artist who has the potential to change real-world conditions by inspiring others. His final self-sacrifice, knowingly fighting in a losing cause like the defeated rebels she had celebrated in 'Felons of Our Land', offers those around him the potential for 'spiritual vision', even though they prove too debased to profit from his example. In *The Deliverer* (1910), a thinly veiled allegory set in biblical Egypt but based on the fall of Parnell, another selfless and idealistic leader is dragged down by the suspicious and quarrelsome tendencies of the subject people he seeks to lead to freedom. The fact that this Moses-figure is an Egyptian who betrays his caste, but is ultimately destroyed by those he tries to help, suggests increasing bitterness on Lady Gregory's part both over prospects for the nationalist cause, and at hostility to her distinctively Protestant brand of nationalism.

The historical tragi-comedy *The Canavans* (1906), set in Elizabethan Ireland but fictive in its action, offers an extreme crossbreeding of genres, and is the most unusual and innovative of her folk-history plays. This three-act political farce repeatedly stages the construction and subversion of political identities, and features an enterprising miller who successfully impersonates Queen Elizabeth as a means to escape from jail. The illusion he creates proves at least as powerful as reality, and is sufficient to expose both the craven lack of integrity of those who profess loyalty to those in power and (as in *Hyacinth Halvey* and *Spreading the News*) the fragility of established constructions of authority. In the extravagantly sustained farce of the final act, the drag-Queen Elizabeth is killed off when the miller hides his costume – a brilliantly satirical staging of political overthrow that seems to have passed surprisingly without comment by contemporary critics. Written in a period when Lady Gregory was dismayed by the self-interested demands of some of the Abbey's actors, by Annie Horniman's hostile directives about the running of the theatre, and by partisan ideological criticisms of the Abbey's productions, *The Canavans* recruits satiric laughter to mock those who lack committed idealism, and condemns the insubstantiality of identities that are merely performative.

The Canavans marks the beginning of a significant shift from the farcical mode which characterizes her 'Cloon' comedies until about 1907 – plays in which the impracticalities and idiosyncrasies of her characters remain predominantly appealing – to a more critical vein. *The Image* (1909), a three-act tragi-comedy, epitomizes the shift, portraying the inhabitants of a remote western peninsula as so vested in local illusion and transient 'talk' that they have ceased to be able to engage meaningfully with reality, preferring, like the paupers of *The Workhouse Ward*, to quarrel rather than to seize their opportunities, but without their partially redeeming linguistic creativity and humour. The two characters with the strongest commitment to illusion in *The Image* are crazed solitaries who live in dreams, and who at first seem to be the butt of the play's satire. But in the end their commitment, however misguided, gives them a certain visionary power, and the play suggests that their stubborn refusal of a sterile reality is preferable to the lazy immersions in small illusions that satisfy their neighbours.

As Lady Gregory signalled in her notes to the play, she regarded visionary commitment as a necessary precondition for transformation of the real, thereby suggesting that true artists must persevere in their quest for higher 'images', since only by doing so might they succeed (unlike the failed visionaries of the play) in returning us to reality with renewed insight: 'if the dreamer had never tried to tell the dream that had come across him, even though to "betray his secret to the multitude" must shatter his own perfect vision, the world would grow clogged with the weight of flesh and clay' (*Collected Plays*, II, 297). In *The Image* telling a 'heart-secret' brings ridicule, but that telling is necessary regardless. The play, in which the surface farce elements clash uncomfortably with an underlying allegorical seriousness, reflects something of the souring strain which Lady Gregory, like Yeats, experienced in the period during and after the *Playboy* riots. In comedies over the next few years, such as *The Full Moon* (1910) and *The Bogie Men* (1912), Lady Gregory would strenuously assert the necessity of escaping the constraints of ordinary social expectations, in favour of a more radical freedom in which the artist-hero is able to pursue their enabling vision untrammelled.

* * * * *

With the death of Synge in 1909, the ending of Annie Horniman's subsidy in 1910 and Yeats's subsequent 'gradual disengagement'[19] from the theatre, Lady Gregory assumed ever-greater practical control at the Abbey Theatre, taking primary charge of its three American tours between 1911 and 1915, and coordinating policy during the turbulent period between the Rising and the end of the Civil War. Her output as a dramatist slowed markedly after 1913, but as she wrote that year, experiment remained for her 'like fire in the blood' (*Our Irish Theatre*, 57), and her later plays gradually take an innovative turn further away from realism. A heightened concern with the 'unseen' marks *Shanwalla* (1914), in which the ghost of a murdered woman returns to ensure justice for her wrongly accused husband, but its supernatural and religious elements jar badly with the clumsy and over elaborate realist main plot, and mawkish melodrama predominates.

With *The Golden Apple* (1916), written as a children's play, however, she developed a mythic, nonrealist mode well suited to her increasing interest in experimental stagecraft, and to her long-running desire to use drama as a means of linking the visionary and the actual. Mythic masterplots as diverse as those of Proserpina, Hercules and Rapunzel swirl richly in the play's account of the quest for a golden apple which cures the king of Ireland's sickness. The play's finale, in which lovers are united, and a witch loses her power, conjures up an optimistic vision of a world in which menace ultimately proves empty – a giant who appears onstage is revealed to be on stilts, for instance – and illusion can be recruited for good ends. As in *The Dragon* (1919), begun in the aftermath of the Rising, a hero-figure helps restore order to a world in which anarchy threatens, and idealistic commitment proves triumphant.

Her most extravagant 'wonder' play for children, however, is probably *The Jester*, written after the death of her son Robert in action in 1918, and not produced during her lifetime. Here, a mischievous Prospero-figure arrives to reanimate a dissatisfied and sterile world by his carnivalesque disruptions, in which people are allowed to change their roles in life and in doing so come to learn the value of cooperation and collaboration. The transforming spirit of laughter sweeps through these plays, which celebrate the possibility of redemption and of unexpected triumph in the face of despair.

Lady Gregory's final 'wonder' play, *Aristotle's Bellows* (1921), written during the Anglo-Irish War, is a sprawling meditation on the effects of abrupt and violent change, a possibility granted to those who find a magic bellows. As in *The Jester*, the wishes of the dissatisfied prove, when granted, rather less satisfactory than they imagined, and in the end they seek a more contented return to their original status. One of the more conservative of Lady Gregory's works in its overall ideological impulses, the play intersperses so much song in its dialogue that, as Ann Saddlemyer has observed, it more nearly resembles 'ballad opera'[20] than traditional drama.

Like all her 'wonder' plays, *Aristotle's Bellows* offers a rich vein of political and autobiographical subtexts – yet to be addressed by critics – and repeatedly suggests intertextual connections with Yeats's work of the period, and with the personal relationship between the two writers. If its old 'Mother', who lives in a half-ruined castle and has largely lost her memory, suggests a satirical self-portrait of the ageing Lady Gregory at Coole, for instance, the scholarly uncle who lives near by and studies from a book he claims 'fell down before him from the skies' (*Collected Plays*, III, 264) evokes Yeats in occult study at Thoor Ballylee; while the play's central tension between the Mother's call for incremental change rather than the violent, apocalyptic transformation favoured by those around her offers a pointed commentary on the difference between Lady Gregory's views on the political turmoil in Ireland and those of her closest friend.

In her final plays religious metaphors and narratives dominate, evoking an optimistic vision of peace and independence for Ireland. *The Story Brought by Brigit* (1924) revisits Christ's passion and crucifixion through the lens of the Irish Civil War, with Christ as the ultimate visionary-disturber whose message might free an oppressed nation and bring unyielding purists and accommodationist cynics to common cause. In the brief verse-play *The Old Woman Remembers* (1923) an old woman in an almost dark room recalls the nationalist martyrs and dead of Irish history, lighting a candle as each of her memories symbolically calls up and illuminates the next. Although poorly played in 1923, this brief work powerfully recruits both Catholic and Republican iconography to dramatize the way in which the act of memory itself might become a 'rosary of praise' (*Collected Plays*, II, 359) and offer ritual comfort and coherence in the face of Ireland's history of conflict and loss. In *Dave* (1927) a boy is granted a divine vision which reveals the materialistic immorality of those around him, and is inspired to devote his life to the good of the poor.

Lady Gregory's final play, however, would be the comedy *Sancho's Master* (1927), a long-planned adaptation from Cervantes's *Don Quixote*. If read as her affectionate reflection on three decades of partnership with

Yeats – years in which she had dutifully served as pragmatic enabler to the flamboyant visionary who publicly overshadowed her – *Sancho's Master* abounds in insider comedy to supplement the already extravagant burlesque of its source material. Quixote-Yeats rises from illness to make one last effort to revive the heroism and romanticism of ancient tales in the face of a modern world which laughs at his Revivalist cause. With the aid of his good-hearted servant – whose name here is wryly given titular status over his more famous master – the 'last romantic' improbably earns the respect of a cynical court establishment.

Characteristically, Lady Gregory's recasting of Cervantes's masterplot offers significant political subtexts beneath its surface humour. The burning of Quixote's books, for instance, is pointedly carried out 'to satisfy the Priest' who deems them 'written by heretics'.[21] In a climate of tightening censorship, which drove Yeats to strident gestures of protest from 1924 onwards, Lady Gregory's play quietly deploys subversive humour to mock the oppressive tendencies of the new dispensation, and to imply that she and her fellow Abbey director would, like their celebrated forebears, ultimately prove moral victors in their rearguard efforts of idealism. Like so much of her work, the play unobtrusively recruits the theatre itself as a forum for political change, and drama as a site where the relationship between idealism and pragmatism can be tested and refined.

Early in her career as a playwright Lady Gregory professed that she and Yeats wanted 'to create for Ireland a theatre with a base of realism, with an apex of beauty' (*Collected Plays*, II, 262). The comment implies a hierarchy – the 'beauty' of Yeats's verse-plays being privileged over her own and others' lesser realism – but it also reflects her characteristically sharp sense of the fundamental interdependence of forms of drama which speak directly to existing conditions, and those which offer the possibility of transcending them, and her wish that the theatre should successfully negotiate the relationship between the real and the ideal. Initially drawn to the theatre by her pragmatic wish to promote the 'beauty' of Yeats's work, in the end her own work embodied a sustained exploration of possible exchanges between the visionary and the real.

NOTES

1. See 'Ireland Real and Ideal', *Nineteenth Century*, November 1898, 770; and *Lady Gregory's Diaries 1992–1902*, ed. James Pethica (Gerrards Cross: Colin Smythe, 1996), 153.
2. Gregory, *Our Irish Theatre* (Gerrards Cross: Colin Smythe, 1972), 19; *The Collected Letters of W. B. Yeats, Volume I*, ed. John Kelly and Eric Domville (Oxford: Clarendon Press, 1986), 386; and *Diaries*, 129.

3. See *Our Irish Theatre*, 19–20; and *The Collected Letters of W. B. Yeats, Volume II 1896–1900*, ed. Warwick Gould, John Kelly and Deirdre Toomey, (Oxford: Clarendon Press, 1997), 128.
4. *Shaw, Lady Gregory and the Abbey*, ed. Dan H. Laurence and Nicholas Grene, (Gerrards Cross: Colin Smythe, 1993), xxv.
5. Unpublished letter, Gregory to Yeats, 24 December 1900 (private collection).
6. *Theatre Business*, ed. Ann Saddlemyer (Gerrards Cross: Colin Smythe, 1982), 12.
7. *The Variorum Edition of the Plays of W. B. Yeats*, ed. Russell K. Alspach (London: Macmillan, 1966), 232.
8. Berg Collection, New York Public Library.
9. *Shaw, Lady Gregory*, Laurence and Grene, xiii.
10. *The Variorum Edition of the Poems of W. B. Yeats*, ed. Peter Allt and Russell K. Alspach (London: Macmillan, 1966), 632.
11. *Cornhill Magazine*, May 1900, 622–34.
12. See note 6.
13. *The Collected Plays of Lady Gregory, Volume I*, ed. Ann Saddlemyer (Gerrards Cross: Colin Smythe, 1971), 280, 283–9.
14. W. B. Yeats, *Memoirs*, ed. Denis Donoghue (London: Macmillan, 1972), 161; O'Casey, *Inishfallen Fare Thee Well* (New York: Macmillan, 1949), 196.
15. W. B. Yeats, *Mythologies* (London: Macmillan, 1959), 326.
16. *Spreading the News* even evokes the Lychehaun murder case that would prove so central to Synge's imagining for the later play; see *Collected Plays*, I, 22.
17. *Shaw, Lady Gregory*, Laurence and Grene, 64.
18. *The Collected Plays of Lady Gregory, Volume II*, ed. Ann Saddlemyer (Gerrards Cross: Colin Smythe, 1970), 280, 283–9, 286.
19. Roy Foster, *W. B. Yeats: A Life, I: The Apprentice Mage, 1865–1914* (Oxford: Oxford University Press, 1997), 444.
20. *The Collected Plays of Lady Gregory, Volume III*, ed. Ann Saddlemyer (Gerrards Cross: Colin Smythe, 1971), ix.
21. *The Collected Plays of Lady Gregory, Volume IV*, ed. Ann Saddlemyer (Gerrards Cross: Colin Smythe, 1971), 241–2.

6

MARY C. KING

J. M. Synge, 'national' drama and the post-Protestant imagination

I

Fogarty: 'Do you mean to say all art is national? That is an awful queer thing for you to say.'

(Synge, *National Drama: A Farce, Collected Works*, III, 225)

In his biography of J. M. Synge, W. J. McCormack contends that we still view the dramatist 'through a mythology broadcast through Yeats's autobiographies and poems'.[1] This mytho-historiography inserted Synge into the Irish Literary Revival as Celtic Ireland's defence against the filthy modern tide. His 'life' became a variant of Matthew Arnold's artistic Celt, enlisted to serve an Ascendancy motivated by cultural noblesse oblige, facilitating interpretation of the plays as peasant drama conceived by Yeats and delivered through sojourns in the primitive west.[2] This chapter interrogates such authorized versions, tracing certain homologous relationships between the almost always repressed life and the plays. Synge's sensitivity to language as action, to the mediated relationship between gallous story and dirty deed, makes him 'in a way one of the most modern of the moderns'.[3]

In his Nobel Prize acceptance speech Yeats constructed his account of Ireland's national theatre movement. He and unnamed friends sought a place to perform 'Irish plays with Irish players', because Dublin theatres were 'hired by English companies'.[4] Ungrateful mobs rejected their Ascendancy legislators who 'thought of everything that was romantic and poetical, because *the nationalism we had called up was romantic and poetical*'. This makes theatre a simulacrum for history and politics, airbrushing their specific complexities into a myth of native Irish deference towards the Anglo-Irish, recently disrupted by urban rancour. With the risk of 'crowded conditions' engendering 'thoughts of murdering your neighbour ... in some kind of revolutionary frenzy ... somebody,' opines Yeats, 'must teach reality and justice'. That saviour materialized in Synge, 'travelling third-class or upon foot, playing his fiddle to poor men'. Yeats declares him 'the man we needed, *because *he was the only man I had ever known incapable of a political thought or of a humanitarian purpose'*. His plays were romantic. Poorer than Yeats, he boasted a 'very old Irish family'. Success came when Yeats directed him to 'that wild island' where he became 'happy for the first time, escaping the nullity of the rich and the squalor of the poor' (*Selected Criticism*, 196–202, passim, my italics).

From McCormack's discriminating life, though, a radically different person and oeuvre emerge. Scion of Protestant ecclesiastical landlord stock whose inheritance and power had been eroded, Synge was not unattracted to Yeatsian Ascendancy. The maturing artist, however, is closer to the critical modernism of Joyce and Beckett than to nationalism based on elitist cultural leadership. He shares protomodernist perspectives with Pater, Wilde, Flaubert, Huysmans and Baudelaire. He admires, with reservations, the Goncourt brothers, Zola and Ibsen, and critically appraises Loti's primitivism and Maeterlinck's impressionistic Symbolism. Religiously agnostic, he mixes in Europe with sceptical writers and intellectuals. He talks with 'peasants' but masters several modern languages, and classical and vernacular Irish. He collects folktales and reads Darwin, Frazer, Spencer, Weber, Hegel, Schopenhauer and Goethe. He meets James Joyce and translates Villon, Dante and Petrarch. Notebooks, letters, diaries, reveal – and cryptically conceal – interests in anthropology, antiquarianism, natural sciences, and ecclesiastical and political history. Synge learnt the violin, won a composition prize, studied Wagner, planned an Irish opera and incorporated Nietzsche's claim that music is a copy of the will into his autobiographical drama, *When the Moon Has Set*.

Far from being apolitical, Synge scandalized his mother by declaring for socialism. He read Marx and Morris but described a Sebastien Fauré lecture on anarchism as very interesting, yet silly. He once campaigned *against* Home Rule, yet acknowledged an anti-Union ancestor and briefly tested, in France, right-wing Irish nationalism. Disaffiliating from 'party' activities, he resolved to work for Ireland in his own way. He visited the Aran Islands not simply following Yeats's advice but shadowing his proselytizing, entrepreneurial Uncle Alex. His studies facilitated sociological appreciation of the economic struggles of the islanders which, in *The Aran Islands*, ironizes the primitivist note, often at his own expense. Student of Henri d'Arbois de Jubainville, he was familiar with French and German contributions to philology and Celticism and alert to their potential for cooption by imperialism and nationalistic essentialism. He dreams uneasily of Captain Dreyfus on Inis Meáin and is traumatized, on Aran Mór, by a 'psychic memory' attached to 'the neighbourhood' (*Collected Works, II*, 99–100).[5] This induces a dream-turned-nightmare of frenzied dancing to music synthesizing folk elements with high art. In 1902 he drafted a sketch about the 1798 Rebellion, interrogating Mother Ireland's life-denying call to arms in plays such as Yeats's and Gregory's *Cathleen ni Houlihan*. On behalf of 'the female women of Ireland' a strong Protestant and a feisty Catholic woman condemn sectarian nationalist fighters and imperialist yeomen alike, uniting against the 'bloody villains is loose in the land' (*Collected Works, III*, 217). This so disturbed Yeats that he evoked it before the Swedish court, to lay its troublesome ghost.[6]

II

'To imagine a language is to imagine a form of life.'
(Wittgenstein)

Synge's practical theatre experience was limited before his debut with *In the Shadow of the Glen* and *Riders to the Sea*. His deployment of language as transformative action is remarkable, given his family's dogmatism. Mrs Synge, rigid evangelical *mater familias*, promulgated the literal authority of Scripture. 'So strict was her rule that it almost paralysed language as an expression of feeling'.[7] This partly explains Synge's dissenting attraction towards the fluid 'peasant' idiom and antipathy towards what he misconstrued as Ibsen's 'joyless and pallid words': he endorsed Ibsen's engagement with contemporary issues (*Collected Works, IV*, 53). In freeing himself from this linguistic straitjacket he owed much to Nietzsche. The philosopher-poet's insistence on words as relational forms of life undermined literalizing theories and theologies. Synge found Nietzsche's teaching practised in the living popular traditions of story, myth and folk memory. Engaging subversively with canonical history, these performatively related to contemporary struggles, while their poetic qualities established that '"literal meaning" is simply figurative language whose complexities have been forgotten.'[8]

Synge's style ranges from high poetry through symbolic romance to earthy realism, violence and swearing. Moreover, settings, place, props and costumes are infused with a supraliteral imagistic power. The dialogue between syntax, imagery, rhythm and represented situation, the transformation of everyday clothes and domestic utensils into semantically loaded emblematic objects, testify to mastery of integrated dramatic form. Capitalizing on and ironizing ideologies of peasant purity and 'poetry talk', the plays foreground the socially mediated nature of what passes for eternal truth. Delimiting the boundaries of the aesthetic, his transfigured realism distinguishes between art and life while rejecting their hermetic separation. To be locked in literalism is to be doomed, like Daniel Burke, Michael Dara, Shawn Keogh and the villagers of *The Well of the Saints*, to visionless mediocrity. Rooted, nevertheless, in time and mortality, acutely aware of dissolution, his plots eschew romantic escape into what he satirized as the 'pearly depths of the Celtic imagination' (*Collected Works, III,* 223).

III
Colonizing Ibsen's *Ghosts*

> Jameson: 'In the little brotherhood of western nations ... everything is common that your controversialists claim for their <own>.'
>
> (Synge, *National Drama: A Farce, Collected Works, III,* 225)

Despite the importance of ethnographical sources, Synge insisted that his reading of Darwin stimulated his creative ambition and explained much of his subsequent development. Appalling him with fears of 'incest and parricide', it inspired him to 'write verses and compose' (*Collected Works, II,* 12). This seems excessive, yet 'when pseudo-Darwin and pseudo-Bible' together 'fuelled the belief that white men possessed an indefinable aristocratic ascendancy', Synge shared Ibsen's counterthesis that evolution had negative connotations of degeneracy for their superannuated class.[9] His personal horror of fathering unhealthy children betrays a deep-seated fear of the terminal anomalies of colonial Ascendancy and its middle-class pathologies. In *The Playboy of the Western World* the laughter associated with Christy Mahon's rebirth as subverter of the Arnoldian poetic type is wrung from tales of incest and parricide. Christy first 'murdered' his da because his father tried to force him to marry incestuously his haglike wetnurse. The comedy contains Conradian *Heart of Darkness* references to the Boers, the Stooks of the Dead Women, mad soldiers, grabbing landlords, rebellious tenants, broken harvests and wars; and to skulls collected from all quarters of the empire and displayed in Dublin: '[w]hite skulls and black skulls and yellow skulls, and some with full teeth and some haven't only but one' (*Collected Works, IV,* 135). The pervasive preoccupation with death makes the attribution of genre to Synge's plays problematic. Those broadly designated comedies are played out in the shadow of mortality. In the two tragedies an almost comic release from fate and troubles foretold comes with the characters' implication into dissolution, their societies in terminal decay.[10]

These pathologies are probed in *When the Moon Has Set*. Synge reworked this dramatized autobiography over thirteen years, accessing diachronically 'an oddly constituted timetable of life' which 'respond[ed] to a series of cultural upheavals as if they were occurring almost simultaneously' (*Fool,* 425). It addresses head on themes more subtly informing the better-known works. Wrestling with ruptures and continuities between the hidden

Ireland of the Ascendancy and the people they colonized, his apprentice piece cancels out, while reinscribing as colonial angst, the sexual/generational mania of Ibsen's *Ghosts*.[11] It explores emblematic family history, insinuating *mésalliance* with a serving-woman, and the birth, and failure to be born, of bastard offspring. A Joycean hemiplegia is induced by fears of transgressing class, ethnic and religious taboos, and related guilt about the colonizer source of family prosperity.

Sister Eileen, nurse and Catholic nun, has ministered to her and Columb's deceased landlord uncle, remaining to tend the wound a vengeful peasant-servant mistakenly inflicts on his nephew and heir. Unlike the mercenary small farmer, Daniel Burke, his landlord-uncle urges Columb, post mortem, to marry for love: 'No man of our blood has ever been unlawful' (912). Columb woos his sisterly cousin, defying proscriptions of blood and religion. Bound to celibacy, poverty and obedience, she plays the harp, donning a green wedding dress intended for the wronged, but not wronged, insane servant, Mary Costello, at once peasant and blue-blooded. The harp is Ireland's emblem and green its national(ist) colour. Making Sister Eileen Catholic, Ascendancy cousin, *and* surrogate for Ireland, Synge betrays an anxiety to annul the guilt of 'the colonizer colonized' and regularize bourgeois incest and promiscuity. The endogamous/exogamous union is eugenically elitist *and* classlessly democratic.

Columb's nationalist friend, O'Neill, ironizes the expunging of colonial history, revealing in a letter from revolutionary Paris the prostituting origins of landlord wealth: 'Mes têtes de mort te saluent. My compliments to the little Irish pigs that eat filth all their lives that you may prosper' (902). Reversing Ibsen's peripety, the plot terminates with a wedding saluting the sun/son. How do these issues inform Synge's peasant drama, distinguishing it from stage-Irish antecedents and from its debased incorporation into the later Abbey Theatre cult of 'look-at-the-Irish, aren't they a scream!' plays for Anglicized audiences?[12] Clues lie in those slippages between class, religion and race in the (displaced) bourgeois family context.

IV

'*The Encyclopedia Celtica*, a brief statement of the facts of the Universe for Irishmen.'

(Fogarty, browsing through books, in Synge, *National Drama*, *Collected Works*, III, 221)

Cairns's and Richards's receptionist reading of *In the Shadow of the Glen* notes the 'considerable attractions' for the Victorian Irish of being 'other-worldly', compared to the 'simian alternative'.[13] For the Ascendancy this choice was unrealizable. Colluding with English views of natives as degenerate, yet feeling betrayed by their Saxon cousins, they cultivated a Celticist distinction from both, claiming descent from poetic avatars in imaginary Western Isles. To the less discriminating English, Celts were, *tout court*, 'as unfit for government as the Hottentots'.[14] Compounding Ascendancy angst, Celticism was being hijacked and Gaelicized by Catholic nationalism. Reclaiming the peasant as its icon of Irishness, this fed on racial essentialism and papal antimodernism. Opposed to Protestant Ascendancy and mixed marriage, it restricted sex to connubial procreation, vigorously supporting small farmer consolidation of land through kinship matches. It was equally necessary for the Ascendancy to secure property through matrimony. As their numbers declined, unions became so introverted that incest and wedlock risked becoming synonymous. Postdated endogamy could not guarantee racial purity to either party: Ascendancy and natives had cohabited long before the emergence of modern imperialist and nationalist racisms.

Synge diagnosed and dramatized the intimate connections between the political and economic discontents of his class and the psychosexual disorders affecting the isolated inhabitants of 'the last cottage at the head of a long glen in County Wicklow' (*Collected Works, III*, 31). Like the saint-worshipping villagers by the 'ruined doorway of a church with bushes beside it' (*Collected Works, III*, 71), or the scandal-hungry frequenters of the shebeen 'near a village, on a wild coast of Mayo . . . on a dark evening of autumn' (*Collected Works, IV*, 55), they shared a state of mental and physical fatigue, which Synge referred to as 'neurasthenia' (*Collected Works, IV*, 210), with their equally bourgeois nationalist cousins. Sexuality and desire were repressed to ensure the stability of an invented – and contested – social world. Experience and observation taught Synge that paralysis and repression were close bedfellows and that the binary essentialisms popularized by Matthew Arnold only exacerbated these conditions and impoverished a more complex human reality. This awareness creatively fissures *When the Moon Has Set* and generates the 'Gael versus Celt' apprehensions of *Deirdre of the Sorrows*, his last Ulster drama whose 'troubles are foretold' (*Collected Works, IV*, 189) is a striking anticipation of future intercommunal strife.

Much of the strength of Synge's 'peasant' drama derives from turning stereotyping discourses against themselves. From *Riders to the Sea* to *Deirdre of the Sorrows* action revolves around poetry-speaking, sexually vital, women. If the male Celt was effeminate, Synge's women scarcely realize either Matthew Arnold's feminizing ideal or its nationalist variants, the virtuous maiden/devoted and sacrificial mother. True in one respect to Arnold's typology, they *are* all poets. But they, and those marginalized idiosyncratic men who have a living voice in the whole world, or a fine bit of talk, reverse the impotence implicit in his debilitating association of poetry with the feminine idiosyncrasy. Far from being emasculated, they release atrophied character into action. Pushed to its dramatic consequence, language as 'feminine' praxis deconstructs the discourses of power confining subjects to subaltern silence.

Like Synge's Aran Islanders, Nora Burke, Mary Byrne, Mary Doul and, most famously, Pegeen Mike, deploy poetry-talk against oppression, greed and conformity. Nora's tribute to Patch Darcy, antitype of 'gentle Jesus', evokes an answering lyricism from the initially fearful Stranger. She and her Tramp exchange a moribund 'doll's house' captivity for the open road, accepting an inevitable but different mortality. Mary Byrne seduces the mercenary priest into heretical protestations against his bishop and restores Michael and Sarah to nonconformity with bourgeois-religious family law. Mary Doul's rejection of the Saint's mediation, her triumphant personal re-transformation of wrinkled skin and tatty locks into 'a face would be a great wonder when it'll have soft white hair falling around it' inspires Martin's dissenting assertion of their right to unorthodox personal vision (*Collected Works, III*, 129).[15] In her great elegy at the end of *Riders to the Sea* Maurya subverts ordination and papal authority when she 'performs the Catholic priestly rite of sprinkling Holy Water on the clothes of her drowned but unrecovered son', compounding the 'subliminal outrage' by 'mumming a scene from the ultra-Protestant prophetic tradition' (*Fool*, 192). This irony is, itself, metatextually ironized when the Authorized Version of the Bible turns the tables on its own colonizing Protestant authority: the mimed passage warns of Jehovah's punishment of Jerusalem for corruption and injustice.[16] Deirdre of the Sorrows kills herself, trusting the power of language to tell how existence under tyrannical Conchubor 'means being denied access to the process of living, and being forced to die into death' (*Dying Acts*, 90).

V

Nora: 'Is it dead he is or living?'
(Synge, *Riders to the Sea, Collected Works, III*, 53)

Synge's poetic women are neither icons of womanhood nor plaster saints. They remain traumatized by specific repressive social, economic and political practices. Nora Burke knows as well as Ibsen's Nora the miseries of conventional loveless marriage. Widowed Maurya and her daughters see their menfolk depart, forced to seek a good price away from home. Mary Doul is decreed poor and ugly by the sainted villagers and condemned to wage-labour, picking nettles. Pegeen Mike, most consciously poetic of all

Synge's 'female women', brutally tortures the man she has helped transform. Succumbing to fear of the law, she loses her only playboy of the Western World. But what of the menfolk?

From the authoritarian, half-dead Daniel Burke and bleating Michael Dara in *In the Shadow of the Glen*, through weedy Michael Byrne and the bullying, maudlin Priest in *The Tinker's Wedding*, to the initially timorous, father-dominated Christy Mahon and his priest-ridden alter ego Shawn Keogh in *The Playboy of the Western World*, Synge's plays dramatize despotic, inadequate 'father figures' paired with emasculated 'sons'. This pairing strips of its aesthetic veneer Arnold's characterization of the Saxon as imperial master and the feminized Celt as merely subaltern, revealing its repressive agenda. Cousins of Joyce's Li'l Chandler, Synge's fearful younger men defer to life-denying authority figures. Consigning Nora to being 'stretched like a dead sheep with the frost on her' (*Collected Works, III*, 55), Daniel Burke contemptuously lords it over Micheal Dara. Pegeen's boozy father despises Shawn Keogh but arranges papal dispensation for their cousin-marriage, for want of anything better. Martin Doul in *The Well of the Saints* temporarily loses confidence in his and Mary's miraculous 'youth in age', deferring to the bullying Saint. He reaches the nadir of subject misery serving at Timmy's forge like a slave. These master-slave pairings, comically inverted in *Playboy* when Christy exits, lording it over an admiring father, anticipate the particular psychic material behind Beckett's *Endgame*: 'the bourgeois routine, emblemized in a *pater familias* dominant in his solitude' (*Burke to Beckett*, 426). Synge, too, 'focuses on such aspects until the family routine – from which they stem – pales into irrelevance'.[17]

Yet his drama also acknowledges that even these characters 'retain a possible worth in the era of [their] decay and parodic rejuvenation' (*Burke to Beckett*, 426). Nora's condemnation, 'It's bad you are living and it's bad you'll be when you're dead' is tempered by interrogative empathy: '[If] it is, Daniel Burke, who can help it at all, and let you not be taking your death with the wind blowing on you . . . and you half in your skin' (*Collected Works, III*, 55). Deirdre's nurse leads the Ulster king, broken in pyrrhic victory, to where, Lear-like, he may pass from imperious tyranny to untitled humanity, to 'a little hut where you can rest Conchubor, there is great dew falling' (*Collected Works, IV*, 269).

VI

'Between poetic euphemisms and discursive barbarity there is indeed precious little room for true art. It is this small in-between that is [Synge's] terrain.'

(Adorno on Beckett)[18]

'[H]is work is infected with the plague-spot of sex.'
                    (Murphy in *National Drama*, *Collected Works*, IV, 223)

The psychosexual realism of Synge's drama, his diagnostic and prescriptive restoration of frustrated desire and the red thread of sex to the Irish theatre, did not endear him to enemies or friends. An aspiring sectarian nationalism which had deployed a high moral line in collusion with its imperial masters to destroy Parnell was unlikely to welcome this 'wounded surgeon' probing the body politic and spiritual, or respond to his Joycean call to awaken from the nightmare that is history (*Fool*, 323). Nor did his own people rush to embrace the analogous inquest into Ascendancy morbidity. None of his immediate family attended Synge's plays in his lifetime. Although *Riders to the Sea* appears to have been greeted and treated from the outset with respect and acclaim, *Playboy*, notoriously, provoked riots to which we shall return. Yeats strenuously defended the playwright while fudging most of the issues. Maud Gonne walked out from a reading of *In the Shadow of the Glen* and led the Daughters of Ireland's premeditated histrionic exodus from its first performance. Unseen and unread, it was roundly condemned by Arthur Griffiths, James Connolly and Padraic Pearse. *The Well of the Saints* was castigated as an un-Irish, anticlerical piece. *The Tinker's Wedding* was not performed in Ireland, lest it incite disturbances. Contrary to Yeats's anachronistic hopes that Synge's dramas would end mob frenzy, they apparently provoked it.

The Synge years at the Abbey Theatre, initiated when *In the Shadow of the Glen* was performed on 8 October 1903, were turbulent. Yeats began the neophyte's promotion in his inimitable way. He 'arous[ed] the curiosity of the [National Theatre Society's] members . . . with hints of an "Avatar" to come', but he tried out *Riders to the Sea* and *In the Shadow of the Glen* with his *London* literary acquaintances before agreeing on any Irish performance.[19] In June 1903 Lady Gregory's reading of *In the Shadow of the Glen* to the Irish Theatre Company triggered a dress rehearsal of Maud Gonne's later theatrical walk-out, and 'the resignation at this "insult to Irish womanhood" of . . . Dudley Digges and Maire Quinn' (*Early Abbey Theatre*, 331). Unquestionably, Synge's portrayal of peasants and women aroused nationalist and Catholic outrage. Any threat to these recently appropriated icons of Irishness was quickly construed as an Ascendancy slighting of national uniqueness, morality and self-respect, while the narrow puritanism of Victorian bourgeois mores produced fevered reactions to any hint of female extramarital sexuality.

It could be said that neither Yeats nor Synge fully understood the complicated feelings and beliefs that fanned the smouldering resentment against *In the Shadow of the Glen* into weeklong protests against *Playboy*. On the first fateful night Lady Gregory prematurely telegraphed to the absent Yeats after Act 1, 'Play great success'. Ten minutes before the end, however, growing disquiet turned into bedlam, causing her to transmit the notorious missive, '[a]udience broke up in disorder after the word "shift"'. Seizing a God-given opportunity, Yeats rushed back to engineer 'his masterstroke . . . a public debate' (*Fool*, 316).

Christopher Morash highlights the multiple causes of audience actions and reactions on the initial and subsequent 'riotous' occasions.[20] They include the symptomatic antagonism of the lower-middle-class Catholic audience to the perceived slight against morality and nationhood, but also their unfamiliarity with the audience decorum demanded by the Abbey. This required respectful silence as opposed to the freer, more vocal and interactive Queen's Theatre tradition. In the Irish context these competing understandings reflected and exacerbated class, sectarian and political tensions, making the battle over the play a political struggle about cultural ownership of theatre. Yeats, Synge and Lady Gregory therefore did the worst possible thing when they imported an 'Ascendancy' Trinity claque, later in the week, to support the performances – these were no friends of the national theatre or its aspirations – and called the police to arrest inhouse troublemakers. Hostility was compounded by Yeats's adoption of a haughty, 'ignorant you versus educated us' stance in press interviews and in his offensive, authoritarian attack on the audiences in the 'great debate' of 4 February 1907.

Synge mounted an altogether more low-key public apologia. He protested, truthfully, but provokingly from his class and religious background, his familiarity with the lives of the peasant people. He pointed out that Douglas Hyde had used the word 'shift', albeit in Irish, in his *Love Songs of Connaught*. Privately Synge seems to have enjoyed the audience response, appreciating the fact that *Playboy* had hit home, if only partially. He wrote, directly after the first protest, to working-class Catholic Molly Allgood, soon to become his fiancée, inclusively claiming, 'Now *we'll be talked about* (my italics). We're an event in the history of the Irish stage' ('All Playboys', 150). He thus democratically affirmed his declaration that '[a]ll art is a collaboration' and his faith in the power of talk (*Collected Works, IV*, 53). Anticipating his more recent acclaim as a modernist, the contemporary satirical account, *The Abbey Row*, declared that with *Playboy*, '[t]he stage became spectators . . . And the audience were players' ('All Playboys', 150).

How did Synge wish his plays to be staged? His attention to their realization has been well documented and new light continues to be thrown by archival research and historical theatre studies. Briefly, the key to understanding lies in his concept of 'Transfigured Realism': neither social realist nor purely symbolic, this was by no means his sole invention.[21] Synge drew upon what he knew of contemporary European drama, music and music theatre, including the theatre of Wagner, Maeterlinck, Ibsen and Jarry. He constantly learnt from, and was in creative opposition to, Yeats, Martyn, Hyde, Russell and Lady Gregory. His theatre art was part inspired by earlier work by Irish playwrights, including Boucicault and Wilde. It was influenced by medieval drama, Shakespeare and Goethe. Formally and ideologically it owes more than has been acknowledged until recently to his and his fellow playwrights' knowledge and championing of Greek theatre.[22] It was shaped by story and folk techniques and by the form, style and content of the (King James) Bible. In post-Protestant fashion Synge carried a Bible, concealed in brown paper, to his death.

The term 'anthropological realism' applied to the Abbey Theatre productions on which Synge advised should perhaps be replaced by 'ethnographic veracity'. His is not 'slice of life' theatre but a highly stylized, liturgical dramaturgy. Experienced actors accustomed to 'stage Irish' noted the strangeness of Synge's language, its artificial rhythms. He coached them rigorously, longing for the formality of musical notation. The delivery he favoured shared something of Yeatsian incantation: language was not reducible to the cerebral. He shared, also, the Abbey actors' predilection for movement as stasis, for remaining still during delivery, and moving with decorum approaching mime or tableaux vivants. Where properties and costume are concerned, sending for pampooties (cowskin shoes) and fabrics to the Aran Islands, and searching for an Aran woman to teach the actors how to keen, are still cited as evidence for preoccupation with 'true to life' reality. This is critically naïve, even if Yeats, for his own reasons, and Synge, when provoked by accusations of inauthenticity, helped to foster such beliefs.

Playing of the drama as peasant social realism, the travesty of Synge propagated by smugly ignorant 1930s' Abbey productions, ignores the need for an informed, dialogic historical imagination striving to meet and match that of the playwright. It jeopardizes the dramatic forcefield between spectacle, diction or melody, and plot. Insensitivity to stage business likewise risks coarsening or suppressing finely tuned socio-historical reverberations. Synge was meticulous about the acquisition and positioning of *new* boards, rope, cake, ladder, coats, spinning wheel, knitting and flannel – and the *absence* of iron nails in *Riders to the Sea*. Boards, ladders and rope had their price in a subsistence economy, and were used for coffin-making and to hang rebel men and women fighting for better conditions. Iron nails suggest crucifixion, as do crossed planks. Nails were also *the* commodity notoriously used to trick those other 'exotic' Islanders, the Tahitians, into yielding women and territory to the colonizing white man.[23] More privately, Synge ironically noted that that cultural colonizer, Yeats, never forgot to see that the Abbey Theatre had enough of them! Synge scrupulously detailed and oversaw the positioning and use of doors, table, utensils, candles, stocking of money and needle, sheet, shawl and stick in *In the Shadow of the Glen*. Nora participates in a self-auctioning black secular Mass, counting out coins on the table-altar with mercenary Michael Dara. She offers a saving, if risqué, last supper of tobacco and pipes to the Stranger with whom she will go forth. Daniel Burke, sadistic impotent antitype of the Good Shepherd, orders her out through the big door: she may knock, but he will never open to her.

Synge notates time and place *with deliberate vagueness* at the opening of *The Well of the Saints* but carefully positions roadside, stones, gap (filled with thorns in Act 3), ruined church, and, later, forge, *broken* wheel and *boarded* well. These details are crucial to the praxis of this highly stylized, ritualistic play, his 'monochrome' theatrical masterpiece.[24] The items listed by Pegeen Mike in *Playboy* matter because they are a wedding list for an arranged cousin-marriage, designed to consolidate family links, but also because, reaching beyond the text, they recall the pathos of lists testifying to the immiseration of the victims of Ireland's Great Famine.[25]

Space does not allow for detailed exposition of the appropriate dramaturgy to be derived from attending to Synge's work in the early Abbey Theatre years. This history is now being recovered, contributing to a freeing of his reputation from Yeats's long shadow. It is to be hoped that a more informed knowledge of his distinctive contribution to Irish theatre will rescue him, also, from undeserved latter-day absorption into touristic cultural consumerism. Theatre practice cannot and should not be fixed in the past, but it should be informed by history. The society which Synge anatomized, ironized and castigated through laughter fed on the pathologies of a patriarchal bourgeois society which underwrote imperialism. Nationalist responses were tainted by their related brand of authoritarianism and racial essentialism. The 'filthy job' of ending prejudice, exploitation, repression, famine, poverty and internecine hatred is by no means concluded (*Collected Works*, *1*, 66). As I write, Ireland is showing less than a hundred thousand welcomes to those modern Strangers at the door, our immigrants and refugees. A speaker on the BBC is voicing fears about the potential of misapplied genetic engineering to facilitate elimination of those we 'Westerners' may judge too unlike our ideal selves. Far from having put away that inauthentic tradition which Yeats finally interrogates in *Purgatory* (1939) and Synge constantly anatomizes in his plays, Western 'culture' may be tempted to revisit our post-Darwinian traumas equipped with more powerful tools than the Victorians or Nazis possessed. Like Christy Mahon's bit of a looking-glass held to face and rear, Synge's dramatic mirror may help us realize that all quests for essentialist perfection of identity, race, nation, religion or gender are chimerical and treacherously flawed.[26] The small terrain between euphemisms and barbarity can be extended only by praxis beyond the action of the stage. Onto that critical gap Synge's decent and courageous post-Protestant drama has opened an imaginary door.[27] No art or artist can do more.

NOTES

References to Synge's works are included in the text in parenthesis. Excepting *When the Moon Has Set*, they are to the following edition: *J. M. Synge, Collected Works Volumes I–IV*, general editor Robin Skelton (London: Oxford University Press, 1962–8). References to *When the Moon Has Set* are to the two-act version edited by Mary King and republished in *The Field Day Anthology of Irish Writing*, general editor Seamus Deane (Derry: Field Day Publications, 1991), Volume II, 898–951.

1. W. J. McCormack, *Fool of the Family: A Life of J. M. Synge* (London: Weidenfeld and Nicolson, 2000), 388.
2. Matthew Arnold's series of articles, collected as *On The Study of Celtic Literature* (1867), followed on from Ernest Renan's 'Essai sur la poésie des races Celtique' (1863) in arguing that the Celts (Irish) had a poetic, feminine sensibility as opposed to the practical, masculine sensibility of the Anglo-Saxons (English). This 'binary essentialism', which reduced the cultures to two opposed, essential characteristics, was highly influential on late nineteenth- and twentieth-century writers and intellectuals.
3. Katherine Worth, *The Irish Drama of Europe from Yeats to Beckett* (London: The Athlone Press, 1978), 1. For a detailed study of Synge's modernism, see Mary C. King, *The Drama of J. M. Synge* (London: Fourth Estate; Syracuse: Syracuse University Press, 1988).
4. W. B. Yeats, 'The Irish Dramatic Movement: A Lecture Delivered to the Royal Academy of Sweden', in *W. B. Yeats: Selected Criticism*, ed. A. Norman Jeffares (London: Pan Books and Macmillan, 1976), 196.
5. Synge's Dreyfus dream occurred on the night of Monday/Tuesday 25/26 September 1899. (See McCormack, *Fool*, 210). His dance nightmare ironizes Celticism and primitivism, linking them together as a form of Gothic terror.
6. For Synge's *Play of '98*, see *Collected Works*, III, 215–7. 'Woman hears' on 216 should read 'Yeoman heard'.
7. Edward Stephens, *My Uncle John: Edward Stephens's Life of J. M. Synge*, ed. Andrew Carpenter (London: Oxford University Press, 1974), 45.
8. Lawrence Gane and Kitty Chan, *Nietzsche For Beginners* (Cambridge: Icon Books, 1997), 157.
9. V. G. Kiernan, *The Lords of Human Kind: European Attitudes to the Outside World in the Imperial Age* (Harmondsworth: Penguin, 1972), 240.
10. For sensitive discussion of this problem of genre, see Fiona MacIntosh, *Dying Acts: Death in Ancient Greek and Modern Irish Tragic Drama* (Cork: Cork University Press, 1994), especially 120–3.
11. Affinities between Synge and Ibsen have long been noted. The biographical-critical homologies are thoroughly explored in McCormack, *Fool*. The

importance of *When the Moon Has Set* for Synge's plays is fully explored in King, *Drama of J. M. Synge*, and reinforced by W. J. McCormack, *From Burke to Beckett: Ascendancy, Tradition and Betrayal in Literary History* (Cork: Cork University Press, 1994) and by Frank McGuinness in his essay 'John Millington Synge and the King of Norway', in Nicholas Grene (ed.), *Interpreting Synge: Essays from the Synge Summer School 1991–2000* (Dublin: Lilliput Press, 2000), 57–66.

12. Brian Inglis, *West Briton* (London: Faber and Faber, 1962), 26–7.

13. David Cairns and Shaun Richards, '"Woman" in the Discourse of Celticism: A Receptionist Reading of *The Shadow of the Glen*', in *Canadian Journal of Irish Studies*, 13:1 (1987), 30–43.

14. Lord Salisbury, quoted in J. L. Garvin, *The Life of Joseph Chamberlain, Volume II* (London: Macmillan, 1933), 49.

15. For a reading of *The Well of the Saints* which emphasizes its Protestant dissenting strength, see McCormack, *From Burke to Beckett*, 241–53.

16. See King, *Drama of J. M. Synge* for discussion of the role of story and folktale in *The Aran Islands*, especially 44–5 for an ironical turning of an Irish translation of the Protestant Bible against Synge's proselytizing Reverend Uncle Alex.

17. Theodor W. Adorno, quoted in McCormack, *Burke to Beckett*, 425.

18. Theodor W. Adorno, *Aesthetic Theory*, ed. Gretel Adorno and Rolf Tiedemann, trans. C. Lenhardt (London, Boston: Routledge, 1984), 47.

19. James W. Flannery, *W. B. Yeats and the Idea of a Theatre: The Early Abbey Theatre in Theory and Practice* (New Haven and London: Yale University Press), 330.

20. Christopher Morash, 'All Playboys Now', in Grene (ed.), *Interpreting Synge*, 135–50.

21. Synge's concept of Transfigured Realism is discussed and applied to his work in King, *Drama of J. M. Synge*. For his definition of the concept, see Chapter 6, 105.

22. For an excellent analysis of the influence of Greek drama on Synge and his Abbey Theatre colleagues, see Fiona Macintosh's comparative studies in *Dying Acts*.

23. See Kiernan, *Lords*, 255–6, for an account of bribery of Tahitians with iron nails. For fuller discussion of Synge's symbolic use of props, see Tom Paulin, '*Riders to the Sea*: a Revisionist Tragedy?', in Grene (ed.), *Interpreting Synge*, 111–8, and also McCormack, *Burke to Beckett* and King, *Drama of J. M. Synge*.

24. Synge wished *The Well of the Saints* to be 'like a monochrome painting, all in shades of one colour' (*Collected Works*, III, xiii).

25. McCormack calls attention to the parallels between props in *Riders to the Sea*, Pegeen's list in *Playboy* and lists given in Asenath Nicholson's *Annals of the Famine in Ireland* (Dublin: Lilliput Press, 1998). See *Fool*, 246–7, 322.

26. I use 'treacherously' here in the sense in which the term 'betrayal' is deployed in *Burke to Beckett*. See especially 17–8.

27. McCormack makes a strong case for aligning Synge with Samuel Beckett and Elizabeth Bowen and reassessing the contribution of post-Protestant dissent to the Irish Literary Revival. See *Burke to Beckett* and *Fool*.

7

RICHARD ALLEN CAVE

On the siting of doors and windows: aesthetics, ideology and Irish stage design

It is difficult to determine precisely whether stage design at the Abbey Theatre was a response to ideological imperatives or to financial constraints. Both probably played a significant part. Certainly after the break-up of the Irish Literary Theatre Society at the close of its third season in October 1901 money was scarce. Between 1901 and December 1904 when the Abbey came into being, theatrical activity was focused on W. G. Fay's amateur group, known first in 1902 as the Irish National Dramatic Company but after 1903 as the Irish National Theatre Society. Though there was a wealth of ambition among the members and varying degrees of staging and acting skills, the budget was markedly limited. Design, of necessity, had in practice to be minimal so the accompanying aesthetic focused on minimalism.

By 1903 Annie Horniman had begun to direct some of her small private fortune to assist in the appropriate staging of Yeats's plays (*The King's Threshold* in 1903 and *On Baile's Strand* for the opening of the Abbey in 1904). Wanting to have a direct hand in the proceedings, she took over the design of the costumes with very little knowledge of the principles which must govern choice and matching of colours to achieve satisfying stage images. Her work on *The King's Threshold* produced a riot of tints, textures and shapes for what is fundamentally an austere morality play. Surviving photographs show the production looking amateur in the worst senses of the word and fully substantiate the criticisms levelled in reviews.[1]

Yeats tried to insist that she exercise more discipline over her imagination when designing *On Baile's Strand* and that she work from books devoted to the history of costume in the heroic age, but the results were equally disappointing. The dress rehearsal for the production is worth recalling. Yeats had a public altercation with Miss Horniman in front of the actors, in which he described the colour and line of their red cloaks as making them look like fire extinguishers or, worse, like so many Father Christmases. Joseph Holloway, the architect of the Abbey who was standing by to report this, opined, 'Candidly I thought some of the costumes trying, though all of them were exceedingly rich in material and archaeologically correct.' Yeats concluded the argument by emphatically denouncing archaeology and insisting, 'It's effect we want on the stage.'[2] This comic showdown proved for Yeats the truth of the dictum that in theatre, less often achieves more.

It was in fact a dictum that in his own distinctive way Yeats had been advocating for some time; his concept found its most concise and impressive statement in his essay 'The Reform of the Theatre' included in *Samhain* for September, 1903. Yeats was theorizing here by reflecting on his own practical experience; and the source of the passion which fuelled that essay derived from his pleasure at the particular staging by Fay's group of his play *The Hour-Glass* in March 1903. This is a morality play set in some unspecified medieval period and has marked affinities with Marlowe's *Dr Faustus*. An Angel comes to the home of a Wise Man to inform him that he has but one brief hour to live, unless he can find someone whose faith has not been undermined by his atheistic teaching. His students and his family laugh at his anxious questioning of them, supposing he is merely testing how securely he has influenced their views. In his dying moments the Wise Man puts his trust in divine mercy and the Angel carries his soul heavenwards in the form of a butterfly. The setting Yeats's stage directions define is of the simplest: a bare study with two doorways (to the house and to the countryside), a desk bearing a weighty book, stools for the students, a bell and an hour-glass: nothing is present for decorative purposes.

Yeats had looked for an Irish designer to complement the Irish actors, director and playwright; but, though Lady Gregory's son, Robert, had sketched a group of male figures clad in simple shades of blue and green against brown architecture, he lacked the practical experience necessary to realize the image as a three-dimensional setting. Sturge Moore, an artist-friend in England who was subsequently to design many of the bindings, dustjackets, colophons and/or endpapers for editions of Yeats's poems, responded with the most economical of settings to Yeats's appeal for help. He created a box-set of undyed jute curtaining which was stretched taut on its supporting frame; a simple cut-out shape for a doorway was situated in the wall to the audience's left and a further door at ninety degrees to this on the left side of the back wall, above which a square, cut-out window revealed a bell suspended outside to announce arrivals. To the right of this door and virtually centre-back was placed a high, narrow desk for the Wise Man, with beside it several low stools for the students, while the hour-glass was placed on a small shelf attached to the front support for the curtaining to the audience's right.

Sturge Moore aimed for an effect of the utmost precision, where everything depended on 'keeping lines straight, the proportions between the measurements exact and on adding no superfluous items'.[3] Photographs of the production show that Yeats took this basic concept but adapted it to the company's scant means: no doorways are visible and it would appear that entrances were effected via a gap in the hanging of the curtains; the hour-glass was placed on a high stand rather than a shelf; and the desk was replaced with a lower trestle table supporting a lectern with illuminated manuscript and alongside this was a high-backed wooden chair. Despite the changes, the principle of an extreme and functional simplicity was carried through in realizing the setting, and that principle was extended to include the costuming and the prevailing colour-scheme. Yeats's note on *The Hour-Glass* makes clear the economy of this design-scheme both in financial and aesthetic terms:

> We always play it in front of an olive-green curtain, and dress the Wise Man and his Pupils in various shades of purple. Because in all these decorative schemes one needs, as I think, a third colour subordinate to the other two, we have partly dressed the Fool in red-brown, which is repeated in the furniture. There is some green in his dress and in that of the Wife of the Wise Man who is dressed mainly in purple.[4]

Less immediately apparent is the ideology that underlies these practical and artistic decisions. The founding of the Irish theatrical movement had had a strong nationalist base. Initially, however, a certain irony prevailed when it came to realizing that agenda in practical terms: there were no suitable Irish theatrical personnel to assist in the venture. For the first three seasons of the Irish Literary Theatre Society, the performers had chiefly come from England (notably May Whitty and her husband, Ben Webster, in 1899; Frank Benson and his Shakespearean company in 1901). If by the time of the staging of *The Hour-Glass* in 1903 Yeats had evolved a wholly new aesthetic of staging, it was in large measure shaped by a deliberate reaction against what he had observed and experienced during the rehearsals and performances of these English practitioners. He saw their acting as artificial in being too confined to dated conventions of playing which had become mannerisms; and he considered the painted backdrops and wing-pieces which made up their scenic arrangements equally jaded and false. Whatever vitality the Irish dramas had sought to promote on these occasions had been steadily dissipated by the lifeless, uninspired *mise-en-scène*. A subversive, anti-English ideology was to be read by discerning audiences into the very differences of subsequent Irish stagings of Irish plays. When Yeats wrote of the need for a reform of the theatre, the aesthetic principles he advocated carried a decidedly political impetus. One can appreciate the daring of this if one compares the design-scheme for *The Hour-Glass* with the setting of a scholar's study for Henry Irving's 1885 production of Goethe's *Faust* with its vast reading-desk, heaps of ancient manuscripts, globes, shelves of books, cases of skulls, a skeleton and dried alligator carcase.[5]

The techniques espoused by Irving and his like were to Yeats and his companions emblematic of all that defined the decadence of English culture with its fixation on materialism, whereas the staging of *The Hour-Glass* pursued a studied simplicity. Yeats's Angel walks matter of factly into the scene without the aid of the gauzes and flying effects which Irving deployed for angelic visitations. What Irving chose to see as 'otherworldly' and so an excuse for theatrical trickery, Yeats accepted as the intrusion of a different dimension of reality into human affairs. Yeats chose to see the difference of mind-set apparent here as proof of cultural difference between England and Ireland, and this fuelled his determination to offer an alternative to the theatrical fare currently being performed on Dublin stages which was in large measure provided by English touring companies promoting values akin to those evident in Irving's work. Yeats sought radical reforms (of acting style, movement, vocal delivery, stage directing and all the elements that constitute design), and for him this meant a refined simplicity, a conscious pursuit of austerity as an aesthetic, cultural and political imperative.

The Gregory/Sturge Moore scheme proved wonderfully adaptable. Dyed gold, the hessian curtaining provided a resplendent 'great hall at Dundealgan' for *On Baile's Strand* (1904) to offset Horniman's costumes in black, green and red; dyed blue-green, the canvas box became the 'dark abyss' of sky and sea appropriate for *The Shadowy Waters* (1906), forming a backing for a huge mast and sail of a darker green and for costuming in shades of green or blue with copper-toned properties and ornamentation. Being basically a tent in shape and manufacture, the design-scheme was constantly employed for drama rooted in narratives drawn from the ancient sagas, such as Lady Gregory's *Kincora* (1905) and Synge's posthumously staged *Deirdre of the Sorrows* (1910). The available performing space at the Abbey Theatre was anything but perfect: the stage was more shallow (sixteen feet) than was ideal for its width (twenty-one feet); the offstage wing-space was absolutely minimal (the stage-left side led immediately by stairs into the foyer-vestibule, while a larger exit to stage right opened straight into the property room); the back wall of the stage was the rear perimeter of the whole building extending along Old Abbey Street, so designers were denied any degree of flexibility in this direction.[6]

Given these limitations, this scheme using the curtained box-set allowed virtually maximum use of the area as a playing space, whereas a conventional box-set using flats to create the three walls would restrict the playing area considerably, since the flats would need angled metal or wooden supports from behind to keep them securely in place. Traditional box-settings of this kind were used for the many peasant-cottage interiors required for Lady Gregory's and Synge's comedies and, in time, for realist dramas by the likes of Lennox Robinson and T. C. Murray. Here, the cramped dimensions could be put to good comic use or to help generate the intense claustrophobia which augments the tragic implacability of a play such as Murray's *Birthright* (1910) or *Maurice Harte* (1912). Gregory even deployed this kind of setting for two of Yeats's heroic plays, *Deirdre* (1906) and *The Golden Helmet* (1908), creating the effect of a primitive hunting lodge like a palisade, where the flats were painted in a repeating pattern suggestive of rough wooden planks. This was stylized realism, whether the situation were peasant comedy or heroic tragedy, and was in its own way as austere as Gregory's curtained settings.

To appreciate how visual austerity links with imaginative richness, it is necessary to go back to the setting for *The Hour-Glass* and look again at its dominant features, which in Sturge Moore's sketch form a carefully spaced diagonal from the rear doorway past the high desk at centre-stage to the all-important hourglass which is elevated on its shelf downstage on the audience's extreme right. The spectator's eye is led inexorably to the door as the highest feature, with the squared window above looking out at a swinging bell. Doorways in conventional realistic drama are simply doorways, the actors' means of entering and leaving the playing space. In Yeats's play the door functions initially in this way as the pupils troop in and out of the Wise Man's study, but once the Angel enters, the door begins to take on symbolic resonance: it has become what T. S. Eliot described as a 'point of intersection of the timeless / With time'.[7] The Angel's return will mean death for the Wise Man, and his anxious watching of the doorway is a measure of the passing of time and the inexorability which will precipitate the action into tragedy, unless some act of faith bring relief. The simply functional has now to be reread by spectators as the focus of the psychological action. The material door has been recreated as dramatic symbol.

Liminality is today a subject of considerable theoretical interest; the Symbolist dramatists and artists of the late nineteenth-century made it a prime subject for representation. Maeterlinck especially chose to focus many of his scenes on closed doors which instil claustrophobia or dread, but which on opening admit death or extremes of terror or joy; and Yeats, influenced in part by Maeterlinck, made liminality a working principle in many of his plays where doorways and what they may or may not frame became the focus of the stage action. *The Land of Heart's Desire* (1894), Yeats's first staged play, exploits the idea of a challenging world beyond the doorway: the forest seen outside the Bruins' cottage excites superstitious fears in all the inhabitants except the heroine, Mary, in whom it induces a poetic sensibility. The mystery which lies beyond the doorway is personified by a dancing faery child who tempts Mary to escape the confined life of dull piety and penny-pinching of the family into which she has married; but, when she attempts to follow the child into the seeming freedom of the 'beyond', Mary dies.

Or consider how Gregory's setting for *On Baile's Strand*, which was dominated by two gigantic doors decorated with shields, provided a focus for the argument between King Conchubar and Cuchulain which occupies the opening half of the play. Conchubar, wishing to renounce the wild days of their youth, seeks to establish a settled community and bind Cuchulain to its confines, while the latter longs for an open life. The great doors are closed when Conchubar's oath-taking ceremony insists that Cuchulain capitulate and show allegiance; but when they next open they reveal a daring Young Man, the very embodiment of the lifestyle which Cuchulain has been extolling, who comes demanding a fight.[8] That Cuchulain is drawn to the Young Man's bravado poses an immediate threat to Conchubar's imposed peace. The doors mark the psychological developments which move the drama inexorably towards tragedy: Conchubar precipitates a fight between Cuchulain and the Young Man which ends in the latter's death. Cuchulain discovers he has slain his own (unknown) son, and as his grief spills over into madness he begins to fight the sea in his rage and is drowned. The climax of the action is reported rather than represented onstage: the Fool, who stands framed in the doorway and stares out, describes what he sees happening on the shoreline to the Blind Man who stays within the hall; the device invites the audience to imagine the catastrophe, to see with what Yeats elsewhere called 'the eye of the mind'.

The imagined offstage world in these plays comes in time to be as important to the resolution of the dramatic action as what is depicted onstage by more traditional means. What impresses is the range and diversity of invention Yeats encompassed in deploying this technique. The quiet round of births, marriages and deaths which define the expected existence of the peasant characters of *Cathleen ni Houlihan* (1902) is disrupted and set at risk by the arrival of the Old Woman with her fierce and mesmeric patriotism which excites Michael, the son of the house, to be her next champion. In *Deirdre* (1906) the seeming haven sheltering the lovers is surrounded by the domain of Conchubar, whose guile has tricked them into coming there; and when finally he enters the stage it is to challenge Deirdre to transcend her dread of being a pawn in his jealous games and find freedom to shape her destiny on her own terms. Invariably in Yeats's plays the agent who comes from the beyond pushes the central character to recognize qualities and potentials in the self which the onstage world has kept hidden or circumscribed. This again is to make dramatic virtue of practical necessity: the material appearance of circumstances is shown to inscribe a limited perception once the 'eye of the mind' is taught to view matters differently.

The elements of design have a precise function to fulfil within the agenda of these plays which, by offering a critique of materialist values, open up a political perspective on the events: Michael follows his nationalist sympathies rather than his homemaking instinct; Deirdre triumphs over Conchubar's masculinist and patriarchal intentions. The visual focus for the psychological process by which spectators come to change their reading of the stage picture is the doorway as threshold, offering entrance to alternative values which prove subversive of what the dramatic action has established as the prevailing status quo. The simplest, most necessary feature of any theatrical setting – the door which allows entrances and exits – ceases here to be merely functional and is invested with a distinct purpose; it is all these plays at the most fundamental level require, the means of defining an inner, as distinct from an outside, space; other elements of a design-scheme help define historical period and social context, but the doorway focuses attention on the psychological enquiry which shapes the action. Even when in 1912 Yeats replaced the original setting for *The Hour-Glass* with a design by Edward Gordon Craig which deployed a curving arrangement of tall, white screens to suggest a long passage approaching the inner recess in which the Wise Man was situated, the presence of a doorway was still evoked in that one of the main sources of lighting for the playing space was angled behind the scenery to suggest a flood of light trying to penetrate into this hidden study which was then personified in the arrival of the Angel (when the lighting apparently intensified). Even though in this instance the doorway was unseen, its presence was forcefully sensed.

It might be argued that in terms of spatial dynamics the intruder from without *invades* the playing space and takes or tries to take possession of the central character's psyche or physical body. Or, to phrase it somewhat differently, the agent from the beyond attempts to colonize and transform the setting which the play has until that moment defined as the central character's own. By exciting resistance or capitulation, that agent invests the central character of each play with his or her heroic stature. Since Yeats associated materialism with English colonialism, what the plays enact is a symbolic repossession of Irish identities by Irish values (Irish, because otherworldly, mystical, spiritual). The action in each of these dramas defines a process of self-discovery and renewal (even if, as in Deirdre's case and Cuchulain's in *On Baile's Strand*, that necessitates acceptance of one's tragic destiny). This narrative emphasis may be on access to selfhood, but the political implications are clear and wide-ranging: the plays are propagandist and subversive of English rule in Ireland. But the challenge is made on the grounds of a superior Irish sensitivity centred in the culture of inner dimensions of being.

While it might be easy to dismiss this as a romantic rather than revolutionary politics, Edward Said argues that the reclaiming of a distinctive national sensibility has a valuable part to play in the political processes which lead to independence from colonial rule. It deliberately contends with the cultural colonialism which is the later, more insidious stage of conquest by focusing awareness on preconquest cultural structures and values and attempting to forge a heritage.[9] However one chooses to appraise Yeats's agenda, it cannot be denied that his deployment of spatial dimensions within a design-scheme privileging a threshold had a precise ideological purposefulness.

Synge, too, recognized the theatrical power of a focal doorway separating a sheltered space from a potentially threatening beyond, but his plays rarely venture into metaphysical experience and the politics is more sharply directed at satire; his overriding preoccupation is with the psychology of his characters. *Riders to the Sea* (1904) is something of an exception in depicting endurance in the face of tragic loss. When the door finally opens to admit the keeners coming to mourn over Bartley's corpse even as Maurya recounts the numerous occasions on which this scene has played itself out, her fate is sealed and her future known. She will no longer need to live in a state of continuing nervous anxiety for the welfare of her menfolk, since all have now drowned in the sea. That anxiety has controlled until now the ebb and flow of the dramatic tension, invariably in relation to who enters or leaves by the doorway: will Bartley dare to go and break his mother's injunction not to do so? Will Maurya return in a state of composure from rushing forth to forgive his hasty departure and offer her blessing on his journey? Will circumstances fulfil Maurya's foreboding of one last death at sea? Always the threshold is the focus of psychological turmoil; though the cottage setting includes fishing nets and fresh planks for shaping a coffin which contribute to the sense of entrapment and to the omnipresence of death within that space, it is the threshold which is the site where the implacability of tragedy is manifest.

Elsewhere in Synge's dramas the satirical impulse is stronger and the arrival of a stranger from the beyond offers the means to criticize those who inhabit or frequent the cottage. What spectators might initially read into the setting of *In the Shadow of the Glen* (1903) are ideas of hardship, a necessary frugality (the furniture is confined to the basic bed, table and chairs) which fire and candlelight endow nonetheless with a degree of warmth and security. But by the time Nora leaves her one-time home in the company of the Tramp, audiences have seen the duplicities residing there, the carefully pursued

adulterous affair, the repeated counting of hoarded money. Nora leaves because she yearns for an alternative to mind-numbing drudgery and constant
penny-pinching. It would be easy to romanticize the life on the open road
which the Tramp offers Nora but he is at pains to define its perils and challenges as much as its delights. The consolation is that at least there are delights
to offset the insecurities: after what we have seen throughout the play, can a
precise value be placed in security? It may have suited Yeats's agenda to see
England as the epitome of a gross materialism; Synge, however, took that
image of the homely peasant interior, so dear to the idealizing sympathies of
the nationalists at the time, and exposed the mercenary ideology on which
it was constructed. Where Yeats espoused engagement with what was to be
imagined as lying outside the actual stage setting, Synge concentrated in *In
the Shadow of the Glen* on the sordid limitations and venality of what precisely lay *within*. Though the emphasis is differently placed, the contrasting of
seen and unseen places in both playwrights' works is a central strategy.
Synge's satire was to bite even deeper in *The Playboy of the Western
World* (1907).

Here, the focal doorway opens to admit Christie, a self-confessed mur-
derer, a cringing, terrified man on the run from the police and a likely hanging. He enters a shebeen where the locals are set in their joyless, humdrum
ways. He brings a welcome touch of excitement to their grey existence, and,
bolstered by their curiosity, he grows in macho confidence with every telling
of his 'story'. Each opening of the door brings more folk anxious to meet
the 'hero', and Christie, who initially feared every opening of that door lest
it admit the police, comes to enjoy the continual arrivals, since every telling
of his deed augments his belief in his own bravado and the truth of his version of events. When this strategy has been pushed to its limits, Synge varies
the pattern (while Christie is away with most of the villagers at their races)
by bringing through the doorway the least expected of arrivals: the murder
victim, Christie's 'da', Mahon, wounded but very much alive and bent on
vengeance.

What should be clear from this brief analysis is the extent to which the
door's movement controls the dramatic tension and the progress of the action
on both narrative and psychological levels. As the play reaches its end the
movement of the door begins to accelerate as Christie returns to confront his
father, is goaded to chase him out to do the murder in earnest, then is dragged
back to be tortured by the shocked villagers who feel suddenly culpable, being
implicated in the violence and needing to assert evidence of a collective moral
conscience. Again the door opens to reveal the injured Mahon, rejoicing that
his son has finally come to manhood and had the courage to stand up for
himself. When the door finally closes it is on father and son swaggering

together out into the world to win themselves an honoured place in other shebeens by telling the tale of the gullible villagers.

Meanwhile the villagers are left all too aware of their lacklustre lives and their desperation at a want of significance in their condition. It is not mercenariness they are guilty of here, but a lack of any secure spiritual or cultural values with which to face experience. The darkest aspect of Synge's satire resides in the fact that the door remains throughout simply a door, a means of effecting entrances and exits, the door which is the traditional scenic mechanism of farce; it never becomes endowed with sustainable symbolic, liminal, mythical or metaphysical connotations, for all the efforts of the characters to invest it with such properties.

By the mid-1920s a new style of scenography inspired by German Expressionist art was being established throughout Europe; it had a subversive ideological agenda, since many of the early Expressionist plays in Germany, for the staging of which this style had evolved, offered powerful critiques of the reductive inhumanities of industrialism, of World War One, and of the conformist tendencies of German society respecting gender, sexual expression and class consciousness. Expressionist stage design was purposefully theatrical in its deployment of the new possibilities of electric lighting to effect distortions of an audience's perceptions and work on a spectator's sensibilities through shock tactics of various kinds. Equally important in explaining its attraction to theatre companies throughout Europe was the sheer economy of means required by such a mode of stagecraft: painted backdrops, wing-pieces and curtains were back onstage but with no attempt at realism. The cultured intelligentsia of Dublin responded with alacrity to this new mode. Denis Johnston captures the mood when he described the New Players as staging 'Ireland's first Expressionist productions in the drawing rooms of private houses with the aid of a complicated set of curtains, wires, cardboard boxes, and sheets of beaver board worthy of Heath Robinson'.[10] The raw, overt politics and the exciting visual potential of Expressionism were what captured Sean O'Casey's imagination as a dramatist with a developed socialist agenda.

Initially, though the locale had shifted from the peasant community to a Dublin tenement, O'Casey's handling of the setting in *The Shadow of a Gunman* (1923) owed much to Synge's example: the focus is on who passes into and out of Davoren's and Shields's room; the inhabitants are questing for a hero like the villagers in *The Playboy of the Western World*, but all candidates are proved sadly wanting; heroic stature is invested finally in Minnie as she rushes out with the incriminating bag of explosives. Setting has a more developed function in *Juno and the Paycock* (1924): again the situation is an impoverished tenement room which emblematizes all that

Juno manages to hold together in the name of a home. The frail door alone keeps her family safe from the intrusive presence of abject poverty and the painful political realities of a civil war. This is most potently realized in the second act when, in the belief that they have come into much-needed money by way of a willed bequest, they have bought a clutter of gaudy furniture and ornaments to create their idea of a middle-class drawing room; their celebrations over their newfound wealth are disrupted by first the sound and later the presence of keening women mourning a neighbour, Mrs Tancred's son, killed for his diehard sympathies. Mrs Tancred's threnody of grief and her black, contained figure, framed in the doorway, challenge the prevailing mood and the stage image which has been built up through the act.

Juno's door will in time admit assassins bent on a reprisal-killing of her son, Johnny, and removal-men who strip every last vestige of furnishing (since the bequest proves an idle rumour and the family is in debt) so that the final scene is played out on the bare boards of the stage floor within the rudiments of a box-set. Juno's worst fears have been realized: home and family have been wrecked. But that process of loss is meticulously linked to social and political causes to depict the desperation that defines working-class poverty and, implicit in this, the need for change. Much of O'Casey's political analysis is to be inferred through his deployment of the setting and the play's visual imagery, most strikingly in the final icon of the drunken father, still vainly celebrating while oblivious of the stark void the stage has become around him. It is the misdirected dynamism in Juno which ultimately is seen as tragic: 'mis-directed', because it could be a creative force but instead is focused entirely on achieving the barest level of security in her home. None of the characters possesses either a developed political consciousness or any degree of political insight into the forces beyond poverty which actually shape their lives.

It would appear that O'Casey had no direct means as yet of representing onstage those larger social forces, awareness of which had tutored his own socialist creed. It is possible to act and to view *Juno and the Paycock* as about character rather than as character moulded by specific political processes. What Expressionism offered was a means of resolving this dramaturgical problem. The first act of *The Plough and the Stars* (1926) pursues a strategy akin to *Juno and the Paycock* in respect of its deployment of a tenement interior with some pretensions to gentility and from which Nora tries hard to expel anyone who is likely to disturb the romantic idyll which she believes her life with her husband, Clitheroe, to be. Act 2 is situated, for the first time in O'Casey's work, in a public place, albeit a bar; importantly, throughout the action the silhouette of a tall figure addressing a crowd in the street outside is to be seen. The figure with his political fervour is representative of the Easter

Rising which is soon to involve every member of Nora's tenement in the repercussions it causes throughout Dublin society, even though many of them attempt to disassociate themselves from the endeavour and its anticolonial motivation. The play examines the impossibility of political neutrality: that shadow of the Speaker looming in the window (the stage directions specify that, 'tall' and 'wide', it should occupy some 'three-fourths of the Back') embodies political process in action. It is a brilliantly economical feat of dramaturgy, communicating a central theme of the play through concise visual and aural effects (sound is to be amplified just as the dimensions of the man are magnified so that his rhetorical gesturing seems to embrace the whole stage area).

This was a first but confident foray into the potentials of the Expressionist style. O'Casey's next attempt was to be remarkably daring. Between three acts conceived in his personal style of realism, O'Casey in *The Silver Tassie* set one whole intense Expressionist scene situated in the trenches of World War One, requiring choric and intoned speech, danced or ritualized action and a setting that was aggressively apocalyptic. Notoriously, the Abbey Theatre directorate led by Yeats rejected the play and have been castigated for their blinkered cowardice ever since. It is worth pondering on this decision. A major practical concern must have been the lack of an accomplished designer; the Heath Robinson-inspired approach to Expressionist sets reported by Denis Johnston would in this instance have been so crude as to be an insult to O'Casey's subject. But the problem went deeper and had a significant history. From the start of the Abbey enterprise Yeats, though content that a means had been found of staging interior scenes economically, was chagrined that no scheme was as readily forthcoming for the staging of outdoor episodes, which would eliminate the need for painted backdrops; these he considered overly artificial, however subtly they might be lit. The painterly literalism of Edy Craig's and Pamela Colman-Smith's settings for Synge's *The Well of the Saints* (1905) was rapidly replaced in 1908 by a scheme devised by Charles Ricketts which was more successful in that the designer insisted that Sean Barlow, the set-builder at the Abbey, should smudge over the work with a sponge to give the impression of a misty, rain-washed landscape.[11]

Robert Gregory had faced the challenge of designing two outdoor scenes for the posthumous staging of Synge's *Deirdre of the Sorrows* (1910) by situating much of the action within tents (curtained box-sets) so that the landscape backdrops were but briefly glimpsed when the curtaining was pulled aside to effect entrances and exits. In the final act the curtains were opened as the stage darkened to reveal a stylized painted backdrop showing the freshly dug graves which awaited Naisi, his brothers and lastly Deirdre herself. It was wholly appropriate that this particular image had a fixed, iconic quality since this is the conclusion to which legend dictates the action must come.[12]

Even greater abstraction was demanded by Yeats for those of his dance plays which are to be envisaged as situated outside: a suitable emblem should decorate a cloth or screen against which the action is played out, a hint merely to the eye of the mind which would then respond imaginatively to the intimations about the setting embedded in the poetic dialogue. Yeats hankered after the freedoms of the unlocalized Shakespearean stage, but too many plays in the Abbey's repertory were in the realist mode to make an attempt along Elizabethan lines at all feasible.[13] It is difficult to see how scenographically the Abbey might, with integrity, have staged Act 2 of *The Silver Tassie* in 1928 (it was eventually to do so in 1935), where that black vision of man's inhumanity to man expresses all the force of O'Casey's cultural and socialist outrage. The rest of the play has to be measured against this evocation of Armageddon.

The visual demands of that act are rich in cultural reference: the walls of a ruined church presided over by a broken crucifix now serve as shelter for a platoon of soldiers who group themselves in sheer weariness over the duckboards supporting a giant howitzer gun; dying figures on stretchers are carried relentlessly over the stage, passing a man strapped in agony to a wheel and another crouching in terror who is racked with horrifying visions. We seem to have entered Dante's Inferno, where in a now-godless world humankind seeks its salvation through the all-powerful gun. The howitzer must dominate the setting, dwarfing all the religious icons 'which have in any case been fractured by shells' and reducing the human figures to anonymous robots going through their militaristic routines. The setting carries the full force of O'Casey's antiwar satire and in serving its demands the actors embody O'Casey's socialist ideology of the need to support all forms of working-class struggle against forces which dehumanize individuals. The stage directions clearly call for the work of a designer with an almost sculptural sense of the potentials of stage space. When the play was first staged in London in 1929 Augustus John designed the setting. There was a degree of irony in this, since his work was well known to Yeats and the circle which met regularly at Coole Park: John had been a friend of Robert Gregory during their training at the Slade School of Art; his sketches of Yeats, commissioned by Lady Gregory, graced several of the poet's publications; he might have been commissioned by the Abbey but the likely expense would have exceeded the budget.

It might seem surprising that the argument of this chapter has focused chiefly on the three major dramatists of the early decades of the Irish theatrical renaissance, but Yeats, Synge and O'Casey were complete men of the theatre: their innovations in dramaturgy required corresponding innovations in the arts which shape performance – acting style and, especially, design. They shaped ways of deploying design for aesthetic and ideological ends which few Irish dramatists have since seen fit to dispense with or even contested. Though Beckett's *Waiting for Godot* (staged in Dublin in 1955) seems to be taking place on an open road in bleak countryside, the apparent realism is quickly undermined by the dialogue so that the stage is shown to be no more than just a playing space, where the crucial factor is who will and who will not next make an entrance. Godot fails to appear, for this is seemingly a godless world where metaphysics has no viable function; instead (a significant anticlimax) either a master with his slavelike attendant, or a frightened boy, arrives. The focus is rigorously on social relations. In terms of the deployment of stage space, have we come so great a creative distance here from Yeats's early plays or Synge's? Even Beckett's *Endgame* (1957) with its simple kitchen door and two tiny windows and its rigidly defined space from which there is no exit is a variation on the same spatial strategy.

Yeats's quest to recover the exciting potential of the wholly unlocalized stage of the Renaissance period, which would effect the ultimate break with the constrictions of stage realism, was realized with his last play, *The Death of Cuchulain* (1939). Here, the action shifts effortlessly between the modern period and the ancient world of the sagas, contracting the complexities of the tales surrounding the hero's demise to a few taut, fragmented scenes modelled in part on the structural technique of the German Expressionist Ernst Toller. The result is a challenge to the audience's imagination, to see settings with the eye of the mind in response to the power of the spoken word and the performers' expressive bodies. Just how liberating such a mode of unlocalized staging can be has been repeatedly demonstrated by Frank McGuinness. In Part 3, entitled 'Pairing', of *Observe the Sons of Ulster Marching Towards the Somme* (1985) the stage is divided into four separate areas as the action shifts between Boa Island, a church interior, a field above Belfast and a rope bridge, each 'place' being evoked either by lighting or by one symbolic property. *Innocence* (1986) takes this experiment further by dispensing with scenery to allow the action to move fluidly about various sites in Renaissance Rome, in and out of dream and vision sequences, and subtle evocations of Caravaggio's paintings. In the Gate Theatre production this threw an emphasis on costuming as signifier, which (taking a hint perhaps from McGuinness's refusal to create a historicized diction, preferring instead twentieth-century demotic Irish) conflated Renaissance and modern styles.

These strategies with words and dress denied spectators the luxury of distancing themselves from the action as merely a 'history' play. Instead the performances carried a decidedly Brechtian insistence on the immediate political relevance of the drama in debating the place of the homosexual artist in a conservative society.[14] The same technique obtained with *Mary and Lizzie* (1989), which imagines a life for the two Irish women, the Burns sisters, who have otherwise been relegated to the footnotes of history as the one-time companions of Friedrich Engels. The spatial freedoms, the modern demotic diction, the fantasized representation of figures such as Queen Victoria or Karl Marx alongside allegorical characters depicting Mother Ireland and the Great Famine all encouraged a rethinking of conventional history, especially of forms of colonization, since the emphasis falls repeatedly on the roles available to women in (Irish) society and in relation to men.

It might seem that this use of an unlocalized space is an abnegation of design, but it is rather a shifting of emphasis to what previously were the marginalized elements of scenography: lighting, costuming and, most importantly, the arrangement of performers' bodies within dynamic spatial relations which approaches the art of choreography (Yeats's experimenting began significantly in this context with his plays for dancers).[15] But whatever the means, there is no loss of political purpose or intensity with this development. Aesthetic innovation has invariably gone hand in hand with a precise ideological agenda, usually acting as the medium in performance to direct an audience to a particular reading of the inner thematic life of a given drama. Design, in other words, is not a matter of providing a suitable background to the action; rather it affords a means to illumination. Much can follow from the particular situating of a doorway in space.

NOTES

1. For a fuller discussion, see Richard Allen Cave, 'Staging *The King's Threshold*', in Warwick Gould (ed.), *Yeats Annual 13* (Basingstoke and London: Macmillan, 1998), 158–75.
2. Robert Hogan and Michael J. O'Neill (eds.), *Joseph Holloway's Abbey Theatre: Impressions of a Dublin Playgoer* (Carbondale, London and Amsterdam: Southern Illinois University Press with Feffer and Simons Inc., 1967), 49–50.
3. These words were part of the annotations accompanying the sketch for the setting now in the collection of Senator Michael Yeats. The annotations are cited in Liam Miller, *The Noble Drama of W. B. Yeats* (Dublin: Dolmen Press, 1977), 82.
4. *The Variorum Edition of the Plays of W. B. Yeats*, ed. Russell K. Alspach (London: Macmillan, 1966), 644.
5. For a full description of Irving's production, see Michael R. Booth, *Victorian Spectacular Theatre 1850–1910* (London: Routledge and Kegan Paul, 1981), 103.
6. For a plan of the Abbey Theatre over the period 1904–51, see Miller, *Noble Drama*, 111.
7. T. S. Eliot, 'The Dry Salvages', in *Four Quartets* (London: Faber and Faber, 1944; rept. 1966), 44.

8. In the Abbey production the importance of the doorway was heightened by changes to the lighting state defining the world outside the great hall: at first the audience saw there only driving grey mist; when the Young Man was first seen it was in silhouette against a topaz sky, which remained constant as an emblem of his fearlessness to the end of the play, gaining in ironic resonance when Cuchulain learns of the boy's true identity. For a fuller description of the setting and lighting, see W. G. Fay, 'The Poet and the Actor', in S. Gwynne (ed.), *Scattering Branches: Tributes to the Memory of W. B. Yeats* (London: Macmillan, 1940), 134.

9. Edward W. Said, *Culture and Imperialism* (London: Chatto and Windus, 1993), 265–88.

10. Denis Johnston, 'The Making of the Theatre', in Bulmer Hobson (ed.), *The Gate Theatre – Dublin* (Dublin: The Gate Theatre, 1934), 12–14. He takes care notably to write of a 'small, educated and sophisticated public for the new venture', though with time he and O'Casey as dramatists, Micheal MacLiammoir as designer and Hilton Edwards as director were considerably to popularize Expressionism in Ireland.

11. Clearly the resulting effect was of a stylized nature, an abstract pattern of subtle colours evocative of a landscape. Ironically Ricketts had never been to Ireland and Yeats had to sketch ideas for him to put him in the right mood for the task, so it was perhaps as well that the finished setting should have an air of indeterminacy. See Ann Saddlemyer (ed.), *Theatre Business* (Gerrards Cross: Colin Smythe, 1982), 275–7.

12. For a full discussion of this design scheme, see Richard Allen Cave, 'Robert Gregory: Artist and Stage Designer', in Ann Saddlemyer and Colin Smythe (eds.), *Lady Gregory: Fifty Years After* (Gerrards Cross: Colin Smythe, 1987), 394–6.

13. The few plays which required outdoor settings were designed in such a way that the action took place against the walls of an appropriate building so there was less need to attempt the representation of trees, hillsides, rocks or grass. This had been Yeats's own decision in 1903 when designing the set for his *The King's Threshold*, which he chose to situate directly before the king's palace. (See Cave, 'Staging *The King's Threshold*'.) When later this setting was replaced by one designed in part by Edward Gordon Craig which opposed two arrangements of stairs at the front of the stage, the backdrop which Jack Yeats painted to fill the spaces between them comprised irregular bands of colour suggestive of grey, threatening sky, distant black mountains and a dark plain. (The design is to be seen in the Yeats Museum at the National Gallery, Dublin.)

14. For a detailed discussion of play, production and design, see Richard Allen Cave, '*Innocence* by Frank McGuinness', in C. de Petris, J. M. E. D'Alessandro and F. Fantaccini (eds.), *The Cracked Looking-glass* (Rome: Bulzoni Editore, 1999), 227–49.

15. Frank McGuinness is not alone in developing this style of work requiring a new concept of what constitutes design. Thomas Kilroy has moved increasingly towards plays which require directing which needs support from choreography, such as *The Secret Fall of Constance Wilde* (1997); so, too, has the range of Tom Mac Intyre's work since *The Great Hunger* (1983), in which he has benefited from the collaboration of Patrick Mason. Mason also brought the style to his staging of Tom Murphy's *Too Late for Logic* in 1989.

8

NEIL SAMMELLS

Oscar Wilde and the politics of style

When Sex Pistols Svengali Malcolm McLaren can convince the *Irish Times* (19 July 1997) that he is planning a film with Steven Spielberg about how Wilde discovered rock 'n' roll in the United States, it is clear that his name has acquired a resonance and currency which even Oscar would have been surprised by. 'Wilde' is now a pop-cultural icon, a multiform signifier of youth, rebelliousness, individualism, sexual freedom, modernity. Indeed the commemorative industry surrounding the centenary of his death in 2000 resolutely commodified him as such: his image is now almost endlessly reproduced on playing cards, ties, T-shirts, mousemats and fridge magnets.

This relocation of Wilde among the ephemera of a supersophisticated consumer culture has been accompanied by an efflorescence of academic interest. Writing in the 1930s Wyndham Lewis dismissed Wilde as a 'fat Dublin buffoon', frozen into a posture of adolescent refusal and revolt: an historical curio who could be consigned to the snobbish 'Naughty Nineties'.[1] These remarks represent the nadir of Wilde's critical reputation, while Christopher Nassaar's *Into the Demon Universe* (1974) marks the beginning of a thorough and almost exclusively favourable reassessment of his writing. Nevertheless, Nassaar, who saw Wilde as 'the last of the great Victorians', repeats Lewis's view that Wilde embodies the last spasm of a dying tradition, with his roots in Romanticism.[2] To Edward Said, writing just a year later, however, he is a pivotal figure: 'nearly every consciously innovative writer since Oscar Wilde has repeatedly denied (or even denounced) the mimetic ambitions of writing'.[3] Since the mid-1980s (and in particular the appearance of Richard Ellmann's biography) it is around this sense of Wilde's modernity that his critical reputation has crystallized.

At the same time the Irish literary-critical industry has rebranded Wilde – who like many Irish writers before and after him left Dublin for the larger stage of London as soon as he decently could – with as much entrepreneurial energy as the Dublin tourist industry. As recently as 1981 Alan Warner could claim – in a guide to 'Anglo-Irish literature' – that '[Wilde's plays] have no Irish dimension' and that we cannot think of him as being moulded by influences which were moulding Ireland in the last decades of the nineteenth century.[4] Now such a verdict looks antediluvian. 'Wilde the Irishman' (the title of a 1998 collection of essays) has become a critical commonplace.[5]

Along with the rediscovery of Wilde's nationality and the insistence on the importance of his sexuality, much recent critical work has concentrated on Wilde as a professional writer in a recognizably modern commercial context. I want to examine this modernity in a specific sense, by exploring his repudiation of what Said called 'the mimetic ambitions of writing', and its consequences for his development as a dramatist. In his poetry convention and genre deploy Wilde, but in his fiction and his plays Wilde deploys and transforms them. To understand the nature and function of these transformations we need to recognize that, despite orthodox approaches to his aestheticism which sum it up as 'art for art's sake', the dominant aesthetic category for Wilde is not art, but style.

Mimesis is based on the notion that art can be a window on to the real, that it can, in some sense, be 'authentic' in its representation of the world. For Wilde, however, art must be self-conscious and deliberate in the way it denies these pretensions to authenticity, and he couples this insistence with a radical erosion of Romantic and Humanist notions of the deep, integrated, authentic self which is discoverable beneath surface appearances and fluctuations. As Wilde put it in the preface to his scandalous novel *The Picture of Dorian Gray* (1891), 'those who go beneath the surface do so at their peril'[6] – perhaps because they will encounter simply a void. Wilde's writing displays a self-reflexive concern with its own surfaces and a pervasive fascination with presenting identity as surface – hence indeterminate, slippery, reversible, a succession of Yeatsian masks that paradoxically intensifies, proliferates and disperses personality. Wilde substitutes style for authenticity, and this fascination with style marks him graphically as our contemporary. In one of his theoretical essays, 'The Truth of Masks', Wilde declared that clothes are 'a most important, if not the most important, sign of the manners, customs and mode of life of each century' (1074). In reading clothes as signs Wilde shows a keen, modern awareness of the semiotics of fashion, but he is also aware of the way fashion can function both as a social code protecting exclusivity, and as a means by which such social exclusivity can be opened up and democratized.

Style, though, for Wilde embraces more than clothes and fashion – it involves 'attitude'. 'In aesthetic criticism', he says towards the end of 'The Truth of Masks', 'attitude is everything' (1078). In matters of style, for us too, attitude is everything: clothes have attitude, music has attitude. What I want to trace is the way in which Wilde's playful and oppositional attitude – a form of camp – informs his development as a playwright. The Society Comedies, which simultaneously flattered and satirized his audiences, brought Wilde considerable commercial success on the London stage in the 1890s; they also display greater and greater degrees of stylization, culminating in that most stylish, playful and political of his writings: *The Importance of Being Earnest* (1895).

Style, for Wilde, is a series of aesthetic choices governing the ways we see the world, the ways we represent it, and the ways we present ourselves to it. And, as he says in 'The Decay of Lying', one of the essays collected as *Intentions* (1891) which theorize style, 'It is style that makes us believe in a thing – nothing but style' (989). Vivian, the insouciant iconoclast in 'The Decay of Lying' insists to the stolid Cyril that 'Truth is entirely and absolutely a matter of style' (981) and Gilbert, in its companion piece, 'The Critic as Artist', declares that 'there is no art where there is no style' (1020). The real artist, Gilbert tells us, is 'he who proceeds not from feeling to form, but from form to thought and passion' (1052). In effect, the central importance of style is subsumed under one of Wilde's most important and modern-looking formulations: that language is 'the parent and not the child of thought' (1023). This appears to anticipate structuralist concerns with language as a sign-system which *creates* meanings, rather than one which is created *by* meaning. However, Wilde is even more markedly our contemporary than this suggests: his ideas are closer to poststructuralism than 'classical' structuralism because he is not merely content to display the processes of signification – he wants to deconstruct them.

Wilde thinks and works *through* form – as is evident in his self-conscious manipulation of well-used and popular theatrical formulae. His willingness to employ conventional plot-devices and dramatic structures has encouraged a critical approach to his plays which is premised on a surface/depth model of analysis perhaps best exemplified in Ellmann's verdict on *The Importance of Being Earnest*: 'amusing as the surface is, the comic energy springs from the realities that are mocked'. According to this enduring model, Wilde is variously seen as either a 'serious' playwright beneath a merely entertaining surface, or as failing to struggle free of conventions which imprison him: both viewpoints begin with the attempt to strip away the veneer of theatrical borrowings and traditions to get at the 'real' Wilde beneath. What I want to suggest, however, is that these plays are *all* surface. Wilde appropriates and displays generic and specific pre-texts. That process of display is a matter of style. His reasons for turning to the theatre, in the wake of disappointing royalties from *Dorian Gray* and the escalating cost of his private life, were unashamedly financial. He anticipated much 'red gold' from *The Importance of Being Earnest*, having earned an extremely welcome £7,000 from the first of his Society Comedies, *Lady Windermere's Fan*, in 1892. Some critics have been encouraged by this to see his commercial success as the result of calculated compromise, the plays described as a 'misalliance of trash and wit'. In fact, despite his studied nonchalance, Wilde worked meticulously through many drafts in refining and polishing his plays, and continued to make changes through production and into publication. His deployment of commercially successful formulae is not the result of compromise or laziness, but rather of assiduous and increasing stylization: a development that is entirely consistent with the theoretical thrust of his essays. Wilde's modernity lies not in the degree to which he dispenses with the old, but in the designs he fashions from it – the style he holds it in.

Lady Windermere's Fan opened on 20 February 1892 and enjoyed the longest initial run of any of Wilde's plays: 197 performances. The novelist Henry James noted, rather sniffily, its 'candid and primitive simplicity' and its 'perfectly reminiscential air'. Reminiscential it may be – of Sardou and of Haddon Chambers's *The Idler*, in particular, while Sydney Grundy accused Wilde of plagiarizing his own *The Glass of Fashion* – but candid and primitive it most certainly is not. Structurally Wilde's play neatly replicates the boulevard successes of Scribe and Sardou, its four acts tracing the familiar formal development from exposition through complication and crisis to denouement. Similarly, Lord Windermere's private bank book, the letter written by his wife explaining why she is leaving him, and the eponymous fan itself, would have been, for 1890s audiences, strongly reminiscent of the manifold documents and misplaced objects which help precipitate the domestic crisis so characteristic of French boulevard theatre. Indeed Lady Windermere – for all the naïvety of her 'character' – knows exactly what sort of play she is in. When Mrs Erlynne – in some respects the stock 'woman with a past' – throws the incriminating letter into the fire, she asks, 'How do I know that was my letter after all? You seem to think that the commonest device can take me in' (411). *Lady Windermere's Fan* simultaneously employs the most familiar of motifs and characters, the commonest devices, and distances itself from them in an ambivalent movement which Susan Sontag has identified as 'camp': affection contradicted by contempt, obsession contradicted by irony.[7] The entire play is in scare quotes. It is a 'Society Comedy' not a Society Comedy.

The crucial point is that Wilde's political and social concerns are not compromised by the knowing, playful, ironic – in short, camp – manner of the way he handles the formulae of society drama, but are, rather exercised by it. Mrs Erlynne clearly provides a focus for his feminist sympathies, for instance (in the late 1880s Wilde edited *Lady's World*, changing the magazine's name to *Woman's World* and introducing content on women's right to equality of treatment with men and to a greater role in public and political life). As female dandy she effects a reversal of gender power-relations, displacing, in Act 2, Lords Darlington and Windermere as the locus of wit, authority and control (on the public stage of the ball, her reentrance into 'respectable' society, she tells Windermere that she can manage the men, but confesses to being afraid of the women). By escaping to Europe with a rich husband and refusing the role of mother she achieves a victory of sorts, for 'cleverness' over morality and the sexual double-standard in particular (she was Mrs Alwynne in early typescript versions of the play). Wilde is aware of the contradictions this resolution implies. Erlynne is the play's most consistent individualist and her fate an example of the kinds of compromises society exacts. Yet, because Wilde holds the situations and resolutions of society drama in such a particular style, the play can claim for itself the kind of transformation of normativity which his essays identify as possible for a self-reflexive, 'critical' art. This style is signalled most clearly by Lady Windermere's fan itself, which signifies nothing so much as the nature of the play bearing its name.

In the final act we find Lady Windermere in an agony of self-recrimination and fear of discovery. She wonders if Erlynne has come clean in Darlington's rooms, told the men of her plan to leave her husband and child and 'the real meaning of that – fatal fan of mine'(420). Wilde, however, prevents any 'real' meaning adhering to the fan as we follow its narrative trajectory, passed from hand to hand, through the play. The fan, the fashion accessory designed at once for display and concealment, floats free of fixed, authentic signification as it acquires shifting meanings in the course of the drama. Darlington notices the fan straight away in the opening moments, where it is offered as a token of the relationship between Lady Windermere and her husband: it carries her name and is a present for her twenty-first birthday. It denotes the domestic and the normative. Act 1 ends with Lady Windermere threatening to strike Erlynne with it; it now represents her unbending puritanism and is a weapon of recrimination.

During the neatly choreographed second act the fan undergoes further transformations. It is handed to Darlington when Lady Windermere confronts her husband. Now it signifies her shifting allegiances and – when she fails to strike Erlynne in what she sees as an act of moral cowardice – she first clutches it then drops it to the floor. In Act 3 Cecil Graham spots it and sees it as an index of Darlington's hypocrisy, thinking he has a woman in his rooms. At this point in the play the fan also serves the purpose of the conventional significant 'stage prop', by bringing the action to a crisis of discovery: it signifies self-consciously the kind of play we are watching. Erlynne coolly picks it up at the curtain drop; now it signifies the self-cancelling confluence of deceit and self-sacrifice. When, in Act 4, Erlynne tries to return the fan, Lord Windermere sees it as a sign of her moral degeneracy. As a gift from Lady Windermere to Erlynne, it signifies both the latter's complicated motherly feelings (she continues to protect her daughter from painful knowledge), her daughter's newfound tolerance and sense of indebtedness, and further multiple concealments: Lady Windermere is keeping the truth from her husband, who is also keeping it from her. Finally, Lord Augustus is allowed to carry the fan – he has been instrumental in the deceit, and is now being duped into marriage by the 'clever' Erlynne. So the fan is appropriated, displayed, passed on and variously transformed as a sign. By the end of the play its multiformity issues a direct challenge to the domestic normativity it connoted at the beginning.

The fluidity of meaning Wilde ascribes to the fan is matched by the indeterminacy of his principal characters. They are opened out, displayed, snapped shut, one surface reversed flamboyantly to reveal another. Lady Windermere is at once the uncompromising puritan and the obverse: a sort of aristocratic Nora Helmer prepared to leave her husband and child. The opening scene brings her into contact with the dandy Lord Darlington, who begins as a predatory opportunist (he and the Duchess of Berwick circle her like social sharks), acts as the spokesman of a high-octane individualism when he tries to persuade Lady Windermere to run off with him ('Be brave! Be yourself!' (404)), and disappears from the play as a confirmed and heartbroken sentimentalist. Lord Windermere begins as a surrogate father and protector, warning his wife against judging Erlynne too severely, but in the final act adopts the rhetoric of puritanism when he turns on Erlynne and cannot contain his horror at this 'divorced woman going about under an assumed name' (423). Erlynne is simultaneously the amoral adventuress, challenging and finally mastering the arbiters of respectability, and the mouthpiece for a social and emotional conventionalism when, in Act 3, she tries to persuade her daughter to return to her doll's house.

Wilde is not revealing psychological depths beneath surface appearances; rather he is creating dramatis personae defined by verbal and theatrical styles, which cancel each other out. As Erlynne says, 'there is a great deal of good in Lord Augustus. Fortunately it is all on the surface. Just where good qualities should be' (407). The characters swap one posture, one surface, one signification for another with a rapid and emphatic theatricality. This self-consciously antinaturalistic method of characterization puts into practice Wilde's theoretical assertion that language is the parent and not the child of thought. Styled by language and literary form, Wilde's characters are dramatic examples of the poststructuralist subject, dispersed and decentred by the processes of signification which simultaneously bring them into being.

Wilde followed the commercial success of *Lady Windermere's Fan* with *Salomé*, a banned attempt to claim for himself honorary membership of the European artistic avant-garde; but the play was for him a false start, and for modern audiences – except in Steven Berkoff's productions in the 1980s which blowtorched the text of its *fin-de-siècle* bric-à-brac – *Salomé* seems preserved in its experimentalist pretensions as in amber.

The development I want to trace reemerges in the next two Society Comedies, *A Woman of No Importance* (1893) and *An Ideal Husband* (1895). The plays scrutinize the English aristocracy in its twin habitats (respectively the country house and London, the imperial metropolis) and the first interrogates associated notions of the 'natural' and – by extension – the normative. The young American, Hester Worsley, bores her onstage and offstage audiences with her smug faith in the great outdoors and the 'natural' values of candour, simplicity, genuineness, and moral straightforwardness, which she believes it signifies and safeguards (and which she also identifies with 'America' and claims for herself). Wilde, however, deploys the idea of the natural only to deny it. 'Here we have the room of a sweet saint,' announces Lady Hunstanton archly, when she and Mrs Allonby visit the 'woman-with-a-past', Mrs Arbuthnot: 'Fresh natural flowers, books that don't shock one, pictures that one can look at without blushing.' 'But I like blushing,' says Mrs Allonby. 'Well, there *is* a good deal to be said for blushing,' comes the response, 'if one can do it at the right moment' (470).

The denizens of Hunstanton Chase allow of no such thing as a natural reaction. To them all behaviour is studied, mannered, part of the social language of flirtation, power, control. Everything is in scare quotes. They also recognize that Arbuthnot is carefully designing her own stage set in which she can play the starring role of penitent sinner. The theatricality with which she presents herself effectively cancels that opposition between manners and morals which Hester insists upon. The whole point of her melodramatic action in slapping Lord Illingworth across the face is that it *is* melodramatic. Wilde is not surrendering to convention and to hackneyed theatricality, but deploying them to a specific end: to show that Arbuthnot's 'natural' behaviour is all artifice, that life imitates art as it struggles for expression. Arbuthnot is as much a part of this self-conscious, artificial world as the female dandy Allonby.

In *A Woman of No Importance* Wilde evokes an English upper-class society which is profoundly superficial in a double sense. He makes no attempt to minimize its casual cruelties, snobbery and general lassitude, but his satiric critique is tempered by the knowledge that it has at least got something right. In its understanding of the importance of fashion and self-consciousness – in short, style – it contains a powerful antidote to the posturing, punitive

Old Testament morality of Hester and Arbuthnot. It realizes the vital importance of being inauthentic. (When Lord Illingworth reads the letter of rejection from his son, Gerald, he comments on its overwrought *fin-de-siècle* style.)

This same cancellation is also at work in *An Ideal Husband*, in which Gertrude Chiltern is as guilty as Arbuthnot of rhetorical excess, in condemning her politician husband for insider dealing. Her moralism is a style among others, though rather less pleasing than most. 'How silly to write on pink paper!' says Mrs Chevely of Gertrude's letter to her husband. 'It looks like the beginning of a middle-class romance.' She then delivers a suitably damning verdict on the handwriting: 'The ten commandments in every stroke of the pen, and the moral law all over the page' (527). Chevely thus neatly reduces her enemy's moralism to a matter of prose style. In so doing she echoes the kind of judgement Wilde's stage directions have already made against *her*. She enters in heliotrope and diamonds, '*a work of art, certainly, but showing the influence of rather too many schools*' (484). Wilde's latest version of the 'woman with a past' is thus judged in aesthetic rather than ethical terms. Her criminality is a matter, principally, of bad taste. But is her taste any worse than Lady Chiltern's?

Wilde's unusually elaborate stage directions are an attempt to establish the manner of *An Ideal Husband* and to reinforce his point that it was written 'for ridiculous puppets to play'. The touchstone is not the real but the artificial. The backdrop to the first act, suitably enough, is a huge tapestry: 'The Triumph of Love' from a design by Boucher. The dramatis personae are each introduced by reference to a work of art, such as paintings by Watteau, Lawrence and Van Dyck. Character is displayed as surface. Wilde's stage directions emphasize that any production wedded to a naturalistic acting style will miss the point. As Richard Ellmann suggests, like the other Society Comedies *An Ideal Husband* does not insist on collective unmasking, but that those characters most voluble in their adherence to the ethical authentic (Lady Windermere, Mrs Arbuthnot, Hester, Lady Chiltern) are also wearing masks, playing roles, though they lack the capacity for varied self-creation which distinguishes the dandies from the dowdies. What is required is a style of layered mannerism, because the play is as inauthentic as its characters. Among the pre-texts Wilde samples are Ibsen's *The Pillars of Society* (1877) and *Ghosts* (1881), Sardou's *Dora* (1877), Dumas's *L'ami des femmes* (1864) and Pinero's *The Cabinet Minister* (1890). In its focus on corruption at the heart of government, its acute recognition that information is a commodity, its exploration of the fraught relationship between public and private morality, and its sceptical view of political correctness, the play looks in some respects the most topical and contemporary of Wilde's social comedies. But *An Ideal Husband* also feels compellingly modern not just because of the topicality of its content but because of its fascination with style and fashion.

Fashion is the subject of almost obsessive comment in the play, in so far as it describes the codes by which a self-consciously disabused society organizes itself. It is a way of keeping ennui at bay, and of conforming, of ensuring membership of a privileged and powerful elite. But the play also explores another – and in some respects contradictory – notion of fashion. The dandy Lord Goring is introduced as *'the first well-dressed philosopher in the history of thought'* (522). We are back to Lord Illingworth and his distinction between those 'who are so absolutely superficial that they don't understand the philosophy of the superficial' (459) and those – like Goring – who are capable of deploying and interrogating the profoundly superficial language of appearances. Fashion, for Goring, is the dominant term in a philosophy of individualism: 'fashion is what one wears oneself. What is unfashionable is what other people wear' (522). For the dandy fashion embodies the opposite of the conformism it entails for others. This is fashion as self-conscious and deliberate style, and Wilde is acutely aware of the irony that fashion can both sustain a privileged elite and act as its solvent. Lord Caversham announces that he never goes anywhere now: 'Sick of London society. Shouldn't mind being introduced to my own tailor; he always votes on the right side. But strongly object to being sent down to dinner by my wife's milliner. Never could stand Lady Caversham's bonnets' (484).

It is a crucial, if throwaway, remark. The milliner's presence represents a potentially threatening social mobility. The charmed circle of the aristocratic elite is being infiltrated by the class it depends upon to supply the 'delicate fopperies of fashion' (522) by which it identifies, sustains and seals itself. Those who produce the material signifiers of style represent a new social dynamic, which is corrosive of traditional hierarchies. Caversham has seen the future and he doesn't like it. The dandy lives as if the exquisite aesthetic future he yearns for, and is attempting to fashion, has already come into being. For Wilde, author of *The Soul of Man Under Socialism* (1891), that is a socialist future in which hereditary wealth and privilege have been disturbed by a social mobility propelled by the excitements of style, and in which an exclusive and exploitative social structure has disintegrated in the process.

In *The Importance of Being Earnest* two kinds of style are again in conflict. Lady Bracknell uses the notions of fashion and style to police the society over which she holds sway. When she hears of Cecily's fortune she is happy to welcome her into the charmed circle, but she must get the signifiers of membership right. 'There are distinct possibilities in your profile,' she says blithely. 'The two weak points in our age are its want of principle and its want of profile. The chin a little higher, dear. Style largely depends on the way the chin is worn. They are worn very high at present' (374). Style, as Lady Bracknell knows, is politics: to maintain the style of her society is to maintain its power, its privilege and its exclusivity. Her celebrated remarks on education and democracy, her prophetic warnings about acts of violence in Grosvenor Square, all betoken a deep-seated conservatism, an institutionally enforced style of normativity, which comes into contact with the pleasure-seeking, liberatory behaviour of the young lovers, and is mocked by the play's comic undercutting of the social rituals of marriage, christening and mourning.

Lady Bracknell does not bother to cloak her political prejudices in moralism. The ethical imperative is voiced instead by Miss Prism (a comic version of the 'woman with a past'), who is persistent in reminding us that 'as a man sows so shall he reap'. Of her novel she says, 'The good ended happily, the bad unhappily. That is what Fiction means' (341). However, for the young lovers fiction does not mean that – it means a self-fashioning freedom from the kinds of authority personified by Lady Bracknell, a stylish refusal of her magisterially ordained normativity. For Jack, as for Wilde, it is a kind of modern heroism: 'To invent anything at all is an act of sheer genius, and in a commercial age like ours, shows considerable physical courage' (375). Cecily and Gwendolen turn their lives into fiction by means of love letters and diaries. Jack and Algy indulge their capacity for invention in Bunburying, and their flair for narrative and drama in constructing Ernest. By putting the novel in the bassinet and the baby in the handbag, Miss Prism unwittingly replicates that privileging of art over life, of the sign over the signified, which characterizes the behaviour of her social superiors. However, what for her is a matter of confusion is for them a matter of style.

The style with which the young lovers fictionalize their lives acts as a solvent on Lady Bracknell's politics. Interestingly, the original four-act version of the play (Wilde cut it to three acts before it opened) sketches its alignment with a nexus of radical politics by making Cecily not just assertive but a comic version of the New Woman. Miss Prism is shocked at her charge's socialistic views: 'And I suppose you know where Socialism leads?' 'Yes,' comes Cecily's reply, which itself declares the politics of style, 'that leads to rational dress, Miss Prism. And I suppose that when a woman is dressed rationally, she is treated rationally. She certainly deserves to be' (342). Cecily puts Algy firmly in his place when trying to transcribe his faltering professions of undying love: 'The fact is, men should never try to dictate to women' (358).

Wilde excised Cecily's waspishly politicized sense of humour in the interests of economy, but the more frequently performed three-act version retains a challenging of conventional gender roles. Cecily and Gwendolen assume the traditionally male qualities of the sexual predator; Jack and Algy busy themselves with the traditionally female interests of clothes and food. It is Cecily who compliments Algy on his hair and asks if it curls naturally: 'Yes, darling,' he relies, 'with a little help from others' (360). This inversion of gender roles has encouraged some critics to see *Earnest* as an exercise in gay politics, as a 'privately coded as well as publicly entertaining play'. (Nicholas Hytner's 1993 London revival at the Aldwych Theatre tried to lay bare a 'gay subtext': Jack and Algy greeting each other with a full kiss on the lips.) But such an approach is premised, once again, on the surface/depth model of analysis. *Earnest* is a gay play 'underneath', a code to be cracked. This is an attempt to locate the play's originary meaning: to stabilize and fix it. However, the radicalism of the play is not to be found by excavating it and returning it to an authentic, specific homosexual politics, but in recognizing the way in which it counters and dissolves a pernicious authoritarianism, personified by Lady Bracknell, with a deliberate and self-conscious emphasis on the liberatory potential of style. *Earnest* is not just about the politics of style, its politics are all style.

In this respect the play's ending is artfully poised. Jack announces that his name is Ernest, after all: 'I mean it naturally is Ernest.' With a respectable family history, a 'name' and position, he is in Lady Bracknell's eyes no longer the rich but threatening outsider. Jack has been respectable 'underneath' all along, and he appears to embrace Lady Bracknell's values by declaring that he has finally realized the vital importance of being earnest. This, then, is the unmasking in which Ellmann says Wilde's dramas culminate: Jack must leave behind the world of 'make believe'. However, the conservatism of this conventional ending (signified by the multiple marriages) is deconstructed by the style Wilde holds it in. From another angle it seems to be not a victory for Lady Bracknell but for Wilde's theoretical essays. As in 'The Decay of Lying', life imitates art because Jack's family history conforms to the role he has been playing. Style defines substance. The final pun celebrates the fluid and arbitrary relationship of sign to signified in a comic denial of the authenticity of meaning, by confusing the name with the quality. It is also self-cancelling: the 'seriousness' of Lady Bracknell is collapsed into its opposite, the 'triviality' of Jack's role-playing as Ernest. The slipperiness of language allows Wilde and his play to elude Lady Bracknell and the limiting, oppressive normativity she represents.

Earnest employs some of the principal characteristics of farce as an act of stylized aggression against 'respectable' drama and its pretensions to psychological realism, seriousness of content and representational authenticity. The staples of farce – mistaken identity, disguise, genderbending as in *Charley's Aunt* (1892), crosstalk – are transformed into a dramatic exploration of the fluidity and multiformity of social and sexual identity, and of the power of language to shape us and the lives we lead. This act of aggression is political as well as stylistic. Wilde associates socialism with a future that is aesthetically as well as materially satisfying, and one in which authority has been deconstructed. The self-conscious playfulness of *Earnest* is an act of faith in that utopian future in which the exquisites, and not Lady Bracknell, will rule.

From a postcolonial perspective Wilde is a colonial subject operating within the discourses of his imperial masters. His subversive project is an 'outenglishing' of English: his characters speak with a style, an elegance and an extraterritorial perfection which exploits English to its own destruction, to the point where it describes only a void: 'Miss Fairfax,' says Jack nervously, as his speech curls back around emptiness, 'ever since I met you I have admired you more than any girl ... I have ever met since ... I met you' (329). Wilde is an Anglo-Irishman contriving to distance himself *within* English, thus registering his paradoxical position in the colonial power-structure linking England and Ireland. As a member of the Anglo-Irish Ascendancy and a nationalist (son of Lady Wilde, the virulently nationalist poet 'Speranza'), Wilde is implicated in English dominion, yet contemptuous of it – a contradiction enacted in his precise deployment, and disarming, of the language itself. However, we should resist any temptation to see Wilde's nationalism as atavistic: it is part of a nexus of radical political allegiances which incorporates his feminism and his socialism as well. Wilde's politics are much more subtle and interesting than a reductive 'anti-Englishness' would imply. Celticism and Irishness were not for Wilde essentialist notions legitimating forms of authenticity, but floating signifiers he could appropriate for his own strategic purposes – principally to define his personal oppositional stance, his 'otherness', his rejection of authority in all forms. Wilde would have been less at home in the 'free', fantasy Ireland of athletic youths and comely maidens evoked by Eamon de Valera's 1943 radio broadcast (whatever his interest in the former) than he was in the English Victorian culture which destroyed him. Besides, Wilde provides his own warning to those who would seek to scrape away the accretions of Englishness to get at his Celtic core, or to define him in terms of sexual, cultural or national authenticity and to trace him back to his roots. When Lady Bracknell hears that Jack's provenance is Victoria Station she tells him he is the first person she has ever met whose origin is a terminus.

NOTES

1. Wyndham Lewis, *Men Without Art*, ed. Seamus Cooney (Santa Rosa: Black Sparrow Press, 1987), 143–4.

2. Christoher S. Nassar, *Into the Demon Universe* (New Haven: Yale University Press, 1974), xi.

3. Edward W. Said, *Beginnings: Intentions and Method* (New York: Basic Books, 1975), 11.

4. Alan Warner, *A Guide to Anglo-Irish Literature* (Dublin: Gill and Macmillan, 1981), 5.

5. Jerusha MacCormack (ed.), *Wilde the Irishman* (New Haven: Yale University Press, 1998).

6. *The Complete Works of Oscar Wilde* (London: Collins, new edn., 1966), 17. All further references to this edition are included in the text in parenthesis.

7. Susan Sontag's 'Notes on "Camp"', written 'for Oscar Wilde', are in her collection *Against Interpretation* (Eyre and Spottiswoode: London, 1967), 275–92.

9

GEARÓID O'FLAHERTY

George Bernard Shaw and Ireland

At the age of ninety, George Bernard Shaw was asked by an Irish newspaper reporter to what extent he thought his mentality had been tempered by the fact that he had been born in Ireland. He responded:

> To the extent of making me a foreigner in every other country. But the position of a foreigner with complete command of the same language has great advantages. I can take an objective view of England, which no Englishman can. I could not take an objective view of Ireland.[1]

David Greene and Dan Laurence have refuted the writer's claim that he suffered from a lack of objectivity when confronted with the subject of Ireland:

> During the period of more than sixty years in which these selections were written, and which Ireland arrived at her final appointment with destiny through bitter political agitation, bloodshed, and civil war, not many Irishmen, whether participants in those events or merely commentators on them, showed as much objectivity as Shaw did . . . It is all the more remarkable therefore that Shaw, who believed he could not be objective on the subject of his native country, could be not only objective but temperate and wise in an atmosphere of rabid partisanship. The reader, knowing that very few of the books which made Shaw famous deal with Ireland, will also be surprised to learn how concerned he was about the problems of his native country and how much of his time and energies was devoted to studying and writing about them (*The Matter With Ireland*, ix).

Throughout his lifetime George Bernard Shaw's affiliation with Ireland could best be described as uncomfortable, a classic love-hate relationship. His association with his native land was from the very beginning ambiguous; the circumstance of birth inducted him into the minority ruling Protestant Ascendancy class, but familial financial misfortune severely restricted the opportunity for further social scaling within this class. If the dichotomy between differing socio-political, religious and cultural allegiances were not cause enough to alienate and exclude Shaw from various sections of the community, his own unique individual approach of offering his opinion on the most diverse range of subjects often sufficed in achieving the same result. Shaw's attitude towards Ireland and the 'Irish Question' vacillated at any given time between disenchanted exasperation and obdurate promotion. It was in essence a very particular Shavian dilemma, often manifesting as a conflict of interest between his emotional and intellectual state of mind. Therefore Shaw's perceptions of Ireland were determined by this impasse in his subsequent fictional, dramatic and socio-political writings, which incorporated an Irish dimension as subject matter.

Explaining in his memoirs why he left Dublin in 1876, Shaw surmised:

> Every Irishman who felt that his business in life was on the higher planes of the cultural professions felt that he must have a metropolitan domicile and an international culture: that is, he felt that his first business was to get out of Ireland. I had the same feeling. For London as London, or England as England, I cared nothing . . . But as the English language was my weapon, there was nothing for it but London.[2]

While reminiscing about his reasons for leaving Ireland in the preface to his first novel *Immaturity* (1879), Shaw referred to Joyce's *Ulysses* in an attempt to explain why it was necessary for any aspiring young artist to leave Dublin – that city of 'derision and invincible ignorance' as he later described it in a letter to the editor of the *Irish Worker* in 1912.[3] The comparison is interesting; James Joyce was of a similar age when he chose to leave Dublin. For Joyce, Dublin had become the 'centre of paralysis' – as if looking through Shavian-tinted glasses the city seemed to repress ambition and in its place offered only lingering obscurity.

Shaw initially struggled to reconcile and objectify his early negative memories of an unhappy Dublin childhood and disillusioned adolescence in *Immaturity*. This disillusionment-with-Ireland motif was further promulgated and embodied by Shaw in the novel. He confronted his previous artistically and socio-politically disenchanted youth working as a clerk in Dublin by incorporating or recreating similar circumstances in a London setting for the main protagonist of his narrative. Robert Smith, a thinly disguised Shavian figure, finds secretarial employment with Mr Woodward, an Irish Protestant member of Parliament. By adopting an English persona with an archetypal English surname, Shaw attempted to exorcize his abidingly negative memories of stultifying Dublin through a process of ironic role-reversal.

Smith, described at one stage as 'the pale scholar of Islington, whose thoughts were like bloodless shadows of conscience and logic',[4] epitomized the young clerical Shaw of Dublin, struggling to release and fulfil his strong, artistic temperament. In *Immaturity* Shaw initially appears to reaffirm the conventional Victorian belief that the Irish disposition was antithetical to the demands and requirements of efficient and effective self-government. On Smith's arrival Mr Woodward's household exhibited all the characteristics of a gregarious, disorderly domicile – personified by the Woodward's butler, Cornelius Hamlet, portrayed as a very un-English manservant, being irreverent, opinionated and so unpredictably susceptible to social solecisms and indiscretions that we are informed he could not be trusted to answer the door after three in the afternoon in South Kensington.

The consequences of introducing the industrious Smith with his English pragmatism and matter-of-factness into this environment are predictable enough – the unconventional Irish household only emphasizes Smith's Englishness, thus allowing Shaw to explore Smith's own latent comic potential and therefore disparage national stereotyping by deviously experimenting with notions of 'stage Irishness' and 'stage Englishness'. Yet the fact remains that it took the introduction of the empirical Smith to bring a sense of order and stability to Mr Woodward's otherwise chaotic public life, and consequently Shaw could be accused of unintentionally falling victim to the very conventions of English cultural imperialism he wished to discredit and which he would return to more emphatically in *John Bull's Other Island* (1904). Indeed, Smith's interactions with the Woodward household, if viewed as an investigation of Anglo-Irish relations, perhaps assumes a further precursory importance or influence over his more detailed analysis in *John Bull's Other Island*.

While the novel is ultimately concerned with the artist-philosopher Smith's search for a positive identity, it also contains one of Shaw's earliest artistic (fictional or dramatic) expositions on the complexity of Anglo-Irish relations, and examines the inadequacies and incongruities of English sensibility towards the Irish. Shaw satirically portrayed Smith rather negatively as an individual going nowhere fast, which was perhaps analogous to Shaw's impression of his own lack of success as an author of fiction. His ambivalence towards his Irish identity during his early years of exile took on a much sharper rejectionist tone despite his later assertive declarations of his Irishness. The original manuscript in the National Library of Ireland discloses the extent of Shaw's identity crisis, since it reveals revisions in the published version apparently designed to obfuscate if not repudiate origin. According to Nicholas Grene:

In one sense, Shaw could be seen in the novel as the provincial with the cultural inferiority complex, deliberately refurbishing himself as more English than the English themselves . . . Shaw was not able to make out of his own Irishness the sort of outsider's distinction he was to achieve with it eventually . . . In so far as Shaw is Smith . . . he takes to himself that superiority of his English persona. He de-Hibernianizes himself and is distanced from what he is ashamed of and dislikes in his own nationality . . . Shaw creates . . . an imagined alter ego, partly wish-fulfilment model allowing him to escape from his provincial status as Irishman, partly caricature of the uptight Anglicized prize he aspired to become . . . Shaw has cast off his family as well as his nationality; the novel represents a blotting out of aspects of the author's life he wanted to forget.[5]

Mr Woodward's daughter Isabella is also portrayed as an unconventional Irish woman equipped with distinctively Shavian objectivity in her opinion of Ireland. She identifies the very things Shaw despised about Ireland and castigates them mercilessly:

But don't fancy that I am disposed to defend my country. I hate Ireland. It is the slowest, furthest behind its time, dowdiest, and most detestedly snobbish place on the surface of the earth (*Immaturity*, 262).

By portraying Isabella Woodward as a convert to Catholicism, Shaw publicized the complexity of diverse religious traditions in Ireland as a further dimension of Irish politics. Isabella personified the multifaceted nature of the Irish question, being of the Protestant Ascendancy ruling class, but also a convert to Catholicism. She sees Ireland in much the same negative light as Shaw saw it, culturally backward and consumed by political, religious and ethnic segregation. Isabella stands in sharp contrast to the other conventional, whimsical 'Irish' characters in the novel; and in certain respects she is very much a forerunner to Larry Doyle in *John Bull's Other Island*. As if echoing Shaw's and Larry Doyle's sentiments, Isabella ultimately concludes that the only sensible institution in Ireland is absenteeism.

The fact that Shaw lived in Ireland for only twenty of his ninety-four years, and that only one of his major dramatic works directly concerned Ireland, has tended to prejudice his contribution to Irish literature. Much conjecture has been made of what if Shaw had stayed to witness the resurgence of Gaelic nationalism? Would he, too, have been swept up in the Irish Literary Revival? Later he at least admitted the possibility. 'If I had gone to the hills nearby to look back upon Dublin and to ponder upon myself, I too might have become a poet like Yeats, Synge, and the rest of them' (*The Matter With Ireland*, x). In reality Shaw's iconoclastic artistic temperament and distinctive sense of Irishness were never suited to Yeats's romantic vision of Ireland. In 1906, two years after he completed *John Bull's Other Island*, Shaw wrote:

> *John Bull's Other Island* was written in 1904 at the request of Mr William
> Butler Yeats, as a patriotic contribution to the repertory of the Irish Literary
> Theatre. Like most people who have asked me to write plays, Mr Yeats got
> rather more than he bargained for . . . It was uncongenial to the whole spirit
> of the neo-Gaelic movement, which is bent on creating a new Ireland after its
> own ideal, whereas my play is a very uncompromising presentment of the real
> old Ireland (*Prefaces*, 439).

Undoubtedly the complexities facing the Abbey Theatre in producing and
staging *John Bull's Other Island* were immense. The stage direction presented
several logistical and financial problems, which were 'at that time beyond
the resources of the Abbey Theatre' (*Prefaces*, 439). Regarding the play itself, Shaw realized all too well the political implications of the stage Irish
conventions. He included them all in *John Bull's Other Island*: the returned
ambitious exile, the industrious if sentimental Englishman, the exploited
peasant, the priest and the Irish colleen. In a review of an 1896 revival of
Dion Boucicault's *The Colleen Bawn* (1860), Shaw announced, 'I am quite
ready to help the saving work of reducing the sham Ireland of romance to
a heap of unsightly ruins',[6] and in 1916 he once again reiterated this fact:
'Ireland is in full reaction against both servility and the stage Irishman' (*The
Matter With Ireland*, 99).

John Bull's Other Island is a perceptive, analytical study of the Irish émigré
confronting the notion of national identity and Anglo-Irish relations. The
play is preoccupied with understanding and revealing modes of national
performance, both Irish and English, which have been constructed and per-
fected over the centuries by colonizer and colonized alike in a manic attempt
to disarm the other for further materialist advantage. Adopting therefore the
Wildean maxim that 'man is least himself when he talks in his own person
but give him a mask and he will tell you the truth',[7] Patsy Farrell assumes
the persona of the stupid, superstitious Irish peasant, which as Shaw reveals in stage direction is 'not his real character, but a cunning developed
by his constant dread of a hostile dominance, which he habitually tries to
disarm and tempt into unmasking by pretending to be a much greater fool
than he really is. Englishmen think him half-witted, which is exactly what
he intends them to think.'[8] Similarly, the empirically minded Broadbent portrays to perfection the role of the good-natured, well-intentioned, liberal
imperialist – and so the performance continues, each pandering to the other's
preconceptions of superiority. But just as at the beginning of the play when
Larry Doyle mocks and undermines the traditional stereotype of the stage
Irishman by exposing the Glaswegian Tim Haffigan as a fraud, the mask has
a tendency to slip, revealing the truth:

Man alive, don't you know that all this top-o-the-morning and broth-of-a-boy and more-power-to-your-elbow business is got up in England to fool you, like the Albert Hall concerts of Irish music? No Irishman ever talks like that in Ireland, or ever did, or ever will. But when a thoroughly worthless Irishman comes to England, and finds the whole place full of romantic duffers like you, who will let him loaf and drink and sponge and brag as long as he flatters your sense of moral superiority by playing the fool and degrading himself and his country, he soon learns the antics that take you in (410).

Broadbent, too, is susceptible to this imperfection at times, proclaiming to Doyle that 'Home Rule will work wonders under English guidance' before cynically and hypocritically adding the proviso, 'We English must place our capacity for government at the service of nations less fortunately endowed; so as to allow them to develop in perfect freedom to the English level of self-government' (412). As the symbolic representative of Shavian exile, and a repudiator of antiquated Irish dreams, Doyle is trapped between his genuine national affinity for his country and his abhorrence of it as a failed economic entity. It is the agony of an Irishman 'whose heart is nothing but his imagination' (410), in the face of English practicality and self-serving imperial efficiency. Keegan, the clerical, symbolic representative of the visionary-dreamer, imagines an idealized de/postcolonized future for Ireland, a utopian alternative to replace the reality which under current conditions is a 'hungry . . . naked . . . ignorant, oppressed land' (451). Ironically this is also Doyle's most secret vision, for 'a country to live in where the facts were not brutal and the dreams not unreal' (415). But it is Keegan who, perhaps in a reflection of Doyle's guilt, sees through this Broadbentian scheme as one which will 'drive Haffigan to America very efficiently' (450), and deliver Roscullen into the possession of his syndicate for developmental exploitation. Shaw was acutely aware of the exploitative side of colonialism, as indicated by the following discussion between Broadbent and Haffigan: 'You know the English plan, Mr Haffigan, don't you?' Broadbent inquires. 'Bedad I do sir, I do. Take all you can out of Ireland and spend it in England: that's it'. Broadbent's chagrined response had something of a hollow ring to it: 'My plan, sir will be to take a little money out of England and spend it in Ireland' (407).

The visionary Keegan understands the reality of the situation; Broadbent is a harbinger of doom for people like Matt Haffigan. They are totally expendable as there is no room in this new world order, or postsyndicated Roscullen, for inefficiency. Keegan acquiesces to this fact, even suggesting that he may vote for Broadbent, because he understands that it is already a fait accompli in the case of Broadbent's commercial redevelopment plans for Roscullen:

For me there are but two countries: heaven and hell; but two conditions of men: salvation and damnation. Standing here between you the Englishman, so clever in your foolishness, and this Irishman, so foolish in his cleverness, I cannot in my ignorance be sure which of you is the more deeply damned; but I should be unfaithful to my calling if I opened the gates of my heart less widely to one than to the other (451).

Similarly, Doyle the cynical realist is left bitter but totally impotent. By the end of the play he has lost both Nora and the opportunity to represent Roscullen in Westminster to Broadbent. He is guilty of complicity in Broadbent's Machiavellian machinations, but like Keegan he accepts Broadbent as Roscullen's most viable option for future economic advancement – resistance is futile, as the alternative does not even bear contemplation:

If we can't have men of honour own the land, let's have men of ability. If we can't have men of ability, let us at least have men with capital. Anybody's better than Matt [Haffigan], who has neither honour, nor ability, nor capital, nor anything but near-brute labour and greed in him (430).

Nicholas Grene has examined the intricacy of Shaw's position as émigré writer in *John Bull's Other Island*: 'Larry Doyle is the most subtle study of the emotions of the Irish exile before Joyce'; Shaw equates the returning Doyle with 'the dream of escape and the fear of return, the guilty shame and self-disgust of nationality'.[9]

Critical research suggests that as well as being his quintessential work on Anglo-Irish relations, *John Bull's Other Island* encompasses an internationalist dimension: Shaw intended to revive a national concern for oppressed nationalities abroad. Sometimes he would exemplify a particular social problem endemic to all societies such as poverty or persecution, and from using one country then universalize the consequences of political apathy and indifference. In his *Essays in Fabian Socialism* (1889) he referred to 'taking the world as one country'.[10] There is much evidence to suggest that *John Bull's Other Island* is as much concerned with a Shavian antimaterialist philosophy and universal class struggle as it is with national self-determination and Anglo-Irish relations – epitomized by Matt Haffigan's and the English valet Hodson's verbal fencing match over the respective social hardships and sufferings of the Irish peasant and English labourer.

Hodson, representing a distinctively Fabian stance, argues that the grievances of the dispossessed, landless Irish peasant pale in comparison with the injustices suffered by the English. He passionately recounts his familial misfortune: his grandfather's eviction at the hands of a capricious landlord, his wife's premature death and his own constant financial insecurity and the uncertainty of seasonal employment – which is now further threatened and exacerbated by an ever-increasing Irish emigrant workforce, all too willing to accept the exploitative capitalist status quo of lower wages, tenement housing and terrible working conditions in industrial Britain. As Tramble T. Turner has remarked, 'Shaw had wanted his audience to question the assumptions of materialistic systems, both English and Irish, and to think about the plight of the common man within such a system.'[11]

If *John Bull's Other Island* was Shaw's attempt to expose the hollowness of racial stage stereotypes through the inversion of national character-types, and a desire ultimately to reeducate his British audience, it was also a damning condemnation of the threat of myopic nationalism. Shaw wrote his *Essays in Fabian Socialism* between 1888 and 1904. If these essays, which represent Shaw's political, economic and religious theories, are studied alongside his reviews of some works dealing with the 'Irish Question'[12] and his own critical essays in his collection *The Matter With Ireland*, one obtains a more definitive understanding of Shaw's 'Irishness' and what he was hoping to achieve with *John Bull's Other Island*. The reviews, according to George Mills Harper, present his detailed description of nationalism's function within his theory of Political Evolution[13] and place the late Victorian fascination with the 'Irish Question' within the perspective of Fabian Socialism.[14] Rereading the play in the context of these topics, Tramble T. Turner suggests it was the result of a typical Shavian process of 'generating lively plays from topical debates. His intent of focusing the audience's attention on long-term issues through comedy also becomes clearer' ('Irish Concerns', 59).

Shaw placed little value on 'nationalism', seeing it more as an unfortunate socio-political aberration, essentially relevant only as a means to an end. In his review of J. A. Partridge's book *The Making of the Irish Nation*, Shaw analysed the nature of English imperialism and concluded that the 'Imperial instinct', governed by the 'appetite for new markets abroad, cheap native labour, and official appointments, civil and military, in newly annexed districts' which were then exploited, was in contrast to the 'philosophical Imperialist', who 'recognises that Federation is a step higher in social organization, and that we must inevitably and quite desirably come to it unless we are content to go backward'. Therefore Shaw accepted nationalism as beneficial only if its ultimate consequence was the formation of a 'federation of nations, each subject only to the whole empire, and not to the nucleus or strongest member of it' (*The Matter With Ireland*, 59).

As early as 1900 Shaw had acknowledged the status quo of global imperialism in his article *Fabianism and the Empire*: 'The partition of the greater part of the globe among such powers is, as a matter of fact that must be faced, approvingly or deploringly, now only a question of time.'[15] In his review of Robert Oliver's *Unnoticed Analogies: A Talk on the Irish Question*, published in the *Pall Mall Gazette*, 25 September 1888, Shaw surmised, '[n]ationalism is surely an incident of organic growth, not an invention' (*The Matter With Ireland*, 21). Sixteen years after he first formulated them in his review of Oliver's *Unnoticed Analogies*, Shaw succinctly recapitulated these sentiments:

> A conquered nation is like a man with cancer: he can think of nothing else, and is forced to place himself, to the exclusion of all better company, in the hands of quacks who profess to treat or cure cancer. The windbags of the two rival platforms are the most insufferable of all windbags. It requires neither knowledge, character, conscience, diligence in public affairs, nor any virtue, private or communal, to thump the Nationalist or Orange tub: nay, it puts a premium on the rancour or callousness that has given rise to the proverb that if you put an Irishman on a spit you can always get another Irishman to baste him . . . Nationalism stands between Ireland and the light of the world (*Prefaces*, 454–5).

Shaw believed that Irish nationalism had to be ancillary to the more essential objectives of international socialism. The constant grievances of Irish nationalists exasperated him, as he truly believed that compared with the hardships endured by the British, the Irish peasant/labourer had never had it so good. As Declan Kiberd has remarked:

> Although they numbered one tenth of the population of Britain, the Irish held the balance of power in the House of Commons, whose business seemed dominated by Irish grievances and questions. Shaw, for his part, was perfectly convinced that Ireland was a far happier and freer country than England. He believed that Britain, too, had unresolved national questions: and Home Rule for England became one of his more lasting hobbies.[16]

Yeats maintained that Shaw lacked a passionate vision, and his portrayal of Irish peasant life was not in the spirit of the Celtic Revival, which stressed a lifestyle uncorrupted by modern progressivism. Shaw condemned this idealization of Irish life and felt his position was legitimated by his intolerance of the 'alleged Arcadian virtues of the half-starved drudges who are sacrificed to the degrading, brutalizing and . . . entirely unnecessary pursuit of unscientific farming.' (*Our Theatres in the Nineties*, II, 31). Shaw was completely antithetical to Yeats's vision of the 'Celtic Twilight', and as a progressive modernist he had little time for the romantic sentimentality associated with certain aspects of the Irish Literary Revival. His portrayal of Irish womanhood completely negated the Yeatsian mythology of

Cathleen ni Houlihan. This mythologized, venerated and apotheosized representation of Irish nationalist femininity – whose purpose was to inspire and incite young Irishmen to battle for the greater glory of Ireland – was utterly anathema to Shaw – as vividly and brutally exemplified by Larry Doyle's description of Nora in *John Bull's Other Island* as 'helpless, useless, almost sexless, an invalid without the excuse of a disease, an incarnation of everything in Ireland that drove him out of it' (Shaw's stage directions, 418).

He later satirized the image of Cathleen ni Houlihan in his short 1915 play *O'Flaherty V. C.* In the play the main protagonist O'Flaherty, an Irishman, joins the British army to fight the Germans in World War One. And just as Isabella Woodward, Larry Doyle and Shaw himself had already chosen absenteeism or emigration, enlistment and war were now added to the preferable alternatives to living in Ireland and facing a life of provincial ignorance, disillusionment and obscurity. The outbreak of war offers O'Flaherty the opportunity to escape from his parochial life in Ireland unbeknown to his Cassandraesque mother, who – in her Cathleen ni Houlihan guise – represents that uncompromising romantic nationalism which Shaw abhorred in Ireland. It later becomes apparent that the fervently nationalistic mother thought her son was fighting on the German side in the war, and she is appalled when she finds papers revealing that her son shook hands with the English king at Buckingham Palace. By implying that O'Flaherty preferred to join the British army and face German guns in the trenches, rather than listen to further belligerent nationalist rhetoric at home, Shaw was attempting to undermine the Anglophobia of militant Irish nationalism and challenge the traditional prejudice and suspicion towards the British by portraying them in a more favourable light. In a letter to Lady Gregory written in 1915 he confessed:

> The picture of the Irish character will make the Playboy seem a patriotic rhapsody by comparison. The ending is cynical to the last possible degree. The idea is that O'Flaherty's experience in the trenches has induced in him a terrible realism and an unbearable candour. He sees Ireland as it is, his mother as she is, his sweetheart as she is; and he goes back to the dreadful trenches joyfully for the sake of peace and quietness (*Collected Letters, II*, 309).

Shaw was wary of the myopic, prejudiced, cultural nationalism establishing a firm foothold in Ireland, so he projected an internationalist or transnationalist vision for Ireland which was often interpreted as unpatriotic, but only because it was modern and certain elements of the Irish Literary Revival/Gaelic League were antagonistic to and found repugnant the notion of Ireland having any association with modernity. Shaw thought much in the manner that James Joyce despised what he construed as the insularity of the Irish Literary Revival, maintaining that its provincial and reactionary driving force was consumed by narrow nationalistic considerations, which consequently stymied the development of true universalist Irish art. Joyce might well have been speaking for Shaw when he wrote the following in his essay 'The Day of the Rabblement':

> If an artist courts the favour of the multitude he cannot escape the contagion of its fetishism and deliberate self-deception, and if he joins in a popular movement he does so at his own risk. Therefore the Irish Literary Theatre by its surrender to the trolls has cut itself adrift from the line of advancement. Until he has freed himself from the mean influences about him – sodden enthusiasm and clever insinuations and every flattering influence of vanity and low ambition – no man is an artist at all.[17]

Gareth Griffith has extended this analogous relationship between Shaw and Joyce to the next stage, referring to similarities in theme and characterization:

> The comparison with Joyce is interesting. Joyce and Shaw are so different, yet in some ways they share the same bleak outlook on Ireland as a land which has missed the boat to modernity. In 'Ivy Day in the Committee Room' from *Dubliners* Joyce reproduced much of what we find in *John Bull's*, the same useless rhetoric, the sense of political futility and, too, an argument based on the overriding need for capital in a country which seems only to produce dreams and anger. Though in Joyce the scene has shifted to an urban landscape, we still encounter similar characters, most notably the shadowy Father Keon, 'a person resembling a poor clergyman or a poor actor', who drifts in and out of the narrative in a manner reminiscent of Shaw's Father Keegan. It is essentially a different scene haunted by the same ghosts.[18]

Philip O'Leary has extensively researched the trials and tribulations Shaw experienced in his search for involvement in the Irish Literary Revival.[19] Shaw had his admirers within the Irish Literary Revival, but he was shunned by sections of the Gaelic League movement because of his uncongenial and uncompromising opinion concerning the Irish language. While he was generally wary and critical of the Gaelic League's objectives, much of the controversy surrounding Shaw's opinion of attempts to revive the Gaelic language stemmed from comments he wrote in *The Freeman's Journal* in 1910; in it he suggested that native Gaelic speakers were critical of formal Gaelic educational practices and in fact preferred writing in English. This was obviously antithetical to the whole Gaelic League ethos. Shaw later went on to argue:

> It happened that long before the Gaelic League was thought of I learnt something about Gaelic from the late James Lecky, one of its rediscoverers. It

presented itself to him as a highly artificial literary exercise, comparable to fifth-century Latin, and having about as much to do with vernacular Irish as fifth-century Latin had to do with the vernacular Italian of that period, or as Trinity College Greek has to do with the Greek actually spoken today in the streets of Athens.[20]

Seán Mac Giollarnáth, editor of the Gaelic League publication *An Claidheamh Soluis* confronted Shaw's perceived suspicions concerning a Gaelic language revival:

> On Monday night last . . . he [Shaw] dropped to the level of the ordinary Britisher, when he expressed his disbelief in the worth of the Irish language. The revival of Irish would, he said, place additional barriers between England and this country, and he failed to see that is just why Ireland is reviving her language. Up with the barriers, they will protect us against a thousand plagues that . . . have come from the land to whose service Mr. Shaw has given himself. They will save us from the new nationality of the author of 'John Bull's Other Island,' and from the politics of Whig, Tory, and Fabian.[21]

The derivation of this attitude towards Shaw, according to Philip O'Leary, lies in 'one of the most important, vigorously debated, and resolutely unresolved literary and ideological issues of the early Gaelic revival, and after – what was the proper attitude to adopt towards Anglo-Irish literature, the work of those Irish authors who by either linguistic necessity or personal choice wrote in the English language'.[22]

In Shaw's case his personal iconoclasm and distinctive brand of 'Irishness' was perceived as threatening by elements within the Gaelic League; and while his ability was never in doubt, for some activists Shaw's views on the Gaelic Revival coupled with his indifference towards the Irish language did raise question marks over his sincerity and commitment to the ethos of the Revival. Certain enlightened Gaelic Leaguers such as P. S. Ua hÉigeartaigh and Pádraic Ó Conaire respected Shaw's work and indeed admired and acknowledged the intrinsically 'Irish', even 'Gaelic', characteristic of artistic creativity, subversive humour and social consciousness incorporated in his writing. This bifurcation of the Gaelic/Literary Revival initiated a dichotomous Gaelic/Anglo-Irish response that was ideologically conditioned and ultimately concerned with the question of representation. Though Shaw championed the cause of Home Rule, and Ireland's inviolable right for national self-determination throughout his life; defied the Lord Chamberlain and Dublin Castle by staging *The Shewing-up of Blanco Posnet* in 1909; ardently and compassionately defended Roger Casement in 1916 as well as vehemently admonishing the British government on the detrimental consequences should it not show leniency and insist on executing the leaders of the 1916 Rising; and cofounded the Irish Academy of Letters with Yeats in 1932: notwithstanding these endeavours he would remain for certain Gaels an obstinate, opinionated outsider.

However, if they 'were always more aware of his prodigality than his patrimony . . . most Gaelic revivalists remained in the end willing to accept him on his own terms as one of their own' ('Lost Tribesman', 64), with illustrative Shavian sarcasm, 'a genuine typical Irishman of the Danish, Norman, Cromwellian, and (of course) Scottish invasions' (*Prefaces*, 440). Much Gaelic opinion concerning Shaw emanated from a particular or distinctive nationalist outlook. The Gaelic Revival and the Anglo-Irish Literary Revival may have had their differences and their own objectives; yet, as was often his wont, Shaw somehow managed to circumvent representing either of them, while ultimately earning their admiration and respect.

NOTES

1. George Bernard Shaw, *The Matter With Ireland*, eds. David H. Greene and Dan H. Laurence (London: Rupert Hart-Davis, 1962), ix.
2. George Bernard Shaw, *Prefaces* (London: Constable and Company, 1934), 642.
3. George Bernard Shaw, *Bernard Shaw Collected Letters, Volume II*, ed. Dan H. Laurence (London: Max Reinhardt, 1972), 127.
4. George Bernard Shaw, *Immaturity* (London: Constable and Company, 1930), 136.
5. Nicholas Grene, 'The Maturing of *Immaturity*: Shaw's First Novel', in *The Irish University Review*, 20:2 (1990), 231–3.
6. George Bernard Shaw, *Our Theatres in the Nineties, Volume II* (London: Constable and Company, 1932), 33.
7. Oscar Wilde, *The Artist as Critic*, ed. Richard Ellmann (London: W. H. Allen, 1970), 389.
8. George Bernard Shaw, *The Complete Plays of Bernard Shaw* (London: Constable and Company, 1931), 417. Further references will be included in the text in parenthesis.
9. Nicholas Grene, *Bernard Shaw: A Critical View* (London: Macmillan, 1984), 75.
10. George Bernard Shaw, *Essays in Fabian Socialism*, Volume XXX of *The Collected Works of Bernard Shaw* (New York: W. H. Wise & Co., 1932), 25.
11. Tramble T. Turner, 'Bernard Shaw's "Eternal" Irish Concerns', in *Eire-Ireland*, 21:2 (1986), 58.
12. Shaw's two unsigned reviews were of J. A. Partridge's *The Making of the Irish Nation* in the *Pall Mall Gazette*, 16 September 1886; and Robert Oliver's *Unnoticed Analogies: A Talk on the Irish Question* published in the *Pall Mall Gazette*, 25 September 1888. Both are anthologized in Shaw, *The Matter With Ireland*.
13. In brief, these theories were developed in his Hyde Park speeches and espoused the common bonds among the international working classes, and the necessity of an antimaterialist religious perspective.

14. For further insight, see George Mills Harper, '"Intellectual hatred" and "intellectual nationalism": the paradox of passionate politics', in Robert O'Driscoll (ed.), *Theatre and Nationalism in Twentieth-Century Ireland* (Toronto: University of Toronto Press, 1969), 49.

15. Fabian Society, *Fabianism and the Empire* (London: Grant Richards, 1900), 3.

16. Declan Kiberd, *Inventing Ireland: The Literature of the Modern Nation* (London: Jonathan Cape, 1995), 62.

17. James Joyce, 'The Day of the Rabblement', in Ellsworth Mason and Richard Ellmann (eds.), *The Critical Writings of James Joyce* (London: Faber and Faber, 1959), 68–72.

18. Gareth Griffith, 'The Irish Question', in *Socialism and Superior Brains* (London: Routledge, 1993), 206. See also James Joyce, *The Essential James Joyce* (Harmondsworth: Penguin, 1971), 439.

19. For an indepth examination of Shaw's relationship with the Gaelic Movement, see Philip O'Leary, 'Lost Tribesman or Prodigal Son?: George Bernard Shaw and the Gaelic Movement', in *Eire-Ireland*, 29:2 (1994), 51–64.

20. George Bernard Shaw, to *The Freeman's Journal*, Dublin, 17 October 1910. (Quoted in Shaw, *The Matter With Ireland*, 59.)

21. 'Up with the barriers', in *An Claidheamh Soluis*, 10 August 1910. This piece appeared in the editor's weekly summary of the news entitled 'Gleó na gCath'.

22. O'Leary, '*Lost Tribesman*', 54. For a more complete discussion, see Philip O'Leary, 'Uneasy Alliance: the Gaelic League looks at the "Irish" Renaissance', in Audrey S. Eyler and Robert F. Garratt (eds.), *The Uses of the Past: Essays on Irish Culture* (Newark: University of Delaware Press, 1988), 144–60.

10

RONAN McDONALD

Sean O'Casey's Dublin Trilogy: disillusionment to delusion

Sean O'Casey is best remembered for his engagement, artistic and otherwise, with Irish history during a crucial period of turmoil and revolutionary change. His most famous and enduring drama – the Dublin Trilogy of *The Shadow of a Gunman* (1923), *Juno and the Paycock* (1924) and *The Plough and the Stars* (1926), and *The Silver Tassie* (1928) which followed it – concerns politically derived suffering: the War of Independence, the Civil War, the Easter Rising and World War One. Formed by these events O'Casey's vision is also manifest in his dramatic representation of them. From the bitter parodies of the Dublin Trilogy to his blistering depiction of the sanctimonious, priest-ridden new state in *The Bishop's Bonfire* (1955) and *The Drums of Father Ned* (1959), O'Casey indulges in a drama of socio-political protest. In some of the later, utopian plays of socialist liberation such as *The Star Turns Red* (1940) and *Red Roses for Me* (1942), the dramatic action often coarsens into agitprop.

Outside the drama the briefest glance at the *Autobiographies* reinforces O'Casey's self-created image as a fierce battler.[1] Throughout his life he was a notoriously pugnacious opponent and proponent in an endless series of professional and personal scraps. It is in one sense an appropriate tribute to O'Casey that the spirit of dispute lives on among his critics. His status as a dramatist is the site of considerable disagreement, particularly as regards his treatment of politics. However, in outlining this debate one can discern elements of O'Casey's achievement which complicate the premises of both his admirers and his detractors. On O'Casey's side we have a longstanding critical orthodoxy which chimes with the great popular fondness for the Dublin Trilogy. These tragi-comic tales of families and communities destroyed by political violence are held close to the hearts of many theatregoers for the colour of the language and the vividness of the characterization. The poignancy and pathos with which the plays end follow a dramatic action imbued with the richest comedy. O'Casey's many devotees admire the warmth and humanity of his vision where, as an early reviewer of *The Plough and the Stars* put it, 'one drop of human kindness is worth more than the deepest draughts of the red wine of idealism'.[2] According to this view, the Dublin Trilogy teaches us to avoid the dangers of political idealism through a demonstration of the terrible destruction these ideals cause to the hearth-and-home humanity usually represented by the women. As two mothers, Mrs Tancred and Juno Boyle, rue the death of their sons: 'Sacred heart o' Jesus, take away our hearts o' stone, and give us hearts o' flesh! Take away this murtherin' hate an' give us Thine own eternal love!'[3] While there are significant differences between these three plays, each seems to indict political rhetoric as the enemy of pity, kindness and common sense, the totem of which is 'motherhood'. O'Casey debunks the mythology of Mother Ireland, who sends her sons out to die for the recovery of her four green fields, replacing it with images of real suffering mothers, of families torn apart by men drunk on ineffable dreams of political utopia and doggedly sober on a doctrine of arid, inflexible political principles.

This aspect to O'Casey's work has had renewed significance since the eruption of the Troubles in Northern Ireland. With its perceived condemnation of 'senseless violence' and debunking of romantic nationalist mythology, the Trilogy had a timely relevance at the moment when nationalist ideology was resurgent in the partitioned Six Counties. Not surprisingly, then, O'Casey has figured in recent intellectual and cultural wars in Irish studies, with *The Plough and the Stars* seen as 'a revisionist play before ever the term was coined'.[4] O'Casey has been adopted before by some ironic sources: militant labour agitator feted by the theatregoing middle class; hardline Stalinist beloved of a generation of American liberal critics during the McCarthy era. That this former Irish Republican Brotherhood man and Gaelic Leaguer should be championed as an antinationalist is the latest of many paradoxical allegiances.

However, some of O'Casey's most prominent critics, such as Seamus Deane and George J. Watson, coming from Northern Ireland, are suspicious of the tendency to graft the politics of O'Casey's Trilogy on to the Northern crisis. Opponents of O'Casey discern a coarse and corrosive political outlook in the Dublin Trilogy, condescending to the characters and inadequate to a complex political reality. Though O'Casey has no shortage of devotees, many critical commentators have found his political thought ultimately unsatisfactory and incomplete. While they differ in emphasis, these critics perceive a simplistic and distorting opposition between politics and humanism in O'Casey's work, particularly his Dublin plays: the political 'principles' of the men versus the hearth-and-home humanity of the women, hearts of stone opposed to hearts of flesh. As G. J. Watson complains of *Juno and the Paycock*:

The politics are a deformation of, and a threat to, the human, and O'Casey's suffering women are the authorially endorsed mouthpieces of this view. There is something simple-minded and sentimental about this . . . Since 'principles' and 'politics' do demonstrably have such a major impact, it is simple-minded to ignore them, and sentimental to pretend that humanity consists in ignoring them.[5]

According to these critics, if O'Casey really wanted to engage in a serious dispute with political and revolutionary thought, it is curious that he failed to include a single serious political thinker in the Trilogy.[6] Since politics is seen solely in its destructive element, with no serious confrontation with a coherent political ideology, politics and family life are constructed not only as hermetically separate, but also in direct hostility to one another. Put bluntly, O'Casey paradoxically regards politics as anti-social. For those who distrust this aspect to his work O'Casey illegitimately presents the 'family' as anterior to the structures which organize society, and more particularly does not recognize, for all his keen awareness of the material plight of the Dublin poor and his own erstwhile political radicalism, the causes of poverty in political terms.

Since for most of his life he was proud to be associated with the hard Left, it is odd that he remains in the Trilogy, if not in his real-life activities nor in his later plays of didactic communism, so resolutely apolitical. It is worth stressing that the hostility to nationalist rhetoric, displayed in the Trilogy, is often indistinguishable from a distaste for politics as a whole, downgraded to so many dry, dangerous 'principles'. O'Casey may have left his beloved Irish Citizen Army because of its lurch towards nationalism and spent most of his life as a staunch communist and unwavering supporter of the Soviet Union, yet the socialists in *Juno and the Paycock* and *The Plough and the Stars* are as deluded and conceited as the nationalist braggarts. Jerry Devine and the Covey mouth static dogmas, but neither contributes anything to ameliorate the practical sufferings of the heroic women. In the Trilogy the political cure always seems worse than the social disease.

Thus goes the case for the prosecution, and indeed there does seem to be a sense that politics is kept, like Johnny Boyle, largely offstage. This eschewal may, as Raymond Williams held, be partly ascribable to the exigencies of the naturalist form, which makes politics (as opposed to domesticity) hard to dramatize: 'As a direct action it is on the streets, and the people crowded in the houses react to it, in essential ways, as if it were an action beyond and outside them.'[7] In other words, the realist form focuses our gaze on the living room, and wider political and social forces tend, almost inevitably, to have a fainter presence. However, the antipolitical import of these plays can be explained only partly by this formal bias. There seems to be a polemical insistence, a thematic as well as stylistic foregrounding, of the intrusion of politics into domesticity.

O'Casey's personal shift from nationalism to socialism has led some to speculate that his target in the Trilogy is nationalism, not politics as a whole. Yet even if the military violence were in the service of a cause which O'Casey considered justifiable, it would not make that much difference to domestic drama of this sort. Even if the trouble in the streets were not, as Juno thinks, down to the stupidity of men, the tragedies of these families would still unfold. The braggadocio and delusions of the characters could have thrived equally in a just, as much as an unjust or futile, war. There were, no doubt, cowards like Donal Davoren, traitors like Johnny Boyle, or martyrs like Jack Clitheroe in the Spanish Civil War, the French Resistance, or – close to O'Casey's heart – the Russian Revolution. Similar plays, with similar dramatic power and a similar tragic action of families torn apart, could have been written about these violent eruptions. The plays do not really engage in political critique at all (save for their antipathy to political rhetoric), rather drawing their energy from the human suffering that all war brings. Whatever one's stance on the events in Dublin during these turbulent years, the truth is that these plays in the final reckoning do not have too much to say about Irish politics, only about war in general, which, it will come as no surprise, is hell.

However, simply to conclude that the politics of O'Casey's drama is coarse and simplistic obscures important, rich seams in the Trilogy. Many elements in his drama brush against the humanist dogma, taken on so credulously by both supporters and detractors of the dogma alike. His effort in the Trilogy to replace nationalist politics with the 'Family' is an uncomfortable transition, which leaves the way open for an intrusion of indeterminate, impersonal historical forces, or 'chassis'. Yet even as it brushes against and fragments the drama's governing polemic, this intrusion and instability can offer suggestive and dramatically effective tensions and conflicts. Many productions, in their emphasis on naturalist coherence and a neat opposition between domestic integrity and destructive political ideology, have glided over this potential and filtered out the alternative voices. The multiple tonal register in the plays – shifting from comedy to tragedy, realism to expressionism, melodrama to vaudeville – could highlight the anguish and dissonance behind the inconsistency and uncertainty of the politics. For instance, the party scene in *Juno and the Paycock*, where the pathos of the Tancred funeral rebukes the revelry in the Boyles' living room, could be presented as the fissured, guilt-ridden, incompatible confrontation it potentially is. However, smoothness and consistency in the dramatic production renders it a much more passive, toothless affair. This emasculates the full dramatic effect, the incommensurability and the conflict which can emerge in productions (such as those attempted by the Irish director Garry Hynes) which, instead of reproducing cosy verisimilitude, are attuned to the restive, expressionistic undercurrents of these plays.

O'Casey's Dublin plays are not so sanctimoniously polar in their opposition between family and politics, women and men, as their ostensible messages would suggest. O'Casey's detractors have unwittingly replicated the erroneous oppositions for which he is praised by his admirers. As well as being a commentator on his times, O'Casey is also a symptom of them, and far from transcending or debunking the rhetoric of political ideology, he is traumatized by it. O'Casey's strongly Protestant upbringing transmuted into the political zealotry of his adult life: as a socialist he believed that human suffering is appalling because it is avoidable. In other words, he was a meliorist. He was a gung-ho participant in the medley of political movements which sprung up in Dublin in the first two decades of the twentieth century (though, significantly, not a combatant in the 1916 Easter Rising). He partook in the dreams of that era but wrote his most famous tragedies when the Irish revolutionary dream had turned into the nightmare of a fratricidal Civil War. In the Trilogy we see O'Casey's optimism, his belief in utopian solutions to social problems, waver. One discovers an underbelly of fatalism, even nihilism, beneath O'Casey's melioristic zeal. It is precisely the resulting conflict, tension and complexity which make these plays dramatically interesting, saving them from the didacticism which often mars his *Autobiographies* and his later drama. The effects of historical disillusionment deeply disturbed his instincts to find a secular, socialist remedy to the problems generated by social and political conditions. The cracks are discernible in the Dublin plays, which thematically oscillate between a materialist and a pessimistic viewpoint, between Juno's plea 'What can God do agen the stupidity o' men!' (70) and Boyle's dissolute recognition that 'th' whole worl's . . . in a terr . . . ible state o' . . . chassis!' (73).

O'Casey maintains a veneer of moral coherence to gloss over these thematic cracks. Discarding his political radicalism for the domestic haven of naturalist drama, he reaches for a humanistic indictment of dangerous delusion, aimed at gullible guttersnipes who believe the bombastic rhetoric visited on them by ideologues such as the Speaker in Act 2 of *The Plough and the Stars*. Yet what energizes the plays is the effect of dissonance, the tensions that emerge when the subterranean pessimism contradicts the overt humanistic fervour. Confusion and embitterment stalk O'Casey's comic and satirical portrayals of Dublin life, as he strives for an idiom to render a disintegrating society cognitively coherent. If there are infelicities in O'Casey's political thought as expressed in the Trilogy, they are not, as O'Casey's detractors often maintain, simply a failure to give politics a fair hearing. His fraught confrontation with social circumstances is not just a refusal of ideology, it is an *alienation* from it. That is to say, his attitude in the Trilogy is not simply an *affirmation* of humanism and the values of hearth and home against the deleterious intrusions of politics and ideology; it is a *renunciation* of the idea of political thought altogether. Behind O'Casey's depiction of political rhetoric as a dangerous delusion preying on credulous individuals is a palpable sense of his own profound disillusionment with politics.

So the Dublin plays, for all the comic overtures, sound a sombre note of confusion, guilt and disappointment. Yet on the surface these tragedies are set on course by the dangers of delusion. In contrast to Synge's Playboy whose delusions of grandeur and heroism give him some dignity and imagination in the teeth of an anaemic community, when O'Casey's characters blind themselves to the 'real world' of domesticity and family obligation, they set about a train of events which ends in terrible tragedy. The exposure of dangerous *delusion* – as a perversion of natural, family values – might seem a directly contrary motivation to the dramatization of a painful *disillusionment*. The first implicitly espouses the 'real world' as an antidote to the perils of dream, the second laments the real world as the enemy of hope. Delusion suggests a normative reality which is dangerously denied; disillusionment suggests the frustration of a worthwhile struggle, the exposure of a cruel illusion at the heart of a noble aspiration. Hence 'delusion' and 'disillusionment' deal in the same thematic currency with directly opposing value systems. In a delusory scene the delusion creates the tragedy; in disillusionment the regrettable return of a brutal, recalcitrant reality creates it. Typically delusion ends in recognition; disillusionment begins with it. O'Casey conflates the two, choosing to indict a delusory politics, which he projects on to his starry-eyed, credulous male characters, as a mask for political disillusionment.

Fortunately this is only a partly successful enterprise. The veneer of anti-ideological polemic has enough cracks to allow contesting discourses to come into dramatically productive conflict. Reading the Trilogy in the terms suggested above, as a conflict between O'Casey's political disillusionment and his compensatory condemnation of political delusion, casts his putative antipolitics in a new light. Nowhere is the opposition clearer than in *The Shadow of a Gunman*. Here, delusion and disillusionment – the respective flaws of Minnie Powell and Donal Davoren – vie for thematic dominance as the chief target of the play. Significantly, however, and unlike the later two tragedies, Davoren's pseudo-poetic disillusionment comes in for O'Casey's most vitriolic scorn. Though a backward projection to the War of Independence, the play bears many disconsolate marks of the Civil War during which it was written. Often regarded as less accomplished than the other two, it is, nonetheless, in one sense the darkest play of the Trilogy. All the characters, save Minnie, are contemptibly cowering and selfish; and all, save Seumas Shields, entwine themselves in a communal heroic fantasy, which masks their true natures. Davoren looks down on the people around him and is too complacent in his effete despondency to allow their projections to unlock his powers of self-realization. Compared to Davoren's world-weary posturing, and to the corrosive, self-serving cynicism of Seumas Shields, Minnie Powell's youthful naïvety and credulity appear almost heroic. Certainly her self-sacrifice in taking the bombs, however ill-founded her intentions, is the noblest action of a drama populated almost exclusively by braggarts and cowards.

The play's most intriguing feature is the disorientation in the dialectic between disillusionment and delusion, despair and false hope. For Davoren's carefully cultivated 'dejection' is just another form of posturing self-deception. Despite his self-assurance at the end of Act 1, Davoren bitterly comes to realize the great danger in being the shadow of a gunman. The recognition, however, brings no catharsis or renewed societal integration because Davoren's self-knowledge is ultimately fraudulent:

> Ah me, alas! Pain, pain, pain ever, for ever! It's terrible to think that little Minnie is dead, but it's still more terrible to think that Davoren and Shields are alive! Oh, Donal Davoren, shame is your portion now till the silver cord is loosened and the golden bowl be broken. Oh, Davoren, Donal Davoren, poet and poltroon, poltroon and poet! (130)

His new knowledge of his cowardice is all too easily assimilated into his practised linguistic rituals; the pretence of brave confrontation, filtered through poetry and melodrama, ironically protects his calloused sensibility. By this point in the play his bogus poetry and affected despondency ring false, as does his repetition of morose Shelleyan fragments – 'Ah me, alas! Pain, pain, pain ever, for ever!' Even as he strives for melodramatic import, his high-flown rhetoric indicates that he is hiding behind his pessimism, rather than confronting his pretentious vanity and culpable passivity. In a curious imbrication of the two dominant yet ostensibly opposing themes, Davoren's disillusionment is *itself* cast as a form of comforting delusion. The recognition of guilt, couched in this overrich idiom, becomes a mockery of itself. Davoren replaces bogus and pseudo-poetic self-delusion with bogus and pseudo-poetic self-knowledge.

O'Casey's move from active militarism and politics into a more rarefied poetic realm is underwritten by doubt and feelings of impotence at his passivity and bitter disenchantment with the course of Irish politics. Donal Davoren, poetic, pretentious and passive, is a sublimated expression of this guilt and frustration. *The Shadow of a Gunman*, though it lacks the breadth and ambition of the later two Trilogy plays, is unique in its self-doubt and embitterment. Moreover, the efforts to transmute harsh disappointment and disillusionment into a meaningful and moral exposure of delusion – the governing motive of the Trilogy – is here most strongly encoded in the action. Ironically the relative inexperience with which O'Casey wrote *The Shadow of a Gunman* is, in one sense, its strength. *Juno and the Paycock* and *The Plough and the Stars* are more accomplished in the concealment of the suppressed motivations behind their construction, smoothed over by a more finessed realist coherence.

Set during the Civil War, *Juno and the Paycock* deals in broken dreams. The narrative uses a stock melodramatic plot – fortune supposedly inherited, then lost – as a mockingly blunt allegory for the disappointments of Irish national independence. The conventional interpretation of the play elevates Juno as the humanist heroine, who keeps house and home together despite the drunken irresponsibility of her feckless husband. Again, there is much in the play which queries Juno's opposition between hearts of stone and hearts of flesh, or at least undermines her status as the play's pragmatic heroine. The verbosity and imagination of the two men, though parasitic and culpably irresponsible, is often more attractive than Juno's dour conformity.[8] We know that it is Juno who keeps the family together, and we admire her for her fortitude and compassion, particularly at the end of the play. Poverty means she can afford the luxury of neither imagination nor politics. However, despite his irresponsibility, the Captain's shenanigans sparkle long after the curtain has dropped. We also witness his selfish, vainglorious bluster and his hopelessly weak, inadequate and immoral rejection of Mary at the end of the play, yet the ambivalence is an antidote to the polemicism into which O'Casey occasionally slides. *Juno* shifts from high tragedy to low farce and back again with such facility that we are often discomfited; yet we are also enabled, appropriately circumspect and cautious about the response the play seems to be demanding. Part of us feels we ought to spurn Boyle, yet we cannot help being lured by his scandalous behaviour, just as we cannot help being somewhat irked by Juno's tedious good sense.

Furthermore, Juno is not always the put-upon heart of flesh. When Mary asks her advice on what ribbon she should wear in her hair, her response, though schooled in the pragmatics of survival, seems troublingly acquiescent: 'It's wearin' them things that make the employers think they're givin' yous too much money' (7). This is certainly not an attitude which O'Casey, dismissed from an early job for refusing to take off his cap when collecting his pay, would endorse.[9] Her instinct for family preservation seems admirably pragmatic when opposed to windy nationalist rhetoric, yet it does not seem so noble when it comes into visible conflict with the interests of others. She criticizes Mary's solidarity with her victimized fellow worker, Jennie Claffey, on the grounds that before the strike Mary 'never had a good word for her' (7). Mary's justification for her action – 'a principle's a principle' (8) – seems solid enough here, however shallowly rehearsed this refrain later becomes. Not all principles are just bombast, as O'Casey's life often admirably attests. Whatever her practical compassion for Mary and down-to-earth realism at the end of the play, there is an element of inefficacy in Mrs Boyle that cannot simply be put down to the vagaries of external forces and unreliable men. Her cures for suffering often do not work. She is signally inadequate in comforting Johnny: 'Tay, tay, tay! You're always thinkin' o' tay. If a man was dyin', you'd thry to make him swally a cup o' tay!' (8).

Juno's relations with Johnny merit close analysis. Having failed to dissuade him from military action, she is unable to assuage the trauma he now endures. This inefficacy contrasts with her clear-sighted support of Mary in her more 'social' crisis at the end of the play. In her relations with Johnny, at least, there is no reason to suppose that Juno's antipolitics is a strength. Nor is there any reason to take on board her description of Johnny's soldiering as 'makin' a fool of himself' (9). If Boyle's talk of 'doin' his bit' in Easter Week is fraudulent bluster, his son's claims to have done enough for Ireland may well be merited. The Captain's comic pretensions to heroism are hardly any more dubious than Juno's dismissal of authentic heroism. Johnny is a complex figure whose story is glimpsed only obliquely, just as he spends most of his tormented time in the adjacent room, offstage. After the bogus posturing of Davoren, Johnny is not just the shadow of a gunman – he has been a real soldier, however physically and psychologically shattered he has become. He is not a fool but a broken man – metaphorically and literally. He is the figure who most represents the Ireland of which, and from which, O'Casey writes. Crushed by Civil War and haunted by the guilt of betrayal of his comrade, which is also a betrayal of his own political idealism, Johnny's greatest hope is escape. News of the legacy provides him with this prospect. Whatever mysterious impulse caused him to betray Robbie Tancred is never disclosed. The betrayal, however, is a pained glance at Civil War Ireland, too traumatic to be more than obliquely incorporated into the main action of the play.

There are other dramatic tensions. There is, for instance, a counterpoint in the play between the pretentiously elevated and the obstinately material, between Boyle's meditation on the stars and the coal vendor shouting outside the window, between Devine and Bentham (the names are ironically inappropriate: no one is less divine than the atheistic Devine, no one less utilitarian than the idealist Bentham). This opposition is not surprising in a text which continually entwines inflated language with squalid reality. As always, the joyful, imaginative principle represented by Boyle leans on the labours of others: his metaphysical musings, like his self-pampering, must suspend the pressing drudgery of material survival. They provide a seductive alternative to reality which for all its comical and imaginative appeal has nonetheless a germ of pathos because it is ultimately fraudulent and parasitic. Just as the characters' verbal eloquence and loquacity mask an oppressive, claustrophobic inability to act, so do imagination, joy and entertainment survive only by covering over a harrowing material reality.

The opposition between inflated language and obstinate reality parallels another conflict in the play. The repeated ascription of a secular, social source for the problems which beset the community is disturbed by an underlying pessimistic fatalism. On the one hand we have the indefatigable Juno attributing the suffering her family endures to human, not divine, sources: 'These things have nothin' to do with the Will o' God. Ah, what can God do agen the stupidity o' men!' (70). On the other hand we have an unravelling tragic destiny, a sense that the events of the play are as mysterious and inscrutable as the stars at which Boyle poignantly gazes, or as supernatural as Johnny's vision of the blood-spattered Robbie Tancred. Jerry assures Mary that 'humanity is above everything' (66), but she refutes his socialist optimism by reciting back to him the pessimistic verses 'Humanity's Strife with Nature', which Jerry read at the Socialist Rooms earlier in their courtship:

> An' we felt the power that fashion'd
> All the lovely things we saw,
> That created all the murmur
> Of an everlasting law,
> Was a hand of force an' beauty,
> With an eagle's tearin' claw.
>
> Then we saw our globe of beauty
> Was an ugly thing as well,
> A hymn divine whose chorus
> Was an agonizin' yell;
> Like the story of a demon,
> That an angel had to tell (67).

The idea of human supremacy over the natural forces of perversion and destruction now seems painfully distant. These verses express a profoundly Manichaean view of the universe. Evil and discord coexist with goodness and harmony, not just because of the 'stupidity o' men', but as a fundamental part of the divine signature. Disenchanted with Jerry's faux-socialist meliorism,

Mary has come to the pessimistic view that human suffering is caused by a fundamental perversion of nature.

O'Casey's prevailing instinct is to subscribe to Juno's belief that the flaws of society are wholly 'man'-made. This is the unambiguous implication of his pre-Civil War political stance and the socialist optimism of his later work. In the Trilogy, however, he is forced to negotiate the supreme let-down brought on by the course of Irish history. O'Casey's belief in reparability is vitiated in the Trilogy – it is his efforts to regain the social element which sometimes lead to the confusion and polemicism of which some critics have complained. However, if we interpret these plays against the grain of their overt polemic, we can observe O'Casey writing not as an impartial observer or a bitter satirist of his country's tragedy, but as a symptom of it.

We see a similar ambivalence in the final play of the Trilogy. Ostensibly *The Plough and the Stars* is a rebuttal of the myths underlying the Easter Rising. Elevating love for Ireland above love for a woman is presented as unnatural and inhuman, equivalent to elevating an abstract, bloodless idealism above the flesh-and-blood familial concerns of hearth and home. However, once again, there are countervailing undercurrents in the play which go against this surface moral. All is not well in the Clitheroe household, even before politics intrudes its ugly head. Mrs Grogan recognizes Nora's 'notions of upperosity' (137) and the rapaciousness with which she sets about her programme of self-improvement: 'She's wipin' th' eyes of th' Covey an' poor oul' Pether – everybody knows that – screwin' every penny she can out o' them, in ordher to turn th' place into a babby house' (138). On the one hand Nora's upwardly mobile ambition to take her family out of the slums – 'She's always grumblin' about havin' to live in a tenement house' (138) – is an understandable and pragmatic aspiration, to be distinguished from the nebulous idealism of the men.

However, as was the case with Juno, it is often difficult to reconcile Nora's material ambitions with her duties to her community. A point sometimes missed is that Nora's much-admired rejection of politics is contingent on a parallel rejection of her society and of her neighbours. Like Juno, Nora's devotion to her family is often not just antipolitical, it is antisocial. For all her own assumptions of independence, and those of liberal-minded critics who espouse the idea that Nora represents an uncomplicated family ideal, her ambitions bear the disavowal of her wider society. Her loyalty to her immediate family is founded in an atomized individualism, based in a denial of social structure and community obligation.[10] In Act 3 a distressed Nora returns with the heroically brave Fluther, who has rescued her from the streets: 'They said th' women must learn to be brave an' cease to be cowardly ... Me who risked more for love than they would risk for hate ...'

(184). This declaration is often brandished as an example of Nora's fierce humanity. Not so often analysed, however, are additional comments in the same scene, which reveal a selfishness contrary to the put-upon benevolence for which she is celebrated. 'I can't help thinkin' every shot fired at Jack'll be fired at me. What do I care for th' others? I can think only of me own self' (184).

At the end of Act 3, when Nora tries physically to impede Clitheroe from proceeding with his comrades, including the gravely wounded and dependent Langon, the audience tends to have an appropriately ambivalent response. Nora claims, with the agreement of many critics of the play, that she is Clitheroe's 'dearest comrade' (195), but his obligations to his friends and fellow-soldiers are now pressing and real, no longer abstract, rhetorical and ideal. The choice is not now between a vainglorious militarism and domestic reality, but between two conflicting and immediate duties. This is a far more pointed, painful dilemma, for the audience as much as for Clitheroe himself. It certainly gives the lie to the opposition usually read into the play: 'Clitheroe puts Ireland before his wife. That is the real tragedy: death before life. Faced with a choice, the Irishman accepts Thanatos before Eros, and so the purpose of life is defeated.'[11] Luckily, from the point of view of interesting drama, the choice is not so simple. The dramatic opposition between Nora's powerful entreaties for Jack to remain with her, and Langon's agonized pleas that they move on, generates a powerful urgency, incarnating the incompatible moral imperatives that war and revolution create. Such moral complexity counters the polemical pacifism and simplistic polarities the play's critics distrust.

Other significant slippages in the play occur in the presentation of the Clitheroe marriage. The relationship between Nora and Jack is a good deal less harmonious than we might suppose, even in the apolitical, domestic sphere which is supposedly the play's idealized realm. Consistently in the play, as befits this version of the Cathleen ni Houlihan myth, love for Ireland is configured in terms of love for a woman, and vice versa. Yet Nora's and Jack's relationship raises serious issues about the nature of desire which remain disturbingly unresolved. Mrs Grogan strikes a significant note when she observes of Jack that, despite his earlier ardour, he is now:

> beginnin' to take things more quietly; the mysthery of havin' a woman's a mysthery no longer . . . She dhresses herself to keep him with her, but it's no use – afther a month or two, th' wondher of a woman wears off (138).

The suspicion is planted that Cathleen ni Houlihan has not lured Clitheroe away from Nora – he was already disenchanted. Fluther believes that Jack's new coolness to Nora comes from infatuation with another woman; the audience, by implication, intuits the rival to be the feminized Ireland of familiar myth.

Nonetheless, the issue of whether Clitheroe was lured into figurative infidelity – delusion – or was already predisposed for it – disillusionment – is left unanswered. Later in the act a love scene takes place between Nora and Jack which supports Mrs Grogan's diagnosis of their relationship. When Jack kisses Nora she rebuffs him, confirming Mrs Grogan's suspicions that he has lost much of his ardour: 'Jack, Jack; please, Jack! I thought you were tired of that sort of thing long ago' (154). Nora is disturbed by the facility with which Jack's desire shifts from her to his political ambitions, and she pinpoints a feature not just of Jack's love, but of desire and satisfaction in general: 'It's hard for a body to be always keepin' her mind bent on makin' thoughts that'll be no longer than th' length of your own satisfaction' (154). It seems that, once satisfied, desire drifts wayward. It is not the charms of Cathleen ni Houlihan which lure Jack away, but a prior sense of dissatisfaction. In the light of her earlier perceptive remarks on the Clitheroe marriage, Mrs Grogan's consolation to the distraught Nora in Act 3 has a sinister double-meaning: 'If you'd been a little longer together, th' wrench asundher wouldn't have been so sharp' (185). It suggests, again, that their desire becomes dormant if satisfied. The implication is that romantic love may be as delusory as the romantic nationalism against which it is placed as a healthy alternative.

So the adulation of hearth and home is a much more complex affair in O'Casey than is sometimes assumed. This is not really surprising given the black depiction of domesticity in O'Casey's next play, *The Silver Tassie* (notoriously rejected by the Abbey Theatre), where cynical mothers and beaten wives encourage men to go to the Front so that they will receive separation money. Here, the women are as vainglorious, petty and self-serving as the men and there is a strong hint that the violence does not intrude into the home from the outside, but rather that war is a symptom of domestic or innate aggression. The priority which naturalist form gives to the home, the coherent domestic reality before our eyes seeming more 'real' than wider social forces, is avoided in the brilliant second act. Using expressionistic techniques O'Casey manages to find a formal expression of fragmentation and confusion, an overwhelming, opaque sense of dark, perverse ritual. Yet the conflict of forms as well as themes which we see in *The Silver Tassie* is nascent in the Dublin Trilogy. It takes a production alert to the conflicts, tensions and contradictions in the plays to resist the reassuring 'moral' messages which slide all too easily from plays performed in a cosy, naturalistic setting. What is dramatically interesting in them is the confusion and disillusionment they incarnate. And, as a later Irish playwright will remind us, 'confusion is not an ignoble condition'.[12]

NOTES

1. Sean O'Casey, *Autobiographies*, 2 vols. (1939–54), (London and Basingstoke: Macmillan, 1981).
2. Quoted in Garry O'Connor, *Sean O'Casey: A Life* (London: Hodder and Stoughton, 1988), 196.
3. Sean O'Casey, *Juno and the Paycock*, in *Three Plays* (London: Papermac, 1994), 72. This edition also includes *The Shadow of a Gunman* and *The Plough and the Stars*. Further page references will be included in the text in parenthesis.
4. Christopher Murray, *Twentieth-Century Irish Drama: Mirror Up to Nation* (Manchester: Manchester University Press, 1997), 94. While the term originates in the 1930s with the journal *Irish Historical Studies*, since the 1980s it has come to be used, by its advocates, as a description of standard 'objective' historical practice which seeks to describe the complex totality of an event and, by its opponents, as an apology for colonialism which denies the trauma of Irish history and removes the actual 'narration' of the nation. O'Casey's treatment of 1916, in its implicit claims to be showing the often unheroic totality of the experience, in opposition to idealizing nationalist versions of the event, is in this sense 'revisionist'.
5. G. J. Watson, *Irish Identity and the Literary Revival: Synge, Yeats, Joyce and O'Casey*, 2nd edn. (Washington DC: Catholic University of America Press, 1994), 265.
6. Seamus Deane makes the complaint succinct: 'All of O'Casey's gunmen are shadows, and consequently his aggression towards politics is a form of shadow boxing.' See *Celtic Revivals: Essays in Modern Irish Literature: 1880–1980* (London: Faber and Faber, 1985), 109.
7. Raymond Williams, *Drama from Ibsen to Brecht* (London: Hogarth Press, 1993), 147.
8. This point is made by G. J. Watson, though he regards it as a dramatic weakness. See Watson, *Irish Identity*, 268.
9. See O'Casey, 'The Cap in the Counting House', *Autobiographies 1*, 339–48.
10. It is significant, then, that as a newly discovered production notebook has shown, O'Casey originally intended the Clitheroes to be a middle-class family, with Jack as a clerk rather than a bricklayer, but was dissuaded by Yeats and Lennox Robinson. See Nicholas Grene, 'The Class of the Clitheroes: O'Casey's Revisions to *The Plough and the Stars* Promptbook', in *Bullán*, 4:2 (1999/2000), 57–66.
11. Peter Costello, *The Heart Grown Brutal: The Irish Revolution in Literature from Parnell to the Death of Yeats 1891–1939* (Dublin: Gill and Macmillan, 1977), 110.
12. Brian Friel, *Translations*, in *Selected Plays of Brian Friel* (London: Faber and Faber, 1984), 446.

11

CATHY LEENEY

Ireland's 'exiled' women playwrights: Teresa Deevy and Marina Carr

'All women are exiles' says the playwright and critic Hélène Cixous.[1] Since James Joyce named exile as one of the conditions of his artistic life it has become associated with Irish writing. The distance exile implies invites an association, in turn, with alienation. However, Seamus Deane argues that while modern Irish literature as a whole 'registers alienation, it is not a literature of alienation'.[2] This comment has a particular resonance for Irish women's writing, and for women playwrights. If women are, as Cixous suggests, already exiles in their own land, how does alienation characterize their work; how might their work be a literature of alienation? The boundaries around Irish women's realities define containment as a form of exile: exile from self-expression, from self-determination. Only the crossing of a boundary makes that boundary visible. How does the work of Teresa Deevy and Marina Carr cross boundaries, and how do those crossings take shape in performance?

Irish plays by women in the 1930s reflect a high register of female alienation which is most thoroughly expressed in the work of Teresa Deevy. Deevy's plays register alienation; but, in the sense that they form a corpus of work expressive of an occluded reality, kept out of the canon of Irish theatrical history, they are also a dramaturgy of alienation. In contemporary Irish theatre the work of Marina Carr pushes the boundaries of theatrical representation to the limit before crossing them to reveal a passionate enactment of exile and alienation.

The crossing of boundaries has a special power in the theatre, since the audience sees the transgression enacted; the energy of human presence in performance celebrates the potential for transformation, and even where the story ends tragically and transformation is denied or delayed, the energizing voltage of performance remains. So, even as Deevy's and Carr's heroines face an impossible future, and are sometimes defeated in the face of that future, what impacts on the audience is the vehemence of their resistance, their will to freedom and fulfilment. In this chapter I will consider two plays by

Deevy, and two by Carr, using W. B. Yeats's *Purgatory* (1939) as a bridge to introduce the extremities of violence and death which are nascent in Deevy's work, and startlingly powerful in Carr's.

I

As a playwright Deevy's impulses were national and contemporary. The issue of alienation in her early one-act play *A Disciple* or *In Search of Valour* (1931), and in her most popular play *Katie Roche* (1936) will focus my comments here. The first play, especially, shows plainly the influence of Synge, and exemplifies the importance of Synge's creations, Christy and Pegeen as the archetypal hero and heroine of twentieth-century Irish theatre.

As a bourgeois Catholic playwright Deevy may easily be identified with what Terence Brown calls 'the dominant political, ideological and cultural consensus of the early years of independence' (*Ireland: A Social and Cultural History*, 102). To see her work in this way would be a mistake. What her social and religious background offered her was an insider's understanding of its barren oppressions. Deevy wrote about those struggling for survival under acute conditions, people to whom the subtler oppressions of privilege might appear attractive, even glamorous; but the glamour is revealed as sham and the privilege offers only another challenge to the ingenuity of the human spirit. When the challenge concerns circumstances dictated by womanhood Deevy's portrayal of it is at its most compelling psychologically and theatrically. Her work is both a reflection on and a challenge to the orthodoxies of 1930s Ireland. By extension, it also explores the individual's negotiation between self and society where the personal is political. Deevy shows us with unflinching honesty the lost horizons and limits of lives most ordinary.

In her work the role of violence is treated with some complexity and its erotic attraction is not denied. Rather Deevy creates dramatic situations where the oppressed are seen to be unable to escape the systems of control to which they have been victim; they then project their fantasies in terms of those systems. The psychological authenticity of this perception is offset against the theatricality of the power struggle between Deevy's heroines, remarkable yet disempowered individuals, and the coercive systems under which they live.

The imaginative wilfulness of Deevy's heroines is *all* that may be celebrated in the plays. In performance it is theatrically the most compelling aspect of the work. Treatment of the play as performance, rather than as text, reveals this emphasis on the vitality of the performer, which runs in ironic parallel to the oppressive conditions within which the character operates.

As Herbert Blau describes it, 'the pretense is the form by which [the actor] coexists with his oppression . . . Illusion, in this sense, is survival'.[3] The living presence of the performer creates a dialectic with the structure of the play itself; the provisionality of performance opens a gap between experience and possibility.

The theme of *A Disciple* is the female impulse towards heroism, and the psychological and ideological contortions that impulse takes. Deevy brings together a character of immense vitality, Ellie Irwin, and an environment of stifling repression in *A Disciple*. Mrs Maher's rundown house is 'between mountain and bog . . . between county and town'.[4] Ellie is her servant, and Mrs Maher runs an employment agency of sorts for female domestics. The setting is expressionist, yet refers, in its isolated and liminal quality, to the Burke cottage, *'at the head of a long glen'* in Synge's *In the Shadow of the Glen*.[5] Ellie's longing for 'spirit' is the positive corollary of Nora's melancholy and hard-earned resignation.

Ellie enters *'with an air of smouldering fury'* (29) which establishes the high emotional register of the whole. Like her namesake in Shaw's *Heartbreak House*, Ellie has been reading Shakespeare, specifically *Coriolanus*. She remembers a school performance of the play in which a professional actress played the eponymous role. The performance, as Ellie says, 'rose me heart in one hour til I seen the scum we are' (35). Ellie's confused identification with Coriolanus is central to the play. Ironically, she has seen Coriolanus played by a woman, therefore why might she not see herself in the same, real-life role? Ellie identifies with the male hero, as women in a patriarchal society tend to do. As Adrienne Rich writes, 'Women – privileged or not – are trained to identify with men, whether with the males in power to whom they may be attached, or – as emotional sympathisers – with men of an oppressed group.'[6]

This identification applies culturally, too. Women are well-practised, when searching for heroes and role models, in cross-gender identification; the female spectator very often participates in the play through the point of view of the hero, even if, by doing this, she feels she is taking part in the objectification and occlusion of her own gender. Deevy's play offers a central female protagonist caught in this identification trap. Ellie's 'rage and despair' (29) grows out of the gap between her imaginative identification with Coriolanus, and the social requirement that, as a woman, her only access to heroism is indirect, through association with a man.

Deevy's representation of the heroic in the play is thoroughly ironic and highly comic. In place of the dreary materialism and cringing piety of her employer, Ellie naïvely looks to the apparent glamour of 'them that lives' as documented in the popular press. She is disappointed, however, in Mr and Mrs Glitterton. When she turns her hungry gaze on Jack the Scalp, a local renegade wanted by the police, the upshot is hilarious; for dastardly though Jack's reputation may be, he is terrified of Ellie. Backing away from her eager advances he protests, 'I'm willing to shoot whoever you'd like but . . . I'm a respectable man.'(47). The scene is a fascinating rewrite of Pegeen's betrayal of Christy in Synge's *Playboy*. In both plays the young man leaves the stage while the young woman is left behind; but in *A Disciple* we are in no doubt as to the craven fear with which Jack views the feminine, while Ellie's lament is not for the loss of one man, but for the failure of masculinity to live up to its own mythology, to be 'Coriolanus-like'.

Deevy was not content to resign herself to the image of disempowerment and defeat which Pegeen so eloquently represents at the end of *Playboy*. Synge places Pegeen as the author of her own inhibition. She actively partakes in the scapegoating of Christy in Act 3, burning him cruelly. In a transformative reversal Synge gives the final triumph to his battered hero, who carries the energy, which the play itself has created, offstage. Synge overturns the ritual of scapegoating so that Pegeen becomes the sacrificial victim who must suffer to maintain the social structure, and the play presents her as the author of her own tragedy. In *A Disciple* Deevy rewrites Synge's fiction in which the inhibited possibilities of the hero are liberated, at a high cost to the heroine who remains trapped in the structure of the play, as she is in her father's shebeen. In Deevy's version Christy is combined with Shawn Keogh in the person of Jack the Scalp. Jack is greatly revered on account of his violent reputation. He asserts power over Mrs Maher and the others through physical threat, but his failure to reach Ellie's expectations means he has no power over her. She maintains control of the stage space when he leaves.

Ellie has no social power, but she does have power as the central consciousness of the play. The achievement of *A Disciple* is that it proposes a dramatic energy of great impact in Ellie, at the centre of a drama of her disillusion and powerlessness. Ellie's yearning for heroic action is, though, like Coriolanus's, a will to power, and contains within it an idealization of violence, disdain for others and amorality. In its treatment of heroism, then, the play is a rehearsal of the attractions of fascism to a proletariat trapped by a stagnant, dreary and impoverished social structure.

The shadow of violence falls across *A Disciple*, in terms both of action and of atmosphere. The violence is disassociated from nationalist concerns and is now dangerously free-floating. Through the image of Coriolanus, Deevy broadens the political terms of reference to include the disturbing tendency towards fascism in both Ireland and Europe. In postrevolutionary Ireland an impulse towards heroism might easily be diverted into reliance on autocratic figures who appeared as a focus for energies and aspirations resistant to the dynamic political threat of communism. Perhaps, then, *A Disciple* is, for all its vivid theatricality and comedy, overloaded with psychic as well as political baggage. A remarkable aspect of the play is that the myths of sophistication and heroism are demolished, but the heroine stands firm, and asserts not grief but fury and frustration: 'There is no MAN living now . . . Why weren't I born in a brave long-ago time?' (47).

Theatrically *A Disciple* creates its own paradox. Ellie is entirely disem-powered at the end, stranded as much as Pegeen was at the end of Synge's *Playboy*. However, dramatically she is empowered. The action and style of the piece create in her an impressive authority despite her social vacuum. The question the play can only pose, not answer, is how a woman may be the author of herself.

Katie Roche is the eponymous centre of Deevy's best-known play. Her mother, now dead, was not married, and Katie bears the surname of the woman who brought her up, but who failed to care for her. She is the domestic servant of Amelia. Stan, Amelia's architect brother, proposes to Katie. He was once in love with her mother; when he declares his intentions to Katie there is a telling confusion. Stan marries Katie, and Acts 2 and 3 track their troubled relationship, or rather lack of relationship.

Notwithstanding the theatrical power of Stan's arsenal of silence, with-drawal and condescension, perhaps the most shocking scene is in Act 2 when the local vagrant, Reuben, demands an interview with Katie. He lectures her on the proper behaviour of a wife, and when she turns scornful, '*Reuben, with surprising vigour, raises his stick, hits her across the shoulders. Katie collapses on to a chair.*'[7] Katie displays absolutely no self-pity. Indeed, the assault gives her the outraged courage to confront him:, 'So you thought to frighten me!' (59). Ironically Reuben holds a wild card: he is her biological father and he disarms Katie with this momentous news. His sternness is unabated, however, and in Act 3 he returns to declare: 'What she needs is humiliation – if she was thoroughly humbled she might begin to learn' (105).

The characterization of Reuben is a theatrical challenge as he is poised between realism and the symbolic; but the frightening visual resonance of his action, as well as the aural resonance of the above exhortation, con-tain the potential to overshadow the surrounding scenes. Reuben's symbolic presence uproots the play from the domestic and places it in the realm of the archetypal.

For present-day Irish audiences Reuben's extolling of humiliation of the deviant female connects directly with recent revelations concerning the in-carceration of Irish women in Magdalen Laundries where they were branded 'sinners'. The original purpose of the laundries was to house reformed prostitutes; by the 1940s the majority of inmates were unmarried mothers. Some were sent there on the mere suspicion that their chastity had been, or was in danger of being, violated.[8] The laundries were secret places, cut off behind gates and high walls. Inmates were robbed of their dignity as individuals: their clothes were confiscated, their hair was cut and they received no pay. This was the secret reality which informed attitudes to all women in Irish society at the time, and which informs Deevy's stress on the strategies of patriarchal power to control Katie's energy and sexuality. As a symbolic dramatic figure Reuben may be seen to represent this unspeakable (in both senses) oppression.

Deevy establishes a theatrical situation onstage, when Reuben assaults Katie, which would not be out of place in melodrama, but the playwright disrupts the theatrical expectations of the audience; Katie's reaction to violence is surprising and ambivalent. She is not cowed by it; she refuses the role of victim. Having invoked, with uncharacteristic coolness, the sanction of the law – 'If you had broken my shoulder you could be put in the court' (59) – she rather attempts to appropriate power through her relationship with Reuben. Despite his heartless disclaimers – 'I have nothing to give you. . . . I've no claim on you – nor you on me' (60–1) – Katie fails to comprehend the degree of her exclusion. The patterning of the whole play follows her misguided attempts to control her reality.

Echoes of Ibsen's heroines in *A Doll's House* and *Hedda Gabler* are present in *Katie Roche*. Unlike Hedda Gabler, Katie is not trapped in the biological female role; she is rendered sexually and socially neutral in her frigid marriage. Unlike Hedda Gabler, she cannot even boast of her paternity; Katie bears the surname of the woman who took her from the convent and exploited her. But, like Hedda's, Katie's frustration is expressed in destructiveness. In the 1994 Abbey Theatre revival of the play Derbhle Crotty as Katie added a piece of business which invited a comparison between Deevy's and Ibsen's heroines.[9] At the beginning of Act 2 Katie wafts her husband's architectural drawings before the fire, recalling Hedda with Lovborg's manuscript saying, 'I'm burning your child, Thea. . . . Your child and Ejlert Lovborg's child. (*Throws the rest in.*)'[10] When we remember that Stan's plans are for a church, – 'The spire . . . with maybe the sun shining on it?' (46–7) – the wonderful mischievousness of this gesture strikes us: the Church as child of the patriarchy, born by immaculate conception, threatened by destruction at the hands of frustrated womanhood.

Katie Roche has been the most performed of any of Deevy's plays. It is the remarkable vivacity of its central character which distinguishes it as a fascinating study of an individual, and a major acting challenge. Joseph

Holloway's view of Katie gives some indication of how unusual she was to this inveterate theatregoer; he called her 'the strangest character [he] ever saw on the stage'.[11] By the time of the 1994 production the puzzlement at Katie which Holloway felt had given way to a perception that Katie is a character of remarkable complexity and quixotic energy, framed by a much too conservative play.

The stresses operating between Katie and Deevy's dramaturgy are especially taut at the end, when Katie must leave with Stan to face an, at best, uncertain future. Jeananne Crowley, who played Katie at the Abbey in 1975, describes the ending as 'open', but the likelihood of fulfilment for Katie is slim. The actress sees the theme of the play as sexual repression. In the closing moments Katie says 'taken away . . . my own fault' (113) and Crowley points out how 'nobody in the play, and specifically none of the women, has the courage to tell her it is not her fault'.[12] Judy Friel and Derbhle Crotty (director and actor in 1994) both found the ending problematic. They tried, in rehearsal, to find a different way of playing Katie's departure, but it did not work.[13] So, almost sixty years after *Katie Roche* was written, the extent to which the heroine is confined and oppressed has become central to the meaning of the performance. If, in the 1930s, Katie was the one who seemed strange, in the 1970s and 1990s it is rather the rest of the play which alienates, and highlights Katie's struggle for autonomous identity. In these later productions the failure of the play to accommodate Katie becomes visible against a changed social context, and offers an acute sense of the claustrophobia of Irish women in earlier decades. The openness of Deevy's work to metaphorical readings is undoubtedly crucial to an understanding of the way in which realist conventions are manipulated, and hence to a recognition of dramatic meaning beyond the currencies of Ireland in the 1930s.

The privileging of literary over theatrical values in part explains why Deevy's work has yet to be recognized as a valuable and integral part of the Irish theatrical canon. As texts Deevy's plays for the Abbey Theatre from 1931 to 1942 may be read as realist enactments of the narrow confinement of socially insignificant women's lives; in performance they become something else. In performance dramatic irony operates so that the energy and vitality which the structure of the play contains and finally thwarts is, theatrically, at the core of the audience's experience.

Death as event forms no part of Deevy's dramaturgy, in contrast with Yeats or Synge; but a sense of death in life intersects with her interest in cycles of sacrifice, return, renewal and attempted transformation – all within a single mortal coil. By the end of the 1930s Deevy's focus had narrowed to concern for the ethics of relationship in a context of unequal access to social power.

Where Irish women were concerned, the contradictions of war, its liberating function, even in the midst of destruction and tragedy, did not effectively disrupt their social exclusion. The painful inability of Deevy's heroines to carve out a future of their own making is testament to the distance travelled from the ideological exhilaration of the cultural renaissance in the early twentieth century, and the distance to be travelled to theatrical expressions of the impact of the feminist movement at the end of the twentieth century. In Deevy's earlier work the ebullience and charisma of her heroines bring the audience to an acute understanding of wasted possibility; in this sense the plays may be described, in Eavan Boland's words, as 'an archive of defeat and a diagram of victory'.[14]

II

The Old Man in Yeats's *Purgatory* murders his son in his revulsion for the polluted genetic inheritance the Boy represents to him. The play romanticizes a version of the contribution of the 'big house' to Irish history and culture, and identifies female desire as the source of degeneration and ruin. It is a ghost play. The performance is a negotiation between the past and the present moment, and the demand of the past for expiation in order that energy be released into the future. The expiation fails and the reason given is the stubborn persistence of the woman's pleasure in desire fulfilled.

Yeats rejected the ending of his source-play, the Japanese Noh drama *Nishikigi*, in which the Buddhist priest releases the souls of the dead lovers. In *Purgatory* the ending is twisted into an image of failure to reach for a future. In a sense the play takes place within a sealed time sequence. The Old Man watches as his mother repeats her 'sin' over and over again. At first the point at which the man stabs his son seems to fracture this time sequence, and confront the audience with a murderous moment in the present tense. However, as the play ends in a return of the sound of horses' hooves on the gravel, it is as if the action begins again; as if the Boy revives, picks up the fallen money, and begins again.

The past wins out over the present; the future is obliterated. *Purgatory* is an extreme image of death in life, an image which mutely underpins the efforts of Deevy's heroines to seize the day, to live in the present, and to project a future, and not be caught in the way things were, with the dead heroes and the impossible heroines. Yeats's inclusion of the savage act of murder, in real stage time, unadorned by reference to ancient myths or heroic legends, opens the way theatrically for direct confrontation with death itself, as well as with the dead, death as something we do, killing as the ultimate performance.

III

In *Portia Coughlan* (1995) and *By the Bog of Cats* (1998) Marina Carr dramatizes the impossibility of life by tracing journeys towards death. Both plays are haunted, literally and figuratively, by the dead, by suicide or killing, by the act of dying. But death is reframed as the final resistance. The heroines, unlike Deevy's, are not the victims of violence but the perpetrators, even more surely when they finally turn violence against themselves.

Ellie and Katie are vehemently struggling to live as fully as their imaginations lead them to believe is possible; society threatens them with the morbidity of containment within the norms of feminine behaviour. Carr's Portia and Hester rush in where Deevy's two fear to tread. They are, literally, terrible women, fuelled by explosive existential and emotional frustration. Having tested what the world might offer them, they redefine 'undead' as a state of becoming. The painful accession of loss and rejection to both characters is an important element in both plays. Reasons are proffered – childhood trauma, incest in the family, the confines of traditional female roles as wife, mother, daughter, good girl – but the furious sense of dissatisfaction exceeds what we might expect these social/political/psychological causes to occasion. The central energy of both plays, in its pure epic tragedy, cuts them loose from the bounds of the local or the national.

Marina Carr's first play was *Ullaloo* (written in 1989), but as this was not performed until 1991, it was *Low in the Dark* (1989) which was the first to be produced. Both plays operate entirely without reference to realist representation, so that with *The Mai* (1994) Carr's apparent adoption of realist conventions such as an identifiable time and place, and focus on individual psychologies, may be guardedly acknowledged, and held in balance with the symbolic structures organizing the action, the use of storytelling, and of direct address to the audience.

In *Portia Coughlan* Carr develops the connection between landscape, grief and the ghosts of the past. The pastoral idyll of Deevy's *Katie Roche* is now the 'dungeon a tha fallen worldt',[15] and both ghost and landscape occupy the stage in the forms of Gabriel, Portia's drowned twin, and the River Belmont in which he drowned. The vivid threat, as well as the beauty, of the natural world, so central to Synge, is here refracted and twisted through the psyche of an awesomely unsympathetic heroine.

Portia's account of the origins of the river centres on an image of agony inflicted by the community on an outsider woman with Medusa-like characteristics: 'If ya lookt her in th'eye ya didn't see her eye buh ya seen how an' whin ya war goin' ta die.' She is an image of Portia herself, 'for she war wan a' thim, on'y a little different' (267). The difference Portia feels is that, without Gabriel, she is only half a person. We, the audience, see Gabriel as Portia does, and hear his heavenly singing, and so we are drawn in to understand how, to her, life is a kind of Hades from which she must escape in death.

The extremity of this image of alienation is emphasized by Portia's relentless refusal of every 'womanly' virtue.[16] She abuses her husband, wants to rape her mother, neglects her young children and fears her impulse to do them harm; she is sexually promiscuous and markedly unhousewifely. More intensely than Ibsen with Hedda Gabler, Carr challenges the audience to acknowledge in Portia a being freed from the value-laden terms conventionally used to define the female. We find Portia compelling as a person whose rage at life exceeds life itself. Paradoxically, she longs for the wholeness of unity with her male twin, an image of gendered complementarity, the yolk and white of the one egg, echoing back through Yeats to Plato.

However, Carr reframes this aspiration through the representation of woman as Portia, angry, violent, obsessed. The play achieves a de-idealized image of woman, yet trusts the trajectory of her emotional journey as the spine of the action. This contrasts significantly with the work of many playwrights of the Irish dramatic renaissance, as well as with contemporary Irish male playwrights' cosmeticized versions of woman.[17] In performance, despite her monstrous aspects, Portia's energy fuels the piece, overtaking the negative images of destruction, failure and suicide and enacting, in their stead, a passionate subjectivity of astonishing vigour.

Carr uses dramatic language and structure to express Portia's place at the hub of the play. *Portia Coughlan* is written phonetically to reflect the idiom and accent of Carr's birthplace, Co. Offaly. All the characters share this language, creating an aural image of tribal otherness. The distance between the dialogue and ordinary standard speech licenses an intensity of image and a colourful syntax which would, elsewhere, seem overpoetic or overwritten. Again, the speech demands performance before its tensile physicality can be felt. Tomred's description of Tilly's utterance in *Ullaloo* captures how the words in *Portia Coughlan* 'start low in the stomach, growl around the gut . . . and finally explode from the tongue'.

The visceral impact of these utterances, established in the opening moments and sustained throughout, make possible an epic structure of feeling (to borrow Raymond Williams's phrase), an emotional intensity which runs off the scale of social or psychological causation. When Portia tells her husband Raphael that there are 'times yar lucky ah don't rip ya ta pieces or plunge a breadknife through yar lily heart' (270), the levels of verbal directness and impact have already been established as so high that we take her at her word. Carr creates a parallel stage world precisely local, yet mythic and archetypal. There is no contradiction here. This challenge to mimesis allows Portia to say the unsayable, to cross the boundaries of what it is to be woman, and the boundary between life and death.

Portia's death (by suicide, it is implied) occurs between the end of Act 1 and the beginning of Act 2. Act 2 opens with a visual *coup de théatre*: Portia's body hauled out of the River Belmont and suspended, dripping, while all excepting Blaize stand in silence, and Gabriel sings (272). The act proceeds with the gathering after Portia's funeral, when the tortured family history of betrayal, deceit and bitterness is exposed. Act 3 takes up where Act 1 left off, on the day after Portia's birthday. This manipulation of chronological time disrupts the relation between cause and effect, and frees both Portia and the audience from the tyranny of closure in death. The antiheroine's reappearance in Act 3 deepens the tragic pain of her life beyond what may be read as the defeat of her suicide. A space is opened up, structurally affirming the privileged centrality of Portia over the demands of chronology: dramaturgy is reshaped to accommodate her, and in the sequence of performance she transcends her own death.

The repugnant expressions of genetic and tribal hatred so prominent in Act 2 of *Portia Coughlan* reflect the eugenic rhetoric in Yeats's *Purgatory*. Portia derides the barman Fintan and his family, 'yar a fuchin' clodhopper liche yar people afore ya an' liche those ya'll spawn ater ya in a weh ditch an a weh nigh' in a drunken stupour' (268), echoing exactly Yeats's Old Man's disdain for his son. Carr harnesses these disturbing tribal impulses against the central figure in her next play *By the Bog of Cats* (1998).

Hester Swane is a quasi-Medea figure: she is an outsider, betrayed by Carthage, the father of her child, powerless to take control of her fate except through murderous violence. The concentrated unity of time and action, which mark the play as a version of classical tragedy, is revealed by the Ghost Fancier in the opening scene. He comes for Hester, mistaking dawn for dusk, and preempting narrative suspense regarding Hester's fate. The audience embark with Hester in full awareness of her doom.

Hester's despair, though, is fundamentally different from Portia's. In *By the Bog of Cats* Carr dramatizes Hester's struggle to live as she wishes, that is, with her daughter and on the Bog of Cats, where she can await the return of her mother, Josie Swane. Portia's longing for her gender opposite is replaced by Hester's for the affirming gaze of her lost mother. It is significant that Hester's child is a girl, since this establishes the line of female connection as the issue. In this way the play is radical in the Irish canon. It is an enactment of mourning for the absent mother; this is not only Hester's mother, but, theatrically speaking, the mother absent from so many important Irish plays. Aside from Carthage's desertion of Hester, and all that goes with it, it is

Hester's longing for Josie Swane's recognition in return that is the central energy of the piece.

The location, the Bog of Cats, works as a limbo metaphor, limbo seen here as cold, white, haunted, betwixt and between. Contrasting with this, Act 2, the wedding feast of Carthage and Caroline, is set in Xavier Cassidy's house. However, the potential settling of the scene into naturalism is quickly disrupted by the appearance of the ghost of Joseph Swane, Hester's murdered brother. Mimesis slips into mimicry as not one, but four bridal figures invade the stage. The ritual of marriage, which has just taken place, is made a nonsense of. This disruption of the ritual structure, which underlies Katie Roche's drama, is here the subject of farcical black humour and absurdity. The act descends into open conflict between Hester and Carthage, and her threat of a 'vicious war'.[18] In the 1998 Abbey Theatre production designer Monica Frawley chose to extend the outdoor settings of Acts 1 and 3 into Act 2. The wedding table was perched incongruously on the snowy bog. This decision added to Carr's formal daring in interrupting the tragic action with carnival upheaval in absurd comedy, while, by maintaining unity of place throughout, it emphasized the play's roots in classical tragedy.

Hester feels 'discarded' (55) by her mother, by Carthage and by society. Her fear is that she will be consigned to a living death, 'on the ashpit', away from her beloved bog, separated from her daughter and robbed of power. She has not 'lived be the rules' (55), as drama so often reminds us women must, to survive. Her 'anomie, itineracy and exile'[19] make a powerful image of otherness. But, in a very different way from Portia Coughlan, the Bog of Cats reflects Hester's reality and offers her sustenance and assertion of her identity, even as it reflects her forthcoming death in the death of the black swan. The painful narratives by which landscape was represented in The Mai, and in Portia Coughlan, are here replaced by images of Hester as the most 'at home' figure on stage. As Melissa Sihra points out, By the Bog of Cats brings the audience into the world of the exile, so that those surrounding her are reframed as outsiders.

IV

There are deep contrasts between the plays of Deevy and Carr which reflect their very different talents as playwrights, as well as the theatres for which they wrote, or are writing. Yet they both negotiate an inherited tradition: of theatrical representations of women, of the role of violence in drama, and of the conventions of dramatic form. They both exploit the energy of the character in performance to resist images of defeat in surrender to the social norms of femininity, or in suicide.

Women's role in theatre, whether as writers or performers, grows out of the dialectic between tradition and innovation. It is in this dialectic that the ambiguity lies, and that performance becomes definitive. Traditionally woman has been the icon, and not the iconmaker. When she becomes the creator of representations the woman playwright must negotiate the representational inheritance in relation to which she inevitably works.

In ways which have been definitive, women were made spectacles of in Irish theatre at the beginning of the twentieth century. The challenge for women playwrights has been to map theatrical landscapes in which their perceptions and experiences might create performances which mark their exile from the tropes and traps so robustly promoted by postcolonial cultural formation.

NOTES

1. Hélène Cixous, *Talking Liberties*, Interview with Jonathan Ree, Channel 4, 6 July 1992.
2. Seamus Deane, quoted in Terence Brown, *Ireland: A Social and Cultural History 1922–1985* (London: Fontana, 1985), 159.
3. Herbert Blau, 'Letting Be Be Finale of Seem: The Future of an Illusion', in Michel Benamou and Charles Caramello (eds.), *Performance in Postmodern Culture* (Madison: Coda Press, 1977), 76.
4. Teresa Deevy, *A Disciple* or *In Search of Valour*, *Dublin Magazine*, 12:1 (1937), 29–47.
5. J. M. Synge, *In the Shadow of the Glen*, in *Collected Works, Volume III: Plays, Book I*, ed. Ann Saddlemyer (Gerrards Cross: Colin Smythe, 1982), 31.
6. Adrienne Rich, 'Disloyal to Civilisation: Feminism, Racism, Gynephobia', in *On Lies, Secrets, and Silence: Selected Prose 1966–1978* (London: W. W. Norton, 1979), 287.
7. Teresa Deevy, *Katie Roche*, in *Three Plays* (London: Macmillan, 1939), 59.
8. *Sex in a Cold Climate* (Testimony Films for Channel 4, 1997). Inmates of the Magdalen Laundries were known as penitents. Their labour was symbolic: the purging of sin by the washing of linen. There were ten Magdalen Laundries in Ireland, run by orders of nuns such as the Sisters of Mercy. It is estimated that 30,000 women passed through the asylums during the twentieth century.
9. See Christopher Murray, 'Introduction: The Stifled Voice', in *Irish University Review*, 25:1 (1995), 7; and Judy Friel, 'Rehearsing Katie Roche', in the same issue of the *Irish University Review*, 117–25.
10. Henrik Ibsen, *Hedda Gabler*, translated by Christopher Hampton in *Hedda Gabler and A Doll's House* (London: Faber and Faber, 1989), 74.
11. Joseph Holloway, *Joseph Holloway's Irish Theatre, Volume II: 1932–1937*, ed. Robert Hogan and Michael J. O'Neill (Dixon, CA.: Proscenium Press, 1969), 52.
12. Jeananne Crowley, interview, Dublin, 13 January 1999.
13. Judy Friel, interview, Dublin, 1 November 1998.
14. Eavan Boland, *A Kind of Scar: The Woman Poet in a National Tradition* (Dublin: Attic Press, 1989), 8.

15. Marina Carr, *Portia Coughlan*, in *The Dazzling Dark*, selected by Frank McGuinness (London: Faber, 1996), 267.
16. See Anna McMullan, 'Marina Carr's Unhomely Women', in *Irish Theatre Magazine*, 1:1 (1998), 14–16.
17. See Riana O'Dwyer, 'The Imagination of Women's Reality: Christina Reid and Marina Carr', in Eamonn Jordan (ed.) *Theatre Stuff: Critical Essays on Contemporary Irish Theatre* (Dublin: Carysfort Press, 2000), 236–48.
18. Marina Carr, *By the Bog of Cats* (Oldcastle: Gallery Press, 1998), 58.
19. Melissa Sihra, 'A Cautionary Tale: Marina Carr's *By the Bog of Cats*', in *Theatre Stuff*, 261.

12

JOHN P. HARRINGTON

Samuel Beckett and the countertradition

At the very end of the twentieth century, more precisely on 22 December 1999, the Mayor of Paris, Jean Tiberi, unveiled a plaque renaming a portion of l'avenue René Coty in the fourteenth arrondissement of Paris in honour of Samuel Beckett. The plaque reads:

> Allée Samuel Beckett
> Foxrock 1906 – Paris 1989
> Ecrivain Irlandais
> Prix Nobel de Littérature

'Samuel Beckett Alley' seems especially appropriate for the writer whose most memorable characters were tramps lacking middle-class values and fond of off-colour jokes. But it is even more appropriate that at the end of the century the French government would recognize and certify that a writer living in France and often writing in French could nevertheless remain an Irish writer. The Irish government essentially did the same much earlier by establishing the Samuel Beckett Centre at his alma mater in Dublin, Trinity College, in 1981. At the end of the twentieth century Samuel Beckett's status as an Irish writer seemed so clear that the Irish critic Anthony Roche, in his study *Contemporary Irish Drama*, could state: 'the presiding genius of contemporary Irish drama, the ghostly founding father, is Samuel Beckett'.[1]

This status was not so clear when Beckett received the Nobel Prize for Literature in 1969. His most influential work had been the play composed at mid-century in French and titled *En attendant Godot*. The setting was specified only as an evening on a country road with a tree, and the play featured two vagabond characters named Vladimir and Estragon. This certainly was not so recognizably 'Irish' as the countryside setting of Synge's *The Playboy of the Western World* (1907) or the tenement of O'Casey's *Juno and the Paycock* (1924). Nor was it the kind of play imagined at the beginning of the century, in 1897, when Lady Gregory, W. B. Yeats and Edward Martyn proposed creating a new Irish drama, of great ambition, in order to create 'a Celtic and Irish school of dramatic literature' which would prove to the world that Ireland 'is not the home of buffoonery and of easy sentiment'.[2] The nature of Irish drama as imagined at the beginning of the twentieth century, the body of work which emerged over the twentieth century, and the place in it of the work of Samuel Beckett are all important dimensions of the history of modern Ireland as well as the history of its literature, dramatic and otherwise.

Gregory, Yeats and Martyn had imagined a single school of Irish drama which would reflect unanimity of values in a single, recognizable style. This would define the tradition of modern Irish drama. Soon work from Synge, O'Casey and others appeared which did seem to create a single school of Irish drama: focused on peasant or working-class characters, especially eloquent but ineffectual men and strong matriarchal figures. The style of production was realistic, often in carefully recreated kitchen settings, and the drama was text-based and language-driven. It was an international success, making the Abbey Theatre a model for other idealistic theatre projects and bringing it the first state subsidy for a national theatre in Europe. But any school of theatre focused enough to be recognized as a tradition would also exclude other visions. One of the first casualties of modern Irish drama as generally recognized was the work of W. B. Yeats, which was often expressionistic rather than realistic and organized on dance rather than text principles. Yeats admitted this late in life in his 'Introduction for My Plays': 'my audience was for comedy – for Synge, for Lady Gregory, for O'Casey – not for me. I was content.'[3]

Throughout the twentieth century there has been tension between the tradition of Irish drama and alternatives to it, and the current recognition of Samuel Beckett as an Irish writer admits this tension between tradition and countertraditions to the story of the national literature. Many prominent Irish writers before Beckett had resided principally outside Ireland, notably George Bernard Shaw, James Joyce, Sean O'Casey and even W. B. Yeats. Many theatre projects thrived in Dublin as alternatives to the Abbey. When the Irish Literary Theatre formed by Gregory, Yeats and Martyn opened its first season in 1899, it inspired immediately, in 1900, an alternative project from Maude Gonne and others called Inghinidhe na hÉireann (Daughters of Ireland), which challenged, among other things, the dominance of the English language on the Irish stage. Another of the founders, Edward Martyn, soon started his own alternative devoted to performance in Dublin of world drama in addition to Irish works. By 1919 the Abbey contributed its own alternative to the national theatre's emphasis on a single recognizable tradition by launching the Dublin Drama League, which staged experimental European dramas. Most famously, in 1928, Hilton Edwards and Micheál

Mac Liammóir founded the Gate Theatre, which quickly mounted Ibsen's *Peer Gynt*, a European masterpiece; then Oscar Wilde's *Salomé*, thus restoring to the Dublin repertoire an Irish writer outside the Abbey tradition; and then Denis Johnston's new play *The Old Lady Says 'No'!*, thus restoring to the Dublin repertoire an expressionistic kind of drama unacceptable to the Abbey. Many other countertraditional venues followed, including the Pike Theatre, in 1953, founded 'to present plays of all countries on all subjects, written from whatever viewpoint'.[4] This theatre produced the first Samuel Beckett play to be performed in Ireland, *Waiting for Godot*, in Dublin in 1955.

One of the beneficiaries of this tumult in Ireland of competing theatrical visions was the young Samuel Beckett. Born in 1906 in Foxrock, a rather affluent suburb to the south of Dublin city, Beckett was educated first at Portora Royal School in Co. Fermanagh, which during his time there was partitioned when Northern Ireland was created, and then, from 1923, or at the close of the Anglo-Irish War and the Irish Civil War, at Trinity College, Dublin. The decade of the 1920s was a distinguished one in the Abbey Theatre's history. Beckett is known to have been a regular attendee at the Abbey with classmates from Trinity. He remembered seeing revivals of the work of J. M. Synge, and he told his biographer James Knowlson that he was influenced by Synge's mix of pathos and humour, by a tragi-comic vision and by the distinctive theatrical language.[5] Others have reported Beckett's memories of seeing at the Abbey revivals of Sean O'Casey's first plays and productions of the plays of Lennox Robinson, T. C. Murray and W. B. Yeats.

In Dublin Beckett also became familiar with alternatives to this tradition of national theatre by attending productions of international classics such as the works of Ibsen, and also by enjoying the great local wealth of popular theatre, music hall and cinema, all of which had influence on his plays. However, his own theatrical vision was not created without experience of the most nationalist and most traditional forms of Irish drama. The Irish writer Anthony Cronin reports in his biography that Beckett attended the opening production of Sean O'Casey's *The Plough and the Stars* in 1926 on both the first and the second nights. On the latter Beckett saw W. B. Yeats enter the stage to confront protesters offended by the play's antinationalist sentiments. Referring to earlier protests over *The Playboy of the Western World*, Yeats imperiously scolded the crowd at the Abbey by telling them: 'You have disgraced yourselves again.'[6] All of this was certainly memorable to Beckett. In 1956, after *Waiting for Godot* had made him internationally famous, he was asked to contribute a greeting to a tribute to George Bernard Shaw on the centenary of his birth. Beckett graciously declined, choosing instead to celebrate, respectively, Yeats's *At the Hawk's Well*, Synge's *The*

Well of the Saints and O'Casey's *Juno and the Paycock* in these words: 'I wouldn't suggest that G. B. S. is not a great playwright, whatever that is when it's at home. What I would do is give the whole unupsettable apple-cart for a sup of the Hawk's Well, or the Saints', or a whiff of Juno, to go no further.'[7]

In 1928 Beckett, who had completed his Trinity degree in Romance languages, left Dublin for Paris, where he took a temporary position as lecturer at the Ecole Normale Supérieure. There he joined the circle of a large number of other young Irish intellectuals and writers interested in international rather than exclusively national issues and aesthetics. Among those who remained influences and friends of Beckett were the poet Denis Devlin and the writer, later Director of the National Gallery of Ireland, Thomas MacGreevy. The elder figure and mentor at the centre of this circle was James Joyce, then at work on *Finnegans Wake* and dependent, through eyesight problems and habit, on assistants for research and composition. In this Parisian context Beckett published his first works: a poem called *Whoroscope*, an essay on Joyce's project (then called 'Work in Progress') and the short story 'Assumption'. Even in Paris in the 1930s, however, Beckett would also write a series of essays on Irish subjects and Irish writers which has since been gathered in the collection *Disjecta: Miscellaneous Writings and a Dramatic Fragment*. Among them were a rather derisory survey of 'Recent Irish Poetry' and an essay on Sean O'Casey which praised his work for dramatic expression of 'knockabout': 'the principal of disintegration in even the most complacent solidities'.[8]

In the 1930s Beckett also published his first books of fiction, *More Pricks Than Kicks* (1934) and *Murphy* (1938). Both dismissed in parody the provincialism of the culture of the newly autonomous country officially designated the Irish Free State. In the novel *Murphy* this incisive parody of Irish culture and impatience with its perceived insularity was stated in quite specific reference to the national theatre. The last will and testament of the title character specifies that:

> With regard to the disposal of these my body, mind and soul, I desire that they be burnt and placed in a paper bag and brought to the Abbey Theatre, Lr. Abbey Street, Dublin, and without pause into what the great and good Lord Chesterfield calls the necessary house, where their happiest hours have been spent, on the right as one goes down into the pit, and I desire that the chain be there pulled upon them, if possible during the performance of a piece, the whole to be executed without ceremony or show of grief.[9]

Unlike Denis Devlin, for example, Beckett used direct references such as this to Irish literature, theatre and culture in order to express his dissatisfaction with its prioritizing a nationalist sense of heritage and identity. Unlike other writers of his generation, such as Thomas MacGreevy, Beckett never returned to Ireland for residence or repatriated his work into an exclusively Irish frame of reference. Thus his work can be termed a countertradition: an alternative vision which is not simply a departure from Irish traditions and practices but a departure fully formed by its dissent from the prevailing aesthetic. There were many influences on Samuel Beckett's drama, including important international ones such as the work of Arthur Adamov, Jean-Paul Sartre, Jean Genet and Antonin Artaud. Among those influences were his experience and intimate knowledge of modern Irish drama, which, in Beckett before most other Irish dramatists, became one influence among others and not a sole set of expectations and ambitions for creative work.

The great cataclysm of the mid-twentieth century, World War Two, was also the critical juncture in Beckett's work and in the path of the Irish nation. Ireland remained neutral in the war, and Beckett famously remarked that he preferred France at war to Ireland in peace. He and his companion, later wife, Suzanne Deschevaux-Dumesnil, fled Paris when it was occupied, returned, then with the onset of anti-Semitic imprisonments and executions fled again. In the course of these events Beckett joined a cell of the French Resistance, survived its betrayal, and for his contribution was decorated after the war with the Croix de Guerre and the Médaille de la Reconnaissance. Beckett and Suzanne returned to Paris at the end of the war in 1945.

Soon afterwards Beckett visited his mother in Dublin, and there and then, his biographers agree, after the war experience and at home again, he experienced a great artistic revelation. The experience would later be represented in his play *Krapp's Last Tape*, where the title character listens to himself at a younger age describing his revelation on tape: 'Spiritually a year of profound gloom and indigence until that memorable night in March, at the end of the jetty, in the howling wind, never to be forgotten, when suddenly I saw the whole thing. The vision at last . . . What I suddenly saw then was this . . .'[10] At that point the character in the play switches the tape off, choosing another more personal memory over the more revelatory one. Beckett explained to James Knowlson that 'Krapp's vision was on the pier at Dun Laoghaire; mine was in my mother's room' (*Damned to Fame*, 352). The nature of the revelation, articulated by Beckett, like Krapp, only indirectly, concerned the bankruptcy of most common organizing principles of life and of work and, consequently, awareness not of personal potentiality but of impotence, failure and ignorance. For Beckett every certainty of value, including assumptions about the intrinsic truth of personal or national identities or the informing truths of theologies or philosophies of life, would henceforth be open to sceptical examination. Corresponding to this philosophical revelation, in his literary work every artistic or theatrical principle, such as characterization, resolution or specificity of scene, would be broken. Much later, and in large part because of Beckett's work, Martin Esslin would invent the term 'Theatre of the Absurd' to describe this kind of drama. Esslin attributed this form of drama to the moment when 'the certitudes and unshakable basic assumptions of former ages have been swept away, that they have been found wanting . . . The Theatre of the Absurd has renounced arguing *about* the absurdity of the human condition; it merely *presents* it in being – that is, in terms of concrete stage images.'[11]

Ironically, Beckett's new understanding of philosophical failure empowered his greatest period of literary productivity and, ultimately, his artistic success. After the war and the revelation in Ireland he began to write in French. This, he said, would make it easier to write without style; that is, entirely apart from the linguistic qualities of French, composition in a second language would serve as a corrective to literary confidence and prevent polished performances of essentially bankrupt eloquence like, he evidently thought, his earlier work. Between 1945 and 1950, in a phase he called 'the siege in the room', Beckett wrote a first play, *Eleutheria*, which was not published in his lifetime; *En attendant Godot*, which would not be produced until later in French and then in English as *Waiting for Godot*; his extremely influential trilogy of novels later translated into English as *Molloy*, *Malone Dies* and *The Unnamable*; and a number of shorter works. Each was original in its total disregard for conventional rules: *Waiting for Godot*, for example, by its total disregard for dramatic development and its repetition in the second act of the situation in the first without resolution or conclusion. The German philosopher Theodor W. Adorno later described this sensibility as quintessentially part of the post-World War Two experience. In an essay devoted to a later Beckett play, 'Trying to Understand *Endgame*', Adorno described scepticism like Beckett's as a product of the horrors of war, holocaust and nuclear destruction; in his context, Adorno believed, the artist must eliminate any illusion of order provided by 'harmonious aesthetic meaning' and purge any 'reified residue of education' in order to describe experience in the new continuum.[12]

Among the certitudes being eroded simultaneously were those about the righteousness of the Irish nation and the artistic accomplishment of its national theatre. Although neutral during World War Two, Ireland could scarcely continue to insist on the sufficiency of the local vision only, or even cultural autonomy, in the context of the postwar economy. After the deaths of W. B. Yeats and of Lady Gregory, the Abbey Theatre had defined its tradition so well that fulfilment of its mission seemed to depend more on repetition than on novelty and experimentation. 'The Irish Play' had become a recognizable genre based on farm, family and religion which was increasingly distant from the realities of Irish life and frequently praised abroad in patronizing fashion. As early as 1937 international critics such as George Jean Nathan were criticizing the Abbey for being a caricature of its former greatness.

During World War Two a conflict between artists and managers at the theatre resulted in the appointment as Managing Director of Ernest Blythe, a government official who would remain in the post for more than a quarter of a century and during that time would attempt with some success to make the theatre more rather than less provincial. The theatre building burnt down in 1951, forcing the company to relocate to the oversized and decaying Queen's Theatre, where its repertoire and its presentation became, all theatre historians agree, mediocre. At the same time, in the 1950s, Dublin, if not the national theatre, experienced a vogue for continental plays and an increase of international commerce of all kinds. Brian Fallon has described the period as 'the old Franco-Irish pull' in which the Irish intelligentsia found it easier to commute to Paris than to live there, and the shuttling back and forth encouraged an international commerce of ideas in Ireland. 'The Joycean tradition of prolonged, voluntary, self-aware exile in France had gone, apparently for good, and though few people at the time recognised it Beckett was in fact the last in his line,' wrote Fallon. 'In this sense, the famous first night of *En attendant Godot* at the little Théâtre de Babylone in Paris on 3 January 1953 was, in retrospect, as much a terminus as a starting point.'[13]

Whatever the significance in terms of literary lifestyles, the opening of *Waiting for Godot* certainly was a radical starting point in both Beckett's work and in the history of modern drama. *Godot* is the most important play of the twentieth century whether judged so because it is found original and effective or because it is found symptomatic of the worst intellectual directions of the modern stage. In the years before its first production Beckett had two playscripts in circulation among the little theatres of Paris: *Godot* and *Eleutheria*. The second portrayed a character named Victor Krapp in a broad satire of contemporary stage devices, including a 'spectator' character on stage. The two plays were considered by the French actor and theatre manager Roger Blin, who was of interest to Beckett because of his successes with classic modernist dramas such as Strindberg's works and also with Irish works by Synge and Denis Johnston. Blin is said to have chosen *Godot* over *Eleutheria* because it had a smaller cast and so would be a more economical production; for whatever reasons, he chose an original conception over a satirical one. *Waiting for Godot* does not ridicule stage conventions but absolutely departs from them. On a country road, which is identified no more precisely, two characters named Vladimir and Estragon wait, without knowing why they wait, for a Mr Godot. A master, Pozzo, with a servant, Lucky, pass by. At the end of Act 1 a boy appears to tell them that Godot will not come that evening. The two characters are left confused and immobile. The second act repeats the situation, with the return of Pozzo and Lucky, with the news from the boy that Godot will not come that evening, and with a closing tableau of the immobile characters. In the course of each act the characters experiment with different ways of waiting, of passing time, such as dancing or thinking. But the only resolution, that fundamental principle of dramatic development, is that there is no resolution.

In retrospect *Godot* can be seen as compatible with Beckett's contemporary work, especially *Molloy*, *Malone Dies* and *The Unnamable*, and the ways he described his revelation in Ireland after World War Two. 'The end', Beckett explained to his Dublin friend Alec Reid, 'is to give artistic expression to something hitherto almost ignored – the irrational state of unknowingness where we exist' (*Last Modernist*, 457). The simplicity of the presentation, with a small cast, austere set and minimal distractions, was a perfect style for an unflinching study of the possibility that sustaining certitudes may be illusions. In the early 1950s, however, Beckett was not widely known, and so the originality of *Waiting for Godot* was itself revelatory: enthusiasm for its conceptual quality grew in Paris, and productions of Beckett's own English translation in London and New York exploited the sensational dimensions of a work reputed to be an exercise in absolute nihilism. Postperformance discussions were popular, with audiences hoping to decode symbolism of impenetrable obscurity, and well-known intellectuals offered verdicts on whether the play was a work of genius or a fraud. The author became a celebrity whose intellectuality was rumoured to have come from past service as James Joyce's secretary.

The play met with the same puzzled and intrigued reception in Ireland when it opened at the Pike Theatre in Dublin in 1955. In its first Irish production *Waiting for Godot* ran for more than a year, transferred from the Pike to the larger and more famous Gate Theatre, and then toured country towns. It was soon translated into the Irish language as *Ag Fanacht Le Godot*. Irish audiences claimed to detect subtle nuances which would be lost on French, English and other audiences, and this claim seems even more credible decades later when the Gate Theatre and its company of Irish actors have become recognized by the world as preeminent interpreters of Beckett's work.

Like *Waiting for Godot*, Beckett's next major play, *Endgame*, was composed in French, as *Fin de partie*. Through a complicated series of scheduling coincidences, the French play was first performed in London, at the Royal Court Theatre on 3 April 1957. Like *Godot*, which includes multiple passing references to Irish places and things, *Endgame* is set in a vaguely European context which is not Ireland and not any other recognizable place. Against the tradition in Irish drama of quite specific local references, Beckett's drama is distinctively vague in regard to scene and setting. At the time of the composition of the first French version of *Endgame*, Beckett also composed, in English, a dramatic fragment called 'The Gloaming' and the radio play *All That Fall*, which was first broadcast by the BBC on 13 January 1957. The first centred on an autobiographical image of fishing in Dublin Bay with his father, while the second, which is quite specifically set in Foxrock and its surroundings, concerns a Mrs Rooney and others in a middle-class and suburban Ireland maintaining modest fictions to offset larger anxieties.

Endgame, which presents the dominant-submissive relationship of Hamm and Clov, eliminated autobiographical dimensions which would distract from the harsh representation of postwar helplessness, which is also suggested by the title allusion to the final stages of a chess match. Though many have pointed to similarities between *Endgame* and works such as Yeats's *At the Hawk's Well* and Synge's *The Well of the Saints*, the accomplishment of Beckett's theatrical representation is better understood by noting the personal and cultural elements he removed: having composed personal expressions of passivity and pessimism in 'The Gloaming' and *All That Fall*, Beckett extricated from those works a more impersonal image of vulnerability most expressive, as Adorno wrote, of the postwar experience.

While Beckett's major plays resist the specificity of place and locality associated with Irish drama, they never fully eliminate the specifically Irish context, and in this tension they find their place as a countertradition to modern Irish drama. *Krapp's Last Tape*, for example, was composed in English and in its earliest drafts was called 'Magee Monologue' for Patrick Magee, an Irish actor whom Beckett had heard in radio adaptations of his own work. The play, which opened in London in 1958, presents the image of an old man listening to himself when younger on a tape recorder describing, among other things, the revelation on the pier that is a fictionalized version of Beckett's at his mother's home. The play refers to several places in Ireland, though in revisions Beckett attempted to minimize autobiographical references, many of which have since been redocumented.

So, too, in *Happy Days*, which presents the image of a woman half-concealed in a mound, then nearly fully concealed, the concluding piece of music was first planned as 'When Irish Eyes Are Smiling'. That song was later dropped in favour of a waltz from *The Merry Widow* as a means of minimizing personal, cultural and national contexts which would distract from the central conception of a person seeking the fortitude necessary to survive intimations of doom. *Happy Days* was first produced in New York, in 1961, though the first production with which Beckett was closely associated was in London in 1964 while he was spending considerable time with Irish actors including Jack MacGowran as well as Magee. Hence the prohibition on 'style' to be sought by composing in French was never complete, and Beckett in the many shorter dramatic works which would follow, as well as in his fiction, continued to vacillate between direct reference to Ireland and analogical representation of it as a place like others.

After the opening of *Endgame* in London, Beckett was arranging for its Dublin premiere at the Pike Theater, as well as a staged reading there of *All That Fall*, and performance of his mime *Act Without Words* (which is usually published with *Endgame*), as part of the Dublin International Theatre Festival of 1958. However, the archbishop of Dublin, who was to open the festival by celebrating Mass, objected to planned performances of Sean O'Casey's *Drums of Father Ned* as anticlerical and to a stage adaptation of parts of Joyce's *Ulysses* as obscene. Beckett was in Dublin at the time to accept an honorary degree from Trinity College. When he learnt that festival organizers had withdrawn the O'Casey and Joyce works because of the archbishop's objections, Beckett withdrew his own work in protest and announced an author's ban of all his works in the country of his birth. Alan Simpson of the Pike Theatre was understandably dismayed. Beckett wrote to him: 'As long as such conditions prevail in Ireland I do not wish my work to be performed there, either in festivals or outside them. If no protest is heard they will prevail for ever. This is the strongest I can make' (*Damned to Fame*, 448).

The ban was not entirely successful because of great interest in Beckett's work among both student groups, including one at his alma mater, and other theatre professionals such as Cyril Cusack, who was mounting a production of *Krapp's Last Tape*. The playwright lifted the ban in 1960. In that same year Beckett contributed a tribute to O'Casey to the *Irish Times* on the occasion of the elder Irish playwright's eightieth birthday. Like that of Shaw, Joyce and Yeats, as well as O'Casey, Beckett's involvement in Irish literary and theatrical activities was not compromised by his miles from Dublin.

A further indication of a mid-century phase in Irish drama much broader than the tradition represented by the Abbey Theatre solely is the parallel example of Brendan Behan. Behan's public personality was as ebullient and excessive as Beckett's was solemn and austere. Behan's orbit, once he became a celebrity playwright on a par with Beckett, linked Dublin to London and New York, as Beckett's did to Paris. Behan's first important plays were composed in the Irish language, as Beckett's were in French. The two met several times, usually in Paris with Beckett as patient host. While there appears to have been no direct influence between their works, both Dublin playwrights, at mid-century, found as their most resonant stage conception an absent character, much discussed, who never appears onstage. This coincidence links Behan's *The Quare Fellow*, staged at the Pike Theatre in Dublin in November 1954, and Beckett's *Waiting for Godot*, staged at the Pike in October 1955.

There are other parallels between their works, but perhaps the greatest comparative significance of their quite different careers is their illustration of the breadth and variety of Irish theatre practices and the reminder that the tradition is not sufficiently represented, even at mid-century, by the works associated with the Abbey Theatre. In a long discussion of related devices and themes in the works of Beckett and Behan, Anthony Roche has observed how these parallel production histories illustrate dimensions of cosmopolitanism not often associated with Irish drama. On the productions of *The Quare Fellow* and *Waiting for Godot*, respectively, at the Pike, Roche notes: 'The first drew the attention of Joan Littlewood at Stratford East and subsequently enabled an Irish playwright like Behan to go international; the second enabled an international play like *Godot* to come home, to find a large local audience in a remarkably short time . . . and through their dual effect a new kind of Irish drama can be seen emerging' (41).

The generation of Irish playwrights who have followed Beckett – especially Brian Friel, Tom Murphy, Thomas Kilroy and Frank McGuinness – have all expressed appreciation of his work without citing it as a direct influence on their own. Beckett as playwright stands as an example to them of options outside the narrowest expectations of what constitutes Irish drama, and the potential of an Irish playwright to exist within both national and international contexts. Those four playwrights have become international figures by virtue of their theatrical practice – opening plays outside Ireland and working within a theatrical infrastructure of directors, casts, designers and business managers who are not Irish. The sense in which the example of Beckett the playwright opened options for them was expressed best by Frank McGuinness, in New York, opening *Someone Who'll Watch Over Me* (1992), a play which does not at all follow expectations of Irish drama's portrayal of the national life at home. 'After Beckett, nothing in the theatre was the same, particularly for Irish playwrights,' McGuinness said. 'He gave me license to write about time.'[14]

A still younger generation of Irish playwrights have moved further in internationalist directions in their theatrical practices and also become more directly influenced by Beckett's work in their own. A playwright such as Marina Carr has written plays in imitation of Beckett (*Low in the Dark* [1989]); others such as Tom Mac Intyre have produced works like Beckett's that are more grounded in movement and image than in text; and still others, like Conor McPherson, have, following Beckett, worked extensively in the form of monologue. Their work has also been influenced by the consistent presence in Dublin theatres of Beckett's work through the efforts of both the Samuel Beckett Centre at Trinity College and the Gate Theatre.

It is perhaps inevitable that at the start of the twenty-first century Samuel Beckett can epitomize Irish drama as much as W. B. Yeats did at the beginning of the century. In his acceptance of the loss of his audience to the writers of comedy, quoted at the opening of this chapter, Yeats assumed there was a single audience for a single kind of Irish drama which was produced by Irish writers for Irish audiences. This was consistent with the optimism of a new national state establishing its autonomy by counteracting colonialism. But the century since then has shown that Ireland was not immune to European and world crises, that separatist policies such as neutrality may prove to be forms of entanglement, that there are distinct constituencies of the state formed by gender and sexual orientations, and that the certitudes of nationalist confidence such as governmental and clerical integrity may, as Martin Esslin wrote in connection with the Theatre of the Absurd, 'be tested and found wanting' (Theatre of the Absurd, 23). Irish drama, by incorporation of both its tradition, as represented by Synge and O'Casey, and its countertradition, as epitomized by Beckett and his younger admirers, establishes its national identity in an international context and so claims its place in the history of the twentieth century.

NOTES

1. Anthony Roche, *Contemporary Irish Drama: From Beckett to McGuinness* (Dublin: Gill and Macmillan, 1994), 5.
2. Lady Gregory, *Our Irish Theatre* (Gerrards Cross: Colin Smythe, 1972), 20.
3. William Butler Yeats, 'An Introduction for my Plays', *Essays and Introductions* (London: Macmillan, 1961), 529–30.
4. Michael O'Sullivan, *Brendan Behan: A Life* (Boulder, CO: Roberts Rinehart, 1999), 175.
5. James Knowlson, *Damned to Fame: The Life of Samuel Beckett* (London: Bloomsbury, 1996), 56–7.
6. Anthony Cronin, *Samuel Beckett: The Last Modernist* (London: Harper Collins, 1996), 56–7.
7. James Knowlson, *Samuel Beckett: An Exhibition* (London: Turret Books, 1971), 14.
8. Samuel Beckett, *Disjecta: Miscellaneous Writings and a Dramatic Fragment*, ed. Ruby Cohn (London: John Calder, 1983), 82.
9. Samuel Beckett, *Murphy* (London: John Calder, 1963), 183.
10. Samuel Beckett, *Krapp's Last Tape and Embers* (London: Faber and Faber, 1958), 20–1.

11. Martin Esslin, *The Theatre of the Absurd* (Harmondsworth: Penguin, 3rd edition, 1980), 23–5.
12. Theodor W. Adorno, 'Trying to Understand *Endgame*', trans. Michael T. Jones, *New German Critique* 20 (1982), 120–1.
13. Brian Fallon, *An Age of Innocence: Irish Culture 1930–1960* (Dublin: Gill and Macmillan, 1998), 131.
14. Bruce Weber, 'On Stage and Off', *New York Times*, 26 February 1993, C2.

13

HELEN LOJEK

Brian Friel's sense of place

In Ireland place always matters. Unsurprisingly, place also matters in the plays of Brian Friel, widely regarded as the island's most successful contemporary playwright, both artistically and commercially. His best-known plays are set in or near Ballybeg (*Baile Beag*, literally 'small town'), an imaginary Donegal town with a significance in Irish literature comparable to the significance of William Faulkner's Yoknapawtapha in American literature. Plays not actually set there usually take place near by. His work maps the northwest corner of Ireland, an area of small towns and rural landscapes, sliced by the border partitioning the island. The plays also map the course of Irish concerns during the late twentieth century. Additionally they map internal, psychic realities of love, family, failure, and the struggle between faith and doubt. Friel picks up the challenge set by the hedge-schoolmaster, Hugh, in *Translations* (1980): 'We must learn where we live.'[1]

Born in Co. Tyrone (Northern Ireland) in 1929, Friel moved with his family to nearby Derry in 1939. Following his graduation from St Columb's College in Derry (also the alma mater of Nobel Laureates John Hume and Seamus Heaney), Friel attended St Patrick's College, Maynooth (in the Irish Republic) and then took teacher-training courses in Belfast. For ten years he taught in Derry. In 1967 he moved six miles from Derry, to Muff, Co. Donegal (in the Republic), and in 1982 he moved further into the Republic, to Greencastle. Throughout the 1980s he was actively involved with the Derry-based Field Day Theatre Company. His personal and professional lives, then, have involved a constant crossing of borders. Derry, the town with which he is closely associated even though he has not lived there for many years, is particularly aware of borders, since partition separated it from much of the northwest it had traditionally served as the major urban centre. Derry is a community of balanced factions: unionist/republican, Protestant/Catholic, English/Irish, colonizers/colonized, urban/rural, haves/have-nots, past/present. Friel's plays are marked by awareness of such factions and boundaries, both geographic and personal. Communities are divided, opinions clash, memories vary, individuals struggle with internal splits. His twenty full-length stage plays map Ireland's divided self.

As a teacher Friel began writing short stories, plays and newspaper pieces. With a *New Yorker* magazine 'right of first refusal' contract and £250 in the bank he stopped teaching, and since 1960 he has made a living as a writer, dropping other genres to concentrate on plays. As a dramatist he has become a powerful force in Irish life and letters, writing in the belief that 'Irish dramatists . . . are talking to ourselves as we must and if we are overheard in America or England, so much the better.'[2]

Philadelphia, Here I Come! (1964) was not Friel's first play, but it was his first real success, and it is the only play from the early period that he chose to include in the 1984 *Selected Plays*. The play was an immediate result of several months Friel spent at the Tyrone Guthrie Theatre in Minneapolis. Director Guthrie, whose family roots were in Co. Monaghan close to Friel's home, gave the playwright a chance to observe rehearsals, and Friel describes witnessing the 'performing side of the art of theatre' and the 'inspired co-ordination' of Guthrie's direction as like 'an explosion in the head'.[3] Friel's only lengthy stay outside Ireland seems also to have sharpened his perspective on home. It yielded a sea-change in his skill and confidence as a writer, and *Philadelphia* became the first Ballybeg play and the first Friel classic.

Philadelphia is set in 1960s Ballybeg. Gareth O'Donnell, like so many real Irish youths of that time, is set to emigrate. Gar is eager to escape the limitations of life in Ireland: the taciturn father who cannot show affection, the girl who married another, the friends caught in a state of perpetual adolescence, the job with little present and no future. The United States represents the proverbial land of opportunity for Gar, but in order to pursue that opportunity he will have to leave the father and the country he – however they madden him – loves deeply. The play catches Gar at the moment of absolute and irreversible transition from one life to another, and he is intelligent enough to sense what that transition will mean. This standard scenario is located in the most conventional of Irish stage sets – the kitchen of a house in the west. Friel's genius is to take stock characters in conventional situations and locations and explode them before audiences can settle into comfortable familiarity.

The set includes not only the public space of the kitchen, but also the private space of Gar's bedroom and a fluid, undelineated space which represents all other locations. Quiet, polite, ordinary Gar Public is balanced by his alter ego, the sardonic, flip, irreverent Gar Private, who first reveals himself in the privacy of the bedroom but later wanders at will, since only Gar Public is able to see him.[4] Public and Private are played by different actors and are not identical, but they are always together and are parts of a whole. Friel's divided stage and divided character incarnate divisions embedded in a particular time and place, and the play is often discussed as a play of emigration. *Philadelphia* is a careful study of small-town, mid-century western Ireland: jobs are scarce; the parish priest fails to make sense of life; the pompous, pub-bound schoolmaster has a mind gone to waste in a stultifying atmosphere; harsh economics make May–December unions common; returning Irish-Americans are sentimental about a world which never was.

The emotions which animate these characters, though, are hardly limited to the play's time and place, and *Philadelphia* is not local-colour drama. Friel's 1972 essay 'Plays Peasant and Unpeasant' (*Essays, Diaries*, 51–6) outlines the limitations of Irish 'cottage' drama, but commentary is not necessary to reveal a richness in this play which goes beyond its consideration of emigration. This is a play about love: Gar's love of his country, his father, his girl, his mothering housekeeper. He fails in all of these loves. He cannot discover a way to make a life in Ballybeg, or to break through his father's reticence. He lacks the nerve to speak to Kate's father, and so loses her to an older man. He does not even seem to realize Madge's love for him.

Failure in love is accompanied by the failure of memory. Madge and Lizzy do not remember Gar's dead mother in the same way, and Gar has no memories at all. He and his father have different memories of the same fishing trip. Failures in love and memory are accompanied by the failures of religion and education. Even emigration will, inevitably, fail. The move which promises to change Gar's life completely will not. Madge, wise in the ways of the O'Donnells, believes Gar will end up just like his father (as Kate's marriage repeats the pattern of Gar's mother's marriage). 'Ireland – America – what's the difference?' asks the American visitor.[5] The play suggests no answer.

For a play about so many failures, *Philadelphia* is remarkably funny, and the good humour is often what audiences respond to most immediately and remember longest. Friel is fond of quoting Brendan Behan saying that the playwright should keep people laughing for five minutes 'and then in the sixth minute, when they're helpless laughing, you plug your message, if you want to plug a message' (*Essays, Diaries*, 6). He also insists that 'the tragedy of theatre is that one assumes that if you laugh, you're being silly' (*Friel in Conversation*, 63). *Philadelphia*, a play full of songs and sardonic jokes and deliberately outrageous fantasies, keeps audiences laughing for the requisite five minutes. It is not, however, a silly play. It may not have a 'message' as such, but it is serious, and angry, about the restrictions of Gar's world, about the failures of his religion and his education, about the limitations of his parents. And it is serious about the difficulties of growing, anywhere, from a boy into a man.

There is an autobiographical element in some of the play's anger. The child of a teacher and a teacher himself, Friel nevertheless speaks harshly of the education he was given:

> For about fifteen years I was taught by a succession of men who force-fed me with information, who cajoled me, beat me, threatened me, coaxed me to swallow their puny little pies of knowledge and attitudes.
>
> And the whole thing, I know now, was an almost complete waste of time . . . I'm certainly not blaming these grim men who prodded me through examinations . . . But surely this isn't education? . . . on second thoughts I am slightly resentful. (*Essays, Diaries*, 39–40)

He can be equally stern about Catholicism, particularly as he encountered it at Maynooth: 'An awful experience, it nearly drove me cracked. It is one thing I want to forget. I never talk about it – the priesthood. You know the kind of Catholicism we have in this country: it's unique' (*Essays, Diaries*, 1). And Friel shares with Gar the pain of an important memory which cannot be confirmed and thus calls into question the entire relationship of past and present, memory and reality. Concluding that his own memory of a fishing trip with his father is unverifiable, Friel decides: 'The fact is a fiction . . . [But] I don't think it matters. What matters is that for some reason . . . this vivid memory is there in the storehouse of the mind. For some reason the mind has shuffled the pieces of verifiable truth and composed a truth of its own' (*Essays, Diaries*, 39).

Philadelphia did well in Dublin and New York. There was talk of making it into a film. Friel's next plays, *The Loves of Cass McGuire* (1966) *Lovers (Winners/Losers)* (1967), *Crystal and Fox* (1968) and *The Mundy Scheme* (1969) were more modest successes. *The Gentle Island* (1971), an underrated play, was a solid success despite the Troubles which increasingly disrupted Irish life. All in all Friel seemed settled in the position of a modestly successful playwright who had had a brief international run.

In the late 1960s Friel occasionally participated in Northern Irish civil rights demonstrations aimed at securing equal employment and housing rights. When British troops killed fourteen unarmed marchers in Derry in 1972, on what became known as Bloody Sunday, though, the playwright had recourse not to the power of demonstration, but to the power of the pen. *The Freedom of the City* (1973) addresses contemporary Irish politics more directly than any other Friel play, and Irish discussions of the relationship of art and politics invariably bring mention of *Freedom*.

In the strictest sense *Freedom* is not specifically about Bloody Sunday, since Friel carefully sets the play in 1970, before the Derry killings with which it is so closely associated. But the location is identified as Derry city, and the Guildhall is a recognizable Derry landmark. The play opens with a photographer taking pictures of a priest waving a white handkerchief and ministering to fallen bodies – a reminder of one of the best-known photographs of Bloody Sunday. In general the play's random, inexplicable shootings so closely resemble actual events that it is often referred to as 'Friel's Bloody Sunday Play'. Outside the Irish community, where Bloody Sunday is less known and discussed, the play has not enjoyed the same success it has in Ireland. In England it is often regarded as a 'green' or Republican view of events; in the United States it is hardly known. As events of 1972 recede and gain a clearer shape in the historical memory, perhaps *Freedom* will gain the wider audience it deserves. If that happens the play's examination of the falsity of imposing *any* shape on history will be an important reminder not to over-simplify the past. Friel's play is rooted in a specific conflict in a specific place, but the human and philosophical queries it poses are not confined to Derry city or to the 1970s.

The play begins at the end, with the dead bodies onstage, so there is never any doubt about how things will turn out. Audiences wonder not 'What will happen?', but 'What does this mean?' As they seek to sort out that meaning, they are in precisely the position of the 'official' commentators whose jargon-studded voices attempt to confine individual experience within a variety of accepted dogmas. In an effective piece of social satire Friel makes the judge English and the sociologist American, but there are a host of Irish commentators to go wrong as well. The commentators are literally as well as metaphorically outside the experience of the ordinary people in the Guildhall. Friel is again using divided stage space to point to themes and divisions in the world of the play. Lilly, Michael and Skinner have taken refuge in the Guildhall, and they are indeed safer in this enclosed world than they would be outside. The refuge is also a trap, and they will need to exit eventually and confront the dangers, but they are most free when they are confined in the Guildhall, where they create a world and a community completely divorced from exterior violence and from commenting voices. Stage space outside the Guildhall is open and unconfined, and this script, like *Philadelphia*, uses lighting to change locales and emphasize different commentators.

As character after character directs towards the audience an analysis of events, viewers are drawn into decision-making, becoming in turn jury, television audience, congregation, sociology class and drinkers listening to a pub balladeer. Astute audiences will recognize that no version approaches reality, though each has elements of validity. *Freedom* also suggests that the truth, if there is one, hovers as far beyond the formulations of a playwright as it does beyond the formulations of these commentators.

The official wisdom of the commentators is balanced by the uneducated, inarticulate voices of the protesters (protesters only in the loosest of ways, since they are all uncertain why they came along at all). Incapable of discerning motive or meaning in their own experiences, they are nevertheless blessed with voices which ring with vigour, authenticity and individuality. Their mocking, cynical, chaotic view of life is richly humorous and acutely perceptive – engaged where the commentators are detached. Audiences may be cast in the role of jury or congregation, but most will yearn to be inside the Guildhall, where three random strangers are having fun building a community and defying the forces which have previously dominated them. The major characters understand and articulate their feelings better than is strictly believable given their limited education and experience, but it is the comedy and the parodic wit for which they are most remembered. Once more, laughter is not the same thing as silliness.

In the Mayor's parlour in the Guildhall, Lily and Skinner and Michael react to the emblems of power and hierarchy. The Union Jack, the baroque chair, the ceremonial sword, the official papers and portraits – all represent established, oppressive, inescapable authority. It is no wonder that these three very different individuals, brought together by the randomness of events they do not understand, are ultimately united by their desire to defy such authority. The postcolonial analysis which has been such an important source of understanding in consideration of Friel's plays provides an interesting perspective on the divisions in the world of *Freedom*.[6] Because the play allows appreciation of and identification with Lily, Skinner and Michael, they emerge as the most distinguished of those who sign the Distinguished Visitors Book. In prompting this realization Friel provides entry into the world of people typically excluded from the pages of history.

Arguing against free directorial rein, Friel often describes scripts as analogous to musical scores which should just be 'played'. Explaining why he does adaptations of works by others, he points to the dangers of using in Ireland 'a score written for English voices and sung by English actors'.[7] Such musical analogies are helpful in considering *Freedom*, since the divisions and contrasts in it are revealed by accent. The measured vowels of the television commentator resonate against the English accent of the judge and the American accent of the sociologist. The priest's northern accent sings in a different key. These voices counterpoint the vibrant, ordinary Derry accents of those inside the Guildhall. The visual divisions of stage space are matched by aural divisions in voices.

In *The Gentle Island* (1971) Friel puts characters in situations where (like Gar in *Philadelphia*) they must balance different memories of the same event, or where they must confront alternative interpretations of events. As Manus says, 'every story has seven faces'.[8] In *Freedom* Friel provides a variety of faces for the story of Bloody Sunday. It is a technique he will use later in very different situations, and it is a recognizable sign of the extent to which his world is one of few certainties and many divisions.

Volunteers (1975) was inspired by debates about the destruction of Viking sites in Dublin in order to erect commercial and public buildings. Like the Viking poems of Seamus Heaney (to whom this play is dedicated), *Volunteers* seeks to dig deep through the rubble, to excavate pieces of the Irish past and examine how they fit with the Irish present. Prisoners on daily parole dig through layers of Georgian cellars and Norman debris to reveal the foundations of a tenth-century Viking house. The Viking house provides a metaphoric as well as a literal foundation for all subsequent layers, including the luxury hotel which will eventually occupy the site. The present builds literally as well as figuratively on the past. The Volunteers of the title are imprisoned for a vague mix of crimes, but their name recalls the Volunteers of the 1916 Rising. The waves of ruins reflect the waves of colonizers who have swept over the island: Vikings and Normans and the English who built Georgian homes – and the Americans, those economic colonists who tour the site and to whom the hotel will cater. Like *The Mundy Scheme*, this play examines the impact of commercialism on Ireland, and it is no accident that Keeney's name reminds us of the lamentation expressed in an Irish keen. This play may be set on the opposite side of the island from Ballybeg, but it, too, involves a deep concern for place.

Like the protesters in *Freedom*, the prisoners occupy a deeply ambiguous space, involving elements of both imprisonment and freedom. They are divided from the prisoners who refused to cooperate with the official excavation, and who will kill them when the dig is over. They are equally divided from the privileged men who supervise them, and whose English names are reminders of ongoing issues of colonialism. The prisoners also realize that every story has seven faces: each offers a specific, convincing story to explain the skull they have named Leif. It hardly matters that the stories cannot all be true, since their major function is not to reveal reality but to create explanations. That those explanations are largely fabricated does not blunt the necessity for their comfort. People need the protection of shape; they cherish the implication that experience is understandable. The stories are 'explanations' as strained and mutually exclusive as the explanations for Bloody Sunday offered in *Freedom*, and Keeney's parody of the visiting schoolteacher's lecture is another clear rejection of official explanations.

Living Quarters (1977) moves back to Ballybeg, the true home of Friel's imagination, to examine again not the way in which divisions and ambiguities affect the lives of people caught up in public events, but how they affect ordinary Irish people far from the centres of power and off the historical record. Family members return in imagination and memory to a key day in their private lives. Sir, the God-like keeper of the 'ledger' of history, sets out to 'organize' their recollections, to 'impose a structure on them, just to give them a form of sorts'.[9] The Butler family members think they want this definitive shape, but in the end each insists on retaining a particular 'face' of the story, and each seeks to modify Sir's supposedly authoritative version. Friel's plot may be 'after Hippolytus', but his characters are (uneasily) in search of an author.

Aristocrats (1979), which continues the exploration of Ballybeg, is one of the Friel plays often described as 'Chekhovian'. It foregrounds the private, the familial, the personal – as opposed to the public or political. *Philadelphia* exploded a series of stock characters and situations; *Aristocrats* has at its centre a stock Irish locale, the 'big house'. The decline of the Anglo-Irish big house is a persistent theme in Irish literature, and Friel here weds that stock theme to some of his own favourite dramatic devices and themes. The ragged lawn outside the O'Donnell house (which has very little relationship to the O'Donnell cottage in *Philadelphia*), for example, has been in turn a croquet lawn and a tennis court. The stage directions specify that 'no trace of these activities remains',[10] but traces remain in the memories of the O'Donnells who grew up there, and who play croquet again in their imaginations. The lawn thus functions as a family archaeological site parallel to the cultural archaeological site in *Volunteers*.

An American academic reminiscent of the sociologist in *Freedom* seeks to make sense of the family and its history, 'to record the truth', but the family's 'remembrance of things past' defeats his effort, because their memories do not coincide. 'There are', says Eamon, 'certain things, certain truths . . . that are beyond Tom's kind of scrutiny' (*Selected Plays*, 309–10). These truths are not the same for everyone, but they are truths deeply rooted in place – not just in the lawn outside the crumbling big house, but in Donegal itself. They are the truths of divisions: among family members, among classes, between past and present, between staying and emigrating.

The power of place to move Friel's imagination was evident from his earliest writing, and *Aristocrats* warrants comparison with early short stories such as 'Foundry House' and 'Among the Ruins'. The power of place for Friel is also evident in the extraordinary productivity of the years 1977–80, during which four major plays, all set in Ballybeg, premiered. Regardless of period or social/economic status, characters in these Ballybeg plays are shaped by realities of place: they are isolated, cut off from the outside world, misshapen by claustrophobic atmospheres; they are also nurtured, enriched, enfolded by places and people they love. In this divided world communication, even between those who love each other, is so difficult that characters seek ways of communicating without words. In *Aristocrats* a shared love of classical music unites those whom words often divide. In other plays other nonverbal communications help compensate for the painful reticence characters demonstrate.

Faith Healer (1979) takes two major Friel themes – the unreliability of memory and the difficulty of communication – and uses them as structural devices for the entire play. The three main characters have shared years on the road, but they communicate poorly with each other and their versions of the years vary considerably. Each speaks in turn to the audience. Frank, the suggestively named faith healer, speaks twice. His wife and manager each speak once. Whatever the awkwardness of their communications with each other, and it seems to have been considerable, they deluge the audience with a flood of words and memories. Audiences are left to sort through conflicts and contradictions to find whatever essence of truth there is, to attempt the sorting out of healing and sickness, faith and disbelief. In some ways the play is another parallel with Faulkner, with whom Friel has acknowledged a similarity in the ongoing exploration of a fictional place. Faulkner's *The Sound and the Fury* is also structured around four monologues, each rehearsing events from a different viewpoint. The monologues of *Faith Healer*, though, are not internal monologues but crafted stories, directed at the audience, and they are most clearly linked to the storytelling tradition of the Irish shanachie (*seannachie*). The play's experimental form is a traditional expression of place.[11]

Fifteen years later Friel returned to similar themes and forms in *Molly Sweeney* (1994), a second Ballybeg tale of faith and healing. *Molly Sweeney*'s monologues are shorter and more interspersed, but they have the same storytelling form. The plays make great demands on audiences and actors. They preserve suspense by reserving full disclosure of the 'end' of things until the final curtain. And like all of Friel's Ballybeg tales, these are tales of failure mitigated by triumphs of the human spirit.

In 1980 Friel and the actor Stephen Rea founded Field Day Theatre Company, whose name echoes Friel-Rea. (Field Day's history is detailed elsewhere in this volume.) Friel's *Translations*, their first production, continues the author's concern with place. It reflects both his personal history (his grandfather was a hedge-schoolmaster; both grandparents were native Irish speakers; Friel and his father were both teachers) and the locale where he had chosen to live (his home in Muff was close to the camp the British army used during its 1830s mapping of Donegal). Friel described this Ballybeg (which he associated with the town of Urris) as 'a dying climate – no longer quickened by its past' (*Essays, Diaries*, 75). The play premiered symbolically in Derry's Guildhall, the setting for *The Freedom of the City*. '[T]his is theirs, boy, and your very presence here is a sacrilege,'[12] declared Skinner in that play, but the building (by then ringed with protective barbed wire because of the Troubles) opened its doors to Field Day in 1980 and housed the company's offices for some time.

Translations excavates the layers of language in Ireland, as *Volunteers* and *Aristocrats* excavate other layers. And it reflects the confusions and divisions of an area split by language and colonialism. Ballybeg in the 1830s was as restricted an environment as Gar O'Donnell found it in the 1960s. The characters' physical problems (lameness, muteness, alcoholism) indicate the deformities of their interior lives. Emigration is a constant temptation. Communication is so difficult that only the lovers, who do not share a language, have discovered how to understand each other. For all this, Ballybeg is deeply rooted in their hearts, and difficult to leave. The play has clear resonances for twentieth-century Ireland, but it does not take sides, urging instead avoidance of the trap of outmoded mental or linguistic landscapes. The origins of Friel (whose background is Catholic) and Rea (whose background is Protestant) on opposite sides of Derry's cultural divide had a symbolic importance emphasized not only by the Guildhall premiere, but also by funding from Arts Councils on both sides of the border and by Field Day's deliberate and publicized incorporation of actors (including Liam Neeson and Rea himself) with roots in the area. The play's impact and appeal are hardly limited to Derry and its environs, however, or even to Ireland. *Translations* has succeeded in most English-speaking countries – and in many countries where the play itself required translation. As Frank Rich observed in a review of *Aristocrats*, 'Mr Friel makes the Irish condition synonymous with the human one' (*Friel in Conversation*, 199).

Translations's sense of place is wedded to sorrow. *The Communication Cord* (1982), which also premiered at Derry's Guildhall and toured Ireland, weds its sense of place to farce. Ballybeg in the hands of the professional preservationists is not a pretty sight, but Friel makes it an amusing one. *Making History* (1988), Friel's meditation on how history has remembered Hugh O'Neill, a sixteenth-century earl of Tyrone, had a similar premiere and production history. The plays touring were dubbed 'Friels on Wheels'.

It was *Dancing at Lughnasa* (1990), though, which demonstrated Ballybeg's phenomenal appeal for the world. The play (which was not a Field Day production) had an astounding success in Dublin, London and New York, winning a variety of prizes including both Olivier and Tony awards for Best Play. Meryl Streep starred in the 1998 film version. The play is often cited as Friel's most sustained portrayal of women, but this is a memory play (one which bears comparison with Tennessee Williams's *The Glass Menagerie* and Frank McGuinness's *Observe the Sons of Ulster Marching Towards the Somme*) – and the memory is a male memory.

Unlike most of Friel's earlier plays, *Lughnasa* avoids juxtaposing radically differing memories or views or approaches. It is true that the sisters differ on a number of issues, but because all events are filtered through Michael's eyes, the play has an overriding coherence of memory and presentation. Like *Philadelphia*, *Lughnasa* has a familiar cottage-kitchen set. Unlike *Philadelphia*, *Lughnasa* does not allow us into the interior space of the bedroom, and the space outside the kitchen is not fluid and shifting but fixed. In this play it is time, rather than space, which shifts, as Michael's present-time narrative shapes and comments on action set in the past. Uncertainty enters indirectly, when we are forced to notice the divide between any nostalgic, pastoral view of 1930s Donegal and the doomed and stunted lives of the Mundy sisters. The dances which seem to embody an ability to communicate without words, for example, are deliberately cut off. Michael's parents dance a farewell. The sisters' famous dance is described as 'grotesque', 'caricatured', like that of a 'frantic dervish', and as Christopher Murray points out, the dance stops abruptly when the uncertain radio cuts out in mid-phrase.[13] Even the radio's name is a warning: Marconi, a brand name taken from the name of the man who (working sometimes on the coast of Ireland) invented the wireless so important in sending out distress calls (like those from the Belfast-built *Titanic*).

The play is built around familiar Ballybeg realities: jobs are hard to come by; relationships do not work out; faith is hard to recognize and harder to hold; emigration lures; failure is inevitable. Friel's awareness of these realities is shaped not only by what he knows of Donegal, but also by what he knows of his own family. His mother's maiden name was Christina McLoone. Loone is related to the Irish word for Monday. Christina McLoone and Chris Mundy. (In *The Mundy Scheme* it is the Irish-American inventor of a plan to turn western Ireland into a supersized graveyard for returning Irish-Americans who shares the family name.) The play is dedicated to 'those five brave Glenties women' – the maiden aunts whom Friel visited in childhood summers. He has said that the story was born one night when he and fellow Irish playwright Tom Kilroy passed homeless people curled up on the streets of London and he was reminded that two of his aunts had ended up in similar circumstances (*Essays, Diaries*, 139). (He had, though, told parts of the story much earlier in such short stories as 'A Man's World' and 'Aunt Maggie, the Strong One'.) Lough Anna, which also shows up in *Philadelphia* and in *Molly Sweeney*, is an actual lake on the map of Donegal, not far from the actual town of Glenties.

Recognizing such geographic and biographical links does not mean that the Mundy sisters *are* Friel's aunts, or that Ballybeg *is* Glenties. The characters and the places are amalgams. Friel's long and deep knowledge of them and affection for them, though, is surely one reason he is able to create this place so convincingly on the stage. Ballybeg has the comfort of familiarity and the danger of any stifling, constricted environment.

Friel's plays test the confinement of Ballybeg by bringing outsiders into it: visitors from the United States in *Philadelphia*, American academics and outsider in-laws in *Aristocrats*, English sappers in *Translations*. In *Lughnasa* the outside world enters with Father Jack and with Gerry Evans. Most interestingly, though, the outside world enters this Ballybeg cottage through the unreliable voice of Marconi. Friel uses mechanical devices in a similar way in *Aristocrats*, in which the tape recorder and the babyminder shatter the staid traditions of the O'Donnell family, but Marconi plays an even more dramatic role. Michael's narration describes the 'voodoo' of Marconi, which he has seen '*derange* those kind, sensible women and *transform* them into *shrieking* strangers' (my italics).[14] Arguably, though, it is Ballybeg which has transformed the aunts, stunting their growth and possibilities so that only through Marconi's voodoo are they able to grasp again some sense of life's possibility and passion. The madness of dancing in the moonlight may be the only source of sanity left them.

Rather than testing the northwest of Ireland by bringing in outsiders, *Wonderful Tennessee* (1993) tests outsiders by bringing them to Donegal. The three couples, linked by bonds of marriage and blood and friendship, have come to a section of coast near Ballybeg. Classical and Celtic mythological references give a spiritual dimension to their vague quest, but they do not find whatever they are seeking. The failure of these middle-class urbanites is different from the failure of the Mundy sisters, but it is failure nonetheless. Among other things the play warns against seeking in supposedly pastoral Donegal, or among the ruins of religious sites, the power of belief and purpose missing from our lives.

Friel's most recent plays – *Molly Sweeney* (1994) and *Give Me Your Answer, Do!* (1997) – are set in contemporary Donegal, continuing Friel's exploration of what time has wrought in the area which remains his home. In *Give Me Your Answer, Do!* it is again an American academic who invades Ballybeg, seeking to appropriate some portion of Irish experience (in this case the novelist's papers) for the benefit of an outside world. The American presence here warrants comparison with similar aspects of *The Freedom of the City*, *Volunteers* and *Aristocrats*. Friel is clearly uneasy about such intrusions – intrusions made increasingly likely by his own remarkable success as an internationally known playwright.

Friel's seventieth birthday in January 1999 was greeted with an outpouring of tributes. Try as he will to retain his privacy by resisting interviews and public presentations, his face is among the most familiar in Ireland. The place he has explored in so many plays, though, seems content to allow him to exist quietly as one of its own, and that is no doubt part of its appeal for him. Friel sees Donegal and Ballybeg through no rose-coloured spectacles, and he is direct about the crippling constrictions so often apparent there. But Donegal is home, and his roots go deep into its rocky soil. At the end of *Philadelphia* Gar Private demands, 'Why do you have to leave? Why? Why?'. Public's stuttered reply, 'I don't know. I – I – I – don't know' (*Selected Plays* 99), is reminiscent of Quentin Compson's confused overinsistence at the end of Faulkner's *Absalom, Absalom!*: 'I dont hate [the South],' he says. '*I dont hate it . . . I dont. I dont! I dont hate it! I dont hate it!*' Deeply divided feelings about Donegal and his imagined Ballybeg are evident in Friel's plays, and they are part of what gives the works power. At the end of *Give Me Your Answer, Do!* Daisy pays tribute to the 'Necessary Uncertainty' that informs her husband's writing. There must be, she says, 'no verdicts, no answers . . . Because being alive is the postponement of verdicts.'[15] Such divisions and uncertainties are evident in Friel's work as well, literary reflections of the borders and divisions of the region which is his home and which he has mapped in a distinguished body of work.

NOTES

1. Brian Friel, *Translations*, in *Selected Plays of Brian Friel* (London: Faber and Faber, 1984), 444.
2. Christopher Murray (ed.), *Brian Friel: Essays, Diaries, Interviews: 1964–1999* (London: Faber and Faber, 1999), 86.
3. Paul Delaney (ed.), *Brian Friel in Conversation* (Ann Arbor: University of Michigan Press, 2000), 36, 38, 35.
4. See Anthony Roche, *Contemporary Irish Drama: From Beckett to McGuinness* (London: Gill and Macmillan, 1994), 72–103.
5. Brian Friel, *Philadelphia, Here I Come!*, in *Selected Plays*, 64.
6. See Shaun Richards, 'Placed Identities for Placeless Times: Brian Friel and Post-Colonial Criticism,' in *Irish University Review*, 27:1 (1997), 55–68; and F. C. McGrath, *Brian Friel's (Post) Colonial Drama: Language, Illusion, and Politics* (Syracuse: Syracuse University Press, 1999).
7. See 'Drama of Love: From One Great Master to Another'. in *Irish Times Weekend*, 1 August 1992, 2.
8. Brian Friel, *The Gentle Island* (Oldcastle: Gallery Books, 1993), 57.
9. Brian Friel, *Living Quarters*, in *Selected Plays*, 178.
10. Brian Friel, *Aristocrats*, in *Selected Plays*, 250.

11. See Roche, *Contemporary Irish Drama*, 106–28, for a comprehensive discussion of *Faith Healer*.
12. Brian Friel, *Freedom of the City*, in *Selected Plays*, 140.
13. Christopher Murray, *Twentieth-Century Irish Drama: Mirror Up to Nation* (Manchester: Manchester University Press, 1997), 227.
14. Brian Friel, *Dancing at Lughnasa* (London: Faber and Faber, 1990), 2.
15. Brian Friel, *Give Me Your Answer, Do!* (Oldcastle: Gallery Press, 1997), 79–80.

14

MARILYNN RICHTARIK

The Field Day Theatre Company

The activities of the Field Day Theatre Company must be seen against the backdrop of the communal violence which preoccupied people in Northern Ireland from 1969 to 1999, when power-sharing arrangements took effect. More than 3,300 people died in the course of this protracted struggle between the more extreme factions of the unionists (mostly Protestant), who want Northern Ireland to remain part of the United Kingdom, and the nationalists (mostly Catholic), who favour some sort of united Ireland. The questions of whether and how to deal with the 'Troubles' worried artists in every medium and genre throughout this unsettled period in Northern Ireland. Failure to confront the atrocities left one open to the charge of ignoring the most vital, dramatic subject matter available. On the other hand focusing too exclusively on current events might make one's art ephemeral while raising suspicions that one was cashing in on the crisis or exploiting other people's pain for personal benefit. Field Day, founded in 1980, represented an attempt by six Northern artists and intellectuals – Brian Friel, Stephen Rea, Seamus Deane, Seamus Heaney, David Hammond and Tom Paulin – to respond to the unsettled political situation in the Province in a manner which seemed to them socially, morally and creatively responsible. The company has now been in existence for more than twenty years, and its legacy includes, in addition to its solid record of theatre production, publications which have set the terms for critical debate in Irish Studies through much of that time. This chapter, however, will focus mainly on the drama produced by Field Day and on its life and achievement as a theatre company.

Rea, an actor who achieved international fame years later as a result of his performance in the Neil Jordan film *The Crying Game*, was the instigator of the Field Day project. He was from Belfast but had long been based in London, where he was steadily employed both on the Fringe and by prominent theatres such as the Royal Court and the National. Despite his success in England, Rea was tired of feeling himself part of an expatriate subculture there and wanted to return to Ireland and perform for Irish audiences. He had met Friel several years earlier when he acted in a production of Friel's play *The Freedom of the City* (1973) at the Royal Court, and there had been an instant connection between them. In 1979 he approached the older man with the idea of mounting an Irish touring production of Friel's next play.

Friel was already regarded by many as Ireland's most important living play-wright (his first international hit was 1964's *Philadelphia, Here I Come!*). He had recently had a bad experience on Broadway, however, where the original production of *Faith Healer* had closed after a mere handful of performances, and he proved receptive to Rea's suggestion. He, too, wanted to speak first to Irish audiences and was concerned about the effect on Ireland of living in the shadow of England and the English language. As a Northerner who was born in Omagh and grew up in Derry, Friel also felt the urge to break away from the Dublin theatre establishment. Together he and Rea decided to open *Translations*, the play he was then finishing, in Derry and to follow the premiere with a tour of thirteen other Irish towns both north and south of the border. The impulse behind the project was thus both populist, in that Friel and Rea were reaching out to new audiences of people who did not usually have the opportunity to attend professional theatre, and parochial in a positive sense. Field Day – rhyming, Friel said, with 'Friel' and 'Rea', but also connoting fun, excitement and opportunity – was funded by the Arts Council of Northern Ireland with the Arts Council of the Republic of Ireland and the Derry city council.

The Derry connection, in particular, became a defining feature of Field Day. Northern Ireland's second-largest city after Belfast, Derry was located on the border between the North and the Republic and was home to a large Catholic majority who had been disenfranchised by unionist gerrymandering for fifty years after partition. The city's unionists and nationalists alike also felt themselves to be victims of neglect by the Stormont government, as the whole northwestern region of Northern Ireland was considered marginal to the interests of the ruling party in Belfast. Following the proroguing of Stormont and the implementation of direct rule from London in 1972, reform of local government in the North ensured that the city council in Derry would reflect the city's electorate more accurately, but relative isolation and high levels of unemployment remained persistent problems.

Nonetheless, the citizens of Derry reacted enthusiastically to Friel's and Rea's request to stage the opening of *Translations* in the city's Guildhall (Derry had, at the time, no civic theatre building). People were delighted that Field Day was bypassing London, Dublin and New York City (not to mention Belfast) as venues for the premiere of a new Friel play; and the power-sharing city council seized on the rehearsals and performances of the play as occasions to demonstrate local pride and solidarity and supported

the venture both financially and politically. In the event, the real-life theatricality of the Derry opening was a crucial part of the impact of the original
production of *Translations*, especially within Northern Ireland. Because of
Friel's stature critics travelled from throughout the British Isles to join locals
in attending the event; and the premiere brought together unionists and nationalists, northerners and southerners, literati and ordinary Derry people
to witness a performance which all seemed to find profoundly moving.

The ecstatic Derry reception of *Translations* was replicated in most of the
Irish towns which Field Day visited with the production and convinced Friel
and Rea that they should not let the energy generated by the production
dissipate. Therefore, in 1981, they formalized the company's organization
by assembling a board of directors made up, in addition to themselves, of
sympathetic friends and acquaintances. Deane, who would turn out to be
the most influential addition to the Field Day project, grew up in Derry
and had known Friel since the early 1960s. In 1981 he was the author of
two collections of poetry and Professor of English and American Literature
at University College, Dublin. Heaney was already the best known of the
'Northern poets', with five volumes of poetry and various pamphlets, essays
and limited editions to his credit. He and Deane had been friends since they
were pupils together at St Columb's College in Derry, and he had likewise
known Friel for years. Like Deane, he was based in Dublin, where he held a
teaching position. Hammond, who lived in Belfast, was another old friend
of Friel. A singer, broadcaster and filmmaker, he had begun his career as a
teacher and then worked for many years for the BBC's Schools Department
before leaving to start his own production company. Paulin, born in Leeds
but raised in Belfast, was an academic based in Nottingham. He was also a
prolific poet, having published two full-length collections and three shorter
books by 1981. The least connected to the other Field Day board members,
Paulin believes he was invited to join the group as a result of his having
reviewed a production of *Translations* in London. His inclusion ensured a
symbolic balance on the board between Protestants (Rea, Hammond and
Paulin) and Catholics (Friel, Deane and Heaney).[1]

Several generalizations can be made about the six men who would determine Field Day's future direction. They were all artists. All except Rea were
or had been educators (Friel had taught maths in Derry before devoting himself full-time to his writing in 1960). All of them had grown up in Northern
Ireland but, with the exception of Hammond, now lived elsewhere, a circumstance which gave them the dual perspective of insiders and outsiders. Their
literal displacement, Heaney explains, was 'only an outward sign of a condition common to most self-aware people, north and south of the border –
namely, that everything was shifting, that the older norms and intellectual

arrangements had to be examined in the light of new political upheavals'.[2] All six felt frustrated by the political stalemate in Ireland and believed it was incumbent on them to engage with the Northern crisis in a fashion which might encourage people to think about it in new ways. Finally, all of them by 1981 were coming from a basically nationalist position which regarded the whole of Ireland as a cultural unit distinct from England and favoured the political integration of the island.

A distinctively Northern feature of their outlook, however, was their dissatisfaction with both Northern Ireland (as part of the United Kingdom) and the Republic of Ireland. One of their basic assumptions was that the political establishments both north and south of the border would not long survive and that Field Day's mission should be to help create a more inclusive notion of Irish identity than the prevailing sectarian versions. Deane hinted at the connection between their cultural goals and a political agenda the following year in a programme note for Field Day's third production:

> If a congealed idea of theatre can be broken, then the audience which experiences this break would be the more open to the modification of other established forms. Almost everything which we believe to be nature or natural is in fact historical; more precisely, is an historical fiction. If *Field Day* can breed a new fiction of theatre, or of any other area, which is sufficiently successful to be believed in as though it were natural and an outgrowth of the past, then it will have succeeded. At the moment, it is six characters in search of a story that can be believed.[3]

Although Deane's formulation overstates the originality of the actual theatre work pursued by the company, a fascination with history as narrative and the faith he expresses in artistic production as a means of effecting social and political change were both hallmarks of the Field Day philosophy.

In many ways Field Day was a very unusual theatre company. For example, from 1983 it carried on significant activities unrelated to the staging of plays, including – in addition to concerts, lectures and special events in Derry – the publication of five sets of pamphlets on various aspects of Irish culture, a series of monographs and essay collections published jointly by Cork University Press in Ireland and the University of Notre Dame Press in the United States, and the massive *Field Day Anthology of Irish Writing*. For a theatre company Field Day had an unwieldy and impractical organization. The only continuity from year to year was provided by the board, the members of which saw their most important job as choosing the play to be produced each year. This emphasis on text was hardly surprising given the composition of the board, but it did mean that performance issues were generally secondary. There was never a core group of actors and directors, although a number of actors and technical support people worked with Field Day more than once. The company and crew thus had to be assembled from scratch every time Field Day wanted to produce a play. There was no artistic director, only a local administrator without much independent authority. Any substantive decisions about the company's policies were made by the board, which included only two theatre professionals (Friel and Rea) and no business people. Furthermore, because the members of the board were scattered around Great Britain and Ireland, it met formally only four or five times each year. At first Friel, who lived just across the border from Field Day's office in Derry, paid close attention to the day-to-day operations of the company, but as he gradually began to withdraw from that level of involvement the diffuse nature of Field Day's governing authority became something of a problem.

To complicate matters further, all six of the Field Day board members had active careers outside the company. Some of their individual work was for Field Day, but much of it was not. Heaney's book *Sweeney Astray*, for instance, was published first by Field Day in 1983, and he wrote *The Cure at Troy* (1990) specifically for Field Day, but in the ten-year period from 1981 to 1991 he also published five books apart from the company. Most of the directors did not like to think of themselves as committed to Field Day indefinitely, so an aura of impermanence suffused the undertaking. Overall Field Day's theatre work was characterized by an ad hoc, improvisatory mode of operation. This conflicted through the years with various forces (including the priorities of the funding bodies upon which Field Day was completely reliant) pushing Field Day to become an independent institution. The Field Day directors mostly resisted these, while managing to coordinate their efforts to the extent necessary to produce and tour, on average, one new Irish play each year between 1981 and 1991.[4] The Field Day 'season', including rehearsals and tour, generally ran from August to December, a little longer if the production transferred to London. Indeed, one could describe Field Day as a part-time theatre company.

One play each year is a relatively small output, and detractors (especially those in competition with Field Day for arts money) have not hesitated to point this out. Moreover, Field Day's publishing activities have tended to receive more attention outside Ireland than its plays. One might thus reasonably ask how significant Field Day's contributions to theatre in Ireland really have been. On this question I would concur with Irish theatre historian Christopher Murray, who sums up a discussion of Field Day by concluding that the company 'generated excitement and hope in Ireland at a time of political and indeed theatrical uncertainty', adding: 'Of the twelve plays staged by 1991 at least three, *Translations*, *Double Cross* and *Pentecost*, stand out among the best Irish plays of the past twenty-five years, while several of the other productions are crucial to any study of modern Irish drama.'[5] In the rest of this chapter I will briefly review the first twelve Field Day productions and venture a few broad statements about the company's work for the theatre.

Translations, Field Day's flagship production, is set in Co. Donegal, Ireland in 1833 and uses education and mapmaking as metaphors for colonial dispossession. At this time Ireland was technically no longer a 'colony' of England, having been integrated into the United Kingdom by the Act of Union of 1800, but, as the official response (or lack of it) to the Irish potato famine of the mid-nineteenth century would shortly prove, Ireland was still considered to be outside the mainstream of British national concern. The introduction of the National School system and the Ordnance Survey's work in Ireland represented attempts by the government to bring Ireland more firmly into the English orbit, but Friel focuses on the negative effect of this attention on the native Gaelic culture, particularly on the Irish language. The plot centres on Hugh, an Irish-speaking schoolmaster, and his two sons: Owen (who is employed by the British soldiers busy mapping the area to 'translate' the local placenames into English) and Manus (who clings stubbornly to the Irish language and all it represents). The doomed love affair between a local girl and one of the British officers provides a subplot.

Though the dialogue is written entirely in English (with a few Irish placenames and a smattering of the Latin and Greek favoured by the hedge-schoolmaster), Friel manages to convince audiences that the characters are speaking both English and Irish, a feat which was commented on by nearly every contemporary reviewer of the play. Despite its undeniably nationalist themes, *Translations* proved to be extremely popular throughout Northern Ireland, while in the Republic it was hailed as an instant national classic, a watershed in Irish theatre.[6] The phenomenal and unexpected success of the play convinced the Field Day directors to try to make the cross-border tour an annual event.

At the same time they were eager to avoid what Friel termed 'the second novel jinx'. This caution may account, in part, for their choice of Friel's version of Anton Chekhov's *Three Sisters* for the 1981 tour: producing a world classic helped to lessen the pressure of expectations on the new company. Friel had long been an admirer of the Russian playwright, and many of his plays, most notably *Aristocrats* (1979), testify to Chekhov's influence. Touring this play demonstrated Field Day's determination to bring quality drama to the people of rural Ireland. There was also a political dimension to the decision, however. The three sisters' unfulfilled longing to go to Moscow was not unlike the frustrated yearning of most people in Northern Ireland for an end to the violence and the political impasse.

Moreover, Friel insisted, there was a fundamental difference between his version of *Three Sisters* and other English-language versions available. He had not adapted the play, changed it to an Irish setting, or tried to underline specifically Irish meanings. Nor was his script a literal translation, since he did not know Russian. What he had written was a 'translation' from English and American versions of the play into the kind of English spoken in contemporary Ireland. He justified his approach by saying that 'with English translations Irish actors become more and more remote. They have to pretend, first of all, that they're English and then that they're Russians. I'd like our audience to see Captains and Lieutenants who look as if they came from Finner or Tullamore. The decolonisation process of the imagination is very important if a new Irish personality is to emerge.'[7]

Three Sisters was an expensive production for Field Day, due to its large cast and heavy set, and in 1982 they needed a show with general appeal. It was fortunate, then, that Friel felt inclined to experiment with the genre of farce. He was worried about the reception of *Translations*, which he felt had been greeted 'much too respectfully', and believed writing a farce would 'release' him artistically.[8] The play he presented as a deflationary companion piece to *Translations* was *The Communication Cord*, set in present-day Donegal. A send-up of academic jargon and of an overly reverent attitude towards the Irish past which would turn it into a museum or theme park, *The Communication Cord* also explores the difficulty of communication. Tim, a university lecturer, borrows a friend's thatched cottage in order to impress his prospective father-in-law, an amateur antiquarian, but the house itself seems to plot against him, sensing perhaps that, as he admits, 'I feel no affinity at all with it and it knows that. In fact I think I hate it and all it represents.'[9] The inability of modern Irish people to possess their own past unself-consciously is a result, in large part, of English colonization, but here the colonial concussion is treated comically rather than tragically. Not surprisingly, the play gave Field Day its second hit.

By 1983 the Field Day directors felt it was time to branch out from the work of Brian Friel and make it clear that the company was interested in a multiplicity of voices. They were particularly anxious to work with a Protestant playwright, since they did not want to be seen as coming exclusively from a nationalist point of view. They approached the dramatist David Rudkin, who had grown up in Northern Ireland, and offered him a commission. The script he produced for Field Day was *The Saxon Shore*, which drew an analogy between the defensive posture of Northern Irish Protestants and that of Saxons transplanted to Roman Britain to help defend that outpost of the empire against the twin threats of hostile Celts and invading Saxons. Field Day eventually decided not to tour this play, probably because the directors were uncomfortable with Rudkin's implied criticism of the Saxons in the play (although he was a Protestant, he was also a nationalist). Instead, at the last minute, the company mounted a tour of *Boesman and Lena*, a 1969 play by the South African playwright Athol Fugard. This portrayal of the abusive relationship of a destitute 'coloured' couple locked, as Eamonn Hughes puts it, in 'an intimacy which does not yield mutual understanding' parallels the relationship between Northern Protestants and Catholics.[10] Field Day probably also intended a broader comparison between Northern Ireland and South Africa, places so deeply divided that accidents like skin colour or the religious affiliation of one's parents could determine one's prospects in life. *Boesman and Lena* was a critical rather than a popular success. Nevertheless, it proved once again Field Day's resolve to look beyond the island for insights about Irish problems.

For the 1984 tour Field Day decided to stage a double-bill, two short Hiberno-English 'versions' of classic plays by two contemporary Irish poets. Paulin adapted Sophocles's *Antigone* in *The Riot Act*, and Derek Mahon translated Molière's *The School for Husbands* as *High Time*. Superficially the two plays could hardly have been more different: Paulin's was a tragedy austerely directed by Stephen Rea, Mahon's a rollicking comedy which directors Mark Long and Emil Wolk of The People Show embellished to play up its potential for broad, physical humour. On closer inspection, however, the two stories turn out to have an almost identical theme: rigidity does not pay. Creon is ruined by a stubborn unwillingness to modify his unjust edict when his niece Antigone challenges it, and the overly strict and controlling guardian in the Molière play loses the opportunity to marry his nubile ward while his more lenient brother keeps the affection of his. Field Day emphasized the connection between the two plays by using the same actors to play similar parts in each, and, since inflexibility on all sides contributed to the Troubles, the production offered a clear warning about the dangers of intransigence.

Owing to organizational difficulties, Field Day did not produce a play in 1985. Instead, early in 1986, the company toured with *Double Cross*, an original play by Thomas Kilroy. As its title implies, *Double Cross* concerns itself both with doubling and doubleness and with betrayal. One idea featured in several of the early Field Day pamphlets was that 'Englishness' and 'Irishness' were social constructs formed largely in opposition to each other. Kilroy plays with that notion in *Double Cross*, which centres on the actual World War Two careers of two Irishmen who attempted (unsuccessfully, in Kilroy's interpretation) to escape their Irish roots and redefine themselves as extreme versions of Englishmen. Brendan Bracken, born to an Irish republican father in Tipperary but often mistaken in later life for an illegitimate son of Winston Churchill, served as Churchill's Minister of Information during the war. William Joyce volunteered as a teenager during the Anglo-Irish War to provide information to the Royal Irish Constabulary, developed an interest in fascism during his twenties, and eventually migrated to Germany where he became (in)famous as a wartime radio propagandist for Hitler (trying, in his view, to save England from itself). These two men (both played by Rea in the Field Day production, in a theatrical tour de force) achieved what Kilroy, in an author's note to the play, describes as 'one kind of mobility, one kind of action across the barriers, the restrictive codes which separate countries from one another'. This kind of action, he adds, is commonly known as treason, and the play was intended to reflect his own belief that '[t]o base one's identity, exclusively, upon a mystical sense of place rather than in personal character where it properly resides seems to me a dangerous absurdity. To dedicate one's life to the systematic betrayal of that ideal seems to me equally absurd.'[11] Despite this pronouncement by the author, it is possible to see the main characters' pathology as having more to do with their denial of their Irishness than with their belief in concepts like Irishness and Englishness in the first place.

Stewart Parker's *Pentecost*, the company's 1987 production, was the only Field Day play to deal directly with the Troubles – indeed, the only play to be set in contemporary Northern Ireland. It takes place during the Ulster Workers' Council Strike of 1974, when militantly unionist workers managed to overturn what had seemed to be a promising resolution to the political crisis. Four characters in their late twenties and early thirties – two male, two female; two Protestant, two Catholic – are stranded together in a house which stands on the dividing line between Protestant and Catholic ghettos on a road which itself is in the middle of an urban redevelopment zone. This house is haunted by the ghost of its long-term occupant, Lily Matthews, whose life story is archetypal of working-class Protestant experience in Belfast during the twentieth century. Besieged by the resurgence of past animosities and an uncertain future alike, the house is a physical embodiment of the working-class loyalism which is responsible for the turmoil in the streets outside it and with which the four living characters (members of Parker's own generation) must come to terms.

Through the action of the play Parker suggests it is self-loathing, projected as hatred of other people, that is at the root of any human conflict, including the Northern crisis. *Pentecost* ends with the four characters sharing stories which illustrate the dramatist's vision of a secular Pentecost which might transcend contemporary discord and division, with one of them proclaiming: 'There is some kind of christ, in every one of us . . . Each of us either honours him, or denies him and violates him, what we do to him is done to ourselves . . . We have got to love that in ourselves. In ourselves first and then in them. That's the only future there is.'[12]

In 1988 Friel contributed *Making History*, his first play for Field Day since 1982. He self-consciously followed the lead of Sean O'Faolain's 1942 biography *The Great O'Neill* in deconstructing the myth of Hugh O'Neill, one of the Gaelic lords of Ulster who led the final, abortive rebellion of that order against the English crown. In retelling the events leading up to and following the Battle of Kinsale (1601) and the storied 'Flight of the Earls' several years later, Friel makes it clear that O'Neill was a flawed and contradictory Gaelic hero – one who had lived in England for many years, spoke with an English accent, had sworn allegiance to the English queen, and had a beloved wife of English stock. Through a coda focusing on the biography which Archbishop Peter Lombard is producing about O'Neill, *Making History* is also a meditation on the process of history-writing, one which makes it clear that any history is a constructed narrative as interesting for what it leaves out as for what it includes. O'Neill pleads with Lombard to tell 'the whole truth', while the latter argues that '[t]his isn't the time for a critical assessment of your "ploys" and your "disgraces" and your "betrayal" – that's the stuff of another history for another time. Now is the time for a hero.'[13]

Terry Eagleton, an English literary critic of Irish descent, wrote *Saint Oscar* for Field Day's 1989 tour. Like *Double Cross* and *Making History*, this play is a stage biography of a well-known (and ambiguously Irish) character: the playwright Oscar Wilde, who, like Brendan Bracken, created a persona for himself which was more English than the English. Eagleton composed *Saint Oscar* in an imitation of Wilde's style and presented its protagonist in the image of himself, an Irish republican and socialist who was drawn to Wilde as a subject when he discovered that 'hardly any of the Oxford students who asked to study him with me realized that he was Irish'. This, he reflects, 'is hardly a grievous crime, though it might be said to be evidence of one'.[14] In two key scenes in Act 2, Eagleton uses the fact that one of Wilde's prosecutors in his sodomy trial was Edward Carson, who later led unionist opposition to Home Rule in Ireland, to draw a connection between Wilde's fate and the vexed politics of the North.

The Cure at Troy, Heaney's version of Sophocles' *Philoctetes*, was Field Day's 1990 offering. Philoctetes is a warrior abandoned by his fellow Greeks on the way to sack Troy when a snakebite on his foot turns it into a mass of rotting, stinking ulcers. Ten years later the Greeks realize they cannot take Troy without the magic bow and arrows belonging to Philoctetes, and Odysseus and Neoptolemus (the son of Achilles) travel to the island of Lemnos to try to steal them from him. Neoptolemus is unable to bring himself to betray Philoctetes, however, and he manages to convince the older man to come with him to Troy of his own free will, where his wounded foot will be cured and he is fated to help win the decisive battle for the Greeks. Like *Three Sisters*, *The Riot Act* and *High Time*, *The Cure at Troy* is written in Hiberno-English dialect, and towards the end of the play the Chorus invokes Northern Irish images (including a 'hunger-striker's father' and a 'police widow in veils') to illustrate the type of human suffering which can make people 'hard'.[15] This encouraged discussion of how Heaney intended the story of Philoctetes to apply to the Northern situation. Interpretations of the play vary from seeing it as a parable about the reintegration of nationalist factions (including the 'men of violence') to regarding it as a comment on the necessity of including unionists in any realistic vision of a united Ireland.

Kilroy's *The Madame MacAdam Travelling Theatre* (1991) was the last of Field Day's annual productions. An English touring company is stranded temporarily in an Irish provincial town during what in neutral Ireland is referred to as 'the Emergency' (known elsewhere as World War Two). The lives of the actors intersect with the schemes of the locals, resulting in a variety of complications, but Kilroy is chiefly interested in the dangerous power of illusion. Madame MacAdam, who had earlier warned against confusing theatre with everyday life, comments on the vicious actions of a squad of the Home Guard with the observation 'that is another lesson to be learned from theatre. Once one puts on a uniform one is in danger of unleashing one's violence. Witness that slaughter out there on those battlefields.'[16]

All in all Field Day presented an eclectic collection of plays during the first twelve years of its existence, but there are a few generalizations which can be made about its body of work. First, despite the company's populist ethos – reflected in a commitment to long tours outside established metropolitan centres – it did not as a rule produce 'popular' drama. Field Day plays were almost invariably challenging and cerebral. Second, though Field Day's publications have been controversial, criticized in some quarters for what critics such as Edna Longley see as unreconstructed nationalism, there was nothing propagandistic about its drama. This is not to say, however, that Field Day's theatrical practice was not political. For one thing the company was Northern-based and always insisted that it spoke with a distinctively Northern voice; at the same time it operated from the beginning in an all-Ireland context, thus making the point quietly but firmly that it regarded the whole of Ireland as a cultural unit. Field Day's plays did, in fact, offer analyses of the Northern crisis, but they did so indirectly, through looking at causes. There was no Field Day play in these years 'about' terrorists, and only one in which the contemporary Troubles featured explicitly. There were, though, several plays which focused on the politics of language, the sort of politics which might be expected to engage writers most intimately (especially in the North where, as Declan Kiberd points out, 'the speaking of Irish was a political act, and where a person who gave a Gaelic version of a name to a policeman might expect a cuff on the ear or worse'[17]). There was also an emphasis on the classics of world drama which helped put Northern Ireland's problems into a comparative context. There were various original plays exploring issues of Irish identity such as 'What does it mean to be Irish?' and 'What sort of cultural common denominator might there be between the island's embattled factions?'. Above all there were plays exploring the idea of history as an imposition on the past of one narrative or another – a process not unlike that of writing fiction, or making theatre. Implicit in Field Day's perspective is the notion that if one version of the past imprisons people, another might set them free. An essential part of Field Day's mission has always been to present alternative visions of the past and present in the hope of opening up new possibilities for the future. In the words of Stephen Rea, the purpose of the company was to encourage audiences to 'choose the history that is enabling to you rather than one that holds you back' (Murray, *Irish Drama*, 208).

NOTES

1. Thomas Kilroy, a novelist, playwright and academic from Kilkenny, later served for four years as a Field Day director, but he was not part of the defining original board.
2. Seamus Heaney, 'A Field Day for the Irish', in *The Times*, 5 December 1988.
3. Seamus Deane, 'In Search of a Story', programme note for the Field Day production of *The Communication Cord*, 1982.
4. In 1995 Field Day produced a version of Chekhov's play *Uncle Vanya* by Frank McGuinness, and in 1998 the company teamed with Belfast's Tinderbox Theatre Company to produce Stewart Parker's *Northern Star*, but the days of annual theatre production were by then in the past.
5. Christopher Murray, *Twentieth-Century Irish Drama: Mirror Up to Nation* (Manchester: Manchester University Press, 1997), 222.
6. Michael Sheridan, 'Friel Play a Watershed in Irish Theatre', in *Irish Press*, 25 September 1980.
7. Brian Friel, quoted in Ulick O'Connor, 'Friel Takes Derry by Storm', in *Sunday Tribune*, 6 September 1981.
8. Fintan O'Toole, 'The Man From God Knows Where' (interview with Brian Friel), in *In Dublin*, 28 October 1982, 21.
9. Brian Friel, *The Communication Cord* (Oldcastle: Gallery Press, 1989), 43.
10. Eamonn Hughes, '"To Define Your Dissent": The Plays and Polemics of the Field Day Theatre Company', in *Theatre Research International* 15:1 (1990), 74.
11. Thomas Kilroy, 'Author's Note', *Double Cross* (London: Faber and Faber, 1986), 6–7.
12. Stewart Parker, *Three Plays for Ireland* (Birmingham: Oberon, 1989), 207.

13. Brian Friel, *Making History* (London: Faber and Faber, 1989), 66–7.
14. Terry Eagleton, 'Foreword', *Saint Oscar* (Derry: Field Day, 1989), vii.
15. Seamus Heaney, *The Cure at Troy* (London: Faber and Faber, 1990), 77.
16. Thomas Kilroy, *The Madame MacAdam Travelling Theatre* (London: Methuen, 1991), 66–7.
17. Declan Kiberd, *Inventing Ireland: The Literature of the Modern Nation* (London: Jonathan Cape, 1995), 616.

15

NICHOLAS GRENE

Tom Murphy and the children of loss

In 1968 Tom Murphy's play *Famine* was staged in Dublin's Peacock Theatre. It was an audacious act of theatrical imagination to represent, in the Irish national theatre's tiny studio space, Ireland's greatest historical disaster. In Murphy's play one family, one village, stand in for the experience of the nation. *Famine* opens with a split scene. The community is mourning the death of a young daughter of the Connor family with the formal rituals of the wake and the keen. At the same time, on the edge of that scene, the men exchange uneasy, disconnected remarks about the potatoes:

> *Mark (nervous staccato voice).* But – but – but, ye see, last year the first crop
> failed but the main crop was good, and this year the first crop failed, but
> the main crop will be – will be – will be . . .
> *Dan.* Hah?
> *Brian.* Oh, you could be right.[1]

The fear of a second year of failure frays their conversation into broken gestures of talk.

This scene preenacts the movement of the play as a whole. A community which has expressed the rhythms of its being in inherited forms – the wake and the keen – has its capacity for utterance and understanding shattered by the magnitude of the calamity which overtakes it. The drama centres on the figure of John Connor, to whom the village looks for leadership – an inarticulate Job who clings stubbornly to the need to maintain principle in the face of impossible adversity. He is, though, a Job whom God forgot; in place of the rewards for his faith given to the Old Testament hero after all his many sufferings, all that comes to John Connor is the deranged 'sacred strength' in which he kills his wife and child rather than see them face death by starvation.

Famine is an extraordinary play in the power of its confrontation with horror, the spare honesty of its dramatic form. But Murphy has always been

aware of the consequences of this trauma of the nineteenth-century famine
as much as the event itself:

> The absence of food, the cause of famine, is only one aspect of famine. What
> about the other 'poverties' that attend famine? A hungry and demoralised
> people becomes silent. People emigrate in great numbers and leave spaces that
> cannot be filled . . . The dream of food can become a reality – as it did in
> the Irish experience – and people's bodies are nourished back to health. What
> can similarly restore mentalities that have become distorted, spirits that have
> become mean and broken? (*Plays: One*, xi).

This had been his subject from his earliest work, the one-act play *On the
Outside*, written with a friend, Noel O'Donoghue, when he was a metalwork
teacher in Co. Galway, not far from the town of Tuam which is his family
home. *On the Outside*, like a provincial *Waiting for Godot* in a minor key,
is about the nonevent of two young men unable to get into a country dance-
hall of the 1950s. It is a cameo study in the petty class constrictions, the
mini-meannesses of a society frozen in moral and economic torpor.

A different dimension to the post-Famine deformations of Irish society was
dramatized in Murphy's first full-length play *A Whistle in the Dark*. This, the
play which made his name in 1961 with a spectacularly successful London
production, brought to the stage the culture of violence by which a family of
Irish emigrants in Coventry attempted to give heroic meaning to their deni-
grated and marginalized lives. In a much more comic key, though a sharply
satiric one, was the play written in the early 1960s but produced at the Abbey
theatre only in 1969, *A Crucial Week in the Life of a Grocer's Assistant*.
The progress of the grocer's assistant, John Joe, through his 'crucial week'
reveals the moral nullity of the small-town life which drives him to leave and
dooms him to stay. *Famine* enacted Ireland's most terrible tragedy; many of
Murphy's other plays dramatize the smaller tragedies, the tragi-comedies,
the dramas of the grotesque which flow from famine for the children
of loss.

That is one way of seeing Murphy's theatre, or rather a way of seeing one
side to Murphy's theatre – historically grounded, precise in social observation, telling the truths of Ireland's experience of the present and of the past.
But take another play of his, performed just three years after *Famine* at the
Abbey. *The Morning After Optimism* has no specific setting, merely a fairy-
tale forest. It has just four characters, two couples set in formal opposition
one to the other: James, a vicious and neurotic pimp, and Rosie his 'dated
whore'; Edmund, a poetical idealist in Robin Hood costume, and Anastasia
the maiden of his dreams. Each character has an idiosyncratic language of
his or her own. James and Rosie speak a worn-down slang of the urban

underworld; Edmund and Anastasia express themselves in various forms of high-flown rhetoric. We are never allowed to know why James is in flight from Edmund, or whether Edmund is really his brother or his half-brother, as the story has it that Edmund was fathered by a king in a casual encounter with James's mother. Is it significant that Edmund, the 'good' brother, bears the name of the 'bad' bastard brother from *King Lear*? Murphy deliberately refuses to offer answers to such questions, just as he deliberately cuts the moorings of this dramatic situation from any 'real' world outside the theatre.

It is possible to read the play as a reflection of Irish social-historical conditions. Such is the reading of Fintan O'Toole, Murphy's most accomplished and authoritative interpreter to date. He sees in the contrast between country and city in the play Ireland's transition to modernity, an exposure of 'a fallen arcadia, a countryside that is not, in fact, free from the realities of history and the commercial system'. Thus '*The Morning After Optimism* is a playing out through a personal psychic history of the recent history of a nation.'[2] Yet such readings feel strained and suppositious with a play which so manifestly declares its status as universalizing fable rather than particularizing representation. James and Rosie are children of loss as much as the characters of Murphy's other early plays, the Carneys of *A Whistle in the Dark*, John Joe in *A Crucial Week*. But they are not creatures of historical conditions. Instead their psychopathology is a given – unsearchable, beyond diagnosis. James and Rosie are haunted by Edmund and Anastasia as the images of what they themselves have lost: goodness, innocence, idealism. James runs from Edmund in resentment, in anger, in fear; he sees in Anastasia an impossible dream of renewal, exchanging his ageing tart Rosie for a happy-ever-after wife. It is never even going to begin to happen, and soon James has reverted to type, kidnapping Anastasia, threatening her with rape. Rosie is equally attracted to the innocent Edmund, and equally frustrated in her failed attempts to seduce him. Caught in this knot of attraction and repulsion to their dream doubles, Rosie and James are driven to murder Anastasia and Edmund in the closing moments of the play.

This strange choreography of innocence and experience in *The Morning After Optimism* escapes from the apparent triteness of the subject by the sheer oddity of its idiom and the compulsiveness of its psychology. Murphy is preoccupied by loss, experienced as some prior state: the mental and emotional distortions it brings, tendencies towards violence and despair with a corresponding urge towards transcendence. Sometimes this is expressed as a socially embedded dramatic situation: the famine as some sort of primal loss in the Irish psyche; the depletions of modern Ireland manifested in emigration, communal conformism, a stricken sterility of the spirit. But equally the state of alienation and dispossession may stand free of originating circumstances, a drama of the heart and its mysteries. In what follows I want to consider a sequence of several of Murphy's major plays to suggest the interaction of these two modes and the styles of theatre used to enact them.

$$* * * * *$$

One of the commonest forms of loss in Murphy is the loss of faith or belief. This is reflected differently in two very different plays originating in the 1970s. *Conversations on a Homecoming*, produced by the Druid Theatre Company of Galway in 1985, is a rewritten version of the earlier *The White House* staged at the Abbey theatre in 1972. It is an ensemble play for seven actors, a group of friends assembling in their local pub in a provincial Irish town on the occasion of the return home from the United States of one of them. It is meticulously naturalistic in style, rendering the night's drinking in all its inchoate movements of gossip, aggression and emotion, unbroken by a theatrical interval, punctuated only by pitstops to the Gents. By contrast *The Sanctuary Lamp* (Abbey Theatre, 1975) is one of Murphy's chamber plays, akin to *The Morning After Optimism*: just three characters in a church in an unspecified city, two of them English, one Irish, brought together by the bonds of common need. It is Pinteresque in its obliquity, in the strangeness of its story and the disconnectedness of the figures in it. Both plays, *Conversations* and *The Sanctuary Lamp*, represent the struggles of disillusionment and despair, the one under the guise of the most ordinary social interaction, the other in a bizarre situation of emotional extremity. In each case I want to look at the nature of failed faith the characters experience, and the divergent theatrical means Murphy uses to express their plight.

The disillusionment in *Conversations* is post-1960s letdown. The small-town pub was given the name of 'The White House', the title of the play in its original two-act form, in the high-Camelot era because of a fancied resemblance of the proprietor J. J. Kilkelly to John F. Kennedy. The group of young people who gathered there saw it as a symbol of the Kennedy era and the spirit of youthful cultural renewal. One of them was to be a writer, another an actor, a third was to have her voice trained. In *The White House* one act was devoted to 'Speeches of Farewell' when the would-be actor, Michael Ridge, is leaving for the United States. *Conversations* is cut back to the one act of Michael's return. His career has gone nowhere, his life in New York has been a disaster, and he comes back in the hope of finding again the hope with which he started. But the ten years have produced changes back in The White House also: the idolized J. J. has turned into a drunk; the pub is barely kept going by his wife, the longsuffering Missus. Tom has never written anything and is stuck in his hated local schoolteacher's job, permanently engaged to, but never marrying, Peggy, whose singing career has not materialized either. The only flourishing presence on stage is the outsider Liam: '*a farmer, an estate agent, a travel agent, he owns property . . . he affects a slight American accent; a bit stupid and insensitive – seemingly the requisites of success*'.[3]

One of Murphy's satiric targets in *Conversations* is Ireland's provincial aping of America and Americanism. The play reaches a comic highpoint with Liam's drunken rendering of 'There's a Bridle Hanging on the Wall', bespeaking Irish enthusiasm for corny country and western music. As Tom puts it, denouncing the Kennedy cult, 'we are such a ridiculous race that even our choice of assumed images is quite arbitrary' (*Plays: Two*, 54). This is an Ireland which may have won its political independence but remains in a state of neocolonial mimicry. It is a provincial community also in its narrowness, its intolerance and sectarianism, features which Michael sees as a betrayal of the White House era. The men mouth patriotic belligerence in their drink, and boast of how they came close to marching north of the border in solidarity with their oppressed fellow-Catholics – came close but of course didn't. Josephine, the new bank clerk who lodges at the pub but is never seen on stage, is regarded with a mixture of salaciousness and puritan disapproval. A partition across the pub, erected at Liam's expense, dividing it into lounge and public bar, denies the classless principle of their original single space.

Tom and Michael, the 'twins' of earlier debates, represent a double study in failure. Tom's hatred of himself and all around him, his exaggerated cynicism, are clearly the product of soured idealism left to curdle and stagnate. Michael's fervent professions of continued belief in J. J. and the past are, equally obviously, driven by the need to compensate for the despair of a directionless life abroad. At one point, with the barest attempt to disguise the fact that he is talking about himself, he tells the story of stripping naked at a New York party and trying to set himself on fire shouting, 'No! No! This isn't it at all! This kind of – life – isn't it at all' (*Plays: Two*, 28). As so often in Murphy's work, Tom and Michael illustrate the no-win psychological situation where wholeness and fulfilment are denied both to those who emigrate and those who don't. The failure is at the source of meaning itself.

A play about stagnation, loss of will, despair barely at arm's length: yet *Conversations* is anything but the glum production this makes it sound. It is alleviated partly by the theatrical energy and skill with which Murphy orchestrates the night's drinking and the rhythms of its talk, from the patter of the opening warm-up, through the contentious, argumentative stages and the later confessional moods, to the last sodden motions of leavetaking. Nothing much happens. The flicker of a possible romance between Michael and Anne, sixteen-year-old daughter of J. J., is snuffed out when Liam, with the support of the other men, warns Michael off. And yet in this male-dominated bull-session, with so much of the futility of the men's talk exposed, Murphy contrives to make the all-but-silenced women's presence count.

There is an awareness of the hardships of Missus, a fine supporting part: *'in her early fifties, carelessly dressed (a dirty house-coat); a worried, slow-moving drudge of a woman, senses a bit numbed by life, but trying to keep the place together'* (*Plays: Two*, 6). It is important that the play begins and ends with the daughter Anne *'smiling her gentle hope out at the night'* (*Plays: Two*, 87). Peggy, suffering under the onslaught of her perpetually hostile perpetual fiancé Tom, who finds her every movement an irritation, is driven at one point to leave. It is as she stands at the edge of the stage, held at the point of departure, that she finally sings the song 'All in the April Evening', J. J.'s song, which she has been prompted to sing all evening. The significance of her singing, and the effect it creates in the theatre, are suggested in the stage direction:

> *She starts to sing – at first tentatively, like someone making noises to attract attention to herself. Then progressively, going into herself, singing essentially for herself; quietly, looking out at the night, her back to us, the sound representing her loneliness, the gentle desperation of her situation, and the memory of a decade ago. Her song creates a stillness over them all* (*Plays: Two*, 81).

Murphy risks a great deal in vesting so much of the emotional climax of the play in the singing of this late-Victorian religious lyric (written by Katherine Tynan, close friend of the young Yeats). But it is a risk which pays off. The singing of Peggy, like the smiling silence of Anne at the end, are made to speak for meanings which the conversations of the men can never express. It is in these expressive theatrical gestures, also, that *Conversations* is revealed as something other, something more than a study of 1970s Ireland and its discontents, a less specific drama of language and gender, of the experience of loss in time.

The Sanctuary Lamp was considered 'the most anti-clerical play ever staged by Ireland's National Theatre', according to one reviewer of its first Abbey Theatre production in 1975; it sparked off, according to another commentator, 'more heated controversy among Abbey audiences than I've seen for two decades'.[4] At a time when the great majority of Irish people were still practising Catholics and the special position of the Church was recognized in Ireland's constitution, it is easy to see why some of the play's passages might have been regarded as scandalously provocative, if not blasphemous. Here is the Irish juggler Francisco, for instance, on God:

> God made the world, right? and fair play to him. What has he done since? Tell me. Right, I'll tell you. Evaporated himself. When they painted his toe-nails and turned him into a church he lost his ambition, gave up learning, stagnated for a while, then gave up even that, said fuck it, forget it, and became a vague pain in his own and everybody else's arse.[5]

Yet *The Sanctuary Lamp* was not designed to provoke an Irish audience: at least, the specifically Irish content of the play is downplayed. When Francisco – not an Irish-sounding name – is first mentioned it is in terms which deliberately occlude his nationality; Francisco, we are told by Harry, his former circus partner, is 'not Italian, not Spanish, a juggler, actually' (*Plays: Three*, 104). It is not until he appears in the second act that he is identified as Irish by his voice and idiom. And at no point does he allude to his Irishness. *The Sanctuary Lamp* is not, like *Conversations*, a play representing the Ireland of its time, even if some of the Irish audiences of the time took umbrage at its treatment of religion.

The play is unlike *Conversations* also in its dramatic form. Where *Conversations* is built around the mood and atmosphere of the group, structured only by the rhythms of the night's drinking, *The Sanctuary Lamp* has a plot, a build-up of action, a climax and a resolution. Olga, contortionist wife of Harry the former circus strong-man, has been unfaithful to him with Francisco – and with many others. After the death of his daughter Teresa, Harry has run away from the performing group formed by Francisco and him, Olga and the dwarf Sam; he is driven by grief and the murderous jealousy of Francisco which he can only just suppress. Down and out, he fetches up in a church where he is hired as clerk/caretaker by the kindly Monsignor, one of his jobs being to keep the candle in the sanctuary lamp always lit. Dossing in the church, he discovers he has a fellow-dosser in the disturbed sixteen-year-old Maudie, an orphan running from the care of her brutal grandparents. The friendship they develop in the first act is disrupted in the second by the aggressive Francisco, who tries to seduce Maudie away from Harry. A violent confrontation between the men is barely averted, and the climax comes with Francisco's revelation to Harry that Olga has died of an overdose. The play ends with the three characters reconciled, settling down to sleep for the night, laid on the floor in the compartments of a confessional.

Fintan O'Toole sees in *The Sanctuary Lamp* a reworking of Aeschylus' trilogy the *Oresteia* (*Tom Murphy*, 186–204). But a more likely and more immediate source may have been Federico Fellini's 1954 film *La Strada*. It, too, turns on the relationship between a circus giant and a waiflike retarded young girl, and the strong-man's violent rivalry over the girl with a clownlike tightrope walker. Fellini's characters are very different, but the configuration of the three might well have prompted the conception of Harry, Maudie and Francisco. And the last 'performance' of the group (less Harry), narrated in bitterly satiric style by Francisco towards the end of the play, takes place at a decadent party reminiscent of Fellini's *La Dolce Vita* (1960). *The Sanctuary Lamp* is like the Italian cinema of Fellini in its focus on the disconnections of a modernity suffering with the anxieties of disbelief. The setting is given as 'a church in a city'. It is a Catholic church, but it could be in any city where, unlike in 1970s Ireland, religious practice is no longer the norm. Harry is in all probability an English Jew, his sense of Christian belief vague and distant. Maudie, though her mother may have been Catholic, has to have the several members of the Holy Family identified for her. Even the Monsignor prefers to read Herman Hesse rather than attend to his church duties. Only Francisco, Jesuit educated, is actively hostile to the church, visiting on it in vicious antagonism his resentment at his upbringing.

The play is iconoclastic in its use of the properties, the symbols, of the church. Harry's test of his self-belief is to lift the pulpit, something he at last triumphantly achieves – with Francisco in it. His act recalls that of Samson, destroying the pagan temple of the Philistines, but in Harry's case it is in a Christian church. In the second act he and Francisco make free with the communion wine. The confessional, already in obvious disuse – brushes and cleaning things are stored there – is upended to provide beds for those sleeping rough. Yet this practical appropriation of sacred things is not just in-tended to represent the obsolescence of religion. The play suggests rather the spiritual needs of the characters, and their attempts to find substitute symbols to replace the now-dead images of traditional Christianity. Harry's long ad-dress to the sanctuary lamp in the first act is a confession, a prayer. He needs sanctuary, he needs the refuge and peace which the place of the Christian sacrament should represent. Similarly, Maudie is looking for 'forgiveness', even though for her it is just a word, not a concept.

Harry and Maudie, like Murphy's other characters, are children of loss and one of the things they share is lost children. Maudie, abused by older boys, has had a baby, Stephen, who died or was taken from her at birth. With this memory, as with Harry's memories of Teresa dancing before him, it is impossible to know how much is fantasy, how much is real. But the experience of loss is a key part of the emotional dereliction which bonds them together. And the desire to escape or transcend this state inspires the homemade theologies which both Harry and Francisco improvise to replace conventional Christian ideas of salvation. This is Harry's imagination of immortality:

> The soul – y'know? – like a silhouette. And when you die it moves out
> into . . . slow-moving mists of space and time. Awake in oblivion actually.
> And it moves out from the world to take its place in the silent outer wall of
> eternity (*Plays: Three*, 158).

The sceptical Francisco questions him about the details of this wall of souls,
but Harry has thought it through; the soul-silhouttes merge in a 'Union
forever of loved ones' (*Plays: Three*, 159). Francisco is impressed in spite of
himself: as a theory of heaven 'it's certainly as good, better, than anything
they've come up with'. But for him the ideal state is that of limbo, the place of
unbaptised babies, those who escape the terrible conflicted states of Christian
belief: original sin, salvation and damnation. His utopian vision of limbo, in
the play's concluding moments, is of a beatific state outside the anguish of
human consciousness which all adults share:

> Oh but Limbo, Har, Limbo! With just enough light rain to keep the place lush
> green, the sunshine and red flowers, and the thousands and thousands of other
> fat babies sitting under the trees, gurgling and laughing and eating bananas
> (*Plays: Three*, 160).

* * * * *

Messed-up lives, dead-end states, the extremes of dereliction and despair –
these provide the staples of Murphy's drama, whatever the form and milieu.
But the very extremity of feeling and situation of his suffering characters generates a need for escape or transcendence. In two extraordinary works of the
1980s such transcendence is sought in the expressiveness of art: in *The Gigli
Concert* (1983), the high-European art of operatic singing; in *Bailegangaire*
(1985) the traditional Irish art of storytelling.

The Gigli Concert is like *The Sanctuary Lamp* in the indistinctness of its
setting. This time, we may guess, it is in a city in Ireland rather than in
England. The stage is occupied by the office-cum-bedsit of the 'dynamatol-
ogist', or quack psychologist, J. P. W. King, who is English but evidently
out of his own country. To the Irish Man, the other main character whose
name we never learn, King is a 'stranger'. The third character, Mona, is also
presumably Irish, and in an Abbey Theatre revival of the play in 1991 she
was played with a Northern Irish accent, making a suggestive trio of voices.
The Irishness and Englishness of the two men are significant in pointing up
the contrast between them. JPW is public-school educated, an upper-class
English drop-out, we may assume; the Irish Man is self-made, an 'opera-
tor' who has built a thousand houses with the help of 'corruption, brutality,
backhanding, fronthanding, backstabbing, lump labour and a bit of technology' (*Plays: Three*, 173). But little of the social reality beyond the stage,
in Ireland or England, is of real relevance to the play. The action is centred

on the encounter between the two men who seem so different from one another in every respect. All they have in common is the desperation voiced in the line each of them speaks independently: 'Christ, how am I going to get through today?' (*Plays: Three*, 166, 173).

The Irish Man comes to JPW with an obsession: he wants to sing like the Italian tenor Gigli (famous in the first half of the twentieth century). The aspiration is a symptom of the state of breakdown he is in; though he protests that he is not insane, he has turned violently aggressive even to his wife and much-loved young child. The Man's obsession with Gigli has reached such a point that, when JPW asks for details of his personal background, what he gets is the story of the Italian singer. The Irish Man impersonates the autobiography of Gigli, just as he hopes to reproduce his singing. We can see the nature of the substitution when we later hear what is probably the real story of Irish Man's childhood – deprived working-class background; abusive, tyrannical older brother; no romantic tale of rise to fame and fortune as in the legend of Gigli. Similarly, the extraordinary operatic arias recorded by Gigli and heard throughout the play in their original versions, represent some sort of ultimate otherness of feeling and articulation, an alternative in their formal perfection to the botched-up, inadequate world in which the characters live.

Irish Man looks to JPW for help, for magical assistance if necessary in his quest for the gift of singing like Gigli. The first aria the Man plays, with the expensive record player he brings along in Scene 4, is 'Dai Campi, Dai Prati' from Boito's opera *Mefistofele*. At first it seems that, in the traditional story of Faust dramatized in the opera, the Man is casting himself for the part of Faust while JPW is intended to be Mephistopheles, the devil who can give him infernal powers. Yet JPW is no magician, but a human no-hoper with plenty of troubles of his own. He himself hardly believes in the shadowy pseudo-science, pseudo-religion, 'dynamatology' that he is supposed to practise. Irish Man is evidently his first customer in years. If Man is fixated on Gigli, JPW has his fixation, too. He is romantically in love with an unattainable woman called Helen, with whom he can communicate only by illicit calls on his cut-off telephone. In his obsession with her he ignores the reality of the love of Mona, the lonely, childless woman with whom he has a desultory affair, and who turns out by the end of the play to be terminally ill. Part of the force of *The Gigli Concert* is how it shows the way in which the two men, in their ego-dominated urge towards transcendence, ignore the bodily reality of love and relationship represented by the sidelined woman Mona.

At the centre of the play, however, is the transfer from the Irish Man to JPW of the yearning to sing like Gigli. JPW becomes the Faust figure, the mortal looking for supernatural powers, while the Man is turned into the tempter Mephistopheles. After a series of frenetic encounters between the two, culminating in an outburst of terrible wordless crying from the Man, he reappears 'cured', revealing that this episode has been just one in a series of such depressive bouts, which he suffers periodically. JPW, who has come to take utterly seriously the Man's obsessive desire to sing, feels completely abandoned, the more so because he has discovered the unreality of his love for Helen and – too late – the substance of Mona's feeling for him. He determines to take on the part of the Irish Man, and sing like Gigli. And this is what we see him do in the play's last scene. High on drink and drugs, alone in his locked office, with the record player turned off, he 'performs' a Gigli aria. It is an extraordinary theatrical moment for an audience. The performance is evidently a fake: we are watching an actor mime an (audibly old) recording of the great Italian tenor singing an aria from Donizetti's opera *Lucia di Lammermoor*. The image of the spaced-out JPW mimicking Gigli is a grotesque one. But it has its own magic, expressive of some sort of human capacity for self-transcendence. After all, though JPW is not actually singing, Gigli is. The last theatrical gesture after the night's ordeal is the exit of JPW, leaving Gigli to sing the aria 'O Paradiso' on endless repeat to the open window. It is a perfectly judged final image, poised between irony and affirmation.

Unlike *The Gigli Concert*, *Bailegangaire* is specifically and explicitly concerned with Ireland and Irish experience. What is more, its setting represents a return for Murphy to a subject he had chosen to avoid at the outset of his career. The one thing on which he and Noel O'Donoghue had agreed, when planning to write what became *On the Outside*, was that it was not going to be set in a kitchen (*Tom Murphy*, 22). The-country-cottage kitchen, by the 1950s, had become synonymous with the stereotypical ruralism of the traditional Abbey Theatre play. Much of Murphy's theatrical experimentalism, through the 1960s and 1970s, had been a search for new forms and styles to replace such conservative representationalism. There was a self-consciousness, therefore, in his choice of time and place for the action of *Bailegangaire*: '1984, *the kitchen of a thatched house*' (*Plays: Two*, 90). *Bailegangaire* uses its old-fashioned, even archaic, setting in a contemporary period (for its original 1980s audience) to create a view of the relationship between past and present in Ireland.

Old Ireland is represented by Mommo, the senile grandmother sitting up in the double-bed which dominates the stage. Mary and Dolly, the two grown-up granddaughters who care for her, stand for the Ireland of the 1980s. From outside the cottage we hear news of the Japanese-owned computer plant down the road. Dolly's house and lifestyle, as she describes it ironically, reflect a relatively prosperous, modernized society. 'I've rubber-backed lino in all the bedrooms now, the Honda is going like a bomb and the *lounge*, my dear, is carpeted' (*Plays: Two*, 107). Dolly and her children are supported by the weekly remittances of her husband working in England. Just how dysfunctional this family arrangement is, however, is revealed in Dolly's account of his annual returns for the Christmas holidays, when he beats her up in revenge for her infidelity. At the time of the play's action she is facing a crisis because she is pregnant, an all-too-evident proof of her unfaithfulness. The older, unmarried sister, Mary, though she succeeded in leaving home and having a successful career as a nurse in England, hardly has a happier life. Having returned in search of some sort of emotional fulfilment, she now finds herself trapped in the role of permanent carer for a grandmother who will not acknowledge her identity, but treats her as an intrusive servant.

The constant accompaniment to the lives of these 1980s women is Mommo's storytelling. Her senile dementia takes the form of repeating always the one story without ever being able to finish it. The story is that of a laughing-contest, a competition between two men as to who could laugh longest, which happened years ago, with disastrous consequences: one of them literally laughed himself to death, the other died shortly after. Mommo tells this as a traditional folkstory, in the style of a formal shanachie. What she never admits is that she herself was involved; her husband Seamus was the 'Stranger' who challenged Costello, the champion laugher of Bochtán village, and it was she, the Stranger's wife, who egged him on, supplying the subject for their laughter: 'misfortunes'. The full dimensions of the tragedy only emerge in the course of the play. While the laughing-contest continued in the distant Bochtán pub, the young orphaned grandchildren (including Dolly and Mary) were left untended, and their brother Tom died in an accident as a result. It is because Mommo cannot face these consequences, because she has never been able to work through the trauma of these events, that she is unable to finish her story or own up to it as hers.

The experience produced by the split drama of past and present narratives in *Bailegangaire* is one of the richest and most resonant in modern Irish theatre. Mommo's storytelling is compelling, hypnotic, given out in a highly wrought rhythmic style, combining Irish-English dialect with showy Latinate vocabulary:

> It was a bad year for the crops, a good one for mushrooms, and the contrary and adverse connection between these two is always the case (*Plays: Two*, 94).

Even for an audience which finds such a style initially hard to understand, there is a delight in the elaboration of the language, the virtuoso skills of the performer acting out all the parts in the story. (The part of Mommo was created by the great Irish actress Siobhán McKenna, in a magnificent last stage appearance.) At the same time the simple dynamic of suspense makes us want to reach the end of the story. We feel thus with Mary, who in the course of the action decides to urge her grandmother on at last to complete the narrative. This she finally achieves. The ending is one of renewal and reconciliation of the sundered and traumatized family, as the story is told to its end, Mommo finally greets Mary by name, and Mary agrees to accept Dolly's still-to-be born baby as her own.

Though *Bailegangaire* is without overt allegorical design, it is hard to see the figure of Mommo without thinking of Cathleen ni Houlihan, Ireland personified as an old woman to be rejuvenated by the sacrifice of her young male patriots. It was an image made famous by W. B. Yeats's and Lady Gregory's 1902 play *Cathleen ni Houlihan*. For Mommo, however, there will be no miraculous rejuvenation; she is a convincingly real old woman at the end of a long life. In so far as there are associations with Cathleen ni Houlihan, it makes for a sardonic comment on the figure: Ireland as a senile old crone unable to forget her past, unable to come to the end of her story. The subject of the laughing-contest is also suggestive of Irish traditions of black comedy as a means of exorcising the memories of deprivation. The frenzied laughter of the contestants and spectators at the laughing-contest turned the village of Bochtán (meaning 'the poor man') into Bailegangaire, the 'town without laughter', where adults never laughed again. Yet *Bailegangaire* works as a theatrical means of living through such memories, and coming to terms with them in the present. And that process is not merely a therapeutic strategy for bringing into consciousness the blocked-out terrors of the past. Storytelling as a skill, an art, in all its energy and brio, is as full-throated a means to expressive transcendence as the arias of Gigli.

* * * * *

Murphy's most recent play, *The House*, produced at the Abbey Theatre in 2000, could be seen as a period piece, a throwback to an earlier style and subject. It is concerned with emigration and homecoming, the theme of *A Whistle in the Dark*, of *A Crucial Week*, of *Conversations*. It is set in the 1950s, and focused on the mass phenomenon of the emigrant workers who come back to Ireland each August, and in two weeks use up in an orgy of drink and talk their accumulated savings of the year. This ritual carnival provides the main theatrical frame for the play. It is intercut with the story of one individual emigrant, Christy, who has an obsessive fixation with the house of the play's title, and the kindly upper-middle-class family, the De Burcas, who represented his childhood ideal in contrast to the brutal bleakness of his own working-class background. Murphy's subject here, once again, is the Irish psychopathology of home and away, the need for an idea of 'home', its distorted construction in the absence of the reality. Yet this need not be seen solely as symptomatic of the Irish situation as such. Alienation, the sense of psychological dispossession, are not, after all, states confined to Ireland. In traditional Marxist analysis they would be seen as the results of capitalist industrialization and modernity. For Freudian interpreters they derive from disruptions of the ego originating in the infantile unconscious; for Christians they are the traces of the Fall and original sin. Murphy's children of loss could be understood in terms of any one of these schemes of belief. The strength and distinctiveness of Murphy's theatre is that his plays, whether set in Ireland or not, reach out to broader patterns of human feeling and behaviour, and cannot be reduced to the confining category of 'Irish drama'.

NOTES

1. Tom Murphy, *Plays: One* (London, Methuen, 1992), 8.
2. Fintan O'Toole, *Tom Murphy: the Politics of Magic* (London: Nick Hern Books, 2nd edn. 1994), 97, 109.
3. Tom Murphy, *Plays: Two* (London: Methuen, 1993), 4.
4. Quoted in Hugh Hunt, *The Abbey: Ireland's National Theatre 1904–1979* (Dublin: Gill and Macmillan, 1979), 225.
5. Tom Murphy, *Plays: Three* (London: Methuen, 1994), 128.

16

CLAIRE GLEITMAN

Reconstructing history in the Irish history play

In a 1983 article the critic Lynda Henderson offered an acerbic critique of the fascination with history which is a hallmark of much contemporary Irish playwriting. 'A concern for history', she wrote, 'is a perverse desire to remain fallen, to make no attempt to rise, to spend your life contemplating your navel . . . Too many contemporary Irish plays bleat plaintively of old wounds.'[1] While Henderson's remarks are particularly damning, she is hardly the first commentator to draw attention to the preoccupation in Irish culture with Ireland's traumatic past. It was Stephen Dedalus, after all, who (in *Ulysses*) described history as the nightmare from which he was trying to awake. Yet Henderson's worry is that recent Irish dramatists are determined to remain asleep: in her view too many keep their gaze stubbornly arrested backwards, like Walter Benjamin's famously retrospective angel of history.[2] It will be the aim of this chapter to suggest something quite different about the Irish history play, a genre which contemporary Irish writers have indeed made their stock in trade. Examples abound: Brian Friel has written about the 1601 Battle of Kinsale in *Making History* (1988); about the mapping of Ireland by colonial forces in *Translations* (1980); and about the horrific events of Bloody Sunday, 1972, in *Freedom of the City* (1973). Tom Murphy has dramatized the Irish potato famine in *Famine* (1968); Stewart Parker's *Northern Star* (1984) concerns the 1798 uprising; the list goes on. This is hardly surprising. Ireland's blood-stained history provides dramatic material aplenty, and it is a rare Irish author who opts to disregard it altogether.

Yet what gives many of these plays their resonant power is their authors' direct engagement with the very issue which troubles Henderson. In this chapter I will examine two works which are emblematic of the best of contemporary Irish history playwriting. Both fix their lens on the frozen backwards stare which Henderson indicts as endemic to recent Irish drama.[3] They do so, however, not by adopting their characters' myopic gaze, but by examining the ways in which the historical past works to invigorate and also to imprison their characters' imaginations. As I shall argue, these plays do not naïvely 'represent' history. Rather they offer a rich analysis of the ideological and psychological imperatives which control the ways in which history is remembered, transmitted and employed, and its potent power to whisper persistently (and sometimes perniciously) in the ear of the present.

It is a commonplace that history tends to be written from the viewpoint of those with the fattest pocketbooks. In self-conscious resistance to this tendency many modern writers prefer to tip history on its side to examine what lies at its edges; for an example, one need look no further than O'Casey's Dublin Trilogy. Following in these footsteps, Frank McGuinness's 1985 play, *Observe the Sons of Ulster Marching Towards the Somme*, explores the experiences of the anonymous class of soldiers whom Falstaff dismissed as 'Food for powder'. More specifically, the play focuses on eight Protestant men of Ulster, a province whose fate hung in the balance during World War One, as England shifted its attention from the knotty problem of Home Rule to the violence engulfing all Europe. In response many thousands of Protestant youths were urged to enlist in the 36th (Ulster) Division as a display of loyalty to the Crown. For their troubles a generation marched headlong into German machine-gun fire, gaining a minuscule amount of ground which was promptly lost again. *Observe the Sons* examines this historical trauma through the eyes of eight recruits whom we follow from the time of their arrival at a makeshift army barracks to the moments preceding their deaths. All of these men subscribe, to some degree, to a unionist politics which serves to unite them, despite the discord which surfaces from the moment they are herded together in a sloppy union of alleged sameness masking manifold difference. As conflicts well up between them the soldiers do their best to remind one another of what they have in common and why they are in France, which is 'For the glory of his majesty the king', 'for the empire's foe is Ulster's foe'.[4]

A predominant concern in the drama is to dramatize the function which such neatly dichotomous thinking fulfils, as these men strive by turns to face and not to face the horrifying end the war has in store for them. McGuinness's soldiers are perched on the precipice dividing a seemingly stable world from the emphatically postlapsarian one which replaced it ('Never such innocence again', wrote Philip Larkin[5]). Raised in communities where it was a point of pride to be able 'to smell a Catholic' a mile away, the Ulstermen endeavour to cling to the secure sense of identity such self-deluding clarity provides. *Observe the Sons* offers a complex analysis of the psychological needs served by a single-minded sense of history and identity in a situation defined by uncertainty, powerlessness and random horror. It is an increasingly desperate desire to give 'slaughter shape' which animates the sectarian gestures exhibited by these men, and it is the character Pyper's capitulation to the need for 'shape' which is the clearest indication of the trauma he suffered at the Somme and the twisted legacy it left behind in the minds of its guilt-ridden survivors.

The eight members of the 36th Division denote, collectively, the spectrum of Protestant Ulster. Among them are rural labourers, the urban working class, and one representative of the old Ascendancy. As men from different places and backgrounds gradually people the stage, the soldiers regard one another with suspicion and even, sometimes, distaste. Still, they manage to form a fragile union initially founded on their mutual hatred for the 'Fenian rats' whom they loathed and sometimes hunted prior to the war. The painful function of this unifying animosity becomes increasingly evident over the course of the play, as the men shroud themselves in sectarian myths which give them the courage to perform a role scripted by commanders whom McGuinness keeps off stage, a role which pits them against an enemy whom we also never see and whom the soldiers seem incapable of fathoming. Mired in their fears and armoured by their myths, the Ulstermen barely glimpse the shadowy figures of authority on whose whims their fates depend.

As its first scene makes plain, *Observe the Sons* is a memory play told from the perspective of Pyper, the sole survivor from the original group of eight. In his older incarnation Pyper is tortured by visitations from ghosts of that July day, who seem to goad him to engage in a kind of compulsive remembrance. Though he shrinks from their decree, Pyper clearly feels a powerful personal compulsion to contort history into a shape which will endow his friends' deaths with transcendent meaning. Once a political sceptic, Pyper has mutated into a tortured fundamentalist, tending the altar of an uncompromising unionism that casts Catholics as usurpers of Protestant mythology as well as Protestant land: 'There would be and there will be no surrender. The sons of Ulster will rise and lay their enemy low, as they did at the Boyne, as they did at the Somme, against any invader who will trespass on to their homeland' (10).

As Pyper's words make plain, the unionism to which he adheres takes its political and military mandate from the blood-sacrifices of the past. This form of radical sectarianism, which holds that past acts of violence justify and even necessitate further ones, is common to both sides of the Irish struggle. What McGuinness does is to show the genesis of this historical orthodoxy as it develops in a man once proudly iconoclastic. While Elder Pyper speaks of his desire to 'rebuild' a world which 'lay in ruins' about his feet (10), his younger self seemed dedicated to deconstructing the tidy world view his comrades carried with them to France. In the play's second scene we are transported to the army barracks where the men first make one another's acquaintance. There, the first character we meet is young Pyper, whose status as anarchic, whimsically satanic truth-teller is quickly underlined. When the other men first see him Pyper is peeling an apple (surely the most overdetermined fruit in nature), and, when he cuts himself, he delivers his first line, which is 'Damnation'. Thus Pyper announces himself as a figure of temptation, a Pied Piper who entrances and repels the other men with his slippery sexuality, his decadent cynicism and his provocative tales of sex with a three-legged French whore. It is Pyper, the seductive homosexual with 'remarkably fine skin . . . for a man', who manages to bring the macho antics of the Belfast pair to a halt by punching one in the groin, and it is Pyper who reminds the others that they are 'the scum' of the army, earmarked for early deaths. As an early dialogue makes clear, Pyper is the forbidden or 'rotten' fruit, despite his fine skin, the 'one bad apple' which has the potential to '[spoil] the barrel' (15). The world as the others perceive it is defined by clear boundaries separating men from women, nuns from whores, the sacred Protestant view of history from the distorted Catholic one. It is Pyper's declared objective to 'take away [the other men's] peace' by undermining such assumptions at every turn (37).

Ironically, Pyper's conversion from provocateur to preacher is juxtaposed with the simultaneous conversion of the others to something like his former nihilism. In Part 3, entitled 'Pairing', the men devote their leave-time to visiting locations which are foundational for their myths. In search (it seems) of a reaffirmation which might steel them for the return to battle, they find they cannot fit back into the roles they occupied in their prewar life. Instead they carry the Front home with them, and that baggage destroys the mythic foundations these places once secured for them as Ulstermen. In 'Pairing's' fuguelike series of exchanges, Roulston and Crawford confront the irrelevance of religion in their present situation, while Anderson and McIlwaine glimpse the same absence of meaning on the Belfast Field where the annual July Twelfth marches (which commemorate the 1690 Battle of the Boyne) are held. Alone in the Field, the very place where they expect their centrality to be affirmed, the Belfast men approach the depths of despondency just as the shell-shocked Moore does, while standing on a rope-bridge in Antrim. 'The whole world is bleeding,' says Moore. 'Nobody can stop it' (49). McIlwaine, in Belfast, concurs: 'The war's cursed. It's good for nothing . . . We're all going to die for nothing' (50).

Once the men no longer feel bolstered by the coherent worldview which once sustained them, they have nowhere to turn except (in Crawford's words) to 'my own sweet self' (48) – or, more positively, to a loving relationship with another doomed man. Part 3 draws to a close with each man clinging to his partner in a moving affirmation of the power of private unions over public ones energized by violence and hate. Yet this shift from a public to a private system of loyalties has an ambiguous status in the play. It allows the men temporarily to discard their patriotic bravado, yet it forces them to accept an absurdist universe without coherence or meaning, one where, to quote Moore once again, 'The whole world is bleeding. Nobody can stop it.' To embrace such a vision while simultaneously marching into machine-gun fire is beyond imagining, and McGuinness does not ask this of his characters. Instead his soldiers prepare for the final march by doing what they can to resuscitate the very mythologies we saw collapsing in Part 3.

Part 4, entitled 'Bonding', stages the lull before zero hour, as the soldiers attempt to divert themselves from what awaits them on that sparkling July morning in 1916. First, McIlwaine amuses the others by recounting the events of the Easter Rising (recent history, in July 1916) with a decidedly sardonic slant. As he tells the tale, a 'boy' named Patrick Pearse 'took over a post office because he was short of a few stamps'. Pearse's mother responded by shooting her son, noting huffily: '"That'll learn him, the cheeky pup. Going about robbing post offices."' When the other soldiers query the truth of McIlwaine's version, he shrugs: 'To hell with the truth, as long as it rhymes' (64–5). Thus the Easter Rising, which holds a central place in the opposing side's catalogue of mythic victories, is rewritten by the unionist as burlesque propaganda. McIlwaine's creative recounting cheers his companions: 'Your man reads the proclamation of an Irish republic. The Irish couldn't spell republic, let alone proclaim it.' But as the moments pass and the battle looms, the soldiers' courage falters. Hence, in an effort to 'make the blood boil', they agree to 'play' the Battle of Scarva, which is the annual reenactment of the Battle of the Boyne held on its anniversary. By restaging not the battle but its annual commemoration, the men inadvertently suggest the impossibility of accessing 'actual history' except through representation. What they enact is a mock Battle of the Boyne which is actually a mock-mock Battle of the Boyne, like something out of Alice's world of reflecting mirrors.

Moreover, the (re-)representation is coopted by the ideological imperatives of unionism in such a way as to pass the poisonous binaries of the past on to the present and future. As Anderson remarks, 'remember, . . . we know the result, . . . keep to the result' (70). Some stories can be tampered with; others, of course, cannot. While the battle is performed the self-appointed director provides appropriate commentary, stressing the virtues of Protestant William versus the vices of the demonized Catholic James. Anderson's 'script' loads the representation with the necessary ideological freight. He cloaks the historical events with the propaganda of unionist myth, adding a conclusion which is pure wish-fulfilment: 'This time James will fall, and with him mighty Rome in this kingdom' (71).

But Pyper, still instinctively subversive, surprises the others by distorting the sacred text. Though his role is to play the Protestant monarch's trusty steed, Pyper trips. His rider, King William, comes crashing to the ground, and James and his horse find themselves the startled victors. As Millen declares woefully, this is '[n]ot the best of signs' (71). Pyper's action works to destabilize the ideologically cathected myth which had provided the thinnest veneer over the terrifying actuality the soldiers are facing, as Pyper himself seems to recognize. Somewhat later he strives to patch up the mythology by delivering a sermon in which he compares this day to the 'glorious' one at the Boyne when God 'scattered our enemies' (80). The play concludes with an incantatory repetition of the word 'Ulster', and the men vanish into the ensuing horror. As they do so one senses that what sustains them in part is the neatly homogeneous sense of history suggested by Pyper's sermon, which permits them to perceive the present as a recapitulation of the past, and to imagine themselves fighting anew the 'Fenian rats' who (they conveniently forget) are fairly well represented in the trenches of the Somme and fighting alongside them. But since the Germans are inscrutable, the soldiers graft on to them the image of the more familiar enemies whom they know from home; Pyper even jokingly remarks that the Germans speak Gaelic 'for badness' (64). The danger of this merging of enemies is that it completely obscures the reality of the soldiers' situation, which may be just as well at this moment, but it is a tragedy for the future of Ulster.

The nature of that tragedy is best revealed in the conversion of Pyper, whose transformation from the gadfly sceptic of 1916 to the righteous scourge of unionism is a dramatic articulation of mytho-historiography. Pyper participates in uncovering the hollow centre of myth at the same time as he helps write another chapter of it. Before enlisting in the 36th Pyper was a sculptor who sought to escape the clutches of unionist indoctrination by fleeing Ireland for France. Once there, he found that his art was contaminated by the relentless bloodlust of his ancestors. 'I could not create,' he tells his lover, Craig, 'I could only preserve' (56). All he could create, in short, was a static repetition of what he had witnessed, which is precisely what he does again by creating the play.

Not only does Pyper instantly give 'slaughter shape' though he says he will not, he imposes on the events of his memory what happens to be a particularly shapely shape. *Observe the Sons* is strikingly schematic in form: its four-part structure is replicated by the arrangement of characters into four pairs in the scene of that name, which itself has four settings. The entire play is framed by the word 'Dance', which ends both the first and last scenes.

Structure, always the most artificial element in a dramatic text, here is forced to the audience's attention because of its heightened artificiality. Structure serves a thematic function for the play as well, as it highlights the artificiality of the historical consciousness, the consciousness which would look into the past to retrieve incidents in such a way as to support a particular political position, or 'give slaughter shape'. The 'truth' of the Boyne or the Somme is that vast numbers of people died brutal deaths in hideously disordered conditions. McGuinness's drama represents the way in which that truth becomes artificially coded into history in such a way as to obscure its full horror.

Yet Pyper's chilling reunion with his younger self in the play's closing moments contains an acknowledgement of the hopelessness of his efforts. 'The house has grown cold,' says Younger Pyper, 'the province has grown lonely' (80). The God to whom Pyper prayed on the battlefield failed to hear his plea ('If you are a just and merciful God,' said Pyper then, 'show your mercy this day' [79]); and the world Pyper now inhabits seems godless despite the fervency of his sermons. Having lost the only meaning his life contained, which he found in a love relationship with another man, Pyper is in at least one regard reminiscent of Pozzo, in Beckett's *Waiting for Godot*, though he has no unlucky Lucky to keep him company. Pyper cries, 'Dance' as Pozzo cries 'On, On', though there is nowhere to go and no reason for dancing except to avoid seeing the hollowness of his own desperate gestures. Bereft of anything resembling a private union, Pyper must cling to public ones, which failed his friends even as they fail him now. Yet this character, like the crumbling world he inhabits, seems trapped in a self-destructive dance, compulsively rehearsing the past in an effort to find meaning and form there.

In a strikingly similar fashion Sebastian Barry's 1995 play, *The Steward of Christendom*, charts the efforts of Thomas Dunne to pick through his memory shards in search of consolation for the anguish of his old age. Like *Observe the Sons*, Barry's drama concerns a man at the margins of history, a former Chief Superintendent of the Dublin Metropolitan Police. The DMP was a British-controlled, Irish police force which (most infamously) clashed with Irish workers and nationalists during the Dublin Lock-Out of 1913 and the Easter Rising of 1916. After the establishment of the Irish Free State, former members of the DMP were vilified by their fellow Irishmen for what was perceived as their traitorous collaboration with imperialist rule. The play's present-tense action is located in 1932, and is set in a county care home where the nearly senile Thomas Dunne is now confined. At the same time the play transports us to various moments in the former Chief Superintendent's past life, as he strives to recapture the orderliness and perfect joy he associates with his personal past and with the Ireland of his youth. For Dunne the pivotal moment of change was 1922, when a nation which was 'shipshape as a ship' detached itself from Britain and swiftly became overrun by 'savagery and ruin'.[6]

Yet woven through Dunne's memories of a serene Ireland, basking in the glow of benign British rule, are constant reminders of how brutal and vulnerable to chaos were the systems of order on which his nostalgia feeds. Indeed, the self-deceiving nature of his memories is underlined by the very manner in which Barry dramatizes them. Just as the grief-stricken old man is on the verge of embracing a precious moment or a lost child, darkness intrudes, the memory vanishes, and Dunne is left to roar 'with pain and confusion' as he finds himself alone again with his regret and loss (20). The sum effect of the string of gapped memories is the recognition, for us if not for Dunne, that there is no past, pure and simple unto itself, which has not always been contaminated by the tendency towards disorder which defines the personal and the political spheres. As Dunne gropes for constancy his daughter Annie confronts him with the implacable fact that dooms his efforts: 'Papa,' she says, 'we've all to grow old' (37).

The Steward of Christendom draws our attention immediately to the gruesome gap between idyllic childhood and dismal old age. The play opens in 1932 in the 'bare room' of the care home, where the furnishings are spare and even the morning light is 'poor'. Dunne's opening lines, which echo the opening of Joyce's *A Portrait of the Artist as a Young Man*, show him taking refuge from his surroundings in a serene recollection of childhood: 'Da Da, Ma Ma . . . Clover, clover in my mouth . . . and Ma Ma's soft breast when she opens her floating blouse, and Da Da's bright boots in the grasses, amid the wild clover' (3). Almost instantly this lyrical evocation is undercut by images which encapsulate much of what will follow: 'and me the Ba Ba set in the waving grasses . . . and the farmhands going away like an army of redcoats but without the coats, up away up the headland with their scythes'. As through metaphor the farmhands are turned into 'an army of redcoats but without the coats', the tranquil scene darkens (though Dunne fails to notice) into an anticipation of his beloved son's death in the trenches of World War One.[7] More than that, the image suggests that order is typically maintained through force and is always on the verge of collapsing into chaos. Dunne's Da Da, lovingly recalled in the first monologue, reappears moments later as a more threatening figure: 'When little Tom no sleepy sleep, big stick comes in and hitting Tom Tommy . . . and all is silence . . . except the tread of the Da Da, . . . except the fall of the big stick' (4).

Add to this Dunne's later evocation of himself in the role of policeman, keeping Dublin 'orderly and safe' with the aid of 300 men (9), and one begins to see how Barry works to undermine the nostalgia for a lost world where 'order was everywhere' because everyone knew his place. Though Dunne marks 1922 as the year when order gave way to a 'tide of ruin', it is clearly his view that things began to fray from the very moment when Victoria no longer held the British throne. Under her exquisite reign, according to Dunne:

> All the harbours of the earth were trim with their granite piers . . . and her mark was everywhere, Ireland, Africa, the Canadas, every blessed place. And men like me were there to make everything peaceable, to keep order in her kingdoms . . . She loved her Prince. I loved my wife. The world was a wedding of loyalty, of steward to Queen, she was the very flower and perfecter of Christendom (14).

Presiding over a perfect chain of being, Queen Victoria functioned as the principle of order which the rest of the world could gladly imitate. In Dunne's mythic reconstruction he strives to link himself into a network of coherence and permanence guaranteed by Victoria, the great mother who worked to web the world into a comprehensible, fixed and peaceful system.

As it happens, Dunne's nostalgia for empire is less political than it is personal – or, at least, the two realms are inextricably intertwined. As he chooses to remember those years, they provided a guarantee of his own patriarchal authority, and they are associated with a cherished period of family stability which rapidly disintegrated – and which in some ways never really existed. This 'Lear in long johns', as Jack Kroll has described him, was not a king but merely a lowly servant of kings;[8] yet Dunne recalls himself as the proud regent of a shipshape domain which mirrored the example set by prince and queen. Married to a woman of whom the king himself approved ('King Edward himself praised her hair,' says Dunne, 'when we were presented in nineteen-three' [25]), he was free to perform his role as Chief Superintendent with warmly paternal efficiency. Meanwhile, at home, 'Dolly my daughter . . . polished my policeman's boots, and Annie and Maud brought me my clothes brushed and starched in the morning' (11).

Yet this image of a beneficently harmonic hierarchy is never really credible. For one thing, we learn early on of Dunne's fervent longing, in his old age, for a suit flecked with gold. The source of this longing is his failure to reach the rank of Commissioner, the reward for which would have been a gold-laced uniform. He never rose to that rank because, he explains, 'that wasn't a task for a Catholic, . . . in the way of things, in those days' (9). Dunne rose as high as a Catholic could in a police force which was a largely powerless puppet of the British army. Despite dogged attempts at self-glorification, he is fleetingly aware of his marginalized status in Victoria's empire, which disqualified him from attaining the kind of success which might have dissipated his haunting sense of failure.

That sense of failure was engendered by the father with the big stick, who upbraided him for failing at his schooling and held him in contempt for joining the police force. Much of Dunne's action in the play can be understood as an attempt to become the man his father assured him he was not. Thus he embraces a political system and a social role which seem to affirm his paternal authority, and also seem to promise to stem the erosion of self and family. But the old man's fragmented memories confront him with nagging evidence of his helpless inability to hold back the 'tide of ruin' which engulfed his family. When his son appears dressed in army uniform to say, 'It's cold in the mud,' he can reply only, 'I know, child. I'm sorry' (17). In another memory-fragment his daughter Annie slips to his bedside to ask why she was afflicted with polio, which has left her back so bent that she despairs of marrying. In response to her plaintive, 'Why, Papa?', Dunne must again confess ignorance: 'Because it afflicts some and leaves others clear. I don't know' (21). As for his adored daughter Dolly, she leaves Ireland for Ohio, because she can no longer endure the scorn her father's former position with the DMP brings upon her.

In fact, Dunne's devotion to the mirage of stability which he associates with empire plays a direct role in the disintegration of his family. Though he might have taken heed of the Cordelia-like Dolly's wise words ('Hats', she says, 'are more dependable than countries' [49]), he is determined that the country should be served. Hence he is dismayed when Willie turns out to be too short to become a policeman. When Willie joins the British army as the next-best way to fulfil his father's aspirations for him, he dies in the mud of France. 'All I got back was your uniform,' Dunne laments, 'with the mud only half-washed out of it' (47). But his relentless desire for a gold uniform of his own displays his unflagging faith in the trappings of power, which can do nothing to compensate for the loss of a child, or to resist the chaos to which order must always eventually yield.

It is increasingly apparent that Dunne's passion for order has its roots in a vexed familial drama whose most striking features are conflict and loss. On the day he watches the reins of power pass from British to Irish hands, he is surprised by the surge of loyalty he feels towards Michael Collins. Though that surge is quickly suppressed, it lays bare the deeper psychological needs which his romance with empire has sought to fulfil. Speaking of the day that Collins took possession of the keys to Dublin Castle, Dunne says:

I could scarce get over the sight of him . . . He would have made a tremendous policeman . . . I would have been proud to have him as my son . . . I felt rough near him, that cold morning . . . There never was enough gold in that uniform, never. I thought too as I looked at him of my father, as if Collins could have been my son and could have been my father. I had risen as high as a Catholic could go, and there wasn't enough braid, in the upshot. I remembered my father's anger when I failed at my schooling, and how he said he'd put me into the police, with the other fools of Ireland (50).

In Dunne's imagination Collins flexibly performs the role of father and son, while also underlining Dunne's acute sense of deficiency. Struck by Collins's glamour, he is dismayed by his own uniform, which lacks sufficient gold because he could never be the son his father wanted him to be, any more than he could be a real 'son' to a British government which used him as a pawn, just as it used his son Willie as cannon fodder.

The other half of the family dynamic, the maternal one, is equally troubled for Dunne. Early in Act 1 he tenderly recalls a morning when he went in search of newly laid eggs which he carried back proudly to his adoring Ma Ma. Later the same image recurs more disturbingly when he recalls a terrible fight between 'my Ma Ma and me' (46). On this occasion he was caught playing roughly with a hidden Christmas toy. In a rage, his mother tossed the toy into a pile of dung, and he retaliated by torturing her favourite hen so that it never laid eggs again. Thus the movement of Dunne's memory (from fresh warm eggs to broken eggs on a dung heap) works against him, unearthing the more turbulent experiences which undermine his cherished memory of benign matriarchs in a world once 'loyal, united, and true' (61).

The story about Dunne and his mother's 'black time' is also resonant because it culminates with a hen whose 'wits go astray' thanks to his abuse of it. This is suggestive of what happens to Dunne himself and to the generation of Irish people with whom he identifies. 'All of them', he says, 'lost their wits and died' (45), or ended up confined with him in the home. The care home, which he repeatedly describes as a madhouse, is a perfect emblem for the world which he both exalted and feared, the world of order restraining the chaos battering at its gates. The madhouse's inmates, like Dunne, linger on in a state of shrivelled bewilderment, 'crying and imagining' because they cannot make sense of what he calls 'the gap between the two things' (16): what was and what is, what they were and what they are. These mad folks are watched over by a man named Smith who, not incidentally, is an *orderly* who carries a 'pacifier' (or billy club) which he does not hesitate to use. Smith, in short, bluntly embodies the figures of parental and civic authority which haunt Dunne's imagination, and whose methods of preserving order now take the distinct form of a 'pacifier'; the very term neatly blends the tenderly parental with the brutally oppressive. As for Dunne (who, as an old man in the home, is stripped naked, unceremoniously bathed, and occasionally whipped), he is now clearly the infantilized subject of the authorities which, in reality, he always was.

Thus the madhouse becomes a kind of nightmarish wish-fulfilment where the order Dunne so obsessively desired is finally brought to bear on him. It was the news of Collins's murder which precipitated the emotional break-down which landed him in the home, and he recalls this event shortly before the play's end. Forced to confront his inability to resist the 'to-do and . . . tur-moil' which descended on his family and nation (62), Dunne asks Annie to slay him with his ceremonial sword. Instead she has him committed. But his memory of his breakdown seems cleansing, as it is followed by the merciful gift of a vision. Like Lear imagining Cordelia's breath on the looking-glass, Dunne is granted the illusion of life in a dead child: Willie appears to him, his 'uniform flecked with gold' (63). As his son helps him to his feet, Dunne utters the words which are inscribed on Jim Larkin's statue on O'Connell Street: 'The great appear great because we are on our knees. Let us rise.' Seemingly embracing the wisdom of his former political enemy, Dunne ap-pears to repudiate the colonial mindset which so debilitated his life. As he admits to his child, 'It's all topsy-turvy, Willie' (63).

Yet even as he seems to embrace Larkin's egalitarian wisdom, his vision of Willie in a gold-flecked uniform cannot help but remind us of the delusions which killed the child, which shattered Dunne's life, and which have not been relinquished entirely. Willie can console his father only when he is garbed in the gold in which Dunne sought to envelop his life, and which Barry persistently associates with delusion. 'Da Da is golden, golden,' Dunne says early in the play, 'nothing that Da Da do takes away the sheen of gold' (4). As Dunne drifts into sleep, Willie lies in close to him and sleeps, too: the lost child is retrieved. Yet, for all its consoling power, this final tableau remains devastatingly sad. Unlike Lear, who is mercifully freed in death, Dunne (according to the play's last stage direction) only sleeps; and the child who is 'not to be lived without' remains irretrievably gone.

Neither McGuinness nor Barry allows us to shrink from Annie's dismal truth – 'We've all to grow old' – nor do they release their kingdomless char-acters from 'the rack of this tough world'. Instead Pyper and Dunne are left to retrace their own footsteps relentlessly backwards into a past which stub-bornly resists the shape they struggle to impose on it. McGuinness and Barry do not collaborate with their characters in their self-deceptions, though they render them with the utmost compassion. Rather these playwrights persis-tently insist on 'the gap between the two things': between the reassuring power of a static and self-affirming view of the past, and the more various, conflicting, confounding and endlessly contestable stories which combine to form that fluid phenomenon we call 'history'.

NOTES

1. Lynda Henderson, 'A Fondness for Lament', in *Theatre Ireland*, 17 (1983), 18.
2. Walter Benjamin, 'Theses on the Philosophy of History', in *Illuminations*, ed. Hannah Arendt (London: Fontana, 1973), 249.
3. It should be noted that both postdate Henderson's article, so she does not, of course, refer to them.
4. Frank McGuinness, *Observe the Sons of Ulster Marching Towards the Somme* (London: Faber and Faber, 1986) 22, 16. Further references are included in the text in parenthesis.
5. Philip Larkin, 'MCMXIV', in *Collected Poems*, ed. Anthony Thwaite (London: Faber and Faber, 1988), 128.
6. Sebastian Barry, *The Steward of Christendom* (London: Methuen, 1997), 50. Further references are included in the text in parenthesis.
7. The term 'redcoats', of course, no longer literally described the British army during World War One, as it had long ago traded in red uniforms in favour of more practical khakis. Hence Barry's suggestive, qualified synecdoche.
8. Jack Kroll, 'Review: *The Steward of Christendom*', in *Newsweek*, 17 February 1997, 68.

17

LIONEL PILKINGTON

The Abbey Theatre and the Irish state

Since the mid-1990s Dublin's Abbey and Peacock Theatres, known formally as the National Theatre Society Limited (NTS) and since 1997 marketed under the title 'The National Theatre', have received approximately £2.5 million per year in state funding.[1] Although occasional debates are held concerning the appropriateness of dedicating this amount of public monies to the NTS in relation to the funding of other Irish theatres, or in relation to other arts activities in the Republic of Ireland, more fundamental issues – such as the question of whether or not the state should support a national theatre in the first place, and the political implications of such support – are generally neglected. Accordingly, this chapter sets out to examine the history of the national theatre movement in terms of its relationship to the state before and after independence, and will consider especially the implications of state support for the role of the national theatre as a forum for social and political critique. My argument is that the determining power of the state is the Abbey Theatre's most important and revealing context, and that this also helps to explain certain dominant trends in twentieth-century Irish playwriting.

Clearly, a national theatre may fulfil many different political and cultural functions, but its primary purpose is to operate as a prestige site for the performance of a society's representative dramatic narratives. Such an operation is useful to the authority of the state in so far as these narratives are designed to engender in their audience an atmosphere of unity and national agreement. To this extent a national theatre encapsulates the core dynamics of a mainstream, European theatre tradition. Its darkened auditorium and illuminated stage encourage the spectator to think of himself or herself as part of a living consensus, which, like the nation itself, transcends internal political divisions. This is a point which has been underlined by theorists as diverse as Friedrich Schiller, Bertolt Brecht and Augusto Boal. Like the citizen's engagement with the nation, the spectator's engagement with the play is constituted as a matter of delegation. Plays work, that is, by having their audiences delegate imaginative authority to their actor representatives on stage. In this respect a national theatre has an important additional function: through its enactment of familiar conventions of action and of representation it helps outline the parameters of political action itself. It is this latter quality which makes the institutional theatre so vitally important to the political authority of the state. A national theatre, that is, serves both as a prominent public site associated with the prestige of national self-representation, and as a means of instituting, or attempting to institute, norms of political agency.[2]

What is so interesting about the history of the national theatre movement in Ireland is the extent to which these ideological qualities are so frankly, urgently and frequently declared. The 'Statement for Guarantors' issued by Lady Gregory and W. B. Yeats in 1897 on behalf of the Irish Literary Theatre, for example, speaks of founding a 'Celtic or Irish theatre . . . confident of the support of all Irish people, who are weary of misrepresentation, in carrying out a work that is outside all the political questions that divide us'. The statement also mentions its hope 'to find in Ireland an audience trained to listen by its passion for oratory'[3] as if, in this instance, an Irish national theatre might somehow miraculously transform Ireland's traditional reputation for subversive orality (from patriotic ballads to the rabble-rousing effects of nineteenth-century 'monster meetings') into the decorous silence of a literary theatre audience.

Written at a time when Ireland's mainly Protestant Ascendancy was entering a period of terminal political decline, the prospect of a national theatre offers an oasis of apparent stability. But this is not to say that the idea of an Irish national theatre was a product of wily Ascendancy opportunism. Catholic, bourgeois nationalist commentators were just as explicit. To them a national theatre was especially desirable because it was regarded as proclaiming the existence of an Irish citizenry and thus would serve as a modernizing cultural force, one which would relegate to the past Ireland's turbulent and embarrassingly recent history of localized insurgency and violent political rebellion. 'We have been living through real dramas,' lamented one critic in an 1895 edition of the *New Ireland Review*, 'and have had no time for dramas of imagination.' For this reason, William Barrett continued, it was all the more imperative that a national theatre repertoire of 'respectable drama' be established at once.[4] Yeats's 1899 use of an expression by Victor Hugo in order to recommend the work of the Irish Literary Theatre bluntly summarizes the point: 'In the theatre the mob becomes a people.'[5]

For a broad cross-section of intellectuals in the late nineteenth and early twentieth century (from separatist nationalists such as Arthur Griffith to unionist MPs such as Sir Horace Plunkett and W. E. H. Lecky), an Irish national theatre was worth supporting because it was considered a forum for plays which would counter crude colonial stereotypes of Ireland, and because a national theatre was regarded as sign and instrument of Ireland's modernization. Thus it was not simply a matter of the physical presence of a national theatre conferring prestige on Dublin as Ireland's capital city and thereby underlining the conspicuous absence of some form of representative national legislature, assembly or parliament. It was also a question of a national theatre demonstrating that Ireland conformed to European norms of state development and, in particular, to the primacy of constitutional politics.

And yet, in spite of this broad agreement, political difficulties arose almost immediately. The difficulties were twofold. First, whereas nationalists such as Griffith tended to interpret the existence of a national theatre as underlining the urgent need for political separation from Britain, most unionists thought otherwise. For them a national theatre was an indication of political normality and a compelling reason therefore why full political independence in Ireland was not needed. The second difficulty relates to the sectarian dimensions of cultural modernization in Ireland. Nationalists may well have thought of modernization as a process which would demonstrate Ireland's readiness for Home Rule, but for many unionists and non-Catholic nationalists there was an added and more problematic dimension: the need to expunge from Irish society the deleterious power of the priest. For Yeats (and implicitly for Lady Gregory) theatre was 'an intellectual movement' which was intrinsically opposed to Catholic 'medievalism': 'as our political disorders and a double share of the medieval man in our blood have given us a dramatic temper, our intellectual movement may begin to speak through the theatre' (*Uncollected Prose*, 163).

The sectarian dimensions of Irish cultural modernization offer one explanation for why the controversies associated with early national theatre productions were so highly charged. More was at stake in the protests and debates which arose in relation to W. B. Yeats's *The Countess Cathleen* (1899) or J. M. Synge's *In the Shadow of the Glen* (1903) and *The Playboy of the Western World* (1907) than any straightforward issue of representation. Many of those who objected so strenuously to the broken statue of the Virgin Mary in *The Countess Cathleen*, to Nora Burke's marital infidelity in *In the Shadow of the Glen*, or to the mention of the word 'shift' in *The Playboy of the Western World* were registering an almost visceral sense of grievance. In impugning Irish Catholicism these plays appeared to contribute to a much broader view about the political inferiority of the Irish people. Within the context of British-dominated Ireland at the turn of the century, that is, anti-Catholicism was a pervasive discourse inextricably connected to the view that an indigenous Irish political life was inherently incapable of autonomy.[6]

What was also in question in those early controversies, moreover, was the theatre's proleptic function in relation to Irish statehood: the particular contested political question of how any representative national institution should relate to its majority population. Whereas for the directors of the Abbey Theatre (W. B. Yeats, Lady Gregory and J. M. Synge) the role of a national theatre lay primarily in its criticism of majority orthodoxies from a minority political perspective, this view was sharply contested by intellectuals and political activists such as T. M. Kettle, James Connolly and Maud Gonne MacBride. These latter individuals argued that the primary function of a national theatre was to give voice to the politically unexpressed views of the majority. 'No play is an impartial transcript,' wrote Kettle in response to Yeats's 1902 argument that the primary role of a national drama was to criticize the cherished beliefs of the majority, before going on to advocate a national theatre aesthetic which would be tendentious and representative:

> Let our poets sing of action, heroic doing, the arduous virtues, be the circum-stance ancient or modern. This melancholy analysis of the prescriptive, the traditional, can be harmlessly indulged only when we have reached our full growth as a nation. Let us climb out of the pit before we aim at scaling the stars.[7]

From the perspective of Ireland today, Kettle's defence of nationalist pre-scription appears authoritarian and intolerant. But Kettle's point was not to lay claim to a permanent theatre aesthetic for Ireland, but to insist in-stead on its historical contingency. The criticism of national orthodoxies for a nation which has political autonomy, he argued, is fundamentally different from that for a nation which does not. A major faultline emerges between, on the one hand, Kettle, Connolly and MacBride, who tend to think of a national theatre along the egalitarian lines of a parliament of democratically elected representatives, and writers such as Yeats, Synge and Gregory for whom a national theatre is envisaged more in terms of a nonelected upper house or senate in which majority views are subject to critical scrutiny and qualification by an enlightened minority.

It was the Yeats/Gregory/Synge view which prevailed. By the time of the third Home Rule bill in 1912–13, the National Theatre Society Limited (as it was by then called) presented itself to the Irish public as an exclusively literary project, a commercially limited private company and as a national theatre institution. None of these attributes were considered to be contra-dictory. Indeed, Gregory's famous 1913 theatre history, *Our Irish Theatre*,[8] expresses this ambiguity so adroitly that, by the time of the book's conclu-sion, the pronoun of the title appears both nationalist *and* patrician. The Abbey Theatre is 'our Irish theatre' in the sense that the National Theatre

Society Limited claims to be representative of the nation, but it is also 'ours' in that it owes its origin to the leisure and far-sightedness of Gregory's own social milieu, Ireland's *soi-disant* Ascendancy. Even if D. P. Moran in *The Leader* and Francis Sheehy-Skeffington in *Sinn Féin* continued to lambast the elitist nature of the Abbey by drawing attention to its propensity for antinational satire, these were now minority viewpoints. Gregory's version of theatre history was broadly accepted and the Abbey Theatre was seen as fulfilling an indispensable role in the process of cultural modernization. Ireland's cultural maturity could be gauged by the extent to which the country had grown to accept Abbey Theatre plays without controversy or protest in contrast to the still violent protests organised by Irish emigrant groups in the United States.

This broad acceptance of the Abbey Theatre as the national theatre of Ireland coincides with a period of relative political stability: a period in which the Irish Parliamentary Party under John Redmond regarded itself with confidence as an Irish government in waiting. It was also a period of considerable cooperation between the Irish Parliamentary Party and the British Liberal Party and one in which the British government considered the appointment of a nonelected Irish senate (composed of eminent cultural figures such as Plunkett and Yeats) as part of its plans for Irish Home Rule.[9] It is wholly unsurprising, therefore, that Lady Gregory's attitude towards Home Rule in this period is so sanguine. In striking contrast to the more alarmist attitudes of the Irish unionist party and some of her Irish Protestant contemporaries, Gregory approaches the issue of Home Rule with *sangfroid*: 'We are not working for Home Rule,' she states in relation to the work of the Abbey Theatre, 'we are preparing for it' (*Our Irish Theatre*, 28).

The unexpected postponement of Home Rule after the outbreak of World War One, the arming of the Ulster Volunteer Force, the nationalist Easter Rising of 1916 and the subsequent protracted executions of its rebel leaders all contributed to a haemorrhaging of political support for the Irish Parliamentary Party. The result was an overwhelming victory for Sinn Féin in the general election of December 1918. For Yeats the 1916 insurrection and its aftermath had dealt a fatal blow to the unifying and conciliatory project of an Irish national theatre. 'All the work of years has been overturned, all the bringing together of classes, all the freeing of Irish literature and criticism from politics,' he wrote to Gregory. 'I had no idea that any public event could so deeply move me – and I am very despondent about the future.'[10]

After the 1918 election Sinn Féin's strategy of establishing a republican counterstate while at the same time engaging the British authorities in a guerrilla War of Independence (1919–21) also entailed a corresponding crisis for the institutional status of the national theatre. Now, despite Gregory's considerable efforts to ensure that the Abbey Theatre abandoned its often rebarbative attitude to popular nationalism, there was a widespread impression of the national theatre's contemporary political irrelevance. In 1920 General Richard Mulcahy of the IRA took to the Abbey Theatre stage to complain that the nationalist struggle had been deserted by 'our poets and literary people,'[11] while in the previous year the unionist-oriented *Irish Times* had referred pejoratively to the theatricality of the Irish counterstate by describing the first Dáil (or parliament) as a 'stage play in the Mansion House'.[12] This latter description implies that the recent upsurge of republican insurgency had led to a lamentable blurring of the distinction between traditional theatrical action and the ordinary norms of civic and political behaviour. From their very different perspectives, therefore, Mulcahy and the *Irish Times* suggest that the terms of political agency in Ireland had now changed. In the context of the Anglo-Irish War, political action had become something which the individual could take for himself or herself, whereas the idea of delegation (so crucial to the proprieties of parliamentary democracy as well as to the institutional theatre) assumed a much lesser importance. This is registered as a serious ontological crisis of national importance.

With the foundation of the Irish Free State in 1922, the ruling Cumann na nGaedheal party (the renamed pro-Treaty faction of Sinn Féin) was faced not just with the formidable task of administering a new state, but also with what it considered to be an urgent cultural requirement: the need to rein in Ireland's anarchic forces of political militancy. This is a point upon which a wide range of intellectuals found agreement. The Catholic primate, Cardinal Logue, lamented that 'the people of Ireland were running wild after visions, dreams and chimeras and turning the country upside down in the process',[13] and Yeats wrote to his friend Edmund Dulac that 'people are trying to found a new society . . . It seems to be the very moment for a form of drama to be played in a drawing room' (*Letters*, 702). A. E. (George Russell), writing in the ex-unionist *Irish Statesman*, argued that boycotts, strikes or political violence would never achieve Irish unity. What was most needed instead, Russell continued, was a programme of education towards a 'social order in which there will be a real sense of identity of interest among our citizens'.[14] For state-building to ensue in post-Treaty Ireland what was required, in other words, was a restoration of the proper distinction between the exaggerated role-playing of theatre and the decorums and conventions of civic and political life.

Sean O'Casey's exposure of the folly of any form of political militancy directed against the state in *The Shadow of a Gunman* (1923), *Juno and the*

Paycock (1924) and *The Plough and the Stars* (1926) accounts (at least in part) for the popularity of these plays with Dublin's new middle-class elite.[15] The lure of playing the part of a gunman for Davoren in *The Shadow of a Gunman*, the absurd role-playing of 'Captain' Boyle in *Juno and the Paycock* or Jack Clitheroe's obsession with military costume and rank in *The Plough and the Stars* constitute a mordant indictment of antistate militancy and, in each of these plays, the deleteriousness of a republican tradition of militancy is diagnosed in terms of a misplaced or misrecognized theatricality. Indeed, the pro-Treaty writer P. S. O'Hegarty was so impressed with this aspect of *The Shadow of a Gunman* and *Juno and the Paycock* that he argued that O'Casey's plays had achieved the apparently transcendental status of history-writing itself: a 'true historical perspective . . . that air of detachment and disillusionment which the historian aims at'.[16]

Cumann na nGaedheal's granting of an annual subsidy of £850 to the Abbey Theatre in August 1925 seems to be directly connected to the NTS's institutional support for the Irish Free State. Given the government's fiscal rectitude and its consistently conservative economic policies in the 1920s, and given that the Abbey Theatre was the first English-speaking national theatre in the world to receive state funding, Cumann na nGaedheal's support for the NTS was, by any standard, an extraordinary political decision. Yeats welcomed the announcement as an expression of the government's benevolence and altruism,[17] but it is more likely that the decision was motivated by a more pragmatic recognition of the role of the NTS in establishing the state as the sole legitimate arena of political action. As the *Irish Times* put it, not only had the Abbey Theatre 'lifted Dublin from the status of a decaying provincial city to that of one of Europe's intellectual and artistic capitals' but, 'more than any other agency', it had managed to rid Ireland of 'superstitions and prejudices that are the relics of a barbarous age'.[18] To this extent it is also relevant that the cabinet members who so strongly supported the Abbey Theatre subsidy in the 1920s, such as Ernest Blythe and Kevin O' Higgins, were also those associated with a leadership cadre within Cumann na nGaedheal which was increasingly concerned with a rowing back from the revolutionary and insurrectionary tendencies of some of their party colleagues.[19]

Maintaining the stability of the Irish state and supporting the Abbey Theatre, then, were mutually reinforcing activities. Again, this was not simply because of the explicitly pro-Treaty sympathies expressed by O'Casey's Dublin plays or, on several occasions, by the theatre's directors themselves, but because of a widely shared assumption that cultural modernization in Ireland required its people to recognize and respect the difference between theatre and politics. A letter from Yeats to his friend Professor H. J. C. Grierson illustrates this well. Writing in February 1926 about the protests against *The Plough and the Stars* Yeats describes to Grierson one republican protester who, having taken to the stage during a performance of *The Plough and the Stars*, interrupted his demonstration to cover the actress playing the part of Mollser (a character portrayed in the final stages of tuberculosis) with a blanket. For Yeats the incident amounted to an epiphany since it exposed the republican enthusiast as so marked by cultural naïvety that he appeared unable to recognize the distinction between O'Casey's fictional character and the actress who was playing the part: 'She was not the actress in his eyes but the consumptive girl' (*Letters*, 711). This, for Yeats, was precisely the point. As in the 1890s, Ireland desperately required cultural education, and a national theatre was ideally suited to this task. Transforming a 'mob' into 'a people' remained the essential project of the NTS in so far as it entailed recognizing a distinction between, on the one hand, an illegitimate theatricality associated with superstition and insurgency and, on the other, a politics sanctioned by the authority of the state. Theatregoing itself, therefore, became a demonstration of an innate cultural sophistication – an automatic recognition, as it were, of the parameters of constitutional politics. To this extent acknowledging the importance of a national theatre was in itself a subtle reinforcement of the authority of the state.

The value of a national theatre institution for the process of Irish state-building also helps to explain why the Abbey Theatre continued to receive government support during almost two decades of Fianna Fáil administration from 1932 to 1948. Despite the association of the Abbey in the 1920s with a pro-Treaty political position and despite initial sharp exchanges between the government and the NTS directorate arising from an Abbey Theatre tour of 'controversial' plays to the United States in 1932–3, de Valera and Yeats very quickly achieved a good working relationship. This is all the more striking considering that many nationalist and Catholic intellectuals of the time expressed strong concern in relation to what they regarded as the anomaly of an Irish national theatre still dominated by a predominantly non-Catholic directorate. Such objections came to a head in August 1935 with the first Dublin performance of Sean O'Casey's *The Silver Tassie* and the protest resignation of Abbey Theatre director Brinsley MacNamara. MacNamara resigned because of the play's alleged anti-Catholicism (the second act of *The Silver Tassie* entails a parody of elements of the Mass), and during the autumn and winter of 1935 the government received numerous calls to terminate the NTS subsidy altogether and to introduce theatre censorship. Not only did the Fianna Fáil government not respond to these calls, however, but within a few years it increased the NTS subsidy. Against many popular objections, the ideological benefits of a national theatre for the Irish state appeared to have had an overruling effect.

For many decades after the 1920s Ireland's national theatre continued to lend an air of gravitas and bourgeois normality to the postindependence state. It did this by evoking an impression of consensus and national unity and also by reinforcing a distinction between political agency authorized in terms of the state and what was seen as the threatening illegitimacy of socialist or republican militancy. Within the context of a resurgence of IRA activities from the mid-1930s, both of these functions were now just as important to de Valera's Fianna Fáil government as they had been to the earlier administration of Cumann na nGaedheal. By the early 1940s the Abbey Theatre repertoire is, once again, dominated by plays which urge the need for an unequivocal allegiance to the state and for an abandonment of antistate republicanism. The bulk of the NTS repertoire in this period – that is, plays by George Shiels, T. C. Murray, Paul Vincent Carroll and Rutherford Mayne – have a familiar thematic emphasis: the urgent need to abandon superstition and antistate loyalties in the interests of modernity and good citizenship. George Shiels's *The Rugged Path* (1940) and *The Summit* (1941) (the former one of the longest running plays in the history of the Abbey Theatre) are cases in point. The narrative action of these plays deals explicitly with the issue of citizenship and its obligations in terms of the legal authority of the state and urges the audience to overcome Ireland's traditional taboo on colluding with the state by informing.

As a national institution, then, the Abbey Theatre's relationship with popular nationalism is fundamentally ambivalent in a manner very similar to that of the Irish state. Committed to the notion of a consensual Irish identity, the NTS nevertheless finds itself pitted repeatedly against the militancy of traditional republicanism upon which the state is founded. As in plays like Bryan MacMahon's *The Bugle in the Blood* (1949), Walter Macken's *Twilight of a Warrior* (1957) and John Purcell O'Donovan's *The Less We are Together* (1957), the NTS repertoire reveals a widening gulf between traditional nationalist views, associated with the foundation of the state, and a modern contemporary world for whom such views appear no longer to be relevant. As Christopher Morash has recently pointed out in an essay on the Republic of Ireland Act of 1949, plays written for the Abbey Theatre in the late 1940s and 1950s show a distinctive 'post-utopian' quality.[20] Within this context Ernest Blythe's appointment as Managing Director of the Abbey in 1941, coupled with his strong and sometimes dogmatic promotion of the Irish language, remained one of the few ways in which the Abbey Theatre was able to overcome this contradiction and express to the nation an unequivocally nationalist identity.

Major social and political changes take place in Ireland in the 1950s and 1960s. Heralded by the landmark Whitaker Report of 1958, there is a new emphasis on the development of an export-based economy and the encouragement of multinational inward capital investment. The resultant economic growth of the late 1950s and 1960s also coincides with a massive expansion of the state in the areas of economic and social planning. The dismantling of economic autarky in Ireland and the slow removal of a paternalistic state apparatus did not mean the state had diminished in power, merely that its mechanisms for the implementation of social policy were beginning to change. Keynesian principles were now installed as the main items on Ireland's developmental and modernization agenda,[21] and, as in the postwar British welfare state, there was now a much greater emphasis on personal pleasure and on individual consumption as the basis for political agency.

Broadly speaking, therefore, the legitimacy of the Irish state tends to be viewed from the 1950s in terms of its responsiveness to the requirements of the individual rather than (as had previously been the case) as a reflection of any dominant national philosophy or ideological position. It is this critical change in the relationship between culture and economics which helps to explain what might otherwise appear a conundrum: the striking coincidence between a widespread impression of the Abbey Theatre's irrelevance in the 1950s and early 1960s and the simultaneous emergence of what has been described as Irish drama's 'second renaissance'.[22] The *Irish Times*'s astringent conclusion that the Abbey was 'not a national theatre'[23] roughly coincides with the first production of Brian Friel's *Philadelphia, Here I Come!* at the Gaiety Theatre in September 1964 Dublin, an event often credited as the starting point of contemporary Irish drama. The trouble was that while Irish economic and social life had changed, the Abbey Theatre had not. As late as 1965, for example, Blythe described the cultural work of the Abbey as 'a constructive influence on public affairs . . . by means of satirical treatments of the Northern Ireland problem . . . and the ventilation of issues to do with Church authority'.[24]

The resurgence of Irish drama as evident in new plays by Brian Friel, John B. Keane, Thomas Kilroy and Tom Murphy which takes place in the 1960s arises because of a general shift away from this more tendentious treatment of popular nationalism. For this younger generation of writers the inadequacy or inappropriateness of traditional nationalist verities tends to be rendered not satirically (as it had been in plays by Shiels, MacMahon, Macken and O'Donovan), but as an existential trauma. In *Philadelphia, Here I Come!* (1964), for example, Gar has no option except to emigrate because Donegal and Ireland are unable to provide any viable alternative to multinational capitalism. And yet emigration – as this play keeps plangently reminding us – will result in an inevitable loss of plenitude. Similarly, in Tom Murphy's *A Whistle in the Dark* (1961), the focus is not so much on the political folly of militant nationalism but on the way in which nationalist rhetoric exacerbates the torment of emigration. The relentless irony of Murphy's play is that in order to achieve an Irish nationalist identity, a west of Ireland family has to emigrate to England and act out the self-destructive stereotype of the 'Paddy'. Whereas the Abbey Theatre of the 1950s and early 1960s was dedicated to the enactment of key *issues* relating to the twenty-six-county Irish state, for younger dramatists such as Murphy and Friel the emphasis was on the experience of the individual within an economy dominated by its increasing dependence on multinational capitalism.

The opening of a newly rebuilt Abbey Theatre in 1966 and Blythe's retirement as Managing Director in 1967 led to a distinct change in the artistic policies of the NTS. With Tomás Mac Anna's championing of Brechtian dramaturgy at the Peacock Theatre and an Abbey Theatre project to bring theatre to working-class areas of Dublin, the NTS presented itself not only as a forum for national consensus, but also as self-consciously politically engaged and as a catalyst for social change. But this impression of a postnationalist horizon did not last for long, since these radical artistic developments also coincided with the reemergence of serious political conflict in Northern Ireland following the civil rights marches of 1968–9. Within the context of stringent antirepublican emergency legislation such as the 1972 Offences Against the State (Amendment) Act, a close alignment between the NTS and the policies of the twenty-six-county state was, once more, in evidence. From the early 1970s theatrical responses to the Northern Ireland conflict at the NTS have been remarkably unified in their tendency to view the Northern Ireland conflict exclusively outside of a political context. The treatment of the conflict varied from satire and farce (as in the 1970 revue *A State of Chassis*, Patrick Galvin's *We do it for Love* [1976] and Stewart Parker's *Catchpenny Twist* [1977]), to an impression of the conflict's tragic inevitability (as in Brian Friel's *The Freedom of the City* [1973]), to a more general concentration on the suffering of the individual (as in Graham Reid's *The Death of Humpty Dumpty* [1979] and *The Closed Door* [1980]). Not until the 1980s, with the performance at the NTS in 1983 of Friel's *Translations* and Frank McGuinness's *Observe the Sons of Ulster Marching Towards the Somme* (1985) and *Carthaginians* (1988), was there an attempt to engage with the cultural and historical dimensions of the conflict, but even these plays are marked by their unambiguous lack of sympathy for republican or nationalist opposition to British rule in Northern Ireland.

Ireland's national theatre movement reflects, therefore, a long and close association with a form of politics organized exclusively in terms of the authority of the state. There are, as we have seen, particular historical reasons for this. At the beginning of the twentieth century the cultural significance of the NTS (and its precursors the Irish Literary Theatre, the Irish National Dramatic Society and the Irish National Theatre Society Limited) lay partly in its demonstration of a longed-for modernity, and was perceived by nationalists, and by some southern Irish unionists as well, as performing a vital role in the struggle for political independence or limited devolution. Though the sectarian aspects of modernization were bitterly disputed and gave rise to some notorious theatre controversies, the presence of a national theatre institution in Dublin was regarded generally as positive proof of Ireland's cultural and social advancement and thus of the need for some form of Irish political independence. The foundation of the twenty-six-county Irish Free State in 1923 in a context in which republican anti-Treaty militants disputed the legitimacy and authority of the state gave this modernizing function an added momentum.

Indeed, a history of the Abbey Theatre in the postindependence period suggests that the primary function of the NTS was that of underlining the authority of the state in the face of a contesting tradition of nationalist and republican militancy. And though there is little evidence of any direct interference by the state in the choice of plays performed at the Abbey theatre and Peacock Theatre, and there is no formal mechanism of theatre censorship in Ireland, the historical and formal association of the NTS with the state has resulted in a perennial anxiety that a distance be established between the authority of the state and an unauthorized national tradition of militancy and insurgency. This has manifested itself in a certain thematic predictability in terms of the Abbey Theatre's treatment of issues relating to the Northern Ireland conflict and in relation to Ireland's colonial history.

NOTES

1. Information correct as of 2001. For further information on the National Theatre Society Limited, see *Assertions, Perceptions and Facts: An Initial Response by the National Theatre Society to 'Views of Theatre in Ireland 1995'* (Dublin: The National Theatre Society Limited). I am grateful to the Abbey Theatre archivist, Ms Mairead Delaney, for her assistance in researching this article.
2. For a detailed theoretical discussion of the ideology of national theatres, see Lauren Kruger, *The National Stage: Theatre and Cultural Legitimation in England, France and America* (Chicago: University of Chicago Press, 1992), 3–29.
3. Quoted in Warwick Gould, John Kelly and Deirdre Toomey (eds.), *The Collected Letters of W. B. Yeats, Volume II 1896–1900*, (Oxford: Clarendon Press, 1997), 123–5.
4. See W. Barrett, 'Irish Drama', in *New Ireland Review* (March–August 1895), 38–41.

5. W. B. Yeats quoted in J. P. Frayne and C. Johnson (eds.), *Uncollected Prose of W. B. Yeats, Volume II:, Reviews, Articles and Other Miscellaneous Prose* (London: Macmillan, 1975), 141.

6. For a more detailed discussion of this topic, see Lionel Pilkington, *Theatre and the State in 20th Century Ireland: Cultivating the People* (London: Routledge, 2001).

7. T. Kettle, 'Mr. Yeats and the Freedom of the Theatre', in *United Irishman*, 15 November 1902, 3.

8. Lady Gregory, *Our Irish Theatre* (New York and London: G. P. Putnam's Sons, 1913).

9. See R. F. Foster, *W. B. Yeats: A Life, I: The Apprentice Mage, 1865–1914* (Oxford: Oxford University Press, 1997), 459, 613.

10. Quoted in Allan Wade (ed.), *The Letters of W. B. Yeats,* (London: Rupert Hart-Davis, 1954), 613

11. Quoted in Arthur Mitchell, *Revolutionary Government in Ireland: Dáil Éireann 1919–22* (Dublin: Gill and Macmillan, 1995), 301.

12. Quoted in C. Kostick, *Revolution in Ireland: Popular Militancy 1917 to 1923,* (London: Pluto, 1996), 49.

13. Quoted in M. O'Callaghan, 'Language, nationality and cultural identity in the Irish Free State, 1922–7: the *Irish Statesman* and the *Catholic Bulletin* reappraised,' in *Irish Historical Studies*, 24:94 (1984), 227.

14. See *Irish Statesman*, 15 September 1923, 4.

15. See Declan Kiberd, *Inventing Ireland: The Literature of the Modern Nation* (London: Jonathan Cape, 1995), 233.

16. Quoted in Robert Hogan and Richard Burnham, *The Years of O'Casey, 1921–1926: A Documentary History* (Gerrards Cross: Colin Smythe, 1992), 146.

17. See *Irish Times*, 10 August 1925, 5.

18. See *Irish Times*, 26 December 1925, 4.

19. For a brilliant recent analysis of this period, see J. M. Regan, *The Irish Counter-Revolution 1921–1936: Treatyite Politics and Settlement in Independent Ireland* (Dublin: Gill and Macmillan, 1999), 246–9.

20. See C. Morash, '"Something's Missing": Theatre and the Republic of Ireland Act, 1949', in Ray Ryan (ed.), *Writing in the Republic: Literature, Culture, Politics in the Republic of Ireland, 1949–1999,* (London: Macmillan, 2000), 71.

21. See R. Breen, D. F. Hannan, D. B. Rottman and C. T. Whelan, *Understanding Contemporary Ireland: State, Class and Development in the Republic of Ireland* (London: Macmillan, 1990), 5.

22. C. Murray, *Twentieth-Century Irish Drama: Mirror Up to Nation,* (Manchester: Manchester University Press, 1997), 162.

23. See *Irish Times*, 20 February 1963, 7.

24. E. Blythe, *The Abbey Theatre* (Dublin: The National Theatre Society Limited, 1965), n.p.

18

VIC MERRIMAN

Staging contemporary Ireland: heartsickness and hopes deferred

'[T]he Free State didn't change anything more than the badges on the warders' caps.'

(Brendan Behan, *The Quare Fellow*)

'Hope deferred maketh the something sick. Who said that?'

(Samuel Beckett, *Waiting for Godot*)

The film *Mise Éire* (1959) was produced at a time of profound cultural change in the Republic of Ireland. Eamon de Valera was about to relinquish executive office to his successor as leader of Fianna Fáil, Sean Lemass. Lemass, with T. K. Whitaker, was embarked on the First Programme for Economic Expansion, the economic logic of Fianna Fáil's abandonment of republican nationalism. In place of an All-Ireland national unity – that grail of the Lemass/de Valera generation – would come a new compact with capitalism itself. The nation would be fulfilled not in the achievement of a complete independence, but in an alignment with global capital. Needless to say, this pragmatism was not publicly promulgated in so many words. It had, however, long been available to consciousness at the lived level of individual, family and class experience.

Mise Éire's triumphalist account of Irish nationalist progression amounted to an almost unchallengeable hegemonic narrative until Northern Ireland exploded in 'The Troubles' of 1969. The film contains one sequence which is of particular interest to a discussion of contemporary Irish theatre. A hoist camera pans across a city street crammed with heaving humanity assembled to greet the 1916 revolutionary Constance Markievicz, on her return in 1918 from incarceration in a British jail. At the height of the crowd's ecstatic celebration, the image of the popular mass is dissolved into Atlantic waves beating against the 'timeless' western coast of Ireland – a key site and trope of nationalist desires. Immortal nature gives way in seconds to the averted gaze of a piece of neoclassical statuary featured on a bridge over the River Liffey, which runs through the heart of Dublin.

The detour into the fabled western seascape facilitates the sublation of radical popular desire into the impassive patrician demeanour accompanying the newly appropriated accoutrements of empire. In the city of Dublin the streets will be avoided in favour of the decorous achievements of a departed elite. This chapter argues that resistance to such a detour has been a key dynamic in Irish playwriting during the twentieth century. The plays chosen for discussion here expose that dynamic, and illustrate the validity of Raymond Williams's observation that 'there is no such thing as the masses, only ways of seeing the masses'. *Mise Éire* reveals that not looking is also a way of seeing. Playwrights such as M. J. Molloy, Tom Murphy and Dermot Bolger challenge these social blindnesses and their consequences, while works by Martin McDonagh and Marina Carr alert us to the partial or selective seeing inaugurated by the emergence of the currently buoyant economy of 'Celtic Tiger' Ireland.[1]

The focus of this chapter is on contemporary theatre from 1990 to 2000, but as Raymond Williams's model of socio-cultural change suggests, no period should be thought of as historically discrete – existing in, of and for itself. Williams suggests the coexistence, at any cultural moment, of practices which constitute the dominant, the residual and the emergent. In the same sense contemporary theatre includes not only new repertoire, but reinterpretations of existing works and traces of what will become accepted as part of what we understand as theatre. It is for this reason that I want to frame the theatre of 1990s Ireland by referring to two productions which came to the stage in the previous decade: Garry Hynes's Druid Theatre Company 1983 production of M. J. Molloy's *The Wood of the Whispering* (1953) and David Byrne's Wet Paint Arts production of Dermot Bolger's *The Lament for Arthur Cleary* (1985).

Molloy's play stages the consequences of the betrayed promises of the Irish Free State by exposing their influences on the lived experiences of the rural poor. As a prophetic corrective to the evasions of *Mise Éire*, in the 'Preface' to *The Wood of the Whispering* Molloy identifies the failures of the neocolonial elite which had assumed office and power in the new state:

> For forty years Ireland has been free, and for forty years it has wandered in the desert under the leadership of men who freed their nation, but who could never free their souls from the ill-effects of having been born in slavery. To that slave-born generation it has always seemed inevitable and right that Anglo-American plutocracies, because they are rich, should be allowed to destroy us because we are poor – destroy us root and branch through mass emigration.[2]

In an echo of what David Lloyd discerns in the poetry of W. B. Yeats, *The Wood of the Whispering* questions the validity of narratives conjured ahistorically from canonized initiating moments.[3] Lloyd locates the purpose of such narratives in their power to erase whole swathes of human experience from public consciousness. *The Wood of the Whispering* restores the particularity of experiences common to those masses elided in the sequence referred to from *Mise Éire*. Its original production in 1953 raged against the official gaze averted from a people exiled in their own country. Memories of communal desires and public betrayals are inscribed on the bodies of the people depicted, in their words and in their silences.

In important ways Molloy's play – usually marginalized in accounts of Irish theatre – may now be regarded as an ur-text for much of what follows, especially in the period 1985–2000. Received critical wisdom locates Molloy as a 'folk' playwright, with the inference that his work is of minor public significance.[4] I want to suggest that *The Wood of the Whispering* is a highly significant play, not least for its recourse to magic realism in the face of a lived reality whose contradictions exceed the representational scope of dominant forms of bourgeois theatre. The Druid Theatre Company's decision to stage it thirty years on from its first performance amounted to an act of what Michel Foucault would call countermemory: it restored to public view the concerns of people erased in *Mise Éire*. 1983 was a high point in more than a decade of economic collapse caused by the deliberate looting of neocolonial elites nurtured by Fianna Fáil from the early 1960s onwards. Druid's production of *The Wood of the Whispering* enabled the vicissitudes of a dark period of recent Irish experience to be historicized in its moment by audiences unborn at the time of the original production.

The play is set in 1950 outside the crumbling gates of a west of Ireland 'Big House'. The fictional world of the play parallels the actual circumstances of peasant communities in that part of Ireland at that time. Many small communities were in terminal crisis due to the disastrous commingling of economically driven emigration, enforced celibacy and late marriage. The dynamics of depopulation are staged all the more starkly in the light of the protagonist's all-consuming desire to bring about marriages and social regeneration. The penultimate scene sees Sanbatch Daly having his friends and neighbours tie him to a tree as a madman. His performance of madness is staged in order to force all around him to see sense, and the eligible couples opt to marry rather than emigrate. The moment is rich in metaphorical material, with Sanbatch as a pagan 'folk-Christ' volunteering to assume the role of one who has 'lost himself' (the vernacular phrase used throughout the play to denote madness) for the greater good of 'saving the village'. It is instructive that much of the critical discussion of the scene interprets it as the resolution of a naïve dramatic narrative: a crude device by which a playwright who had essayed an unwieldy theme gets himself off the hook.

At the symbolic level Sanbatch's performance of madness amounts to a realization of the regenerative power of fellowship in an organic community: a practical enactment of the communal values invoked and betrayed by neo-colonial elites. In this perceived 'structural flaw' *The Wood of the Whispering* anticipates by nearly forty years the aesthetic strategies of such plays as Dermot Bolger's *The Lament for Arthur Cleary* and Donal O'Kelly's *Asylum! Asylum!* (1994). In all of these works I read the intrusion of the symbolic into the literal as a manifestation of a common postcolonial form; magic realism.

For Peter Szondi, in *Theory of Modern Drama*, classical drama is impossible in modernity, with its alienated subjects and fragmenting social orders.[5] His analysis exposes aesthetic crisis in metropolitan dramatic practices, and finds absent the conditions wherein mimesis can approximate reality. In a social order with a colonial past and a neocolonial present, the crisis in realism is evident. It is simply inadequate to the task of staging popular desire. If the persistence of realism is an analogue for attempts to posit a stable social reality as imagined by a comfortable elite, the intrusion of heightened imagery – the symbolic – manifests the persistence of utopian dreaming. Magic realism is a hybrid cultural discourse which exemplifies Edward Said's contention that '[i]n the cultural discourses of decolonization, a great many languages, histories, forms, circulate'.[6]

In the final scene of *The Wood of the Whispering* the resurrected Sanbatch offers a quasi-theological reflection on the state of things past, and the hope of things to come:

> In the English Army, as soon as wan man is killed they enlist another. And that's God's plan, too: for each person that dies, a child to be sent into the world. But around here we reckoned we were men of brains, as good as God, and we reckoned we could do without ye, and God never said wan word only let us go ahead and ruin ourselves: and then Himself scattered all women and girls away from us to the ends of the world . . . But may less be now He thinks we have enough good sense got again, and may be soon He'll bestow children on the village again. If He does, we'll have nothing more to want or to do, only wait for the death, and then die happy because we will be leaving room for more (192).

The final image is of Sanbatch and Sadie – rescued from self-imposed withdrawal from the world by her long-postponed, but now imminent, marriage to Hotha – sitting on a log among the ruins of Sanbatch's improvised camp. Outside the rusting gates of the departed colonial aristocracy they envisage a frugal future, both of and beyond this world. In this moment of closure *The Wood of the Whispering* fatalistically attributes its economic predicament to the blind hubris of peasant manhood and appears to evade the play's profound articulation of desires for identity, community and national liberation. All these desires could be realized through human acts, yet they are consigned to ineffable fate in Sanbatch's discourse. The speech, a complex and heady mix of utopian discourses delivered by a ragged peasant man to a ragged woman, amplifies the power of the metaphorical pairing of physical wretchedness and doomed, melancholic Irishness in the visual composition of the scene. Its ironies are manifest in the metaphorical significance of the pairing, and the persons, of Sanbatch and Sadie, redeemer and redeemed – saved too late, but safe at last.

Apart from his appearance, language and longings, which identify him with the pristine peasant of national myth, Sanbatch's cultural coordinates are English. In Act 1, Stephen reveals that his unusual name derives not from his father, but from a local landowner: 'Sanbatch is his nickname evermore since he used to be training dogs for oul' Captain Sanbatch' (135). The Irish peasant's aspiration to a social order run according to the harmonious precepts of the divine is made flesh in the macabre efficiencies of 'the English Army'. The evocation of the colonizer's military enforcer as a social ideal is no idle gesture in this metaphorical collage. It indicates the full impact of Sanbatch's near-destruction of himself and his devastation of his temporary camp. The anticolonial struggle produced only a set of conditions which must themselves be resisted in the very habitations and bodies of the people if their desires for liberation – however circumscribed – are to have any hope of fulfilment.

Garry Hynes's work on Molloy, Synge and Murphy exposes the inscriptions of economic, cultural and political failure in the homeland of nationalist myth: the rural west of Ireland. Druid's reclamation of Molloy and Synge, and Hynes's staging and restaging of Murphy, force the bodies and experiences of the rural poor into the public domain. The aspirations and sacrifices of the period of anticolonial struggle haunt these plays, and their restaging provided opportunities for realizing metaphors savage in their damnation of the Ireland so ruthlessly analysed by J. J. Lee in *Ireland 1912–1985* as the one 'we' have settled for. Significantly, plays such as *The Wood of the Whispering*, Murphy's *Famine* (1968) and Synge's *The Playboy of the Western World* (1907) are formally innovative, and are marked by the use of heightened poetic language. All of these characteristics return in Dermot Bolger's first play, *The Lament for Arthur Cleary*.

Just as Molloy's play staged the disappointments and inequities of rural Ireland betrayed, *The Lament for Arthur Cleary* is an urban drama of intranational betrayal. It is also a drama of Ireland's complex relationships with Europe. The play's episodic structure foregrounds narrative as opposed to plot. It operates as a montage, and makes use of strategies such as repetition of scenes, direct address to the audience, and heightened poetic language. All of these devices are deployed in order to enable the significance of key actions to emerge in production. From the point of view of performance, the convention of actors playing multiple roles clearly serves the needs of narrative over plot, privileges the representation of role over the assumption of character, and prepares the ground for a type of complex seeing, threatening to received ways of staging who 'we' are.

The Lament for Arthur Cleary began life as a narrative poem of the same name, a creative response to the eighteenth-century lament by Eibhlín Dhubh ní Chonaill for her murdered husband Art Ó Laoire, *Caoineadh Airt Uí Laoire*. Bolger's play was commissioned by Wet Paint Arts for performance to audiences in various locations in the many Dublin suburbs which subsist as economic, social and cultural wildernesses. Touring to a series of what Fintan O'Toole refers to as 'places without history',[7] the play accepts the challenge of testing the poem's assertions with audiences for whom dispossession, exile and fruitless return are experiences first, metaphors second. What the play does, relentlessly, is force audiences to look at an Irishman as the alien he is regarded as in the 'common European home'. As the play develops, so the menacing significance and the gathering juxtapositions of the repeated border crossings become familiar as an enactment not only of exile, and of calamitous return, but of a prophetic scene for the future. This is made explicit in Arthur's final conversation with the Frontier Guard:

> *Frontier Guard.* So many trains run through here, day and night, in all directions, all times, coming and going.
> *Arthur. (looking down at platform)*: Who's on that one? Where's it going?
> *Frontier Guard.* Europe . . . The future . . . Her children.[8]

Arthur, the representative of a generation of 'Strangers in their own Country', contemplates an image of Ireland's future as diaspora.

The poem, like its source, gives voice to the woman's narrative. When the lyrics of her loss emerge in the spoken language of the play, that voice is positioned as a key organizing element of the drama. The moment of Arthur's death is densely narrated in choric verse by Kathy, before it occurs in the temporal experience of the audience. His relationship with her is impossible because the fifteen years which separate them encompass a cultural change so great as to appear to be a complete break with history. This gives Arthur's double significance, arising from his derivation from the historical figure of Art Ó Laoire, an important role to play. Rooted in the Gaelic past invoked in nationalist rhetoric as an exemplary social state, Arthur restores a sense of the participation of historical experience in contemporary narratives of identity.

The memorial Dublin he had domesticated to the requirements of the state of exile was fixed. It became unalterable because it was never examinable against the changing circumstances of the actual city. Confronted on his return with so many signs of familiarity, Arthur's devotion to a personal myth precluded engagement with social reality as it had developed for Dubliners of his class.

The persona of the returned exile, displaced in an Ireland which has changed out of all recognition, is a familiar device in Irish cultural production. Arthur Cleary, however, emerges as a truly new figure in Irish theatre, exposing a world made complex by urbanization and mass communications. It is an existence in which the failures, omissions and exclusions of independent Ireland are made manifest. The heroin economy into which he returns is completely implicated in the overt economy, driven by commodity consumption, accelerating in range and quantity. The historical past of the source poem maintains a presence which shadows the contemporary drama but there can be no question of escaping into its narrative. The business of this play is Ireland now, and as it confronts its audience so its audience must confront its reading of this present as not just immediate but strange.

Centring Arthur's experience in the play involves the audience in acts of identification with the experience of wandering, and thus exposes to critical view the assumptions underlying notions of home and experience which authenticate official homogenized narratives of Irish identity. Perhaps the most significant achievement of the Wet Paint Arts production was registered at the level of cultural politics: the place of performance was that of the class whose experiences it stages. These people were also the play's primary point of address, and so occupied their place on the cultural map and must be considered part of the public sphere. In the wake of this play Irish cultural production which does not envision this public as constituting part of its audience is obliged to acknowledge this choice and to address the reasons why.

The 1990 election of Mary Robinson, a postcolonial President, was a moment of extraordinary significance in independent Ireland. Robinson's rhetoric of inclusion, elaborated in her careful handling of symbols, amounted to a political and cultural watershed. One year after she had issued her invitation 'come dance with me in Ireland', Brian Friel repositioned Field Day, the most coherent attempt at a contemporary project of cultural nationalism, by offering a new play to the Abbey Theatre. The play was *Dancing at Lughnasa* (1990), and within two years its director, Patrick Mason, had succeeded Garry Hynes as Artistic Director of the Abbey and Peacock theatres, or – as he deliberately reminded everyone – the National Theatre Society (NTS). Mason read the mood of the postcolonial moment accurately, programming repertoire from the Abbey's past, staging a brilliant reinter-pretation of Frank McGuinness's 1985 *Observe the Sons of Ulster Marching Towards the Somme* and Part 1 of Tony Kushner's *Angels in America*. He gave young directors their head, and entered into partnerships with some of the exciting new theatre companies which emerged in towns and cities outside Dublin during that period. He also initiated the Abbey Outreach Programme, and played a central role in the debates around culture, citizen-ship and public policy which marked Michael D. Higgins's period in office as Minister for Arts, Culture and Gaeltacht (1993–7). Mason's sampling of international repertoire, and his commitment to touring the work of the Abbey and Peacock to other countries, made a statement about the status of the national theatre and its role as public educator. His subtle accentu-ation of the homoerotic in McGuinness's play responded to and amplified the emergence of gays and lesbians into full – decriminalized – formal citi-zenship. In short, Mason's directorship of the NTS restated some of Yeats's, Gregory's and Synge's foundational questions about both drama and nation: why would one found a stage for a nation's stories; who can narrate such stories, and how; for whom, and to whom are they to be told?

These questions resonate at the very core of *Dancing at Lughnasa*. Open-ing the play at the Abbey Theatre marked a symbolic acknowledgement of the enduring status of the stage of the NTS as a site of interrogation of the nation and its core questions. The question of narrative voice is highly prob-lematic in all Friel's work, and produces extraordinary energy in his best plays. In *Dancing at Lughnasa* it is most obviously inflected in gender pol-itics as the narrator constructs the remembered world of the Mundy sisters around events of significance in his own life. He is also a bourgeois, and as a result of this his memorializations are themselves a form of amnesia, as subtly achieved as in the sequence in *Mise Éire* alluded to earlier. If the film editor uses seascape to disengage from engaging with the plenitude of human experiences, Friel's Michael deploys distance and a nostalgic tone in order to avert the gaze from the relationship between the socio-economic predicament of the Mundys and the enduring inequalities of the Ireland he occupies. Reception of the play has tended to misrecognize the dance at its core as a celebration – an error compounded in Frank McGuinness's screen-play by moving this most private frenzy out of doors, and framing it as an affirmation of sisterhood rather than a cry of pain. It is a frenzied 'Yes!' to life desired: a physicalization of the terrifying recognition that postponement of desire has produced conditions in which it will never be fulfilled. This is accentuated by the historical fact that in 1936 – the year in which the re-membered action takes place – de Valera's draughtsmen were busy refining *Bunreacht na hÉireann* (*The Irish Constitution*), a document which would drastically limit the life opportunities available to women in the state. In the very fabric of Friel's writing there is, not for the first time, an aversion of the gaze from the realpolitik involved and encapsulated in the daily struggle to live an ordinary life in independent Ireland.

Dancing at Lughnasa is haunted not only by the boy's remembrances of his aunts, but also by the spectre of modernization itself. The social ruptures of progress with a native accent cut deep in the threat to cottage-based piecework posed by the opening of a knitting factory, and reports of the attraction of young people in the village to consumer goods and places far away. It is also present in the absolute power of the priest to determine the staffing of the local school: this will be modernity with a peculiarly Irish accent, in which the inchoate and apparently benighted will coexist with, and be mobilized to domesticate and endorse, 'the latest thing'. In these senses *Dancing at Lughnasa* is a very useful matrix for reading not the 1930s but the 1990s. In its silences, hints and tracings it reveals the signatures of a profound cultural change which would engulf independent Ireland before the decade was out.

On the occasion of her election in 1990 Mary Robinson announced the importance of our ability to tell our own stories about ourselves, to ourselves and to others. For many people on the margins of independent Ireland, the period of Robinson's tenure as President (1990–7) marked a newfound affirmation of the rich material potential of the symbolic. Fintan O'Toole, in reviewing the condition of naturalism in contemporary Irish theatre some years ago, remarked that it was no longer possible to stage images of a coherent struggle for or against a social reality when the reality itself had fractured into multiple centres of identification in which ideas fundamental to the coherence of a social order were being challenged and contested by positions derived from the experiences of everyday living. As Ireland resounded to the first roars of the Celtic Tiger economy, the organs of public legitimation and social pedagogy began to busy themselves with offering new accounts of who might now constitute a national 'we'.

The Celtic festival of Lughnasa provides a mythic fabric for the events staged in Friel's play. The Celtic festival of Samhain or Hallowe'en is an inbetween time, a moment when the membrane separating this world from that of the dead, of ghosts, visions and the unnamable becomes permeable. Unquiet spirits wander between worlds at this time. Premiering at the Abbey Theatre at Hallowe'en 1998, Marina Carr's *By the Bog of Cats* offers a compelling insight into what crucial wanderings, sightings and unsightings might be assembling to dance a new Ireland into being. Unable to critique an *us*, unwilling to confront the construction of *us* at the expense of *them*, mainstream contemporary Irish theatre has returned to the past in order to interrogate its own representations of *us then*, and, in its treatment of such representations, to construct mythic images as parables for the predicaments of the present. Hallowe'en itself provides a striking example of how the ritual celebration of a culturally sacred moment can be coopted and transformed into another node in the network of conspicuous consumption. Dreamed and developed in Ireland, it was recognized by the genius of American capitalism as a unique marketing opportunity. Its characteristic emblems are distorted, despised grotesques.

Along with Martin McDonagh, Carr is one of the most celebrated Irish playwrights of the 1990s. In an apparently bold oppositional stance, their successes have been built around plays which stage Ireland as a benighted dystopia. At a time of unprecedented affluence Carr and McDonagh elaborate a world of the poorly educated, coarse and unrefined. The focus is tight, the display of violence inhering in the people themselves, grotesque and unrelenting. Carr's *By the Bog of Cats* and *Portia Coughlan* (1995) take as their point of departure the condition of being poor in contemporary Ireland. Both plays travesty the experiences of the poor, both urban and rural. Introducing a category of internal outsider known in the United States as 'white trash', they posit worlds in which material poverty and moral bankruptcy map on to one another, eerie partners in a dance of death. In McDonagh's case the Leenane Trilogy of *The Beauty Queen of Leenane* (1996), *A Skull in Connemara* (1997) and *The Lonesome West* (1997) stages a sustained dystopic vision of a land of gratuitous violence, craven money-grubbing and crass amorality. No loyalty – communal, personal or familial – can survive in this arid landscape. Death, affection and responsibility appear as meaningless intrusions in the self-obsessed orbits of child-adults.

While dystopic visions of Ireland are nothing new in theatre – 'The Love Scene' in Tom Murphy's *Famine* being perhaps the most fully realized – such stagings populated by violent child-adults repeat the angriest colonial stereotypes as a form of communal self-loathing. The dramatis personae of these plays specifically mark out figures of the poor which are overdetermined in their Irishry. Gross caricatures with no purchase on the experiences of today's audiences, their appeal to the new consumer-Irish consensus lies in their appearance as ludicrous Manichaean opposites – the colonized simian reborn. In each belly laugh which greets the preposterous malevolence of its actions there is a huge cathartic roar of relief that all of this is past – 'we' have left it all behind. The problem, from a postcolonial point of view, is clear: these plays implicate audiences in particular stances towards the poor, the past and Irishness.

The cultural tone of contemporary Ireland is structured around a notion that the past is best forgotten, as its hopes and struggles have lost their relevance. Success is everywhere evident. The argument that the apparent ironic playfulness of McDonagh's work marks the nation's ability to laugh at itself claims the plays as manifestations of a postcolonial maturity. However, while the plays are replete with violence – matricide in *The Beauty Queen of Leenane*; death through drink-driving, attempted murder and the desecration of the bones of the dead in *A Skull in Connemara*; parricide and suicide in *The Lonesome West* – the entirety of the trilogy stages not one moral voice, save that of the ludicrous Father Walsh . . . Welsh. His contribution ends in a suicidal walk into the lake at Leenane, leaving the fictional world of the west of Ireland with nothing to counter the craven barbarity of its inhabitants, except the strong possibility that they will one day wipe each other out. No Syngean anthem to robust paganism this. These plays offer a kind of voyeuristic aperture on the antics of white trash whose reference point is more closely aligned to the barbarous conjurings of Jerry Springer than to the continuities of an indigenous tradition of dramatic writing. Importantly, the repellent figures presented turn out to be representations of those most fully betrayed by indigenous self-rule: emigrants, undereducated peasants, bachelor smallholders, women abandoned in rural isolation by economic collapse.

Each play in the trilogy posits a single fictionalized west of Ireland as the locus of its stage world. All the *dramatis personae* encountered, with the exception of the neutered Father Walsh, are of this world, and their actions conform to barbaric norms established at the plays' outset and left intact at the end. Neither challenge, change nor redemption is available to the persons of the play. The denouements to which the audience is led are all signalled in acts of destruction of persons and objects which can be fully accommodated within the terms of this fictional social order. As the lights fade on Maureen's cottage in *The Beauty Queen of Leenane*, the question as to whether her responsibility for her mother's death will ever emerge is all but negated by the onset of mental illness, and the proposition that, in any neighbouring cottage, a similar set of barbarities is probably in train. The grotesqueries of *A Skull in Connemara* and *The Lonesome West* confirm this. In *The Lonesome West* Father Welsh states, 'I'd have to have killed half me fecking relatives to fit into this town.'[9] The trilogy presents a world where the only available conflicts are between competing lusts which must be sated. Complicity can be purchased for 'a Kimberley biscuit'. The murders of dogs and daddies attract only passing comment, and no opprobrium whatever, not to speak of redress or retribution. Against the formal surefootedness of the Leenane Trilogy, the apparent naïvety of Molloy's *The Wood of the Whispering* appears as an heroic attempt to force theatre form to perform modest possibilities in impossible circumstances.

Marina Carr's *Portia Coughlan* and *By the Bog of Cats* opt for worlds even more tightly sealed than McDonagh's, but here, too, coarseness of accent signals economic, cultural, emotional and spiritual poverty. The nod to Shakespeare in *Portia Coughlan* goes no further than crudely ironizing the white-trash world of Portia against that of the gentle Venetian lady of *The Merchant of Venice*. *By the Bog of Cats* is largely a rewrite of concerns staged in *Portia Coughlan*: the troubled woman as outcast, the incestuous family, the brutal father, the haunting by a dead brother, the corrosive climate of the outcast woman's home. Its frame of reference is that of Euripides' *Medea*, with a playful nod to Shakespeare. As Act 2 opens, Carthage Kilbride's mother is found photographing her sequinned shoes in deference to the price she paid for them, and the thrift necessary to purchase them: 'I saved like a Shylock for them.'[10] Mrs Kilbride is a monster, even if she has an amusing acquaintance with the Bard of Avon.

By the Bog of Cats is primarily a play about travellers, the land and rural Ireland. Carr specifically grounds Hester Swayne's predilections for violence, deceit and unnatural urges in her identity as a traveller. In Act 2 Hester appears in a wedding dress, gate-crashing the monstrous petit-bourgeois wedding of Carthage, her daughter's father. Mrs Kilbride's racist epithet 'Ya piebald knacker ya' (54) at this moment brought the house down at the Abbey, Ireland's National Theatre. In a subsequent scene the bride's father shoves a loaded shotgun under Hester's skirt in an image of gross brutality so gratuitous that it risks rupturing the boundaries of the fictional world altogether. In the play's denouement Hester slits her daughter's throat from ear to ear. By representating their own countrymen as 'others', and scorching them in the heat of their derision, McDonagh and Carr offer bourgeois audiences course after course of reassurance. Hester Swayne, traveller, is beyond the pale, a constant figure in a mutating social order desperate for points of otherness against which to imagine its own impossible consistency. The movement of the characters of *By the Bog of Cats* and the Leenane Trilogy to central positions in Irish theatre enables such figures to occupy and redefine the coordinates of cultural space. In celebrating the new Irishness of the audience for such spectacles, they simultaneously negate the interrogation of the conditions in which such images are produced and have points of reference. In this way they revisit the editorial strategy detected in the *Mise Éire* clip described, and expose contemporary Ireland's turn away from public inquiry into the actually existing social order. In settling for – or refusing to critique – a divided society, theatre institutes a lesser public role for itself than envisaged by the founders of the Abbey Theatre.

Irish drama's claim to social significance rests on the pledge that in acts of theatre something more than box-office success, or the reputation of an individual artist, is at stake. Theatre is part of a broader cultural conversation in which the questioning stance of dramatic artists is essential to the development of critical citizenship, without which no social order can remain healthy. When Synge produced his *Playboy* to inhabit civic space opened up by the national theatre, he demonstrated the critical vigour and political significance of performative images themselves. Far from demanding space for a rarefied 'aesthetic' position, the theatre of Yeats, Gregory and Synge inaugurated a conversation with 'Ireland'. Their use of ambivalent narratives and images of community to critique emergent nationalism established Irish theatre as a site of public conversation about the moral health of the social order as it mutates in history. The works by Molloy and Bolger cited in this chapter take up that challenge as they differentiate from the figure of the Irish masses individual fictional histories. Sanbatch Daly and Arthur Cleary, and the social relations they make visible, contain within them questions fundamental to the health of the social order. McDonagh's plays, and Carr's, substitute for human vitality a set of monsters frozen in the stony gaze of the triumphant bourgeoisie.

NOTES

1. The phrase is used to describe Ireland's economic 'leap' forwards, which was initiated in the late 1980s and reached an acme such that, in 2001, the Organization for Economic Cooperation and Development registered Ireland at the top of its growth league.
2. M. J. Molloy, 'Preface', *The Wood of the Whispering*, in Robert O'Driscoll (ed.), *Selected Plays of M. J. Molloy* (Gerrards Cross: Colin Smythe, 1988), 111. Further references are included in the text in parenthesis. A 'neocolonial' elite refers to those of the indigenous (Irish) population who occupy the positions once held by the departed (English) colonists. In this sense political power is transferred while the social structure (and its inequalities) is unchanged. As argued by David Fitzpatrick, 'if revolutions are what happen to wheels, then Ireland underwent a revolution between 1916 and 1922 . . . social and political institutions were turned upside down, only to revert to full circle upon the establishment of the Irish Free State'. *See Politics and Irish Life, 1913–21. Provincial Experiences of War and Revolution* (Dublin: Gill and Macmilan, 1977), 232.
3. See 'The Poetics of Politics: Yeats and the Founding of the State', in David Lloyd, *Anomalous States: Irish Writing and the Post-Colonial Moment* (Dublin: Lilliput Press, 1993), 59–87.
4. Christopher Murray states that 'Molloy's main interest was as a folklorist; he wanted to capture and immortalize the manners, customs, language and people he knew intimately in County Galway . . . This is a dangerous aim for a playwright and too often Molloy simply lapsed into quaintness.' *See Twentieth-Century Irish Drama: Mirror Up to Nation* (Manchester: Manchester University Press, 1997), 146–7.

5. Peter Szondi, *Theory of Modern Drama* (Cambridge: Polity Press, 1987).
6. Edward Said, 'Yeats and Decolonization', in Terry Eagleton, Fredric Jameson and Edward Said, *Nationalism, Colonialism and Literature* (Minneapolis: University of Minnesota Press, 1990), 86.
7. Fintan O'Toole, 'Introduction,' in Dermot Bolger, *A Dublin Quartet* (Harmondsworth: Penguin, 1992), 1.
8. Dermot Bolger, *The Lament for Arthur Cleary*, in *A Dublin Quartet*, 67.
9. Martin McDonagh, *The Lonesome West* (London: Methuen, 1997), 34.
10. Marina Carr, *By the Bog of Cats* (Oldcastle: Gallery Press, 1998), 47. Further references are included in the text in parenthesis.

19

BRIAN SINGLETON

The Revival revised

Throughout the twentieth century the Literary Revival provided a template for subsequent writers and theatre practitioners for decolonizing Ireland on the stage. The political idealism of the prerevolutionary plays of the Revival's founders could be judged only by the realities of postrevolutionary guerrilla and civil warfare. And almost as a continual act of unconscious amnesia, Abbey Theatre audiences, fed on a diet of 'jog-trot nationalism' and 'comfortable images of their own Irishness',[1] decried all attempts to break away from naturalism as the dominant theatrical form. So entwined has political nationalism been with theatrical practice that Irish theatre has struggled to find deviant voices, or to find a form beyond heightened political and poetic rhetoric. Contemporary writers complain of the expectation laid on them to uphold the tradition of writing the nation. But while writers in Northern Ireland have not been afraid to reflect the everyday realities of armed struggle, in the Republic of Ireland writing on contemporary political realities has rarely been a major part of the theatrical landscape. The Abbey, by far the single greatest producer of new Irish plays, has always felt its 'national' tag as a filter for the issues of those produced. This part of its national project has been to expand the 'canon' in the mould of its founders, as well as to revive the early canon in a spirit of deference and national triumph.

Revivals are safe programming choices in times of economic hardship and thus O'Casey's early Dublin plays came to be the mainstay of Irish theatre throughout the twentieth century while the poetic-allegoric work of Yeats and Lady Gregory fell out of favour and the repertory. This has as much to do with the length of their plays, which can fill only a small slot in an evening's programme, as their unfamiliar antinaturalist form. More significantly, the plays' blatant calls to arms seemed inappropriate for middle-class urban audiences in the late twentieth century who wished to distance themselves from the atrocities committed in their name north of the border, and who now tacitly supported processes of peace. Censorship, and what was essentially a theocratic republic from 1937 onwards, also ensured that theatrical modernism would take a back seat. The safety of the repertory which had accompanied the birth of the nation would be reproduced without any threat to the new morality which was sending the country's greatest figures into exile. Only the early O'Casey plays were canonized (despite the original hostile reception to the plays' politics); his later work, which breaks from the cosy familiarity of stock comic figures, and naturalistic form, was not seen as part of the national project. Modernist writers such as Beckett retreated into exile and were reclaimed only in the latter part of the twentieth century as the nation entered a new phase in its history.

The revival of the canon of Irish theatre writing is as difficult to locate in time as it is in its composition, but it continues to expand: Beckett's work was embraced in a 1991 festival produced by Dublin's Gate Theatre, and Brian Friel achieved canonical status in the last year of the century in an all-theatre retrospective. Perhaps the simplest way of determining the canonical in Irish theatre is to isolate writers whose work has been 'festivalized', embraced by the trend of single-author marketing which recognizes that great theatre writers are the mainstay of Irish cultural capital. These writers and their works are celebrated by international recognition, and so by festivalizing their opus their lesser-known and less popular works can be consumed on the international markets, thus reinforcing their canonical status.

Locating the Revival revised in a timeframe is best understood by taking as the marker the last decade of the twentieth century, which witnessed seismic shifts in the economic and political climate of the country as well as a huge demographic change. 1990 is seen as the beginning of the change, with the election of Mary Robinson to the Presidency, the first woman and the first socialist. Her unique ambassadorial skills, as well as popularity at home, constituted a marked change from the succession of retired politicians in the post and she carved out for Ireland a role on the international stage. Popular cultural successes on the sporting and musical stages created a cultural feelgood factor, and European Union grants for infrastructure and investment in information technology put Ireland in a very strong position economically. This combined with a highly educated young workforce who, no longer forced to seek their fortunes abroad, could capitalize on this wealth. By 2000 half the population of the Republic was under the age of twenty-seven, and they lived in one of the fastest-growing economies in the world.

The economic boom of the 1990s had a significant effect on theatre culture. Investment in theatre training in the period began to produce theatre-makers interested in experimenting with form, and challenging the messages of the canon. In O'Casey's work armed struggle took second place after the representation of social injustice, while the jingoism of Yeats's plays became secondary to the quest for new performance practices for his poetic allegories. Young practitioners no longer struggled with their identity as diasporic exile became a matter of choice rather than necessity. Theatregoing, once the preserve of the middle-aged, also changed. New companies began to emerge with new messages, new forms and new idioms. Reviving the Revival was no longer the safe bet it once was, as new audiences sought novelty and revision. Reclaiming the economic exiles to shore up the workforce was mirrored culturally as exiled playwrights such as Samuel Beckett acquired new currency and relevance. The phenomenal upturn in Ireland's economic fortunes in the 1990s makes the decade a suitable place for the examination of the early revival, and also necessitates the embrace of those playwrights of the old Ireland who helped shift the theatre out of a theocratic headlock.

O'Casey's Dublin Trilogy (*The Shadow of a Gunman, Juno and the Paycock* and *The Plough and the Stars*) constitutes the bedrock of the Revival, with the plays' familiar domestic settings against a backdrop of the struggle for independence. With its pseudo-historical figures, its political rhetoric, and its contested representation of revolution, *The Plough* can be singled out as the touchstone for the shift in representation in the last decade of the twentieth century. Historically it marked the beginning of the tenure of the first female Artistic Director of the Abbey in modern times – indeed, the first woman of power since Lady Gregory. Garry Hynes, who had achieved significant success with her Galway-based Druid Theatre Company, with notable productions of the plays of Tom Murphy and J. M. Synge, chose *The Plough* as her inaugural production in May 1991 to mark the seventy-fifth anniversary of the Easter Rising. With a woman as head of state, and a woman as head of the National Theatre (NT), these were changing times. Significantly, Hynes chose as her literary adviser the respected *Irish Times* columnist and critic Fintan O'Toole, whose socialist politics and sharp critical thinking were influential on what was to be one of the most radical productions of the Revival ever witnessed. Hynes's production interrogated a century's tradition of representation, stripped the play of its comic accretions, and questioned the legacy and injustices of postindependence politics.

Hynes's designer, Frank Conway, stripped the stage to an almost white box. The furniture of the tenement interior was covered by a washed-out Union Jack, and on the top of the proscenium was inscribed the slogan of the Irish Citizen Army: 'We Serve Neither King Nor Kaiser but Ireland.' This was a faithful textual icon to the cause of nationalism, but it became increasingly ironic as the drama emphasized the appalling social conditions giving rise to the rasping breathlessness of an emaciated Mollser; the domestic violence of Jack Clitheroe against his wife Nora; the revision of Fluther as a jolly drunk into a man whose consumption of alcohol fuelled his rages and fits of temper; the reconstruction of Rosie Redmond from a healthy, happy middle-aged prostitute to one not long left school whose prostitution was out of economic necessity.

At the opening of the production the faded Union Jack was stripped away to leave a bare stage peopled by women in rust-coloured, raglike dresses and closely cropped hair which suggested that they had arrived at a point where their sexuality was so irrelevant it had been removed completely. In such a costume design (by Consolata Boyle) O'Casey's women became bonded by their labour and their struggle to keep family intact. Nora's exceptional physicality with her husband Jack clearly demonstrated women's needs and desires, which were rejected by a man whose overriding needs lay outside the domestic sphere.

The Act 2 pub scene, traditionally the male preserve, was held up to ridicule. A large mirror was flown in, and the audience was reflected on it. The Speaker, whom in tradition and text is placed in silhouette outside the pub window, was now physically present within the audience. When he stood up the mirror reflected his image back on to the audience, who saw themselves positioned around him as his supporters. For many this was an uncomfortable experience, made all the more uncomfortable by scenically forcing them to be identified with his vacuous political rhetoric. His rose-tinted vision of a new Republic was clearly at odds with the onstage representation of a hungry young woman being forced to sell her body, and another emaciated through ill-health caused by her social conditions. The vacuity of the rhetoric of the Speaker, dressed in a modern suit, was clearly an attack on the successive governments of the Republic.

The contemporary 1991 situation was highlighted to be no better than when under the yoke of imperialism. Indeed, within five minutes' walk of the Abbey one would have found some of the worst housing conditions and greatest heroin addiction in Western Europe, and a government still insisting that lack of public spending was the price of independence. At the time many suspected that corruption at the highest levels of government was to blame, and this was to be borne out in a succession of scandals, revelations and public tribunals throughout the 1990s. O'Casey's focus on the marginalized in a society at such a momentous period of history, and not even giving a name to the politician, was further politicized by Hynes siting him in the margins. As Fintan O'Toole observed, 'O'Casey . . . was taking very marginal people and saying we can make those central to the way we look at the event. Pearse and Connolly . . . are on the margins of it.'[2]

Citing the Speaker's rhetoric amid the audience implicated their own inability to elect governments which could change social conditions and tackle injustice. Further, the notion that the real struggle is the elimination of social inequity rather than the expulsion of a colonial master is evidenced in O'Casey's juxtaposition of revolution in the public sphere with chronic social injustice in the domestic sphere. The success of a revolution and the achievement of independence seemed a hollow victory in the light of the lack of progress in the material and social conditions of ordinary folk. Hynes's emphasis on the domestic and the social thus caused Mary O'Donnell to write in the *Sunday Business Post*: 'No other production [of the play] has made such a potently political statement in such a global context about the warmongering path of human endeavour.'[3]

This production, more than any other in the decade, caused the biggest division among critics and the largest flurry of comment on the Letters page of the *Irish Times*. Hynes's directorial approach was compared to a celebrated, revived production of *Juno and the Paycock* first directed by Joe Dowling at the Gate Theatre in the previous decade. Although many critics marvelled at the attention to detail in the replication of poverty, this production was not so much a revision but a reinscription of tradition by locating the play in the mire of naturalism. Thus when the comedy of the bombast Boyle and his slippery sidekick Joxer was inserted into a naturalistic environment, it seemed to endorse social conditions rather than challenge them. Frank Rich in the *New York Times* marvelled at the accuracy in 'a panorama of poverty so grim that one might think the rear wall of the playhouse had been torn away',[4] while Michael Billington of *The Guardian* concurred that the depiction was 'a masterpiece of dilapidation'.[5] Those characters belonged there, they appeared happy given their comic routines, and they didn't seek change. In Hynes's *Plough*, however, their setting was uncomfortable and alienating. Wiping out the comedy and naturalism thus challenged the acceptability of poverty. Traditionalists, denied the cosy familiarity of their favourite comic characters, were prevented from laughing by a representation which provided no comic relief from the seriousness of the politics and the violence surrounding it.

Though no riots accompanied this revival, unlike the fourth-night debacle in the auditorium in February 1926, it was clear that the motivation for such large-scale critical disapproval had remained throughout the sixty-five years of the play's production history. Relatives of the executed revolutionaries Padraic Pearse and Tom Clarke were in the audience of the original production, and objections to O'Casey's desentimentalizing of revolution came out of historical proximity to and experiential memory of actual events. Such representation was seen as a betrayal of the national ideal and it was almost as if in the intervening period directors had sought to restore that national ideal in their productions by eliminating O'Casey's social indictment. Thus a tradition emerged of character representations happy with their lot; jolly in their alcoholism (Fluther); stoic in their tuberculosis (Mollser); resigned to domestic violence (Nora Clitheroe); and content to sell her body (Rosie Redmond). When, on the first day of rehearsals, Hynes's initial request for props was met with the original bassinet used in the 1926 production, it was clear that production of O'Casey's plays was trapped in an unchallenged tradition of sentimental accretions. Something had to be done. Hynes rejected that original bassinet on day one and signalled that the museumlike accretions which had restored the early O'Casey plays to canonical status were to be swept away by the contemporary agendas of the decentred and marginalized voices which had been written out of the national cultural agenda.

In 1991 Hynes laid down the theatrical gauntlet by making social injustice contemporary and equating its imperial with its postcolonial manifestation. She focused on the plight of woman in a patriarchal society, as part of a spirit-of-the-age movement which swept the first woman to power in presidential elections, preceding subsequent referenda on legalizing divorce (successful) and abortion (unsuccessful). Theatrically she adopted a distancing style which aimed at defamiliarizing the play. Many of the stock comic lines were spoken as part of whole scenes rather than as engineered claptraps and, moreover, comic lines spoken by characters who were clearly anything but funny were emptied of all comedy. This production more than any other revision challenged the Revival's retreat into self-congratulatory comic sentimentality, and pointed out that theatrically Ireland had fallen into the trap of a postcolonial replication of the stage-Irishness of the old colonial order, which the Revival had once aimed to repair.

Reviving productions which are no longer considered part of the Revival, even though they were contemporaneous and very much part of it, is an indictment of Irish theatrical historiography. Written out of the canon because they did not deal directly with the national questions, or mythologized a premodern Celtic past, are a host of comedies by the largely overlooked Lennox Robinson, who managed and directed productions at the Abbey after Yeats. Many of Robinson's plays imitate Yeats's interest in European modernism. *Church Street* (1934), for example, is a scathing social satire of hypocrisy dealing with such taboo issues as abortion, and, more importantly, is written in a self-conscious metatheatrical form which owes much to Luigi Pirandello's *Six Characters in Search of An Author*. His early plays, however, are based on a premodern, well-made play structure. *The Whiteheaded Boy* (1916) is a tightly woven and intricate study of a rural bourgeois Catholic family, the Geoghegans, struggling to cope with a mother's obsession with a favourite son who, in reality, is a profligate and lazy gambler rather than a medical student at Trinity College. His further betrayal of his family by being sent down from college is enough to bankrupt the family, since he is betrothed to local girl Delia Duffy, whose father threatens to sue for breach of promise. Shipping him off to Canada is a solution not taken up, and the play winds a twisted path through a series of transactions which reveal an ever-increasing world of petty provincialism in which fear of shame and other heart-ruled obsessions govern rational thought and sensible decisions and provides much of the comedy.

By 1997, however, despite his position in Irish theatre history, Robinson's play had been written out of the canon as a contrived satire. In that year the relatively young physical-theatre group Barabbas . . . The Company, trained in the mime of Jacques Lecoq and Marcel Marceau, used it as the textual base for their physical inventions. Formed in 1993, Barabbas was an innovation on the Irish theatre scene, presenting a theatre motivated by the body and not by the word. The Revival, which had done so much to establish a body of indigenous theatrical literature, had to a large extent denied the Irish actor a body. Barabbas injected the stage with the poignant and bitter-sweet antics of red-nose and other clowning traditions, characterizing the Irish in a new form. Up to 1997 their devised shows had reached a small niche audience, and the choice of *The Whiteheaded Boy* was directed by a desire to broaden their audience base. Though the play may have been written out of the canon and left untouched by the main stages for many decades, *The Whiteheaded Boy* had become a very popular choice on the enormously successful and extensive amateur drama circuits. Its choice by these groups was understandable: this was a comedy of manners, with easily identifiable characters and situations with comic twists. The choice proved successful, the company supplying demand with national and international tours, as well as three runs in Dublin, the last in the Olympia Theatre, the largest surviving proscenium-arch theatre in the city.

Directed by Gerry Stembridge, Barabbas's invention was radical in the extreme, with four actors playing twelve characters, an actor often having to play opposite himself within the one scene. The play began with three actors in loose grey clothing peering into a model box of a set for the well-made play the audience expected, complete with footlights, furniture and wallhangings. The life-size actors made very clear the joke that they were too large and too modern for such representation. Behind them was a two-dimensional black-and-white panorama of the main street and shopfronts of the Munster village of the action. The actors began by performing the stage directions, and audiences were able to identify what precisely the director had chosen to retain within the model of a set design from the past, and what to appropriate and bring to life. The actors, however, did not perform these self-consciously as stage directions but embraced them as part of their characters' lives and environment.

The narration continued as dead characters were commented upon, with the other actors, offering parenthetical expressions such as 'God rest his soul', turning solo narration into dialogue and creating the effect of an ensemble creation where no one actor embodied or represented one single character. When living characters were mentioned by one actor, another adopted the physical leitmotif for the character; these leitmotifs were spelled out for all characters at the beginning so that during the action proper, when actors were jumping from one character to another, the audience could follow readily. Character descriptions were played out physically and altered as the description proceeded, often forcing the actor to alter the demeanour as the description evolved. This vocabulary of characterization had its strict codes: some characters were performed in either left or right profile, some front on, and an actor never performed a character of the same sex. Further, in some cases the actors never fully embodied a gesture, denying the parody of exaggeration which this crosscasting tended to suggest. For instance, Mrs Geoghegan, performed by Raymond Keane, never really cried at her son's increasing misfortune, but would instead hold a handkerchief up to her face as if to stop tears but use it as a tool to translate her psychological gesture, punching out her words in stoicism. This distancing device had the effect of separating actor from character, but also separating gestural and vocal expression from the governing force which drove and motivated character. This was a very self-conscious physicalization to expose the rampant hypocrisy of these lives: a harsh but very cruel exposure of what lies behind the mask of the land of 'a hundred thousand welcomes'.

The Whiteheaded Boy himself, a Pirandellian 'otherworld' character, was dressed 'realistically' in cream suit and scarf, and smoking a cigar. The colour difference from the grey world of the country characters separated him instantly from the parody. He was a product of these grey characters' own fiction and consequently he appeared as a hand-tinted character in a black-and-white film. Such was the exaggeration of the fictionalizing of the character that Raymond Keane as mother greeted her stage son by leaping on to the boy's waist and was lifted aloft in a physical exaggeration to mirror the textual fiction. Towards the end of the play, when reality bites and Denis the White-headed Boy is accepted for what he is and not what the other characters would like him to be, the colour of his clothes changed to grey.

Eighty years after its first performance, when the representation of Irish characters was judged according to accuracy and national mythologizing, the exposure of hypocrisy through Barabbas's theatrical idiom pointed up clearly why Robinson's portrayal of the rural Catholic bourgeoisie was written out of the national canon. The peasantry, in whom the original vestiges of nationalism were deemed to reside, was swept away and replaced by a scathing attack on the middle classes who espoused nationalism but displayed none of its ideals, middle classes who made up much of the National Theatre's clientele and yet had no justification for inclusion in the national project. While such mocking exposure of values had been blamed on an English class system, the contemporary audiences for this revival – the rural amateur movements and the young urban avant-garde – firmly embraced them as their own. Barabbas's disinheriting of each character of the body of an actor further contributed to the debate that a newfound performativity, and the primacy of physicality on the stage, might unsettle the stability of an indigenous theatre and might now be prepared to include more heterogeneous forms of cultural self-representation, which, as Anna McMullan points out, led to a 'crisis of authority'.[6] Barabbas's bodies unsettled and destabilized fixity and tradition of character representation, doubling the mocking of an idealized homogenous Catholic nation already begun by Robinson.

Such performativity would have been anathema to Yeats, who once demanded that his actors stand still and become vehicles for his oratory. But the paradox of Yeats's desire was that his poetic oratory and Symbolist dramaturgy were themselves manifestations of theatrical modernism. The enshrinement of his plays within nationalism, however, marked their theatrical deathknell. More importantly, contemporary programming trends which dictate a two-hour show with interval have banished Yeats from the stage. His short political allegories, some in the form of esoteric Japanese Noh drama, with their ritualized and conventionally undramatic forms, have found no place in contemporary practice. However, the concept of the Irish nation made world famous by its literature and drama is a rich mine for tourist-board marketing, and the reputation of the Revival dramatists within the academic establishment also has marketing potential. Yeats has acquired his own annual summer school in Sligo where enthusiasts and scholars gather, reflect on and debate his work.

In 1989 the American academic/director James Flannery sought to reclaim Yeats from the academic establishment and move him back into the theatre through the first of five annual International Yeats Festivals which ran during the summer tourist season at the National Theatre's studio theatre, the Peacock. Each of the Festivals had a theme and the plays presented were chosen to explore that theme.[7] The idea behind the festivals was that of a Yeats Drama Foundation which was founded in 1988 'out of a desire to commemorate the fiftieth anniversary of the death of W. B. Yeats in an appropriate manner'.[8] The National Theatre's Artistic Directors during the period (Vincent Dowling and Garry Hynes), though endorsing the project, had no direct input. All the money came from private overseas sponsorship and the organization was led by Flannery, who directed most of the productions.

Commenting on the very first festival, Fintan O'Toole saw it as an attempt to reclaim the relevance of Yeats and help it compete 'with Star Wars and Batman rather than with Ibsen and O'Casey'.[9] The popular comic-book approach to the early work was, though, combined with lectures by academics, exhibitions, concerts and even an ecumenical service!

Despite press support, however, these seasons failed to become part of the theatrical fabric of the emerging, young 'Celtic Tiger' nation, in which the new youth positioned themselves in a technological global village and saw no need to beat the old drum of anticolonial nationalism or canonize theatrical memorials. The impetus behind this Revival came from the nostalgia of the diaspora, not from the drives of home-based practitioners, though the experimental creativity of the practitioners involved (particularly in choreography and music) would leave a legacy in performance elsewhere beyond the Yeats summer festival. The dispossessed Cathleen of old had become a contemporary irrelevance as this Revival failed to restore Yeats to the repertory.

Academic summer/spring/autumn schools now abound and focus on the cult of the author: Synge, Wilde and Yeats are perhaps the biggest and most successful. Authenticity and the original sites of the authors' exploits, or those of their fictional characters, turn the study of the author into pilgrimages. The Synge school takes place in Wicklow, the Yeats in Sligo. And though they engage in contemporary criticism, to a certain degree they are preservation societies for the works of those authors abandoned by contemporary theatrical practice. Yeats's plays, now fallen into disuse, are kept company by Synge's, with the exception of *The Playboy of the Western World*, performed once by the Abbey Theatre in the time period in question, and Patrick Mason's direction of what was seen as a 'discovery production' of *The Well of the Saints* in 1994 focusing on the controlling presence of religion, a topic very much in vogue in the new media at the time. Thus, since there is no longer any revision of the Revival, the schools mentioned above fulfil the function of reclamation.

Another Irish author in the Yeatsian modernist tradition, Beckett, has replaced Yeats to a large extent in the theatrical canon, if not in historical significance within Irish theatrical tradition. As he was in exile in Paris from 1937 to his death in 1989, Beckett's work has struggled to establish its identity within national parameters. In 1986, for example, Tom Bishop, the American organizer of celebrations of Beckett's eightieth birthday at the Centre Georges Pompidou in Paris, was asked by Dublin's Gate Theatre Director Michael Colgan about the intended Irish presence. The response was that no reason could be envisaged for having such a presence. Colgan swiftly dispatched to Paris Professor Terence Brown to lecture and a one-man show by Barry McGovern entitled *I'll Go On*, based on Beckett's work. However, Beckett's work did have some presence on Irish stages; in the 1950s the now-defunct Pike Theatre premiered his work, and *Waiting for Godot* has had the occasional mainstage production, though by the 1990s Beckett had become the preserve of student theatre companies. Colgan consequently saw a marvellous marketing opportunity in a three-week Beckett-fest, in the summer-school tradition, and in the increasingly prevalent festivalizing trend which has now become the bane of Irish cultural practice.

Colgan's Beckett Festival, which ran from 1 to 20 October 1991 and was hailed as a collective masterpiece which toured and was revived extensively, was an attempt to reclaim Beckett as Irish, a reclamation from the hijacking of Irish culture by both Britain and France.[10] It included all of Beckett's stage plays in nine bills, the shorter pieces programmed in bills of three and four, with *Godot*, *Endgame*, *Happy Days* and *Krapp's Last Tape* standing on their own. The reclamation was an attempt to situate Beckett within an Irish theatrical tradition, 'to give back some of the fundamental Irishness to a South Dubliner who expatriated himself'.[11] What caught the attention of most reviewers was the accent of the actors, most of whom were from Dublin, the accent itself an act of reclamation from the received pronunciation of an English class system. Working-class Dublinese was used in Walter Asmus's production of *Waiting for Godot*, and the pauses as moments of reserved anguish were ridden over roughshod as Didi and Gogo (Barry McGovern and Johnny Murphy) delivered their lines as firecrackers, obliterating the silence with their humour. But this was no stage-Irish comic accretion which Garry Hynes had dusted off O'Casey earlier in the year. This was a siting of Beckett's tramp-poets amid the wanderers of Synge and Yeats, their displacement made all the more poignant and, indeed, political by the locating nature of their accents.

Casting David Kelly as Krapp in *Krapp's Last Tape*, directed by Pat Laffan, was truly a revival, as he had been in the play's Irish premiere in a professional production in Trinity College's Players' Theatre in 1959, when he was far too young to play the role. Now more appropriately aged, Kelly's TV sitcom persona of the hapless working-class Irishman displaced in England brought out Krapp's anger as he accidentally hit his hanging lamp in a moment of rage, with huge theatrical consequences; the lamp's swinging in real time mirrored Krapp's own attempt at composure and denied the Dublin audiences' desire to laugh with him. Similarly, *Endgame*, directed by Antoni Libera, featured another hapless character portrayal, an angular and awkward Clov, played by Barry McGovern, in a set by Robert Ballagh which was a grey representation of the inside of a human skull complete with eye sockets for windows. But what was most significant in all these productions was not so much the scenographic locations or directorial invention, but the delivery of text by Irish actors, a delivery of 'discovery' rather than 'novelty',[12] made possible by the native speakers' approach to 'Hiberno-English cadence and syntax'.[13]

With Radio Telefís Éireann's simultaneous radio and television broadcasts of Beckett's work, and an academic symposium with video installations at Trinity College, Dublin, the Gate Theatre move together two major cultural trends: festivalization and the (summer) school as means by which the largely unmarketable canon of Beckett's work might be staged. For though on the world stage Beckett with Irish accents is acceptable – indeed, desirable given the current cultural chic attributed to Irishness – Beckett's work outside such a huge marketing venture remains unapproachable. Perhaps it was only the caché of the event which was the success, rather than the work itself, as his plays, like those of Yeats, still remain outside the contemporary repertoire.

The Revival of, with the rare exception of Garry Hynes's exceptional, though notorious, production of *Plough*, continues to be revived as a tourist-board enterprise. It rarely takes liberties with style and form, and panders to the basest popular taste of the ex-patriot Irish, returning on summer holidays, and seeks to recapture a (theatrical) vision of the old country locked in minds at the moment of emigration. But it is not all the fault of diasporic taste: a permanent company of actors at the Abbey and a succession of artistic directors who treated the canon as weapons of national defence, and a nation anxious to exclude outside influence, all share culpability. Experimentation and revision are not part of postcolonial nostalgic recovery. Ireland and Irish culture need to be trapped in the poor rural idyll of mythology, struggling to shake off the colonial master. Since the Famine ships of the nineteenth century and subsequent economic hardship transported Ireland's children overseas, that necessity to abandon the home and the family must be justified continuously by trapping Ireland in that socio-economic timeframe. The reality of what has happened to Ireland economically in the 1990s is a severe challenge to that myth, and the cultural preservation of the myth, in realistic revivals of 'the largely ruralist canon',[14] certainly on Dublin's stages, looks increasingly unjustifiable. The fact that these continue to be revived rather than revised points to a crisis in theatre and a possible split: the main stages might pander to the myth of the ex-patriot returnee, desirous of rural realism, and the preservation of the theatrical canon, with the smaller stages appealing to the vast majority of the youthful population, employed in global-technology industries in which the simulacrum speaks more than the real. Thus, through most of the twentieth century, middle-aged theatre aficionados yearned nostalgically, not for the Symbolism of Yeats and the Expressionism of O'Casey, but for the realism of the Revival's revival. The

Hynes/O'Casey Expressionism, the Barabbas/Robinson corporeality, and the Gate Theatre's Absurdist and Symbolist experiments remain touchstones of creative relevance to Irish theatre's entry to the modern world, once signalled by the founders of the national theatre as part of the movement of European modernism, but thereafter sidelined as formalist deviants in the nationalist project of mythologizing. The examples examined here, therefore, are not so much recent attempts at revival of an original Revival, but more exponents of the art of theatrical recovery.

NOTES

1. Nicholas Grene, *The Politics of Irish Drama* (Cambridge: Cambridge University Press, 1999), 138.
2. Fintan O'Toole, Transcript, *The Arts Show*, RTE, broadcast 7 May 1991.
3. Mary O'Donnell, 'Plough Beaten Into Swords', in *The Sunday Business Post*, 12 May 1991.
4. Frank Rich, 'Poverty and Decay in Irish Microcosm', in *New York Times*, 22 June 1988.
5. Michael Billington, 'Purity Among the Predators', in *The Guardian*, 12 August 1987.
6. Anna McMullan, 'Reclaiming Performance: The Contemporary Irish Independent Theatre Sector', in Eberhard Bort (ed.), *The State of Play: Irish Theatre in the 'Nineties* (Trier: Wissenschaftlicher Verlag Trier, 1996), 35.
7. The Five Festivals were as follows:
   1989: The Poet with a Thousand Faces (*At the Hawk's Well, The Green Helmet, On Baile's Strand, The Only Jealousy of Emer, The Death of Cuchulain*)
   1990: Masks of Transformation (*Cathleen ni Houlihan, The Dreaming of the Bones*)
   1991: Sacred Mysteries (*Deirdre, A Full Moon in March, The Shadowy Waters*)
   1992: *The Countess Cathleen*
   1993: Art and the Spiritual (*The Hour-Glass, The Words Upon the Window-Pane, The Cat and the Moon*)
8. Programme note to the 1989 festival, 'A Memory and a Prophecy', by James Flannery.
9. Fintan O'Toole, 'Coca-Cola Yeats Could be the Real Thing', *Irish Times*, 16 September 1989.
10. William Rocke, 'Bringing Beckett Home', in *Sunday Press*, 29 September, 1991.
11. Matt Wolf, 'National Pride in the Waiting Game', in *The Times*, 16 October 1991.
12. Iriving Wardle, 'Play it Again, Sam', in *The Observer*, 22 September 1991.
13. Barry McGovern, quoted in Wolf, 'National Pride'.
14. Declan Kiberd, *Inventing Ireland: The Literature of the Modern Nation* (London: Jonathan Cape, 1995), 653.

GUIDE TO FURTHER READING

The range of critical material available on late nineteenth- to twenty-first century Irish theatre is vast but variable: coverage of Synge and O'Casey is extensive, that of Carr and McDonagh understandably less so. And the same variations are discernible within historical periods: Friel and Murphy both began their careers in the 1960s, but studies of Friel far outweigh those of Murphy. Many of the books listed below carry their own bibliographies, particularly Murray (1997), Grene (2000) and Morash (2002). Individual journal articles are generally not included, but readers are directed to Irish literary-cultural journals, particularly *Irish University Review*, *The Irish Review*, *Irish Studies Review*, *Eire-Ireland*, *Etudes-Irlandaise* and past issues of *Bullán* (now discontinued). Also useful is the theatre journal *Modern Drama* whose annual bibliography, along with that of *Irish University Review*, is a sure way of keeping up to date with an expanding area of study.

Acheson, James (ed.), *British and Irish Drama since 1960*, Basingstoke: Macmillan, 1993.

Andrews, Elmer, *The Art of Brian Friel: Neither Reality Nor Dreams*, Basingstoke: Macmillan, 1995.

Ayling, Ronald (ed.), *Sean O'Casey: Modern Judgements*, London: Macmillan, 1970.

Ayling, Ronald (ed.), *The Dublin Trilogy: A Casebook*, London: Macmillan, 1985.

Barnett, Gene A., *Denis Johnston*, Boston: Twayne, 1978.

Becket, Fiona, 'A Theatrical Matrilineage?: Problems of the Familial in the Drama of Teresa Deevy and Marina Carr', in Scott Brewster, Virginia Crossman, Fiona Becket and David Alderson (eds.), *Ireland in Proximity, History, Gender, Space*, London: Routledge and Kegan Paul, 80–93.

Beckson, Karl (ed.), *Oscar Wilde: The Critical Heritage*, London: Routledge and Kegan Paul, 1970.

Boland, Eavan, *A Kind of Scar: The Woman Poet in a National Tradition*, Dublin: Attic Press, 1989.

Bort, Eberhard (ed.), *The State of Play: Irish Theatre in the 'Nineties*, Trier: Wissenschaftlicher Verlag Trier, 1996.

Brown, Terence, *Ireland: A Social and Cultural History, 1922–1985*, London: Fontana, 1985.

Byrne, Ophelia, *The Stage in Ulster from the Eighteenth Century*, Belfast: Linen Hall Library, 1997.

Cairns, David, and Shaun Richards, *Writing Ireland: Nationalism, Colonialism and Culture*, Manchester: Manchester University Press, 1988.

Casey, Daniel J. (ed.), *Critical Essays on John Millington Synge*, New York: G. K. Hall, 1994.

Cave, Richard Allen, 'Staging the Irishman', in J. S. Bratton et al., (eds.), *Acts of Supremacy: The British Empire and the Stage, 1790–1930*, Manchester: Manchester University Press, 1991.

Clark, Brenna Katz, *The Emergence of the Irish Peasant Play at the Abbey Theatre*, Ann Arbor: UMI Research Press, 1982.

Costello, Peter, *The Heart Grown Brutal: The Irish Revolution in Literature from Parnell to the Death of Yeats 1891–1939*, Dublin: Gill and Macmillan, 1977.

Danson, Lawrence, *Wilde's Intention: the Artist in his Criticism*, Oxford: Clarendon Press, 1997.

Dantanus, Ulf, *Brian Friel: A Study*, London: Faber and Faber, 1988.

de Búrca, Séamus, *The Queen's Royal Theatre Dublin 1829–1969*, Dublin: Séamus de Búrca, 1983.

Deane, Seamus, 'Irish Politics and O'Casey's Theatre', in Thomas Kilroy (ed.), *Sean O'Casey: A Collection of Critical Essays*, Engelwood Cliffs, NJ: Prentice Hall, 1975, 149–58.

Deane, Seamus, *Celtic Revivals: Essays in Modern Irish Literature 1880–1980*, London: Faber and Faber, 1985.

Delaney, Paul (ed.), *Brian Friel in Conversation*, Ann Arbor: University of Michigan Press, 2000.

Dollimore, Jonathan, *Sexual Dissidence: Augustine to Wilde, Freud to Foucault*, Oxford: Oxford University Press, 1990.

Dorn, Karen, *Players and Painted Stage: The Theatre of W. B. Yeats*, Brighton: Harvester, 1984.

Edwards, Philip, *Threshold of a Nation: A Study in English and Irish Drama*, Cambridge: Cambridge University Press, 1979.

Ellmann, Richard, *Oscar Wilde*, London: Hamish Hamilton, 1987.

Eltis, Sos, *Revising Wilde: Society and Subversion in the Plays of Oscar Wilde*, Oxford: Clarendon Press, 1996.

Etherton, Michael, *Contemporary Irish Dramatists*, London: Macmillan, 1989.

Ferrar, Harold, *Denis Johnston's Irish Theatre*, Dublin: Dolmen Press, 1973.

Fitz-simon, Christopher, *The Irish Theatre*, London: Thames and Hudson, 1983.

Flannery, James W., *W. B. Yeats and the Idea of a Theatre: The Early Abbey Theatre in Theory and Practice*, New Haven: Yale University Press, 1976.

Frazier, Adrian, *Behind the Scenes: Yeats, Horniman, and the Struggle for the Abbey Theatre*, Berkeley: University of California Press, 1990.

Gagnier, Regenia, *Idylls of the Marketplace: Oscar Wilde and the Victorian Reading Public*, Aldershot: Scolar Press, 1987.

Genet, Jacqueline, and Richard Allen Cave (eds.), *Perspectives of Irish Theatre and Drama*, Gerrards Cross: Colin Smythe, 1991.

Gibbs, A. M., 'Bernard Shaw's Other Island', in Oliver MacDonagh, W. F. Mandle and Pauric Travers (eds.), *Irish Culture And Nationalism, 1750–1950*, London: Macmillan, 1983, 122–37.

Gonzalez, Alexander G. (ed.), *Assessing the Achievement of J. M. Synge*, Westport, CT: Greenwood Press, 1996.

Greaves, C. Desmond, *Sean O'Casey: Politics and Art*, London: Lawrence and Wishart, 1979.

Grene, Nicholas, *Synge: A Critical Study of the Plays*, Basingstoke; Macmillan, 1975.

Grene, Nicholas, *Bernard Shaw: A Critical View*, London: Macmillan, 1984.

Grene, Nicholas, *The Politics of Irish Drama: Plays in Context from Boucicault to Friel*, Cambridge: Cambridge University Press, 1999.

Grene, Nicholas (ed.), *Interpreting Synge: Essays from the Synge Summer School, 1991–2000*, Dublin: Lilliput Press, 2000.

Grene, Nicholas (ed.), *Talking About Tom Murphy*, Dublin: Carysfort Press, 2002.

Griffiths, Trevor, and Margaret Llewellyn-Jones (eds.), *British and Irish Women Dramatists since 1958*, Buckingham: Open University, 1993.

Harper, George Mills, '"Intellectual Hatred" and "Intellectual Nationalism": the Paradox of Passionate Politics', in Robert O'Driscoll (ed.), *Theatre and Nationalism in Twentieth-Century Ireland*, Toronto: University of Toronto Press, 1969, 40–65.

Harrington, John P., *The Irish Beckett*, Syracuse: Syracuse University Press, 1991.

Harrington, John P., *The Irish Play in New York 1874–1966*, Lexington, KY: University of Kentucky Press, 1997.

Herr, Cheryl (ed.), *For the Land They Loved: Irish Political Melodrama, 1890–1925*, Syracuse: Syracuse University Press, 1991.

Hogan, Robert, *'Since O'Casey' and other Essays on Irish Drama*, Gerrards Cross: Colin Smythe, 1983.

Hogan, Robert, and James Kilroy (eds.), *Laying the Foundations, 1902–1904*, Dublin: Dolmen Press, 1976.

Hogan, Robert, and James Kilroy (eds.), *The Abbey Theatre: The Years of Synge, 1905–1909*, Dublin: Dolmen Press, 1978.

Hogan, Robert, and Richard Burnham (eds.), *The Years of O'Casey, 1921–1926: A Documentary History*, Gerrards Cross: Colin Smythe, 1992.

Hogan, Robert, Richard Burnham and Daniel P. Poteet (eds.), *The Rise of the Realists*, Dublin: Dolmen Press, 1979.

Hogan, Robert, *After the Irish Renaissance: A Critical History of the Irish Drama since 'The Plough and the Stars'*, Minneapolis: University of Minnesota Press, 1968.

Howes, Marjorie, *Yeats's Nations*, Cambridge: Cambridge University Press, 1996.

Hughes, Eamonn, '"To Define Your Dissent": The Plays and Polemics of the Field Day Theatre Company', in *Theatre Research International*, 15.1 (1990), 67–77.

Hunt, Hugh, *The Abbey: Ireland's National Theatre, 1904–1979*, Dublin: Gill and Macmillan, 1979.

Johnson, Toni O'Brien, *Synge: The Medieval and the Grotesque*, Gerrards Cross: Colin Smythe, 1982.

Jordan, Eamonn, *The Feast of Famine: The Plays of Frank McGuiness*, Bern: Peter Lang, 1998.

Jordan, Eamonn (ed.), *Theatre Stuff: Critical Essays on Contemporary Irish Theatre*, Dublin: Carysfort Press, 2000.

Kearney, Richard, *Transitions: Narratives in Modern Irish Culture*, Dublin, Wolfhound, 1988.

Kenneally, Michael (ed.), *Cultural Contexts and Literary Idioms in Contemporary Irish Literature*, Gerrards Cross: Colin Smythe, 1988.

Kerwin, William (ed.), *Brian Friel, A Casebook*, New York: Garland Publishing, 1997.

Kiberd, Declan, *Synge and the Irish Language*, Basingstoke: Macmillan, 2nd edn., 1993.

Kiberd, Declan, *Inventing Ireland: The Literature of the Modern Nation*, London: Jonathan Cape, 1995.

Kilroy, Thomas (ed.), *Sean O'Casey: A Collection of Critical Essays*, Engelwood Cliffs, NJ: Prentice Hall, 1975.

King, Mary C., *The Drama of J. M. Synge*, London: Fourth Estate; Syracuse: Syracuse University Press, 1988.

Kleiman, Carol, *Sean O'Casey's Bridge of Vision: Four Essays on Structure and Perspective*, University of Toronto Press, 1982.

Knowland, A. S., *W. B. Yeats: Dramatist of Vision*, Gerrards Cross: Colin Smythe, 1983.

Kopper, Edward A. Jnr (ed.), *A J. M. Synge Literary Companion*, New York: Greenwood Press, 1988.

Krause, David, *Sean O'Casey: The Man and his Work*, London: MacGibbon and Kee, 1960.

Lawrence, Dan, and Nicholas Grene (eds.), *Shaw, Lady Gregory and the Abbey: A Correspondence and a Record*, Gerrards Cross: Colin Smythe, 1993.

Lee, J. J., *Ireland 1992–1985 Politics and Society*, Cambridge: Cambridge University Press, 1989.

Leeney, Cathy, and Anna McMullan (eds.), *The Theatre of Marina Carr: Before Rules was Made*, Dublin: Carysfort Press, 2002.

Leerssen, Joep, *Remembrance and Imagination: Patterns in the Historical and Literary Representation of Ireland in the Nineteenth Century*, Cork: Cork University Press, 1996.

Lojek, Helen, 'Difference *Without* Indifference: The Drama of Frank McGuinness and Anne Devlin', *in Eire-Ireland*, 25:2 (1990), 45–53.

Lowery, Robert G., *O'Casey Annual*, nos. 1, 2 and 3, London: Macmillan, 1982–84.

Lowery, Robert G. (ed.), *A Whirlwind in Dublin: The Plough and the Stars' Riots*, Westport, CT: Greenwood, 1984.

MacCormack, Jerusha (ed.), *Wilde the Irishman*, New Haven: Yale University Press, 1998.

MacDonagh, Oliver, W. F. Mandle, and Pauric Travers (eds.), *Irish Culture And Nationalism, 1750–1950*, Macmillan, London, 1983.

MacIntosh, Fiona, *Dying Acts: Death in Ancient Greek and Modern Irish Tragic Drama*, Cork: Cork University Press, 1994.

Maxwell, D. E. S., *Brian Friel*, Lewisburgh, PA: Bucknell University Press, 1973.

Maxwell, D. E. S., *A Critical History of Modern Irish Drama 1891–1980*, Cambridge: Cambridge University Press, 1984.

McCormack, W. J., *From Burke to Beckett: Ascendancy, Tradition and Betrayal in Literary History*, Cork: Cork University Press, 1994.

McCormack, W. J., *Fool of the Family: A Life of J. M. Synge*, London: Weidenfeld and Nicholson, 2000.

McDonald, Ronan, *Tragedy in Irish Literature*, Basingstoke: Palgrave, 2002.

McMullan, Anna, 'Marina Carr's Unhomely Women', *in Irish Theatre Magazine*, 1:1 (1998), 14–16.

Mickail, E. H. (ed.), *The Abbey Theatre: Interviews and Recollections*, Basingstoke: Macmillan, 1988.

Moore, John Rhys, *Masks of Love and Death: Yeats as Dramatist*, Ithaca: Cornell University Press, 1971.

Morash, Christopher, '"Something's Missing": Theatre and the Republic of Ireland Act, 1949', in Ray Ryan (ed.), *Writing in the Republic: Literature, Culture, Politics in the Republic of Ireland, 1949–1999*, London: Macmillan, 2000, 64–81.

Morash, Christopher, *A History of Irish Theatre 1601–2000*, Cambridge: Cambridge University Press, 2002.

Murray, Christopher (ed.), *Irish University Review* (Special Issue on Tom Murphy), 17:1 (1987).

Murray, Christopher (ed.), *Irish University Review* (Jubilee Issue on Teresa Deevy and Irish Women Playwrights), 25:1 (1995).

Murray, Christopher, *Twentieth-Century Irish Drama: Mirror Up to Nation*, Manchester: Manchester University Press, 1997.

Murray, Christopher (ed.), *Brian Friel: Essays, Diaries, Interviews: 1964–1999*, London: Faber and Faber, 1999.

O'Brien, George, *Brian Friel*, Dublin: Gill and Macmillan, 1989.

O'Connor, Garry, *Sean O'Casey: A Life*, London: Hodder and Stoughton, 1988.

O'Flaherty, Gearóid, 'George Bernard Shaw and the Irish Literary Revival', in P. J. Mathews (ed.), *New Voices in Irish Criticism*, Dublin: Four Courts Press, 2000, 33–42.

O'Leary, Philip, 'Uneasy Alliance: The Gaelic League looks at the "Irish" Renaissance', in Audrey S. Eyler and Robert F. Garratt (eds.), *The Uses of the Past: Essays on Irish Culture*, Newark: University of Delaware Press, 1988, 144–60.

O'Leary, Philip, 'Lost Tribesman or Prodigal Son?: George Bernard Shaw and the Gaelic Movement', *in Eire-Ireland*, 29:2 (1994), 51–64.

O'Neill, Michael J., *The Abbey at the Queen's: The Interregnum Years 1951–1966*, Ontario, Canada: Borealis, 1999.

O'Riordan, John, *A Guide to Sean O'Casey's Plays, From the Plough to the Stars*, London: Macmillan, 1984.

O'Toole, Fintan, *Tom Murphy: The Politics of Magic*, Dublin: New Island Books; London: Nick Hern Books, 1994.

Parkin, Andrew, *The Dramatic Imagination of W. B. Yeats*, Dublin: Gill and Macmillan, 1978.

Peacock, Alan (ed.), *The Achievement of Brian Friel*, Gerrards Cross: Colin Smythe, 1993.

Pelletier, Martine, 'Field Day and "The Irish-English Collision"', in *European Journal of English Studies*, 3:3 (1999), 327–41.

Pilkington, Lionel, *Theatre and the State in 20th Century Ireland: Cultivating the People*, London: Routledge and Kegan Paul, 2001.

Pine, Richard, *Brian Friel and Ireland's Drama*, London: Routledge and Kegan Paul, 1990.

Pine, Richard, *The Thief of Reason: Oscar Wilde and Modern Ireland*, Dublin: Gill and Macmillan, 1995.

Pine, Richard, *The Diviner: The Art of Brian Friel*, Dublin: University College, Dublin Press, 1999.

Powell, Kerry, *Wilde and the Theatre of the 1890s*, Cambridge: Cambridge University Press, 1990.

Raby, Peter (ed.), *The Cambridge Companion to Oscar Wilde*, Cambridge: Cambridge University Press, 1997.

Richards, Shaun, 'Refiguring Lost Narratives – Prefiguring New Ones: The Theatre of Tom Murphy', in *Canadian Journal of Irish Studies*, 15:1 (1989), 80–100.

Richards, Shaun, 'Field Day's Fifth Province: Avenue or Impasse?', in Eamonn Hughes (ed.), *Culture and Politics in Northern Ireland 1960–1990*, Milton Keynes: Open University Press, 1991, 139–50.

Richards, Shaun, '"Suffocated in the Green Flag": The Drama of Teresa Deevy and 1930s Ireland', *Literature and Society* 3rd Series, 4, (1995), 65–80.

Richtarik, Marilynn, *Acting Between the Lines: The Field Day Theatre Company and Irish Cultural Politics, 1980–1984*, Oxford: Oxford University Press, 1995.

Roche, Anthony (ed.), *Colby Quarterly* (Special Issue on Contemporary Irish Drama), 27:4 (1991).

Roche, Anthony, *Contemporary Irish Drama: From Beckett to McGuinness*, Dublin: Gill and Macmillan, 1994.

Roche, Anthony (ed.), *Irish University Review* (Special Issue on Brian Friel), 29:1 (1999).

Saddlemyer, Anne (ed.), *Theatre Business: The Correspondence of the First Abbey Directors: William Butler Yeats, Lady Gregory and J. M. Synge*, Gerrards Cross: Colin Smythe, 1982.

Saddlemyer, Anne, *In Defence of Lady Gregory, Playwright*, Dublin: Dolmen Press, 1966.

Sammells, Neil, *Wilde Style: the Plays and Prose of Oscar Wilde*, London: Longman, 2000.

Schrank, Bernice, *Sean O'Casey: A Research and Production Sourcebook*, Westport, CT and London: Greenwood Press, 1996.

Sekine, Masaru, and Christopher Murray, *Yeats and the Noh: A Comparative Study*, Gerrards Cross: Colin Smythe, 1990.

Simmons, James, *Sean O'Casey*, London: Macmillan, 1983.

Simpson, Alan, *Beckett and Behan and a Theatre in Dublin*, London: Routledge and Kegan Paul, 1962.

Sinfield, Alan, *The Wilde Century*, London: Cassell, 1994.

Trotter, Mary, *Ireland's National Theaters: Political Performance and the Origins of the Irish Dramatic Movement*, Syracuse: Syracuse University Press, 2001.

Ure, Peter, *Yeats the Playwright: A Commentary on Character and Design in the Major Plays*, London: Routledge and Kegan Paul, 1963.

Varty, Anne, *Preface to Wilde*, London: Longman, 1998.

Watson, G. J., *Irish Identity and the Literary Revival: Synge, Yeats, Joyce and O'Casey*, 2nd edn., Washington, DC: Catholic University of America Press, 1994.

Watt, Stephen, *Joyce, O'Casey, and the Irish Popular Theater*, Syracuse: Syracuse University Press, 1991.

Watt, Stephen, Eileen Morgan and Shakir Mustapha (eds.), *A Century of Irish Drama, Widening the Stage*, Bloomington: Indiana University Press, 2000.

Welch, Robert, *The Abbey Theatre 1899–1999: Form and Pressure*, Oxford: Oxford University Press, 1999.

Worth, Katherine, *The Irish Drama of Europe from Yeats to Beckett*, London: The Athlone Press, 1978.

Worthen, W. B., 'Homeless Words: Field Day and the Politics of Translation', in William Kerwin (ed.), *Brian Friel, A Casebook*, New York: Garland Publishing, 1997, 135–57.

INDEX

Index

CAMBRIDGE COMPANIONS TO LITERATURE

CAMBRIDGE COMPANIONS TO CULTURE